Terrorism IV

CULTUREAMERICA

Erika Doss
Philip J. Deloria
Series Editors

Karal Ann Marling
Editor Emerita

Terrorism TV

Popular
Entertainment in
Post-9/11 America

Stacy Takacs

University Press
of Kansas

Published by the University
Press of Kansas (Lawrence,
Kansas 66045), which was
organized by the Kansas
Board of Regents and is
operated and funded by
Emporia State University,
Fort Hays State University,
Kansas State University,
Pittsburg State University, the
University of Kansas, and
Wichita State University

Library of Congress Cataloging-in-Publication Data

Takacs, Stacy.
Terrorism TV : popular entertainment in post-9/11 America /
Stacy Takacs.
p. cm. — (CultureAmerica)
Includes bibliographical references and index.
ISBN 978-0-7006-1837-8 (cloth : alk. paper)
ISBN 978-0-7006-1838-5 (pbk. : alk. paper)
1. Terrorism on television. 2. Television programs—Social
aspects—United States—History—21st century. 3. Fear—
Social aspects—United States—History—21st century.
4. September 11 Terrorist Attacks, 2001—Influence. 5. War on
Terrorism, 2001–2009—Influence. 6. September 11 Terrorist
Attacks, 2001—Psychological aspects. 7. War and society—
United States—History—21st century. 8. Terrorism—United
States—Public opinion. I. Title.
PN1992.8.T47T35 2012
791.45′72—dc23   2011046020

British Library Cataloguing-in-Publication Data is available.

Printed in the United States of America

10 9 8 7 6 5 4 3 2 1

The paper used in this publication is recycled and contains 30
percent postconsumer waste. It is acid free and meets the minimum requirements of the American National Standard for Per-
manence of Paper for Printed Library Materials Z39.48-1992.

This book is dedicated to Betsy Myers, whose

energy, patience, and intelligence know no bounds.

You are a constant inspiration to me.

Always, S.

CONTENTS

Acknowledgments ix

Introduction: The Long Information War 1

Chapter 1. 9/11 and the Trauma Frame 30

Chapter 2. Spy Thrillers and the Politics of Fear 59

Chapter 3. Reality Militainment and the Virtual Citizen-Soldier 97

Chapter 4. Fictional Militainment and the Justification of War 122

Chapter 5. From Virtual Citizen-Soldier to Imperial Grunt 144

Chapter 6. Contesting the Politics of Fear 168

Chapter 7. The Body of War and the Collapse of Memory 206

Epilogue: Trauma and Memory Ten Years Later 238

Notes 245

Bibliography 281

Television Bibliography 309

Index 313

ACKNOWLEDGMENTS

As this project has been a decade in the making, there are many people who deserve thanks and praise for their support. First, thanks to my parents, Robert Takacs and Monica Perdue, for your constant support. Thanks to my colleagues in English and American studies at Oklahoma State University, especially my various bosses, Michael Willard, Amilcar Shabazz, Laura Belmonte, and Carol Moder. Without the latter two, this project would never have come to fruition, and I want you to know I appreciate your efforts on my behalf. Thanks also to the wonderful staff and board members of the Oklahoma Humanities Council for reminding me of the value of humanities work and keeping me sane in the reddest of red states. Lt. Col. Todd Breasseale, Hollywood liaison for the U.S. Army, spent over two hours with me one day in July 2008, going over the various programs that received (or not) army assistance. He was very generous with his information and his time, and I thank him for his insights. Research grants from the Oklahoma Humanities Council, the OSU Department of English, and the OSU College of Arts and Sciences enabled me to travel to collections to perform much of the research for this book, so thanks. Research for this project was conducted at the UCLA Film and Television Archives and the Wisconsin Center for Film and Theater Research, and I appreciate the aid of the archivists at both locales. Finally, thank you to the anonymous reviewers of the manuscript for helpful comments, particularly about the shifting ground of the television system. It is a better book for your efforts.

The portion of chapter 6 dealing with the alien invasion series has previously appeared as "Monsters, Monsters Everywhere: Spooky TV and the Politics of Fear in Post-9/11 America" in *Science Fiction Studies* 36, no. 1 (March 2009): 1–20 (© SF-TH, Inc. 2009). The portion of chapter 6 addressing the sitcom *Whoopi* has previously appeared as "Burning Bush: Sitcom Treatments of the Bush Presidency," in the *Journal of Popular Culture* 44, no. 2 (April 2011): 417–435 (© 2011 Wiley Periodicals, Inc.). Much of chapter 7 has appeared as "The Body of War and the Management of Imperial Anxiety on US Television" in the *International Journal of Contemporary Iraqi Studies* 3, no. 1 (2009): 85–105 (© Intellect Ltd. 2009). I thank the editors and guest editors of all of these journals for their assistance and the publishers for permission to republish.

Introduction: The Long Information War

On September 11, 2001, Islamic extremists associated with the international terrorist organization Al Qaeda hijacked four jetliners, driving two into the World Trade Center towers in New York, one into the Pentagon in Washington, and another into a field in Pennsylvania (the presumed target was the White House). By staggering the attacks on New York in such a way as to ensure the presence of live news coverage, they also managed to hijack the U.S. media for their own propaganda purposes. The attacks were, as French philosopher Jean Baudrillard acknowledged, a pure media event.[1] Not only were they orchestrated to maximize media exposure; they were designed with primarily symbolic, rather than strategic, goals in mind. The point was to signify defiance of the global system of power and privilege promoted by the United States. Al Qaeda leader Osama Bin Laden viewed the attacks as a sort of advertisement for jihad. The 9/11 attacks could thus be described as a first salvo in what has become a very long information war. From the crumbling of the Twin Towers to Operation Anaconda, the "Shock and Awe" bombardments of Iraq, and the recent spate of foiled bomb plots, including the "shoe bomber," the "underwear bomber," and the "Times Square bomber," media systems have become key battlegrounds in the global War on Terrorism, and media consumers have become key stakes in these virtual battles.[2]

Both Al Qaeda and the U.S. government have worked hard to ensure their messages are broadcast over the global airwaves and to control the contexts for the reception of those messages. Al Qaeda, for example, has not only commandeered official media channels using spectacular strikes on symbolic targets; it has also leveraged the competitive environment of satellite news to its advantage, using the promise of an "exclusive" or "scoop" to secure an open conduit to the Arab masses watching Al Jazeera, Al Arabiya, or one of the other new satellite channels available in the region. Al Qaeda's media and publicity committee also creates and disseminates its own media content, using state-of-the-art video production and editing techniques to package its fundamentalist ideologies for popular consumption.[3] These propaganda tapes circulate through a global network of mosques, madrasas, and Islamic cultural centers and via peer-to-peer video and file sharing. These alternative networks exist beneath, beyond, and beside official media conduits and confirm Arjun Appadurai's insight that global mediascapes are uneven, porous, disjunctive systems subject to "backdraft."[4] A key facet of this backdraft is the appropriation and recontextualization of mainstream media content. Al Qaeda is adept at using found footage from Western media outlets to create a receptive context for its jihadist messages. Its propaganda videos are full of images of U.S., UN, and Israeli military forces firing on innocent civilians, for example, or running from rebels in Somalia, Bosnia, and the West Bank. The images are ripped from their original contexts and embedded in elaborate video montages whose net result is to portray Western powers as cowardly, weak, and morally degenerate. It is a textbook example of how "global communications saturated with images of the United States can dramatically backfire when used by global terrorists for their own ends."[5]

Of course, the U.S. government and its allies have undertaken an equally well coordinated campaign to control the flow of information about the War on Terrorism and to condition the reception of news about that conflict. Much of this work involves the deliberate and calculated promotion of pro-U.S. propaganda.[6] For example, the George W. Bush administration created its own alternative media networks in Afghanistan and Iraq to "cut through the hateful propaganda that fills the airwaves in the Muslim world."[7] The coordinators of these networks (Radio Sawa, Alhurra, and the Iraqi Media Network) admit to having a dual function: "reporting the news honestly" but also "reminding their Arab audiences of all the good America does." The result is "less news than propaganda."[8] The Department of Defense has also contracted with a public relations firm called the Lincoln Group to plant positive stories about the U.S. invasion of Iraq in independent Arab media outlets. According to the *New York Times*, the Lincoln Group not only wrote and distributed these communiqués, often pretending to speak from an Iraqi perspective; it paid Arab news outlets to run them or funneled stories through reporters on its payroll, never acknowledging the source or the payments involved.[9] In addition to undermining the objectivity of Arab news outlets, the Bush administration used corporate advertising and public relations techniques to try to "sell America" as a brand to Middle Eastern and Islamic media consumers. Under the leadership of advertising executive Charlotte Beers, the Office of Public Diplomacy and Public Affairs produced a series of video advertisements, pamphlets, and educational materials for distribution in the

Middle East and elsewhere touting the "shared values" of Americans and Muslims. Not surprisingly, these "ads for America" were recognized by Muslims as superficial "spin" and criticized for failing to address issues of American foreign policy in the region. Arab media outlets refused to run the ads, and the campaign was discontinued after only a month.[10]

The Bush administration's PR tactics were much more successful at generating domestic support for the War on Terrorism. Karl Rove's sophisticated communications strategy promoted tight message discipline and exploited every opportunity for generating good press. Rove's team hired stage managers and lighting consultants from Hollywood to help construct the best possible image of the president, paid political pundits to stump for presidential policy initiatives, and even filled the White House Press Corps with conservative flacks paid to ask leading questions.[11] In the aftermath of 9/11, the administration flooded the media with spokespeople all touting a unified message supportive of war, and the media provided an open mike. Eager to maintain access to the inner circles of power, journalists and editors also filtered out alternative perspectives and framed information in ways that would support administration policies.[12] For example, CNN chair Walter Isaacson directed his news staff to "balance" images of civilian casualties in Afghanistan with images and reminders of the 9/11 attacks, claiming "it seems too perverse to focus too much on the casualties and hardships in Afghanistan."[13] Journalists at MSNBC were ordered to present two conservative pundits for every liberal voice included in a broadcast to avoid an illusion of "imbalance."[14] Editors at local and regional newspapers, such as the *Tennessean* in Nashville, reported printing more pro-war letters to the editor than antiwar letters to avoid accusations of "bias," even though the volume of antiwar mail exceeded the volume of pro-war correspondence by more than 3 to 1.[15] Overt government censorship, though not absent, was virtually unnecessary, as news organizations censored themselves to avoid upsetting the administration or angering an audience presumed to be supportive of war.

The Bush administration took particular advantage of journalistic gullibility during the run-up to the war in Iraq. Recognizing that an invasion of Iraq would be a harder "sell" than the invasion of Afghanistan, the White House tested its rationale for the invasion using focus groups and polls before disseminating it in a coordinated blanket campaign through multiple media outlets.[16] When the first message (regime change) did not sell well, the administration settled on Secretary of State Colin Powell's suggestion of disarmament and began what Karl Rove called a "meticulously planned strategy to persuade the public." The strategy included a staged photo op on the first anniversary of 9/11, shot from Ellis Island because it offered "better camera angles" of the Statue of Liberty. Rove and his team then set a March 2003 deadline for the invasion because, as White House Chief of Staff Andrew Card told reporters, "you don't introduce new products in August."[17] Between September 2002 and March 2003, the Bush administration campaigned for the war by systematically distorting intelligence reports regarding Iraq's weapons programs. As a Carnegie Endowment for International Peace report concluded in 2004, "the president, the vice president, and the secretaries of state and defense" made frequent public statements "to the effect that 'we know' this or that when the accurate formulation was 'we suspect' or 'we cannot exclude.'" The "caveats, probabilities and expressions of uncertainty" that littered the original reports were eliminated or rephrased in order to make the case for war seem airtight.[18] The coup de grâce of this marketing campaign came in late 2002 when the administration exploited the liberal reputation of the New York Times to lend credence to its pursuit of war in Iraq. As reported in an episode of the PBS program Bill Moyers Journal ("Buying the War," 2007), administration officials first leaked (faulty) intelligence about Iraqi attempts to purchase enriched uranium from Niger to the Times, then cited the resulting story as "proof" of administration claims on the Sunday morning talk shows. Thus, by the time the administration dispatched Powell to the United Nations to present the administration's case against Iraq to the world, the American public was already primed to accept the evidence as irrefutable. The presentation itself—with its dazzling imagery, techno-speak, and selective interpretation of the facts in evidence—looked like nothing so much as an episode of CSI or Law and Order.[19] Familiarity with such legal procedurals lent additional credence to the evidence, as all viewers of these programs know the evidence never lies. Predictably, American popular support for the war in Iraq grew as a result of Powell's pitch.[20] The Daily Show with Jon Stewart (2/5/2003) provided the lone voice of sanity, declaring that the presentation proved only that "America is second to none in the field of Power Point presentations."

Image management also saturated the military campaign from beginning to end. The opening salvo of the war, for example, was advertised in advance as "shock and awe." The memorable "rescue" of wounded PFC Jessica Lynch from a hospital in Nasiriyah was filmed and carefully edited to resemble a scene from a Hollywood action movie and later turned into a Hollywood movie with the assistance of the Pentagon.[21] The iconic toppling of Saddam

Hussein's statue in Firdos Square was manipulated by a Marine Corps psychological operations unit to appear spontaneous and was framed so tightly as to make the scant crowds of revelers, many of them Iraqi children incited by marines using bullhorns, seem like thousands of Iraqis, all grateful to the U.S. military for their liberation.[22] The triumph of spectacle over reality was confirmed with George W. Bush's dramatic tailhook landing on the USS *Abraham Lincoln*, where he cynically declared major combat operations complete and the "mission accomplished."

A key facet of the administration's strategy for managing the information war at home was to coopt the media's representatives in the field. It accomplished this by permitting reporters to embed with military units during the invasion of Iraq. Not surprisingly, this strategy was the brainchild of another public relations specialist, Victoria "Torie" Clarke. A long-time employee of the PR firm of Hill and Knowlton—the same firm responsible for concocting the "Iraqi baby atrocity" scandal of the first Gulf War—Clarke was appointed undersecretary of defense for public affairs in 2002. She quickly recognized that embedding reporters with the troops would both constrain their views of the war and ally them with their protectors in ways that would benefit the military and the Bush administration. Studies of the subsequent news coverage show Clarke was right. According to Stephen Cooper and Jim Kuypers, reports from embedded journalists were invariably more positive than reports from those behind the lines.[23] While many of these reports provided compelling descriptions of the grim realities of combat, they were limited in perspective and rarely attempted to contextualize events on the ground in relation to some larger whole. By inviting journalists to assume a military perspective, the tactic of embedding positioned the domestic U.S. population literally and figuratively "behind the troops."

Objective Hearts and Minds: Popular Culture and the War on Terrorism

Embedding was but one facet of a larger strategy of media cooptation embraced by the Bush administration to win the hearts and minds of the American people to its foreign policy vision. As James Castonguay argues, one overlooked locus of this strategy has been the entertainment media.[24] Producers and personalities from the film, television, radio, advertising, and videogaming industries helped legitimate the War on Terrorism by translating war into entertainment. In the aftermath of the 9/11 attacks, for example, the major television networks offered, at great financial expense, twenty-four-hour real-time news coverage of the recovery efforts without commercial interruption. They also donated air time and resources to produce a star-studded telethon to collect donations for victims of the catastrophe and their families.[25] As I argue in chapter 1, much of this coverage used melodrama to depoliticize the actors and events in ways that proved useful for the Bush administration. By the time President Bush announced his plans to invade Afghanistan, the broadcast media had already primed the public to accept war as the only "just" response to terrorism. This priming function was confirmed by a Pew Research poll of public opinion regarding the media's handling of 9/11. A majority of the public thought the media had done a good job of both being "objective" and "standing up for America" in its coverage.[26] Recognizing the economic viability of ethnocentric and jingoistic coverage post-9/11, the news networks transformed themselves into megaphones for administration propaganda, amplifying the administration's message regarding the need for war in both Afghanistan and Iraq.[27] When National Security Advisor Condoleezza Rice asked the news networks to cease transmitting Al Qaeda videos for fear of disseminating "coded messages" to sleeper cells in the United States, for example, CNN, Fox News, MSNBC, and all three major networks complied with the censorship request. As Fox owner Rupert Murdoch plainly put it, "We'll do whatever is our patriotic duty."[28] The public, for its part, approved of such censorship, especially when it came to military matters.

Even such compliant news coverage failed to please administration officials, however. Claiming "there's a lot of other ways to convey information to the American people than through news organizations," they increasingly took their case to the entertainment media. For example, Pentagon officials assisted in the production of several reality TV series focused on combat operations in Afghanistan (chapter 3) and collaborated with the producers of JAG to tout the military tribunal system later ruled unconstitutional by the U.S. Supreme Court (chapter 4). The DOD provided material and other forms of assistance to a variety of filmmakers and TV producers willing to produce a compelling image of the military lifestyle, and, in 2003, Secretary of State Colin Powell even appeared on MTV to pitch the administration's case for the war in Iraq.[29] The use of non-news and soft-news venues to transmit political messages was a deliberate strategy to depoliticize the War on Terrorism and enlist the public in its continuation by evacuating the negative consequences of war. As the body of this book will demonstrate, such entertainment programming was unabashed, though not unconflicted, in its defense of the United States and its strategies for combating terrorism. Consciously and unconsciously, such programming justified the War on Terrorism and solidified the identification of the U.S. public with its goals, specifically the militarized extension of U.S. hegemony.

Popular cultural producers did not wait to be solicited to contribute to the war effort, however. In many cases, they pitched in voluntarily. Advertisers, for example, created patriotic-themed ads to express their sympathy with the suffering nation and its political leaders in the aftermath of the attacks. The nonprofit public service agency the Ad Council called on the advertising industry to help "inform, involve and inspire Americans to participate in activities that will help win the war on terrorism."[30] They orchestrated a public-service campaign, called the "Campaign for Freedom," whose tagline echoed the Bush administration's depiction of 9/11 as an act of "hatred" directed at our "freedoms." It read, "Freedom: Appreciate it. Cherish it. Protect it." Commercial advertisers, also, began incorporating American flags, red, white, and blue bunting, and images of firemen and policemen, the designated heroes of 9/11, in their advertising imagery. The McCann Erickson agency even cribbed President Ronald Reagan's famous "Morning Again in America" campaign ads (1984) to create for General Motors an ad linking consumption of its vehicles to national recovery. The ad featured a sunrise and the following text: "The flags are back up. They're playing football again. And people are once again experiencing the simple joy of buying a new car."[31] Like the 1984 Reagan ads, this ad culminates in an assertion of American pride and strength indexed to economic vitality and well-being. It evokes the old adage "what's good for GM is good for America" and connects patriotism to consumption in ways that reinforced the Bush administration's post-9/11 injunction to "go shopping" and "visit Disneyland."[32] By exercising their "freedom to consume," the logic went, U.S. citizens would demonstrate the nation's resilience, advertise the American Dream, and help rebuild the nation's economy, thereby defeating the terrorists on a number of fronts. Such patriotic advertising contributed to a jingoistic climate that encouraged the popular withdrawal from public debate regarding issues of foreign policy. Good citizens, such ads implied, would "live their lives and hug their children" and trust their political leaders to handle the rest.[33]

The radio industry also played an important role in generating a popular consensus supportive of war. In response to the 9/11 attacks, two of the largest radio networks in the country, Clear Channel and Cumulus, spontaneously banned from the airwaves songs deemed to be "inappropriate" to the new climate of seriousness post-9/11 or in "poor taste" given the nature of the attacks. The list of banned songs ranged from Bruce Springsteen's "I'm on Fire" and the Cure's "Killing an Arab" to Alanis Morissette's "Ironic" and Cat Stevens's "Peace Train." The inclusion of the latter two songs illustrates the post-9/11 antipathy to critical distance and dissent, however mildly expressed.[34] This intolerance toward dissent led Cumulus to sponsor boycotts of the country music group the Dixie Chicks after lead singer Natalie Maines told a London audience Texans were embarrassed to say the president came from their state. Local Cumulus DJs even held CD-smashing parties in a number of cities. In addition to advocating the censorship of free speech, conservative talk-radio hosts openly advocated for the president's war policies and served as a conduit connecting administration officials to their conservative "base." In the run-up to the invasion of Iraq, for example, Clear Channel sponsored a series of "Rallies for America," hosted by conservative radio personality Glenn Beck. These rallies were basically advertisements for the war, often staged in military towns and showcasing military technology and military careers. Vice President Dick Cheney and President Bush both appeared on the *Rush Limbaugh Show*, the most popular conservative talk-radio program in the country, to enlist Limbaugh's listeners as foot soldiers in the battle to win American hearts and minds. Not only did Limbaugh provide an open mike for administration officials, he aggressively defended the administration's war strategies and tactics, even dismissing the Abu Ghraib scandal as a collegiate hazing ritual.[35]

While much of the support within the culture industries for the Bush administration's policies post-9/11 was spontaneous and "bottom-up," some of it was funded and coordinated by government agencies. Video-game developers, for example, have long collaborated with the military to produce simulations for training purposes, which could later be modified for release in the commercial market. The collaboration enables game makers to offset some of the costs of research and development while allowing the military to lower the costs of combat training.[36] It is a win-win situation for all involved. The collaborative relationship between game developers and the military reached its apotheosis with the development of a Pentagon-Hollywood cofinanced Institute for Creative Technologies at the University of Southern California.[37] The facility is designed to enhance research and development into virtual reality and artificial intelligence by combining the monetary and mental resources of the university, the Pentagon, Hollywood studios, and commercial game developers. The Pentagon paid $45 million for the first five years of the facility's operation to get access to cutting-edge technologies for enhancing the realism of its training simulators. The university gets research money, and Hollywood studios and game creators get a chance to refine their special effects and lower the costs associated with them. Everyone benefits.

Recognizing the importance of gaming to contemporary popular culture, all branches of the service now make video games and gaming equipment available to troops in the field to enhance morale. The army has even created its own video game, *America's Army*, to assist with its recruitment and retention efforts. The game immerses players in the military lifestyle and allows them to "play war" with maximal realism. As Roger Stahl reports, the game reproduces "military realities of low strategic sensitivity" in elaborate detail, for example, varying the type of explosion by grenade type, making sure breathing and heart rate affect targeting on its virtual firing ranges, and even punishing "soldiers" for failing to follow military rules of engagement.[38] The army ensures this level of realistic detail by shipping programmers out to play war games twice a year at the Pentagon's expense.[39] Because the game is designed for teen audiences, however, the realism is highly selective, emphasizing the high-tech weaponry and skilled training available in today's army but glossing over the negative consequences of combat. *America's Army* does not show, for example, how contemporary weaponry rips bodies apart or turns them to ash. It does not depict death as painful or long-lasting. Players simply crumple to the dust and then start over again. The result of such selective realism is to produce an emotional rush that cathects young players to the military lifestyle.

More troubling, the military also assists commercial developers to enhance the realism of games based on former combat operations. Games such as *Medal of Honor* and *Conflict: Desert Storm* give players the chance to reenact battle scenes from past wars based on logistical field notes and reconnaissance information from the actual operations. Like *America's Army*, such games function as advertisements for the military lifestyle, which is why the military collaborates in their production. The online game *Kuma/War* takes the process of military interpellation to its logical extreme by inviting players to play the War on Terrorism virtually as it happens. According to Stahl, *Kuma/War* "gives players a chance to re-enact dramatic military scenes just weeks after they play out on television news."[40] The creators of *Kuma/War* are all former military men who draw on their military connections to gather logistical information for their interactive combat scenarios. They feed the combat teams information that real military combat teams would have, such as satellite imagery of the terrain of battle, and ask the players to "game" the war scenario. More than just an advertisement for the military lifestyle, Kuma/War helps to militarize society by transforming ordinary civilians into "virtual citizen-soldiers."[41] Like America's Army, Kuma/War offers an illusion of authenticity that effaces the material effects of warfare on civilians and soldiers, thereby intensifying the player's identification with militarism as a project. Jennifer Terry reports, for example, that the gamed version of the 2004 marine assault on Fallujah, called Fallujah: Operation Al Fajr, rescripted the conflict in such a way as to transform U.S. soldiers into protectors of Iraqi civilians trapped inside the battle zone when, in fact, it was the U.S. military cordon that trapped them in the first place and U.S. soldiers who constituted the gravest threat to their existence. Three hundred of the 800 fatalities from the assault on Fallujah were civilians, including the elderly, women, and children, a fact conveniently belied by the game-play.[42] The success of Kuma/War convinced the U.S. Army to develop its own multiplayer online war game called Asymmetric Warfare Environment (AWE). The game reportedly "will allow hundreds of thousands of players to simultaneously train in combating terrorism. Starting with Baghdad, the plan is to model every hotspot the world has to offer."[43] Games such as Kuma/War or AWE demonstrate how interactivity, far from heralding the liberation of the media consumer, may more fully identify him or her with the logics of the state and its military apparatuses. The apparent freedom of choice involved in playing these games makes the transformation of citizens into soldiers far more efficient and effective than older strategies of information control, such as censorship or propaganda.

Hollywood producers and performers have also openly collaborated with the White House, the Pentagon, and the various intelligence agencies to produce a supportive environment for the rebirth of U.S. militarism. For instance, Hollywood media executives, screenwriters, and directors met with representatives from the FBI a mere month after the terrorist attacks. The FBI asked these cultural producers to concoct a series of potential terrorist scenarios for use as intelligence training modules. The next month Karl Rove himself met with high-profile media moguls and producers, such as Motion Picture Association of America (MPAA) president Jack Valenti, Viacom owner Sumner Redstone, Fox owner Rupert Murdoch, executives from the major studios, and screenwriters and directors, to enlist their support. White House spokesman Ari Fleischer described the meeting as an opportunity for the White House to "share with the entertainment community the themes that are

Video games such as *Full Spectrum Warrior* and *Kuma/War* mimic news reports and incorporate actual reconnaissance data to create as real a simulation of the "war game" as possible.

being communicated here and abroad: tolerance, courage, patriotism."[44] Of course, these themes were to be associated exclusively with the United States and its citizens. While Jack Valenti insisted "content was off the table" during the meetings, he also described the meetings as "quite affectionate to behold" and suggested Hollywood could "try to tell people how America has been the most generous country in the world. We have fed and clothed and sheltered millions of people without asking anything in return."[45] As Justin Lewis, Richard Maxwell, and Toby Miller conclude, the meeting was really "an intelligence briefing designed to bring the Hollywood power elite up to date on the White House's war aims."[46]

The immediate result of this confab was the production of a Showtime docudrama recreating the movements of Bush administration insiders in the days following the 9/11 attacks. Called *DC 9/11: Time of Crisis*, the film worked to reassure viewers that President Bush was a man's man, firmly in control after the crisis. Indeed, the program presents all major policy developments, as well as all public relations talking points, as originating from Bush himself. To make room at the center for Bush, the producers have to deliberately sideline Vice President Dick Cheney, who is reduced to his nickname "Vice," continually dictated to by the president, and later sequestered off-site in an underground bunker at the president's order. Cheney appears in all subsequent scenes, including all cabinet meetings, via a tiny television screen positioned on the margins of the room and out of sight of the TV viewers. Lest we miss the point, Ari Fleischer explains that the "Cheney-runs-the-show myth" is false and "what is really going on" is that the president holds all the reins.

Also sidelined, of course, is Richard Clarke, director of the Counter-Terrorism Security Group at the National Security Administration, who had been advocating for a more aggressive posture toward Al Qaeda since January of 2001 to no avail.[47]

Bush's authority in the film is grounded in his physical superiority and masculine performance style. Each "day" in the narrative chronology begins, for example, with a scene of the president jogging or pumping iron, with low-angle crotch shots being the preferred method of composition. A sequence of brusque but provocative pronouncements also positions Bush as a Western hero out for righteous retribution. As Susan Faludi puts it, "the Showtime Bush was part Hulk Hogan ('We're gonna kick the hell outta whoever did this! No slap-on-the-wrist game this time!'), part Rambo ('This will decidedly not be Vietnam!') and part Dirty Harry ('If some tinhorn terrorist wants me, tell him to come over and get me! I'll be at home waiting for the bastard!')."[48] To underscore his authority, Bush orders his inferiors to stop calling him "Mr. President" and start calling him "Commander in Chief." Cheney clarifies the implications of this position for the White House staff: "We'd better remember in the weeks, and months, and perhaps even years to come that we work for the President, the political Head of State, but we also take orders from the Commander-in-Chief and *his instincts take precedence when necessary over our opinions*" (emphasis mine). The overall message is that Bush's authority is natural, inevitable, and not to be questioned. Even experience and informed judgment must give way before his manly instincts. These are clearly marching orders for the nation, as well: fall in line or suffer dire consequences.

To underscore the implicit threat, the docudrama cuts actual footage of the 9/11 attacks into every scene transition and, whenever possible, interjects images of weeping Americans as reminders of the costs of inaction. These scenes are not designed just to authenticate the story; they are designed to manipulate public emotion and "remind" the nation, two years post-9/11, of the reasons we fight. The National Day of Mourning and the president's speech to the Joint Session of Congress are both reenacted in full, for example, and fade between the fictional drama (the faux Bush re-presenting stirring speeches) and the documentary fact (shots of weeping Americans, including Bill and Hillary Clinton, responding to the message) in ways that tug at the heartstrings and validate the proactive message of the film. In all, DC 9/11 offers an unalloyed endorsement of neoconservative foreign policy doctrine, especially concerning the need to attack Iraq.[49] "The danger of not acting . . . far outweighs all other problems," Bush instructs us in the film, "[in] this post–Cold

War world . . . weakness is despised. Strength is admired. . . . Decisiveness. Action. That is vital." The Iraq conspiracy theories of Paul Wolfowitz and Donald Rumsfeld receive prominent mention in the proceedings, as Bush himself links Saddam Hussein to the World Trade Center attacks "in 1993, if not this one." "That man surely means us no good," Bush opines, "and he is developing weapons of mass destruction." By connecting 9/11 to Iraq in this way, DC 9/11 seeks to drum up support for a policy that, by fall 2003 (when the film aired), was already seen to be failing. In all, the film takes a page directly from the Bush administration's public relations playbook. It propagates fear and anger in order to legitimate a more proactive domestic and foreign policy agenda. Unlimited war, it suggests, is the only cure for national trauma.[50]

In response to the visit by Rove and Co., Hollywood also began producing a spate of military-themed films designed either to tout military technology (Stealth, 2005) or to reduce war to an intimate experience of "brotherhood" and self-sacrifice. The subgenre of the "noble grunt" film has become especially important in the representation of contemporary conflicts, as the conduct of these conflicts has assumed the form of a video game.[51] Foregrounding the "drama of the fighting man," these revisionist narratives disavow postmodern abstraction and return the human element to war.[52] According to Pat Aufderheide, the trend began in the 1980s with the memorialization of the Vietnam War in films such as Platoon and Casualties of War, films that "celebrate survival as a form of heroism, and cynicism as a form of self-preservation." The function of these films is largely therapeutic: they are designed to rehabilitate "bad war[s]" and make it OK to love the military again.[53] Films such as Saving Private Ryan (1998), Thin Red Line (1998), Pearl Harbor (2001), and the HBO mini-series Band of Brothers (2001) (re)popularized this romantic, if not necessarily romanticized, view of war immediately before 9/11, but the trend picked up speed in the wake of the terrorist attacks. Films such as We Were Soldiers (2002), Black Hawk Down (2002), Windtalkers (2002), Gods and Generals (2003), Jarhead (2004), and The Great Raid (2005) all evacuated the political contexts of war and focused instead on the intimate details of the fighting.[54] Documentary depictions of the war in Iraq—Gunner Palace (2003), Occupation Dreamland (2004), Combat Diary (2006), The War Tapes (2006)—have likewise assumed this form, offering decontextualized images of combat as the "reality" of war.[55] The culmination of this trend has been the creation of no less than three military television channels (the Pentagon Channel, the Military Channel, and the Military History Channel) devoted to the realistic representation of the "grunt'" perspective and running films such as Band of

Brothers in an almost constant loop. The military is also using YouTube and Google Video to deliver mini–noble grunt films directly to the populace.[56]

The intensely realistic depictions of combat in these films have led many critics to describe them as antiwar statements. In fact, the films use conventions of documentary realism (consciously mimicking the style of "direct cinema," for example) to persuade a cynical, media-savvy audience of the continued importance of military ethics and values. The assumption is that straightforward military propaganda, of the sort used during World War II to push for U.S. involvement, will not work in today's society. "We're never going to see a 'Strategic Air Command' with Jimmy Stewart being made again," says the U.S. Air Force's Hollywood liaison, Lt. Col. Bruce Gillman, "That doesn't interest audiences, anymore. They've become more sophisticated."[57] Contemporary war films eschew mythic representations of American infallibility in favor of lovingly detailed, hyper-realistic combat sequences. The emphasis on action obviates the need for reflection about the political necessity or morality of war and invites viewers to identify with the skill and professionalism of the soldier, who need not be a "patriot" to be admired. Indeed, professionalism eclipses patriotism as the emotional core of the contemporary war film. The soldiers in these films do not fight for their country or some set of abstract values, but for their buddies and the love of a job well done. As *Black Hawk Down* concludes, "It's about the man next to you." This emphasis on military professionalism ensures that even military defeats, such as the downing of a Black Hawk helicopter in Somalia, can be recuperated for military promotion. By reducing war to an interpersonal encounter, noble grunt films celebrate combat as an occasion for the moral development and personal growth of the individual. War becomes a sort of moral proving ground in which Americans demonstrate bravery, loyalty, discipline, and self-sacrifice. The films thus promote military principles despite the "antiwar" sensibilities occasionally displayed. This explains why the Pentagon has provided either full or courtesy assistance to the producers of all of these films.[58] In essence, the films are military-media coproductions.

Hollywood has also helped fashion a new series of "strategic fictions" supportive of the War on Terrorism and the military and intelligence communities responsible for fighting it. Strategic fictions are "tales of future wars" that are "written as propaganda for or against a particular course of action."[59] In this case, tales of apocalyptic terrorist plots prepared national subjects to accept the need for more intrusive surveillance by the state and its agents. The blockbuster *The Sum of All Fears*, for example, imagined a nightmare scenario

Black Hawk Down (2001) is an example of the "noble grunt" subgenre of war films. In this subgenre, war is no longer about politics or strategy, but "about the man next you."

of nuclear terrorism that conformed almost perfectly to President Bush's political rhetoric. In the 2002 State of the Union Address, Bush justified the need for preemption by asking Americans to "imagine those 19 hijackers with other weapons. . . . It would take one vial, one canister, one crate slipped into this country to bring a day of horror like none we have ever known."[60] This nightmare scenario is precisely the plot of *The Sum of All Fears.* Sensitive to the administration's desire to separate the War on Terrorism from a war on Muslims or Arabs, the film's producers replaced its Arab terrorists with neo-Nazis. In exchange the Pentagon "rented Paramount a small military force" including several bombers, fighter jets, and helicopters, access to the National Airborne Operations Center, fifty soldiers and marines, and an aircraft carrier.[61] The CIA likewise assigned a special Hollywood liaison to train star Ben Affleck in counterintelligence procedures and allowed the production team to measure and model its CIA headquarters in Langley, Virginia. The film was, as Doug Davis suggests, one long advertisement for the military and intelligence agencies that would be fighting the War on Terrorism. Producers even offered a special screening of the film for senators, Bush cabinet officials, and officials from the Pentagon and CIA. Paul Wolfowitz, undersecretary of defense and author of the defense planning memo that first advocated "regime change" in Iraq, allegedly lauded the film for its "realism" and called it "life-affirming," despite the fact that the nuclear catastrophe at the film's heart wipes out half of the eastern seaboard.[62]

Collusive relations such as these have led many to speculate on the existence of a "military-industrial-entertainment complex" whose shared goal is to secure U.S. global domination through the coordination of the nation's hard and soft power assets.[63] Hollywood, according to this theory, constitutes little more than a propaganda arm of the state, which is itself but a servant of capitalism. In truth, however, media collusion in the production of the War on Terrorism has been far less conscious and coordinated than in previous wars. During World War I, for example, President Woodrow Wilson established the Committee on Public Information, also known as the Creel Committee, to produce and disseminate propaganda promoting the U.S. entry into the war against Germany.[64] Among other things, the committee dispatched an army of public speakers—called "Four Minute Men" for the length of their speeches—to the nation's movie theaters to detail the degeneracy of the German enemy and inspire patriotic zeal for the U.S. war effort. Exhibitors also incorporated patriotic newsreels and propaganda films shot by the CPI's own Division of Film into the regular theater program, thereby transforming the nation's theaters into sanctioned spaces for the enactment of patriotic rituals.[65] The committee also encouraged Hollywood filmmakers to create their own propaganda films to assist with the war effort. In exchange for making and exhibiting so-called Hate the Hun films, the film industry was given greater license to monitor their own film content and business practices without government interference.

During World War II, the government established an Office of War Information (OWI), which, through its Bureau of Motion Pictures (BMP), effectively conscripted the Hollywood studios into the war effort. Among other things, the BMP distributed a pamphlet to industry leaders called the "Government Information Manual for the Motion Picture Industry." This pamphlet encouraged industry self-censorship and established rules for the distribution of overseas films that made the projection of a "positive" image of America and its allies the primary criterion of consideration. Studio heads who wanted to secure an export license for their films had to ensure they would "help win the war" by not maligning U.S. allies or presenting "unattractive" aspects of life in the United States.[66] Far from balking at these requirements, the major Hollywood studios pitched right in to help. On their own initiative, they organized and supported a military film unit, the 1st Motion Picture Unit, which was headed by Lt. Col. Frank Capra and staffed by the likes of Ronald Reagan and William Holden.[67] This unit created the famous training/propaganda series *Why We Fight*, as well as numerous other training films and promotions for war bonds, recycling efforts, and victory gardens. Exhibitors again contributed theater space and time to military propaganda efforts, and the Academy of Motion Picture Arts and Sciences even awarded an Oscar to the Marine Corps for its documentary short *With the Marines at Tarawa* (1944).

All of this goes to show that the culture industries were far more integrated into war efforts, and constrained in their ability to criticize the U.S. government or its military, during twentieth-century conflicts than they are today. Rather than a conspiracy, the media-military collusion in the War on Terrorism is a product of a loose convergence of interests. The military agrees to assist Hollywood filmmakers because it views Hollywood films as tools for recruitment, retention, and agenda setting. Hollywood products not only give the military easy access to millions of potential recruits, they also serve as vehicles for "product placements" and congressional appeals. For example, the Air Force coerced the producers of the NBC miniseries *Asteroid* (1997) into including its new airborne laser in the series, rather than conventional weaponry. The laser blows up the rogue asteroid of the title and saves the world.[68] By inserting its "global engagement themes" and expensive technologies into Hollywood films, the Department of Defense hopes to create a climate conducive to increased military spending.[69] In return Hollywood filmmakers get cheap access to otherwise expensive sets, props, and extras, which enhances the authenticity of their dramas. Meanwhile, the multinational conglomerates that run Hollywood receive an abundance of favorable trade and tax benefits.[70] While there is clearly a political-economic convergence of interest between Hollywood and Washington, however, the recourse to conspiracy to explain this convergence oversimplifies very complex processes of social control and implies the public plays no role in the formation, maintenance, or alteration of power relations.

The biggest flaw in this conspiracy theory is its assumption that military-media coproductions always achieve the desired ideological effect—support for the United States and its military. Castonguay insists, for example, that the constraint and management of the "war on terror text" in U.S. popular culture "create[s] a context of reception with limited possibilities for oppositional or politically progressive readings."[71] Yet, a film such as *Black Hawk Down*, which clearly supports the military lifestyle and implicitly advocates for war as the proper response to terrorism, has also been interpreted as an antiwar film and as propaganda for U.S. military weakness. Saddam Hussein allegedly used the film to psyche up his troops before the invasion of Iraq in 2003. Al Qaeda has offered its own "oppositional" reading of the pro-militarist *Rambo* films, suggesting that, like Rambo's body, the U.S. military presents a façade of indomitable might that masks its inherent cowardice: "They are a superpower only in Hollywood and in films. Their heroes are only mythical like Rambo and they won't come to Afghanistan."[72] More importantly, U.S. citizens have used the film Black Hawk Down, and its video game spin-off, to produce multiple online video parodies that deconstruct the noble grunt film's romanticization of combat.[73]

It is important to remember that Hollywood texts now circulate in a global marketplace where they are articulated to different social circumstances. The complexity of contemporary media systems, including the dissemination of technologies of production and the proliferation of channels of distribution, makes it difficult for any single agent—even the sole remaining superpower—to control the political narrative absolutely. Indeed, competition between media outlets for consumer attention encourages audience fragmentation and dispersal and works against the maintenance of a national consensus. As Lynn Spigel argues, "the new media environment does not lend itself to unifying narratives of patriotism. . . . Nationalist popular culture does, of course, exist (and obviously rose in popularity after 9/11), . . . [but] it appears more as another niche market . . . than as a unifying cultural dominant."[74] While media conglomeration clearly does constrain public discourse, narrowing both the range of topics available for discussion and the array of responses to those topics, even conglomeration cannot guarantee the production of a singular or consistent "war on terror text."

Thus, political economy gets us only so far in understanding the role of the media in the coproduction of the War on Terrorism. To understand why it was so easy for the Bush administration to enact its permanent war solution, one must also look at the informal social mechanisms that promoted a convergence of sentiment and interest around the militarization of counterterrorism. Raymond Williams once called these informal mechanisms a society's "structures of feeling."[75] The term designates not just the shared assumptions every society has about itself, its history, and its status in the world, but also the way those assumptions are lived or felt emotionally by individuals. Political and cultural discourses in any society tend to converge, in part, because they draw from a shared pool of ideas, images, myths, and narrative strategies and, in part, because they define a repertoire of proper behaviors. Popular culture is the repository of these ideas and the main engine for the dissemination of behavioral norms. The media circulate and naturalize a society's power relations, but they are more then mere tools of elite propaganda or mass deception. They actively constitute social identities and norms, which individuals aspire to, invest in, and activate in their everyday lives.

To understand how the War on Terrorism became possible, then, it is necessary to examine the regimes of knowledge and affect circulating in and through the popular media. Which journalistic practices, narrative themes, and popular forms were particularly useful for the construction of a pretext for the War on Terrorism? How were political authorities able to leverage extant popular culture to generate affective investment in this "new kind of war"? Why was this process so easy to accomplish? How did the media then feed back into the system, perpetuating a refined set of norms and values conducive to the use of war as an instrument of peace? These are the questions at the center of this text.

Why Entertainment Television?

There are many studies dissecting the role of broadcast journalism in the construction, dissemination, and perpetuation of the Bush administration's militarized security discourse post-9/11.[76] Only a handful of works examine how entertainment formats have participated in that process,[77] and most of these either dismiss television out of hand or treat only a few touchstone texts in isolation. This book offers a more sustained examination of the role of television as an industry, a technology, and a cultural form in the construction, maintenance, and renegotiation of a discourse supportive of militarization post-9/11. One immediate difficulty involved in such a study is distinguishing between the informational and entertainment properties of the medium.

The commercialization of contemporary media systems has increasingly blurred the boundaries between programs designed to inform and those designed to divert. News production budgets have been slashed, and the intense competition for viewer attention has led news producers to include more and more "human interest" elements and "soft news" items. News stories increasingly mimic the structure of melodrama and reduce every social problem to a clash between good and evil with clear villains, victims, and vindicators (often the journalists themselves). Not only is the news more entertaining, but media conglomeration makes every media space a potential space for the promotion of the corporate brand, its artists, and its products. Thus, entertainment increasingly *becomes* news, reported alongside foreign policy and domestic politics and with equal seriousness. Meanwhile, the revitalization of unscripted programming, so-called reality TV, blurs the boundary from the other direction. Producers and viewers alike tout the ability of reality formats to convey information about human relations and social psychology. They speak of such programs as "experiments," rather than amusements or diversions, and evaluate them in terms of the aesthetics of documentary film.[78]

Rather than reimpose some false distinction between information and entertainment, nonfictional and fictional programming, my approach is to treat all program types as simultaneously entertaining and informative. Put somewhat differently, I will treat all TV formats as elements of culture, and culture as a form of "history-in-the-making."[79] Thus, for example, chapter 1 treats news representations of the 9/11 attacks, but it does so by considering how popular cultural myths and narrative structures shaped the presentation of the event as news. Other chapters examine program types often identified with "entertainment" and "escape" (thrillers, military dramas, science fiction TV) but with the aim of demonstrating how these "amusements" also carried information that helped knit together a certain understanding of how the world works, or ought to work.

As I use it, the term "entertainment TV" owes more to the etymological history of the term "entertain" than to modern usages of it to distinguish among television program types. The word "entertainment" derives from the French *entretenir*, which means both "to keep up" or "maintain" and "to hold together" or "support." Thus, my project is about "entertainment TV" in the sense that it examines how U.S. television representations helped to "maintain" the discourse of national security and "hold together" a national consensus favoring the use of war to achieve peace during the Bush years. I argue that the discourse of security, like all discourses, "structures cognition," shaping the way we think about the world.[80] By foregrounding a restricted set of words, images, and combinations of these, discourse makes some ideas and actions appear logical and others illogical, or even unthinkable. For instance, the description of the 9/11 terrorist attacks as "acts of war" makes a military response appear necessary and just. Who would argue against the right of a nation to defend itself against aggressors? As the language of war assumes center stage, however, other strategies of response (diplomacy, modes of legal redress, programs to alleviate the frustrations that engender acts of terrorism) become unthinkable. Discourse takes root in a set of social practices that then reinforce the discourse. Once materialized in this way, discourse takes on a life of its own and becomes virtually self-perpetuating.[81] It becomes common sense.

As the above discussion makes clear, the methodological approach of this text is heavily influenced by the work of French philosopher Michel Foucault. Foucault posits an intrinsic and mutually reinforcing relationship between knowledge and power and examines social discourses as instances of power's articulation. For Foucault, power is not just negative; it is a productive force shaping individual identities and social relations in ways that engender pleasure for some and pain for others. As Foucault puts it, "What makes power hold good, what makes it accepted, is . . . the fact that it doesn't only weigh on us as a force that says no, but that it traverses and produces things, it induces pleasure, forms knowledge, produces discourse."[82] Power, in this conception, is not (or not only) a top-down affair but a subtle, purposive, yet nonsubjective and highly unstable phenomenon that saturates society even down to the level of the individual psyche and body. Power "comes from everywhere" and is implicit in every relation, including one's relation to one's own body.[83] Power in its most institutionalized forms (the state, class domination, paradigms of thought) is but the culmination, or ultimate effect, of the local force relations that individuals enact in their daily lives. Television is a key site for the articulation—both the announcing and the aggregating—of these local force relations.

Foucault's work influences this text in two key ways. First, it impacts the way I approach public discussions of national security. Rather than assuming terrorism is or should be a central problem of the state, I ask how it has been constructed as a state problem. There is an obsession with terrorism in the United States that is out of all proportion to the actual occurrence of terrorist activities in or against this country.[84] Since 9/11, the volume of this discourse has only increased. Though riddled with fantasy, the discourse on terrorism has generated very real material effects. It has reoriented social policy away from domestic needs and toward foreign affairs, sanctioned the conduct of wars with questionable strategic merit, institutionalized surveillance and the suspension of civil liberties within the United States, and promoted an imperialistic expansion of U.S. power that many in the world find threatening. It has created a whole new set of industries and individuals—security agencies, defense contractors, beneficiaries of Homeland Security grants, academics, and media personnel—with vested interests in the continuation of the phenomenon of terrorism. Finally, it has saturated the social fabric and conditioned the behavior of individuals toward their fellow men and women. Skill-ful political actors, including but not limited to those in the Bush administra-tion, have exploited the public's sensitivity to terrorism in the wake of 9/11 and used it to extract power for themselves and to impose control on others. *Why* this has happened is fairly obvious, but *how* it has happened is not. Discourse analysis directs our attention to questions of *how*: How is power articulated, disseminated, and consolidated? Under what conditions and through what mechanisms? By assuming national security is a socially constructed and his-torically contingent discourse, this method also assumes that it can be decon-structed, contested, and shifted in new directions. Examining the techniques of power's operation is a first step in this process.

In terms of the politics of fear mobilized around the concept of terrorism, the key question becomes: How does one turn a free and democratic citizenry into "a people for bondage," not only willing to "let their freedom be taken from them, but often actually hand[ing] it over themselves?"[85] An emphasis on the negative and repressive aspects of power cannot answer this question. Instead, we have to ask: What does the overemphasis on terrorism and coun-terterrorism in security discourse offer individuals? Why might they be willing to invest in the perpetuation of this discourse despite its repressive aspects? I suggest the discourse of security offers a comforting sense of national identity and belonging to individuals threatened by the rapid economic, political, and cultural transformations associated with globalization. In a world character-ized by flux, the discourse of security offers clarity by dividing the world into categories of "us" and "them." David Campbell argues that such boundary definition has always been the raison d'être of foreign policy. "The articula-tion of danger associated with foreign policy . . . instantiates 'the political,'" by giving political communities a sense of themselves as bounded, sovereign entities opposed to other entities in a conflict-ridden world.[86] In the United States, a sense of the "foreign" has been especially important to the formation of national identity since the United States is a settler colony comprised largely of immigrants who come from elsewhere and, therefore, lack a shared ethnicity, language, or sense of history. The identification and persecution of "enemy-others" gives "Americans" a sense of themselves as a singular com-munity. Put differently, the process of identifying and demonizing the "for-eign," which is central to foreign policy, also *produces* "Americans." The resulting sense of identity and belonging is a positive inducement to go along with political methods and practices that seem to serve the state's best inter-ests, even when they may not serve the interests of the individual. This is particularly true for women, queers, and racial and ethnic minorities, who have historically been marginalized within symbolic constructions of national identity.[87] Take, for example, Francisco (Frank) Silva Rocque, a Latino, who gunned down Balbir Singh Sodhi in Mesa, Arizona, four days after the September 11 attacks, claiming it was an act of patriotism. Rocque had confused all Arabs and Muslims with terrorists and then assumed Sodhi fit that category because he wore a turban (Sodhi was actually an Indian Sikh). When the police came to arrest him, Rocque purportedly shouted, "I'm an American. Arrest me and let those terrorists run wild?"[88] While extreme, this episode illustrates quite clearly how 9/11 reoriented domestic racial politics in ways that entailed a conditional expansion of the symbolic and social terrains of citizenship. As sociologist Robert Putnam put it, U.S. citizens developed a "more capacious sense of 'we,'" but one that was still predicated on the exclusion of Arab and Muslim Americans.[89] How this marked expansion of the circle of "we," and its concomitant quarantining and policing of Arab and Muslim "others," was promoted via TV programming will be a central focus of the analyses to follow.

Television has traditionally played an important role in the production, reproduction, and dissemination of national identity.[90] TV programs contain regular references to the nation and to national belonging, and TV viewing is one ritual, among others, that helps to concretize the experience of national communion. Television "naturalizes the idea among the mass public that 'the nation' takes precedence over other forms of collective identity and perpetuates notions of distinctiveness and superiority over other cultures."[91] The nationalist orientation of U.S. television persists even in the face of a global reorientation of the cultural industries, largely because U.S.-based producers still dominate the global trade in TV programs and the U.S. market is still the largest (and most closed) market for cultural goods.[92] Because television helps instantiate national identity and make it a banal aspect of everyday life, it is an important place to look for the production and reproduction of security discourse.

The second way Foucault's theories influence this study is in the approach to television. As the medium has moved away from a centralized network model of organization and toward a more flexible, dispersed "neo-" or "postnetwork" model, Foucault's theories of power seem best able to capture the contours of this new system of circulation. Changes in the industry have increasingly fragmented and dispersed the mass audience, making it difficult to argue for the continued relevance of TV in the processes of national subject formation.[93] That TV no longer hails viewers en masse (except on rare occasions, like 9/11) does not mean, however, that it fails to aggregate individuals into groups and to articulate those groups into a critical mass. Foucault's capillary model of power directs attention to processes of asynchronous and dispersed aggregation, that is, to the ways that micropolitical expressions of power coalesce to create tightly knit discursive and institutional frameworks of control. Critiques of the "military-industrial-entertainment complex" largely adopt an arterial model of power that presumes it flows from the center outward, or from institutions to individuals. Such an approach may produce valid insights about the inner workings of those institutions, but it sidesteps the problem of audience fragmentation. It can tell us little about how culture instantiates power relations at the local level and articulates them across an increasingly disjunctive national-political terrain. The arterial approach also cannot account for the emergence of a "participatory culture" in which individuals assume greater control over the narratives, images, and technologies once controlled absolutely by state and corporate authorities. As participatory culture empowers individuals, it makes it more difficult for those "in power" to impose order and consensus.[94] One need not imagine media as tools of social revolution to understand how participatory culture might change the rules of the prevailing game.

The fragmentation and dispersal of the national audience enabled by new technologies of control and choice demands a more sophisticated approach to the question of how TV participates in the construction of a national public. Instead of looking from the top down, we need to examine how power is articulated, where and how it flows, and how it links up to form a comprehensive system even though no single individual or corporate entity may be directing traffic and no two individuals may be accessing the system at the same time and in the same ways. In the case of the War on Terrorism, there is clearly a significant amount of overlap between the Bush administration's official rhetoric and the TV industry's portrayals of terrorism and counterterrorism. Yet, the theory of a state-corporate conspiracy can account for only some of this overlap. In most cases, media representations respond to local conditions of intentionality, whether that is a reporter's unconscious ethnocentrism, a television producer's sense that patriotism will sell, or a filmmaker's attempt to appease Arab media watchdog groups by changing a film's villain from an Arab to a neo-Nazi. The net result may still reinforce the larger strategy of power, but that result cannot be guaranteed or assumed in advance.

Rather than assuming an automatic propaganda effect, this text seeks to map the dynamic role of U.S. entertainment television in the formation of public discourse and practice in the wake of the 9/11 attacks. I approach television as a dynamic, nonlinear system for the production of knowledge about the world and the conditioning of behavior within it. In this system, relations of cause and effect are neither simple nor straightforward; inputs do not necessarily correlate with outputs in either scale or substance. TV producers may invest heavily in patriotic-themed entertainments, for example, only to find these rejected by the mass of TV viewers. Though TV's specific outputs cannot be guaranteed, TV still plays a crucial role in "the construction of modern regimes of knowledge and perception."[95] Indeed, as cultural studies theorists are fond of arguing, popular media are constitutive of reality as we know it. They help frame our understanding of the shape of the world and project normative notions of being and belonging that, in turn, establish the terms and techniques of power's operation within society. I am interested in the way that television helps construct and disseminate common sense assumptions about the nation, its peoples, its values, and its position in the world. Occasionally, the media may be consciously manipulated for strategic purposes, but such manipulation works only if individuals are already familiar with and invested in the cultural common sense of the society—its discourses, practices, and regimes of knowledge and pleasure.

Chapter Outline

The project proceeds roughly chronologically from the immediate aftermath of 9/11 to the end of the Bush tenure. The first two chapters address the politics of fear marshaled after 9/11 to encourage the public to fall in line behind President Bush and his new, more aggressive policies of national security. Chapter 1 examines news coverage of the 9/11 terrorist attacks and its role in producing an emotional context favorable to war. I argue that journalists deployed the conventions of melodrama to personalize the tragedy and package it as a familiar tale of innocence violated. This violation seemed to cry out for vengeance as a solution; thus, the news media helped prime the public for war even before the Bush team called for such a policy. Journalists were not alone in this endeavor, however. The initial framework for interpreting 9/11 quickly circulated through popular television representations of the catastrophe on "soft news" programs such as *America's Most Wanted* and in scripted dramas such as *Third Watch* and *The West Wing*. These sources refined the construction of the terrorist-villain and furthered the call for strong, manly heroes to protect the nation.

Chapter 2 examines the representation of counterterrorist discourse in television thrillers such as *Threat Matrix*, *The Grid*, *The Agency*, *Sleeper Cell*, and 24. It argues that such programs do not reflect threats to U.S. security objectively; rather, they construct abstract and expansive notions of "threat" in order to legitimate the militarization of counterterrorism and the redirection of social authority and public expenditure this requires. The way these programs constructed their terrorist villains and patriotic heroes helped normalize the state of emergency and promote the acceptance of policies of surveillance, detention, and interrogation that were fundamentally antidemocratic. Much of the work of legitimating these policies was performed not at the level of ideology—where there was a good deal of variation among the programs—but at the level of affect—where the programs consistently propagated a sense of urgency and anxiety that led audiences to desire extreme action as a means of alleviating the perception of pressure. By targeting the sensations and emotions of viewers at least as much as their intellects, the programs made affect productive and put it in the service of a particularly pernicious (because antidemocratic) political agenda.

The next three chapters consider the proliferation of "militainment" formats that accompanied the invasions of Afghanistan and Iraq. By "militainment," I mean entertainment programs with strong military content and themes. The term is often used to describe a formal collaboration between the military and the culture industries, but I am equally interested in programs that do not receive overt military assistance, may even position themselves as antiwar statements, yet end up reproducing the conditions of war production. Chapters 3 and 4 examine the military-media coproduction of Operations Enduring Freedom and Iraqi Freedom in programs such as AFP: *American Fighter Pilot* (ABC), *Making Marines* (Discovery), *Profiles from the Front Lines* (CBS), and *Military Diaries* (VH1), and the scripted series JAG. Policies of press censorship ensured that reality TV series offered some of the only images of the early war U.S. citizens had access to. The fly-on-the-wall camera style of these series aligned viewers with the American soldier's perspective and helped normalize the culture of militarism by presenting it as a mundane reality, or lifestyle choice. In this way, the programs helped transform U.S. citizens into what Roger Stahl calls "virtual-citizen-soldiers." Meanwhile, the fictional series JAG—a legal thriller devoted to the exploration of the military character—incorporated high-profile instances of bad press related to the conduct of the

War on Terrorism in order to rewrite the outcomes in ways that flattered the U.S. military. By exonerating U.S. soldiers of intentional wrongdoing in instances of friendly fire, collateral damage, or excessive force, the program materialized the myths of American innocence and exceptionalism that lay at the heart of the Bush doctrine. Ultimately, the show's "remediation" of war coverage was designed to "premediate" the future memory of war and ensure its continued availability as a tool of foreign policy.[96] Together, these scripted and unscripted military series helped transform war from an experience to be avoided into a force that gives us (the United States) meaning.[97]

As a preventative war, undertaken by choice, and conducted through the use of questionable tactics, the war in Iraq strained the "Just War" narrative to its breaking point and undermined the complacency of the public with regard to the use of war as an instrument of foreign policy. Chapter 5 charts the transformation in public attitudes toward war by examining the transformation in the rhetoric used to justify the invasion. It examines the combat series *Over There* (FX) and *Generation Kill* (HBO), which presented the invasion as a botched frontier expedition that could, nevertheless, be salvaged with the right techniques and tactics. The emergence of both series coincided with and symbolically reinforced the shift toward a smaller-scale, more specialized strategy of counterinsurgency warfare in Iraq and, by celebrating the skill of the professional gunslinger, implicitly argued for the extension of that strategy to other sites around the globe. Thus, despite their antiwar sentiments, they ended up helping to turn the "virtual-citizen-soldier" into an "armchair imperialist."[98]

Whereas the first five chapters are largely concerned with the manufacturing of popular consent for the new security policies, the last two examine the emergence of popular ambivalence, anger, and dissent against those policies in a variety of television programs and formats. Chapter 6 examines how satiric and fantastic programs, from *The Daily Show* and *Whoopi* to *Lost, Invasion*, and *Battlestar Galactica*, opened a space in the cultural terrain for dissent to be elaborated, explored, and consolidated. Satiric programs used humor to puncture the pretensions of political authorities and open political discourse to a broader range of voices and ideas, while science fiction programs used political allegory to interrogate the post-9/11 politics of fear and the security policies that followed from it. While none of these programs articulated an alternative approach to security, they all paved the way for such articulations by showing how "counter-terrorism is complicit in creating the very thing it abominates."[99] That is, they showed how state violence begets terrorist violence in an endless, escalating, and self-perpetuating cycle and, in that way, sought to transform the way individuals thought about their world.

Chapter 7 returns to more literal representations of the War on Terrorism to examine the proliferating images of wounded soldiers in entertainment formats from 2004 onward. As news media increasingly drifted away from war coverage after 2005, images of violated soldier-bodies emerged in entertainment formats across the spectrum. From daytime talk shows (*The Montel Williams Show*) and primetime reality series (*Extreme Makeover Home Edition, Off to War*) to a variety of high-profile dramas on network, cable, and premium channels (*ER, Bones, Law and Order, Without a Trace, Kill Point, Six Feet Under*), mentally and physically wounded soldiers became a staple of the TV landscape. I argue that these wounded soldiers served to return the repressed realities of war to U.S. society. By detailing the human costs of war, they begged U.S. citizens to bear witness to and assume responsibility for the policies being enacted in their names. In some cases, this entailed a simple emotional catharsis that produced nothing more than identification with U.S. soldiers, but, in other cases, these images drew attention to the structural conditions underlying the suffering, thereby prompting a more ethical mode of witnessing.

Ultimately, the aim of these two chapters is to illustrate how television continues to function as a "cultural forum," or site for the negotiation of social contradictions and crises.[100] The cultural forum approach has never been about discovering how TV transmits a singular ideology through a singular text. Rather, it is interested in how TV texts collide and, in that collision, mark out the boundaries of social discourse—the limits beyond which a society will not go but within which individuals may entertain a range of ideas and engagements. Amanda Lotz, for one, argues that the processual approach offered by the cultural forum model is uniquely suited to contend with the fluidity and complexity of contemporary television because it asks how messages traverse the televisual system, rather than how they inhere in particular texts.[101] By asking how "texts brush up against other texts, institutions, technologies, and practices," the model allows us to account for the aggregation of publics across the length and breadth of the intermedial system that now constitutes "TV."[102] It enables us to grasp how television continues to provide shared experiences of reality despite the death of the mass audience.

Terrorism TV offers one highly contingent attempt at "working through" the mass of televisual data related to the War on Terrorism and identifying points of convergence. It is neither exhaustive nor definitive, in part because the sheer volume of material is so vast. What it does do is outline certain patterns of presentation that emerged from 2001 through 2008 across some of the more recognizable programs and program types. While television as a whole has clearly reproduced key aspects of the political discourse and practice associated with the War on Terrorism, it has also provided opportunities for viewers to process events in new ways. It has even modeled how to do this by entertaining ethical questions and inciting viewers to assume responsibility for resolving them. In short, it has constituted viewers as active witnesses of history, responsible for making sense of what they see and what they can't or won't see. Ultimately, the study aims to remind readers that culture is a complex site of social formation, articulation, and modulation. As a process, it offers big rewards but no guarantees—not even to those who control the central institutions of society. While it may work on individuals, shaping them into certain types of "citizens," it may also work through them, affording them an opportunity to transform behavioral and social norms. To determine the outcomes, you have to examine cultural texts in their contexts of production, circulation, and reception. That is what this study aims to do.

1 9/11 and the Trauma Frame

When American Airlines flight 11 crashed into the North Tower of the World Trade Center (WTC) at 8:45 AM EDT on September 11, 2001, local, national, and cable network news organizations rushed cameras to the scene and, thus, were on hand when the second plane, United Airlines flight 175, crashed into the South Tower. Adhering to the "Breaking News" format of news production, broadcast journalists scrambled to gather the facts and provide a sense of the on-site experience for viewers located elsewhere. Early coverage featured live shots of the burning towers, eyewitness accounts of the devastation, commentary from official sources, and very little context or analysis. According to one study, as much as "76 percent of the [initial] coverage dealt with the presentation of facts"; only 19 percent offered analysis, and much of that eschewed history or politics in favor of references to Hollywood films or biblical apocalypses.[1] The goal of the early coverage was simply to set the scene. After the towers crumbled and the dust cleared, TV news took on a new mission, which was to package the events for ongoing consumption. The catastrophe was translated into a chronological narrative, accompanied by visual loops, and repeated at regular intervals as if to reassure viewers that life still had order and meaning. TV news acted, in other words, as a "shock absorber," taming the "wild footage of the wild world" and presenting it to viewers in a form they could recognize and identify with.[2] Specifically, news of the events became a form of public drama complete with spectacular settings, compelling characters, and emotional themes of loss and perseverance reminiscent of fictional television dramas.[3]

This melodramatic style of news coverage helped translate the events of September 11, 2001, into the national trauma that would become known as "9/11." As Neil Smelser notes, there is nothing inherently traumatic about historical events. Rather, trauma is a socially constructed and culturally conditioned way of *responding* to events.[4] By framing the story of the September 11 attacks in traumatic terms, news media primed the public to interpret the events in certain ways and to conveniently "forget" other aspects of the story, such as the failure of the government and intelligence services to anticipate or disrupt the threat. 9/11 became "a morality tale about patriotism, loss, victimhood, and heroes," organized almost exclusively around appeals to emotion.[5] The result was a simplified narrative of national violation that echoed and legitimated the Bush administration's call for retributive violence.

How the news media borrowed the tropes of melodrama to shape 9/11 into a form of national trauma will be the focus of the first part of this chapter. It will show how the media's intense concentration on the spectacle of individual suffering produced a sense of collective victimization that seemed to cry out for redemption through violence. The second part of the chapter considers how entertainment programs responded to the attacks in ways that amplified these trends. Specifically, it examines how the special 9/11 episodes of the television programs Third Watch, America's Most Wanted, and The West Wing used the conventions of news coverage to reinforce the construction of terrorism as a simple conflict pitting "innocent" Americans against "evil" others. Featuring eyewitness interviews, objective styles of camera positioning and movement, and direct address, these programs deliberately confused the information and entertainment functions of television in the hope of redeeming entertainment from charges of frivolity and irrelevance in the new age of "seriousness." West Wing Executive Producer John Wells acknowledged as much when he said the special 9/11 episode of that program was designed to "make people talk and think" in a way that promoted civic engagement.[6] Its use of direct address and incessant dialogue mimicked TV news as much as its content replicated the Bush administration's characterization of terrorism as abstract "evil." By reading news media in conjunction with entertainment programs, I hope to show how the lines between realism and documentarism, melodramatic and civic modes of discourse, became hopelessly blurred in the aftermath of the attacks, and how this blurring encouraged individuals to accept the consolidation and extension of state power. Indeed, these special 9/11 episodes heralded the administration's more deliberate approach to the use of entertainment as a mode of information provision and, thus, demonstrated the importance of the domestic terrain—the winning of U.S. hearts and minds—to the conduct of contemporary modes of war.

The Melodrama of American Innocence:
Breaking News Coverage of 9/11

Breaking news coverage of the attacks on the Twin Towers emphasized emotional appeal at the expense of political and historical context.[7] The goal was less to explain the events than to bring viewers close to the suffering and dismay—to create an experience of live witness that would envelop viewers into the unfolding drama. Given the difficulty of gaining perspective on events that are still unfolding, the news media's reflexive emphasis on liveness and proximity are understandable. The standards of objective journalism in a privatized and commercialized media system dictate that description dominate over analysis in such circumstances. The explicit goal of such coverage may be to present the facts, yet the focus on eyewitness testimony and sensational detail ultimately privileges an intimate and personalized perspective, which lends itself easily to conversion into public melodrama. Very quickly the focus shifts from generalized discussions of emotion to individualized stories of suffering and triumph. Victims, villains, and heroes emerge as character types, and their interplay provides a narrative coherence to the chaos. Viewers familiar with the conventions of melodrama know what to expect next: good will triumph over evil, and the existence of moral order will be reaffirmed.[8] They start to look for redemption, usually through the violent elimination of the villain. In the case of 9/11, the melodramatic frame nurtured a powerful sense of American grievance and provided an incentive to support the militarization of counterterrorism, for in melodrama punitive violence brings catharsis.

The first step in the process of melodramatic framing was to emphasize the scale of the attacks in order to make them appear exceptional in kind and quality when compared to all previous terrorist incidents. CNN reporters were obsessed with issues of "magnitude," a word they repeated like a mantra at the start of every interview. "Give us some historical perspective," they begged of their sources. Rather than seeking to reduce the scope of the events, such pleas were designed to set the day's events apart from history as an "exceptional" experience. Indeed, when the deputy mayor of New York reminded Aaron Brown that mass casualty disasters of this sort were neither "unexpected" nor "unique" in the history of New York City, Brown responded vehemently: "It may not be a unique occurrence, but it is *a very rare and extraordinary one.*" Anchor Judy Woodruff, suffering all day from a case of severe emotional discombobulation, likewise used her experience in journalism to mark the day's events as exceptional: "I have to say in my 30 years as a journalist I have *never seen anything like this*. Never covered a story of the *dimensions* of this." According to Amy Reynolds and Brooke Barnett, the most frequently repeated descriptive keywords in the early hours of the coverage were "horrible," "horror," "horrific," "horrendous," "disturbing," "unbelievable," "extraordinary," and "terrible."[9] Joey Chen's late afternoon recap of the day's events is typical, using all of these words, multiple times and with unusual dramatic emphasis: "*Extraordinary* coverage there from the rooftops in New York of this *extraordinary* and *horrific* series of events that we have been watching throughout the day here at CNN. Acts of terrorism at *such an unprecedented scope and scale*, it is really quite difficult to follow."

The inability to "follow" events led to some reflexive reconstruction of events in more familiar terms. Specifically, reporters and anchors quickly focused on the personal stories of the victims and survivors. These tales of ordinary Americans struck down in the prime of life displaced historical, political, and ethical reflection and invited viewers to empathize with the victims. Just a few hours into the attacks, for example, Brown encouraged CNN viewers to set aside "the facts" and "pieces of information" and, instead, "absorb" the events: "There were 50,000 or so people who came to work on a beautiful, late summer morning here in New York in those two towers that are gone now. These are people with families, with children, people who had offices and have them no more, people whose lives are forever changed." NBC's Matt Lauer and Katie Couric framed the events in similar emotional terms: "It's important to remember," Lauer noted on September 12, "that we're talking about personal stories here. Each person who is lost has families and friends and loved ones."[10] Newspapers provided readers with detailed biographies of the victims, which emphasized their roles as husbands and wives, mothers and fathers, community leaders and all-around good folk.[11] They also regaled their readers with tales of the random occurrences that spelled the difference between life and death that day—a late train, a doctor's appointment, a fateful decision to switch work shifts, and so on.[12] The focus on the arbitrary nature of fate reinforced the ordinariness of the victims and encouraged viewers to imagine themselves in similar circumstances. By personalizing the attacks in these ways, the media put a face on the tragedy for viewers otherwise remote from the events and folded them into a shared experience of national trauma.

As Susan Faludi notes, gender politics were quickly summoned to affirm the innocence of the victims and forge heroes from the rubble. In U.S. culture, innocence is a property usually associated with women and children, while heroism tends to be associated with men. Thus, in media portrayals of 9/11, female subjects were most often used to represent "victimization" despite the fact that male victims outnumbered female victims 3 to 1. As Faludi reports, "the media foregrounded the few pictures they had of men tending to injured or at least distressed women," while neglecting to focus on either the women who tended those injured in the attacks or the many men who needed such assistance.[13] Meanwhile, New York City firefighters emerged as the privileged incarnations of heroism because their actions that day—running into the buildings as others ran out—distinguished them from the other victims. The overwhelmingly male character of the NYFD as an institution naturalized the conflation of such heroic activity with men and masculinity. Newspaper columnists such as Peggy Noonan and Phil McCombs began celebrating the rough masculinity and "strong backs" of the firemen and praising them for their old-fashioned, boot-strapping, "get-the-job-done" attitudes.[14] As Faludi argues, such melodramatic tales of innocent female victims attacked by dastardly dark villains and rescued by manly white heroes recall nothing so much as 1950s Westerns, and the familiarity of such tales went a long way toward preparing national subjects for a war against terrorism.[15]

The personal tales of suffering and redemption were quickly converted into nationalist narratives of trauma and triumph. Journalistic habits of objectivity and neutrality gave way to open celebrations of American nationalism. News programs hastily assembled computer graphics decked in red, white, and blue and paired these with jingoistic slogans such as "America under Attack" (CNN, MSNBC), "Attack on America" (CBS), and "Terrorism Hits America" (Fox). The references to "America," rather than the United States, were designed to privilege the emotional experience of communion over the intellectual experience of political community, thereby obviating questions about U.S. foreign policy and its potential for blowback. What brings us together, the banners indicate, is a shared love of nation, not a shared responsibility for state policy. News anchors embodied the love of nation by appearing on camera wearing flag pins on their lapels and exhibiting absolute deference toward the president and his policies. Even liberal CBS news anchor Dan Rather expressed his loyalty to the chief executive in a famous appearance on The Late Show with David Letterman: "George Bush is the president," Rather averred. "He makes the decisions, and you know, as just one American, wherever he wants me to line up, just tell me where."

Such invocations of American unity were less descriptive than proscriptive. They sought to produce the unity they pretended to describe and defined

"unity" in a very narrow way—as bipartisan cooperation and absolute deference to presidential authority. News coverage featured a veritable parade of
political elites pledging allegiance to President Bush no matter what actions
he decided to take. Even Republican arch-nemesis Hillary Clinton affirmed
"this was an attack on America. And the President of the United States is our
President. And *we will support him in whatever steps he deems necessary to take.*"
Statements like these contrasted sharply with eyewitness accounts, which
tempered anger with wariness about the consequences of an American overre-
action. "I have feelings of revenge," said one eyewitness, "but I sure hope the
government doesn't just arbitrarily select an enemy and, for political reasons,
obliterate that enemy."[16] Such popular ambivalence belies the illusion of a
"naturally" unified American response and exposes the disciplinary function
of such political performances, including and especially the "spontaneous"
singing of "God Bless America" by politicians on the Capitol steps. As CNN's
Wolf Blitzer acknowledged, these rituals of national unity were calculated "to
send a message" to the public. By modeling proper "patriotic" behavior, political elites circumscribed the boundaries of national identity and belonging
and stifled dissent by coding it as "unpatriotic." News producers abetted
these strategies of control by failing to incorporate alternative perspectives.[17]
Elite consensus and deference to the president thus became the model of
proper citizenship in the aftermath of the attacks, and unity behind the president and his policies became a veritable mandate.

References to religion, religious belief, and religious iconography sancti-
fied this vision of national unity and expanded the connotations of "American
innocence" in ways that would serve the Bush administration's future policy
decisions. Reynolds and Barnett counted sixty-one references to God and the
words "pray" or "prayer" during the first twelve hours of CNN's coverage of
9/11.[18] These counts only increased as the reporting moved into the "rescue
and recovery phase," which included live coverage of the national service in
honor of the victims and the National Day of Prayer.[19] What is most striking
about the early coverage is the degree to which such religious references were
being expressed by journalists themselves, not necessarily their interview subjects. CNN's Larry King, for example, prompted eyewitnesses to the morning's tragedy to frame their salvation in religious terms. He asked one of his
guests, a survivor from the South Tower of the WTC, *twice* to explain "why [he]
didn't go back up." Clearly fishing for a reference to God, he showed obvious
dissatisfaction when the man responded mundanely: "it seemed like the sen-
sible thing to do at the time." With the next interviewee, King did not make

the mistake of asking obliquely. He simply affirmed, "you are probably resort-ing to prayer." Judy Woodruff also famously signed off from the first day of CNN's coverage with a very personal statement of belief. She began by asking God to "bless the souls of those who have lost their lives today." She then de-nied even the possibility of a nonreligious interpretation of the events by sug-gesting "even those out there who may not believe that there is a God . . . reach out for a higher being" at "times like this." "We want to believe that there is someone who can bring us salvation," she concluded. Her recourse to the pronoun "we" powerfully constructs the nation as a community of believ-ers. Again, this is less a neutral description than a proscriptive dictum that im-plies nonbelief—the refusal to "reach for a higher being" to explain the events—is abnormal and "un-American."

Religious rhetoric ultimately connected the exceptional moment of na-tional suffering to a tradition of American exceptionalism, which holds that the nation is inherently "good" because of its foundation on principles of lib-erty and equality. In John Winthrop's famous phrase, America is "a shining city on a hill" destined to lead the world by example and deed.[20] Such rhetoric quickly converts into a ready excuse for military adventurism since moral lead-ership demands that one act when faced with "evil." Thus, U.S. politicians have long appealed to exceptionalist rhetoric to justify militarism as a "de-fense of civilization." According to this rhetoric, the United States does not undertake violence lightly or in pursuit of selfish goals; rather, it goes forward "to defend freedom and all that is good and just in our world."[21] By evoking religious language, the media helped frame the attacks as acts of "evil" that posed a threat to humanity and, thus, required a military response.

In short, the melodramatic framing activated apocalyptic structures of be-lief that absolutized the conflict in ways that made militarism appear neces-sary and inevitable. The news media's construction of 9/11 as an "exceptional" experience of unprecedented "dimensions" ripped the events from their his-torical context and permitted an interpretation of them in cosmic terms. A struggle between real world political foes became, instead, a struggle between abstract good and abstract evil for the soul of humanity. As Jack Lule notes, apocalyptic rhetoric has historically been used "to ready a people for conflict and strife, suffering and sacrifice."[22] Though journalists may not have in-tended to produce such a frame, or to use it to justify war, the effect of the vi-sual and verbal choices made on 9/11 was to prepare the public to accept the White House's depiction of the conflict as a clash between the forces of "civi-lization" and the forces of "barbarism." The construction of "America" as an "innocent" victim of a "monstrous" attack coded the U.S. state as the embodiment of the "good" and made its resort to retributive violence seem a "moral imperative."[23] It also stifled political debate about security strategy by implying any response other than militarization amounted to an abdication of the moral responsibility to "fight evil." Dissent was presented as "immoral" and "un-American," not part of who "we" are.

The Bush administration did not coerce media institutions into conceiving of 9/11 in these terms; it did not have to. The commercialization of news production—and the intense competition this engenders—has shifted the priorities of news producers. As Brian Monohan argues, the newsworthiness of a story is increasingly determined not by the value of the information in itself, but by its human-interest quotient: Does the story have a compelling setting and interesting characters? Is it dramatic enough to keep viewers coming back for more?[24] This shift has been underway since the deregulation of the television industry in the 1980s, and, not coincidentally, television coverage of the first "War on Terrorism" provides an eerie precedent for the construction of 9/11 as a national trauma. As Bethami Dobkin has shown, news coverage of televised terrorist spectacles during the 1980s also used melodrama to frame political events in personal and emotional terms and to direct popular energy toward identification with the state and its leaders. Multidimensional social conflicts were reduced to a form of identity politics whereby "America" was constructed as innocent, godly, and good in contrast to the terrorists, who were coded as "evil."[25] Key to defining American innocence was to redefine the state and its representatives in private, rather than public, terms. For example, the U.S. hostages being held at the Iranian Embassy from November 1979 through January 1981 "were identified with the private sphere, allied with family, emotions, and domesticity, rather than diplomacy, officialdom or politics."[26] Images of their families and their lives as private citizens dominated the coverage, making them appear to be "typical Americans," rather than government functionaries. The trope of the "family under siege" generalized the experience of "terror" and evacuated questions of history and politics.[27]

In sum, news of terrorist events in the 1980s offered U.S. citizens mini-morality plays in which the representative "innocence" of the victims made the terrorists appear not just "guilty," but "abnormal" or "degenerate." Terrorism was naturalized through association with terms such as "contagion," "cancer," or "pestilence" and attached to certain societies (Middle Eastern, Arab, Muslim) in ways that made members of those societies seem pathologically violent. The effect of these patterns, as Dobkin points out, was to make the most extreme measures of control seem desirable, even necessary, for the protection of the "average" citizen: "When US journalists tell their stories about terrorism using the conventions of melodrama, replete with paper tigers [as villains] and video postcards [of victims], these news narratives become structurally aligned with an ideology of foreign policy driven by military strength and intervention."[28] Indeed, the Bush Doctrine of preventative war was first advanced during the 1980s by Secretary of State George Shultz as a means of dealing with Libyan leader Muammar Qaddafi's alleged support for terrorism.[29] Thus, journalists and politicians both had ample precedent for constructing 9/11 as a national trauma, and they drew upon an existing body of discourses and practices to portray terrorism as a threat to civilization, that is, the private sphere and family life. The competitive, commercial context of contemporary news production, which encourages the conflation of information and entertainment, just made the recourse to myth that much easier.

The Construction of Terrorist Villainy in Primetime

The interruption of regular television broadcasting in the wake of 9/11 reinforced the sense of dire emergency being constructed in the news coverage itself. As Meaghan Morris notes, we live in a time of such televisual saturation that any interruption in the routine processes of television production is "experienced as more catastrophic . . . than a 'real' catastrophe."[30] Thus, the return to regularly scheduled programming was considered an immense relief and a sign of the return to normalcy.[31] Yet, the content of entertainment programming was not unaffected by the events of 9/11. Producers scrambled to edit out visual references to the Twin Towers in programs set in New York and to eliminate "disturbing" footage that might recall the attacks. The *Law & Order* franchise, for example, cancelled a blockbuster miniseries bringing together three of its programs because the topic was an anthrax attack on New York City. *The Agency*, a series about the CIA, pulled its pilot episode because it featured an incident of Al Qaeda–related terrorism, and a scene of a plane exploding in midair was cut from the techno-thriller 24 (more on these programs in chapter 2).[32] In general, television producers interpreted 9/11 as a signal to change the dominant themes and emphases of their programs. Said producer Sean Daniel, "There's an understanding from television and the CSIs and Law & Orders and the 24s that there's a desire to see the bad guy gotten. It weighs in the story conferences and in the staff meetings. It just does."[33] The

turn toward new, more black-and-white modes of storytelling was but one attempt by a newly self-conscious industry to counter charges of frivolity leveled
at the media in the wake of the attacks. For example, Robert Bresler blamed
the "silliness" and escapism of popular culture for leaving Americans unprepared for the challenges of life in a dangerous new globalized world. He and
other commentators celebrated the "end of the silly season" and looked for
popular culture to assume a new gravitas more suited to the context of war.[34]
The Bush administration also called for a more serious tone in entertainment
when Ari Fleischer infamously admonished comedian Bill Maher for daring to
describe long-range bombing as a "cowardly" style of conflict: "Americans . . .
need to watch what they say, watch what they do. This is not a time for remarks like that; *there never is.*"[35]

The rapid production of primetime programming related to the attacks
and their aftermath, thus, seemed calculated to raise the public profile of a beleaguered industry. The dedication of free airtime to benefit concerts and rituals of mourning was but one way the industry shifted its emphases toward
more civic-minded modes of presentation. Stars were literally relegated to the
background within these live performances (the likes of George Clooney and
Julia Roberts answered hotline phones as viewers called in to make donations) so that an ethic of national unity and copresence could be generated via
direct appeal.[36] Several primetime programs also produced special episodes
dedicated to presenting the "story" of 9/11 and its survivors more explicitly.
These episodes all self-consciously sought to balance storytelling with information provision, producing a semidocumentary effect that was deliberately
civic-minded in nature. They were designed not just to tell a story about 9/11
but to engender and sustain an experience of national communion. In an era
of audience fragmentation and dispersal, such programs sought to resurrect a
long-discarded public service function for commercial television. The producers of these programs appealed to notions of civic duty and honor to explain
their creative decisions. Recognizing that TV provides a shared vocabulary of
references and norms that might help knit disparate individuals into an imagined community, they sought to provide the emotional support and reassurance the public craved.[37] They understood that television has a unique
potential, by virtue of its familiarity and immediacy, to serve as an engine of
national incorporation, and they sought to revive that function. In the
process, however, they helped define new and troubling notions of proper citizenship. How they balanced national reassurance with calls for subservience
and unquestioned allegiance is the focus of the remainder of this chapter.

As I've suggested, the various 9/11 special episodes were marked by a "documentarist" impulse, which subordinated realist narrative to naturalist description and more direct modes of address. As John Corner explains, such documentarism is designed to "[elicit] certain kinds of investments of self" and to "call viewers into empathy and understanding; to create a 'virtual community' of the commonly concerned, of vicarious witness; to cut through accommodating abstraction with the force and surprise of things themselves."[38] It is designed, in other words, as a civic mode of address that hails individual subjects as national citizens and, in that way, engenders imagined community. NBC's Third Watch, a scripted program about firemen and emergency personnel working in New York City, provides a perfect example of this process. In the wake of the attacks, the producers replaced the season premiere with a two-hour documentary featuring the show's consultants, many of whom were active emergency personnel and assisted with the rescue efforts on 9/11 ("In Their Own Words," 10/15/2001). According to actor Skipp Sudduth, who played NYPD officer John "Sully" Sullivan on the show, the program was designed to acknowledge the loss of normalcy in real life before moving on with the show: "We decided that the only appropriate way to continue was to first honor these people by giving them the opportunity to tell their own stories, in their own words, before we return to telling our fictional stories." As a break from the timeline of the program and its regular brand of narrative realism, this episode reinforces the sense of 9/11 as a historical rupture after which "nothing would ever be the same." The documentary testimonials that comprise the content of the show echo the news media's framing of the attacks almost verbatim. Like journalists, the emergency workers reported being "totally unprepared for the magnitude of what [they] saw" that day. NYFD Lt. Bill Walsh called it "too colossal to take in," while NYPD Officer Anthony Lisi likened it to Armageddon: "You felt like . . . it was the end of the world. . . . It was like hell. Hell on Earth." Interviewees also echoed the media's depiction of "unity" and "resolve" as uniquely American character traits. NYPD Officer David Norman, for instance, reported feeling "proud" of the survivors "because strong people were helping those that were injured or weak." He implied such behavior was a "unique" character trait of Americans in times of crisis, something we "always" and inevitably do while others do not. In all, the subordination of drama to documentarism interpellates an imagined national community scarred by trauma and bent on vengeance. When the program resumed its regular pursuit of realism, rather than naturalism, these themes would be at the core of the drama.

Producers of *Third Watch* also scripted two new fictional episodes designed to address the events. Together the episodes illustrate the cataclysmic shift in perspective caused by 9/11. The first, "September 10" (10/22/01), emphasizes the mundane day-to-day routines of a pre-9/11 world, with characters fretting over false emergency alarms, impending nuptials, home renovations, football, and sex, among other things. Initial scenes are shot using a handheld camera to create a sense of intimacy with the ordinary while a nostalgic piano score creates a rosy glow around the events and transforms the everyday into the poignant stuff of tragedy. Using dramatic irony, the script exploits audience knowledge of the impending catastrophe to magnify the sense of dislocation post-9/11. At one point, for instance, Carlos Nieto (Anthony Ruivivar), an EMT with the NYFD, complains to his partner, Doc Parker (Michael Beach), about how slowly the shift is going. Doc replies sarcastically: "I'll see if I can order up a tragedy so the shift can go by faster for you." The shocking line yanks viewers out of their complacent identification with the story and induces critical reflection on the difference between "then" and "now." The sense of foreboding constructed in such pieces of dialogue is reinforced by the use of on-screen temporal markers and a musical score that shifts in pace and intensity as the episode progresses. By 8:20 AM on September 11, the score sounds like the countdown from the horror movie *Jaws*. The episode ends as each of the characters learns of the first plane crash and rushes to the World Trade Center to assist. In all, "September 10" provides American viewers with an opportunity to vicariously reexperience 9/11 and reinforces the journalistic construction of the events as a national trauma that has yet to be worked through.

The second of these scripted episodes, "After Time" (10/29/01), won a Peabody for its sensitive portrayal of the effects of the attacks on the lives of the first responders. It begins two weeks after the attacks and shows the rescue workers struggling to cope with both their private emotions and their public roles as heroes. The episode literally walks the audience through the stages of grief (denial, anger, bargaining, depression, acceptance) alongside its main characters, especially the character of Alex Taylor (Amy Carlson), a firewoman whose father was killed in the line of duty on 9/11. While it begins with death—specifically the image of Jimmy Doyle, a fictional firefighter killed on 9/11— the episode concludes with the recovery of Doyle's body and the birth of a healthy baby at the scene of a traffic accident. Like the so-called 9/11 babies (babies born to the pregnant widows of men slain on 9/11), this child is presented as a symbol of collective hope and recovery. Her existence testifies to the "exceptional" resilience of the American character in the face of extreme trauma and signifies the creeping return of a "normal" existence. The message seems to be that life will go on despite the tragedy. In that sense, the episode appears to challenge the depiction of 9/11 as an exceptional historical event. Yet, "After Time" also likens U.S. victimization to a form of impotence and laments the failure of the state to "do something" about the tragedy. Its circular narrative structure—the episode opens and closes with slow-motion shots of rescue workers heading to and from "the pile," as the WTC rubble is called—creates a palpable feeling of frustration that virtually cries out for heroic remedy. Like modern-day Sisyphuses, the workers seem condemned to roll boulders ineffectually in hell forever, and we viewers feel condemned to suffer along with them. This is a profoundly melancholy image of American powerlessness that begs for redemptive action. Frustrated viewers are invited to identify with the hot-headed Maurice "Bosco" Boscorelli (Jason Wiles), who declares: "Give me a parachute and a pistol and drop me down in there, and I'll shoot [Bin Laden] in the head myself."

Third Watch was not the only primetime series to produce a special 9/11 episode or to stoke the popular desire for vengeance. The primetime political drama The West Wing and the reality program America's Most Wanted (AMW) also generated special episodes devoted to the attacks that combined elements of documentarism—most notably eyewitness testimony and direct address—with melodramatic narrative and visual techniques to reinforce the news media's depiction of "America" as an exceptionally innocent and good nation. Though designed for different purposes, both shows addressed their audiences using the same language of civic responsibility that shapes the ethos (if not the content) of news production, and, like news coverage of the attacks, they imagine they are serving an explicitly national purpose. Thus, in both form and content, these programs reinforced the dynamics of abstraction initiated by news depictions of 9/11 and circumscribed public discourse in ways that stoked popular desire for a retributive form of justice.

The special episode of AMW, called "America Fights Back: Terrorists" (10/12/01), was actually commissioned by the Bush administration and featured an interview with then–attorney general John Ashcroft at the conclusion of the episode. A clever piece of public relations, it was designed less to identify the perpetrators or solicit "tips" on their whereabouts than to consolidate the national consensus necessary for the pursuit of a war against terrorism. John Ashcroft admits as much when he describes the administration's rationale for participating in the program: "We're going beyond governments.

Attorney General John Ashcroft appears on *America's Most Wanted* (10/10/2001) to "shine the light of justice" on terrorists. The show was designed to elicit support for the War on Terrorism.

We're going into the hearts and minds of individuals, and we're saying . . . these were assaults against civilization, and what you do and what you say . . . can work again like it has in the past on this program." As entertainment, rather than news, the program addresses its audience in a familiar manner, promising a confused and disoriented populace they can recapture a measure of control over their lives by participating in the "hunt" for terrorists. "We're working with the White House to launch *you* on the most important manhunt of our lifetime. . . . You really *can* make a difference," host John Walsh concludes. The familiar "you" powerfully interpellates the viewing audience into an imagined national community aligned with the White House and its policies. Viewers should be "proud," Walsh says, "that the White House has chosen . . . [them] to join their fight to catch the seemingly uncatchable."[39] By hosting this episode from outside the White House gates, Walsh assumes the authority of a political reporter and promises his viewers exclusive access to the inner circle of the Bush administration. This illusion of access is really a means of stifling democratic debate, however, as viewers are asked only to assent to or reject established policy, not help shape it. In short, *America's Most Wanted: Terrorists* (AMWT) defines "American identity" in narrow terms—as allegiance to the Bush administration—and invites viewers to embrace their own political pacification as an expression of "freedom" (a free choice).

AMWT constructs this normative American identity through contrast to the "evil" terrorists the United States opposes. A longer, more dramatic version of the news media's "crime script," *America's Most Wanted* specializes in the production and dissemination of such bipolar worldviews. It stages a weekly public confrontation with the "abject"—the unclean, the impure, that which disturbs identity, system, order—to shore up the boundaries between innocence and guilt, "good" and "evil."[40] Dispensing with the justice system's presumption of innocence, AMW invites viewers to become "good Americans" by condemning the "abnormal" criminals it puts on display. The criminals, more than the crimes, are its central focus. As media critics have noted, the emphasis on identity that structures the "crime script" evacuates questions of context or motivation in favor of biological explanations for criminal activity.[41] In the lexicon of AMW, terrorism, like mundane crime, becomes less a calculated political act than a pathological condition of certain individuals or social groups.

In keeping with the crime script, AMWT begins by referencing the "victim's story," recounting the scope and scale of the tragedy incurred on 9/11 and celebrating the "heroic" perseverance of those left behind. "This special," as Walsh himself puts it, "is about getting justice for innocent victims."[42] "I was in NY just yesterday," Walsh tells his audience,

> and it's just amazing. The ruins from the World Trade Towers are still smoldering. Brave crews are working around the clock, pulling out body parts. Many victims were totally vaporized in the collapse, and nothing of them will ever be found. They say the average age of the victims in the towers was only thirty-nine years old. As many as 10,000 widows and orphans were created as a result of this tragedy—men, women, and children whose lives are changed forever.

Walsh emphasizes the brutality of the crimes in order to present the suffering of the victims as exceptional. As in media accounts of 9/11, this exceptional suffering is then used to justify a call for war. "That's why we've got to get these cowards," Walsh says. "That's why we've got to stop terrorism, and we can't give up, no matter what." The statistical averages Walsh cites present the victims as "ordinary folk" and underscore the sense that "it could have been any of us." This strategy not only generalizes the experience of trauma; it transfers the "innocence" of the victims onto "America," which comes to stand for all that is good, pure, righteous, and rational. The program basically replicates President Bush's depiction of the United States "as a nation . . . that rejects hate, rejects violence, rejects murderers, rejects evil," even as it declares an expansive War on Terrorism.[43]

By contrast, terrorist activities are described in the program as "cowardly," "vicious," "evil," and "savage," and the terrorists featured are called "psy-chos," "cowards," "low-lifes," and "dogs." Viewers are urged to help authori-ties "hunt [them] down." The program's graphics work to clarify the moral distinctions between "us" and "them" by literally fulfilling the president's mandate to "expose the *face* of terrorism." The producers overlay headshots of the twenty-two "Most Wanted Terrorists" on top of images of the effects of their crimes; this directs viewer attention toward the similarities between the visages of the "perpetrators" and away from the patterns of similarity that de-fine their actions. The effect is to naturalize the popular association between Middle Eastern ethnicities, Islamic religious practices, and terrorist propensi-ties. Terrorism has a face, these images say, and that face is brown and bearded. The program also uses the metaphorics of "light" and "dark" to clar-ify who is "good" and who is "evil." Photos of the various terror suspects are encircled by a halo of bright yellow light that literalizes the attorney general's promise, quoted in the opening montage, to "shine the light of justice" on these shadowy terrorists.

The end result of this melodramatic visual and narrative construction of "terrorism" is to affirm the Bush administration's depiction of the War on Terrorism as a cosmic struggle between the forces of "good" and "evil," "civi-lization" and "savagery." Indeed, AMWT concludes by providing a platform for the repetition of this official narrative in the form of an "interview" with Attorney General Ashcroft. This "interview" is really more of a conversation, as Walsh peppers the AG with tagged declaratives that merely affirm the ad-ministration's positions. "So it's a long haul. It's a global war, the American people have to be patient, don't they?" Walsh "asks." Such pseudo-questions allow Ashcroft to transmit, rather than defend, administration policies. He reaffirms the depiction of terrorists as "outlaws against civilization" and en-joins "citizens of the world who believe in civilization, who are against the savagery of terrorism" to call the various tip lines established to aid law en-forcement officials. The problem with this appeal to the "hearts and minds" of the world's peoples, aside from the fact that the program would be viewed only in the United States, is that AMWT's profiles in villainy have already de-fined "suspicious behavior" as being brown and practicing Islam. Arab popu-lations, in particular, are not likely to assist in the prosecution of a War on Terrorism that pits the "good" West against a monolithic and "evil" Orient.

What is perhaps most important about AMW is the way it prepares citizens of all sorts to accept, even embrace, surveillance as a social good, a tactical weapon in the "fight for freedom." Viewers are instructed to internalize the surveillance ethic as a condition of their inclusion into the community of "Americans." You have a "duty as an American to call 1-800-crimetv," as Walsh puts it. Viewers are thus transformed into conduits for the capillary dissemination of state power. In the words of Colin Powell, whom AMWT quotes, the public becomes a "force multiplier" giving the State Department "millions of additional pairs of eyes and ears to be on the lookout." But surveillance can work both ways, a point driven home by the graphic depiction of a large, unblinking eye that leads into and out of the commercial breaks. This eye simultaneously stands in for and stares back at the viewing audience, evoking deep-seated cultural fears of "Big Brother watching." Why do such fears fail to register with AMW's audience (at least as evidenced by the show's twenty-plus-year series run)? Because the show presents surveillance not as an oppressive imposition of government, but as a freely internalized aspect of the "American character." The willingness to surveil oneself and others is a point of entry into communal identity—part of what it takes to be a "good American." Inclusion in this normative symbolic community is a reward the program offers its viewers for internalizing and multiplying state power. In short, AMW elides the function of surveillance as a mode of social control by making the exercise of power seem positively pleasurable—a laudable exercise in communal bonding. It confirms the Foucauldian insight that power works best when it is positive and productive, rather than repressive.

By rooting social conflict in issues of identity and culture, rather than politics, the pathologization of terrorism evidenced in *America's Most Wanted: Terrorists* serves a dual disciplinary function with respect to the Bush administration's War on Terrorism. On the one hand, it sanctions the use of extreme measures of interdiction and punishment against those accused of "being terrorist." If terrorists are "deformed," "irrational," "psychotic" beings unresponsive to reason, then measures such as open-ended detentions and "tough" interrogation tactics (i.e., torture) come to seem necessary and just. Indeed, if "Americans" are "innocent" and "good" by definition, any actions they might take in pursuit of the War on Terrorism are excused in advance. On the other hand, the pathologization of terrorism also disciplines the domestic public by defining a normative standard of citizenship that is extremely limited in range. Absolute unity and allegiance to America's political leaders becomes the sine qua non of U.S. citizenship. Within the terms of this discourse, dissent comes to seem "abnormal," hence akin to terrorism and equally deserving of repression. By constructing a difference between "evil terrorists" and "good Americans," and rooting that difference in ontology, AMWT helps consolidate a national consensus favoring the pursuit of a "war" on terrorism and exonerates the United States in advance for any actions it might take in pursuit of that war. It is, in short, a powerful act of political propaganda designed to reclaim militarism as an element of foreign policy.

The West Wing (NBC, 1999–2006), a primetime series that dramatized the inner workings of a fictional Democratic presidency, could hardly be accused of supporting conservatives or their issues. Indeed, real-life conservative pundits condemned the program as hopelessly "liberal in orientation" and criticized its tendency to caricature the beliefs of conservative groups, especially the religious right.[44] Yet, in response to 9/11, West Wing creator Aaron Sorkin penned a special, stand-alone episode on terrorism that differed only slightly from the Bush-approved depiction of the "terror problem" in AMWT. It, too, pathologized terrorism, promoted "American innocence," and disciplined its audience to embrace social authority as a condition of "American" identity. Yet, The West Wing courts its viewers in a different way and offers a more expansive, "pluralist" conception of the national community. Like AMW, it invites people to identify absolutely with the representatives of state authority, but its image of the "proper patriot" is more racially, sexually, and ideologically diverse. In both its form and content, "Isaac and Ishmael" touts "pluralism" as the antidote to terrorism. The result is what David Holloway calls "allegory lite," a displaced interrogation of contemporary political problems, which, by offering something for everyone, ends up offering nothing for anyone.[45] Put differently, by staging an illusion of political debate, "Isaac and Ishmael" effectively preempts the threat of genuine dissent and promotes in its stead a sense of patriotic fellow-feeling grounded in the über-ideology of political liberalism (what Samuel Huntington calls "The American Creed").[46]

NBC president Jeff Zucker and West Wing executive producer John Wells both positioned the special episode as an attempt to intervene in and shape the national processes of grief and mourning. As Zucker put it, the episode was created with the aim of "helping the dialogue in this country and continuing the healing process." "Hopefully," Wells added, "we can say something that's useful."[47] Both men claim they were motivated to sacrifice the $10 million in ad revenue this special episode would cost the network by a high-minded desire to perform a public service in a time of national crisis.[48] Yet series creator Aaron Sorkin, who penned the special episode, was more frank about his motives:

I was thinking selfishly. I didn't want [West Wing] to suddenly become quaint, to suddenly be about a time that seems long ago when our biggest problems were repealing the estate tax and the strategic petroleum reserve . . . one [in] which Republicans fight with Democrats and the White House fights with Congress and that's the fun of the show. So I was thinking "Gee, I've really got to stop and pause and take a moment with the series. It's what feels right. I've got to do something to somehow protect my livelihood and the livelihoods of a couple hundred people that I work with."

Critics and viewers were quick to pick up on the "selfishness" involved and rejected the episode almost before it was aired.[49] The shift from West Wing's routine snappy dialogue and fast pacing classed the program among the "earnest" appeals of tabloid programs such as America's Most Wanted and turned off even regular viewers (bulletin board commentary was full of state-ments like: "that's the episode that made me stop watching"). USA Today's Robert Bianco called it "a crashing and often condescending bore" while Time's James Poniewozik credited the episode with almost single-handedly re-viving the need for irony: "If irony had been dead, it has by now clawed itself out of its coffin and is roaming the moonlit countryside looking for re-venge."[50] And Sorkin himself later acknowledged the episode was a mistake: "I don't think that it was a good episode of 'The West Wing' . . . I'm not even sure it was good television. But what I do know for sure is that it was well-intended."[51]

The "good intentions" of the producers are marked from the beginning by a break in the fourth wall, as the characters step outside their roles to address the public and beg assistance for a variety of charitable organizations. This appeal to charitable giving channels citizen concern toward privatized and emotional modes of response and away from political engagement, thereby preparing for the episode's primary argument, which is about the need to em-brace the imminent expansion of state authority. The stated moral of the episode is to "remember pluralism" and "keep accepting more than one idea." The pluralism on display is a pale shadow of informed political debate, however, and its expression seems to be bought at the expense of acquies-cence to sovereign authority. The decision to incorporate virtually every avail-able opinion on terrorism, from the notion that terrorists ought to be tortured to the old adage that one man's terrorist is another man's freedom fighter, levels important distinctions between historically informed and reasoned

THE WEST WING ENCOURAGES YOU
TO GIVE WHAT YOU CAN TO THE
FOLLOWING ORGANIZATION

West Wing and other special 9/11-themed episodes used a civic mode of address to create an illusion of imagined community. Here, "President Bartlet" speaks directly to viewers and invites them to contribute to various 9/11 charities. ("Isaac and Ishmael," 10/3/2001)

analysis and reactionary spleen-venting. Moreover, we seem to be encouraged to entertain these many opinions only on the condition that we let the authorities handle the actual operation of the country. By offering lip service to tolerance and pluralism while promoting a highly circumscribed conception of civic responsibility that infantilizes the public vis-à-vis the state and its patriarch du jour, "Isaac and Ishmael" ultimately endorses the extreme countermeasures adopted to combat the terrorist bogeymen.

The story itself begins when a routine Internet search for the name of a suspected terrorist turns up an alias that matches the name of a low-level White House functionary. This sends the White House into "crash," or lockdown, mode. A diverse group of fresh-faced high school students from the "competitive" Presidential Classroom program get caught in the lockdown. Deputy White House chief of staff Josh Lyman (Bradley Whitford) herds the children into the White House mess hall and proceeds to lecture them, with the assistance of other staff members, on the fundamentals of U.S. governance, foreign policy, and terrorism. These lessons are contrasted with a different sort of lesson, enacted by White House chief of staff Leo McGarry (John Spencer), who aggressively interrogates the suspected terrorist mole. As Jasbir Puar and Amit Rai have argued, this "double frame" illustrates the tight connection between the repressive and productive modes of state power. The presence of the "monstrous terrorist . . . provides the occasion to demand and instill a certain discipline on the population."[52]

The students are clearly stand-ins for the mass public, and their docility and receptiveness to authority are presented as the very model of proper citizenship during a time of crisis. While they occasionally challenge aspects of the lessons Josh and the other characters convey, they rarely pose alternative theses of their own. Indeed, most of their questions are rhetorical, designed to elicit elaboration and detail, rather than to challenge the soundness of the lesson. They listen attentively as Josh compares Islamic terrorism to the "[Ku Klux] Klan gone medieval and global" and fail to question communications director Toby Ziegler's (Richard Schiff) comparison of the Taliban in Afghanistan to the Nazis in World War II. No one ever disputes the relevance of such analogies or asks about the contemporary historical and political relations obscured by them (the history of the Saudi regime, for example, or the Israeli occupation of Palestine). They accept without question deputy communications director Sam Seaborn's (Rob Lowe) depiction of terrorism as rooted in eleventh-century Islamic culture and thus inherently foreign to America and Americans. When asked by one student "weren't we terrorists during the Boston Tea Party," Sam replies, "No one got hurt during the Boston Tea Party. [Just a] couple of nancy boys who didn't have anything to wash down their crumpets with." The upshot of these discussions is to define terrorism as antithetical to "Americanness." In contrast to terrorist zealots, "Americans" are defined by their "pluralism." "You want to get these people," Josh tells the students, "I mean you really wanna reach in and kill 'em where they live. Keep accepting more than one idea. Makes them absolutely crazy." A visual pan of the diverse faces—male and female, black, white, Asian, and Hispanic—affirms the importance of continuing to embrace tolerance for others since such tolerance distinguishes "us" from the "fascist," "Klan-like" extremists.

To underscore this last point, the other narrative of "Isaac and Ishmael"—the interrogation of the staffer-cum-terrorist-threat—presents what happens when Americans abandon tolerance in the pursuit of security. While Josh and company are entertaining the children in the mess hall, the Secret Service bursts into the office of the accused staff member with guns drawn and orders him to answer some questions. The interrogation scene is blocked and lighted in clichéd ways and offers a direct contrast to the bright, airy, and open mess hall. The background is all but obscured by low-key lighting that emphasizes the contrast between the accuser and the accused. Close-ups of the accused get tighter and tighter as the interrogation wears on, hemming the suspect in and making him appear guilty, while subjective shots from the accuser's point of view align the audience with his ideological perspective. The conventional setup is a dodge, however. The interrogation scenes are really a form of "epic theatre" designed to shock viewers from their complacency.[53] The identification with Leo McGarry's authority, once established, is repeatedly undone by jump cuts and revealing dialogue. The most shocking example of this technique comes at the culmination of the interrogation when Leo asks Ali why he was once accused of phoning in a bomb threat to his high school:

Ali: "It's not uncommon for Arab Americans to be the first suspected when that sort of thing happens."

McGarry: "I can't imagine why. . . . No, I'm trying to figure out *why* anytime there's terrorist activity people always assume it's Arabs. I'm wracking my brain."

Ali: "I can't tell you that Mr. McGarry, but I can tell you it's horrible."

McGarry: "Well, that's the price you pay."

Ali: "Excuse me. . . . The price I pay for what?"

Leo does not answer, leaving the audience to fill in the blanks. It is the price Arabs pay for being Arab—for "having the same physical features as criminals," Leo later says. The contrast between the platitudinous discourse on pluralism taking place in the cafeteria and the racism structuring the interrogation of Arab Americans could not be clearer.

Yet, by exposing the ideology of racism to view, the program makes it easier for its liberal audience to swallow discussions about the need to curtail civil liberties in the name of security, the beneficence of American military power, and the need to trust in the authority of the executive branch. Josh literally tells the students/audience: "Don't worry about [terrorism]. We've got you covered." The program ends with a pseudo-apology to Arab Americans for the persecution they have suffered that can only be construed as condescending. Leo visits Ali in his office where, instead of actually saying he regrets his racist comments, he congratulates Ali for demonstrating "American" self-discipline: "Hey, kid, way to be at your desk." Nothing in the episode suggests that the racial profiling of Arab Americans will or should cease. Indeed, Leo's discomfort during this scene suggests he, literally, knows what he is doing is wrong, but will continue to do it anyway, the very definition of enlightened false consciousness. By cynically lamenting the necessity of such distasteful measures, "Isaac and Ishmael" prepares its liberal audience to accept the "new realities" of a post-9/11 world.[54]

In all, the program promotes an infantilization of the U.S. public that is not unlike that performed by the Bush administration. Whereas president Bush tells tales about "evil-doers" and "monsters" lurking under American beds, *The West Wing* reduces the Arab-Israeli hostility responsible for the bulk of contemporary terrorism to a family melodrama. The paternal President Josiah Bartlet (Martin Sheen) and his wife Abbey (Stockard Channing) tell the "kids" a fairytale about how the conflict between the Jews and Arabs began with the biblical parable of Abraham, Isaac, and Ishmael.[55] Abraham's wife, it seems, wanted his illegitimate son Ishmael cast into the desert so that Isaac could receive his full birthright. This, the students are told, and not the brutal colonization and occupation of Palestine, is responsible for contemporary Arab hostility toward Jews. "And so it began," Abbey opines, "the Jews the sons of Isaac. The Arabs the sons of Ishmael. But what most people find important to remember is that, in the end, the two sons came together to bury their father." This story is not only condescending; its metaphor of humanity as a patriarchal family urges a kind of blind obeisance to paternal authority that has its political corollary in the approval of the imperial presidency of George W. Bush. Like Ishmael, U.S. citizens are urged to respect the paterfamilias no matter what he does in our name.

Like AMWT, "Isaac and Ishmael" stages a spectacle of difference in order to constitute a symbolic American community—now multicultural and gender-inclusive in its contours—unified behind the president and his policies. Its dual narrative frame provides something for everyone and, in that sense, operates as a technology for managing dissent. Both programs offer intimate access to the president and his advisors as a substitute for political engagement and promote an emotional identification with the state that makes dissent difficult to articulate.[56] In short, by constructing a particular sort of terrorist menace, they also construct a particular sort of U.S. citizen—the "docile patriot" willing to support the president no matter what steps he decides to take to combat terror.[57]

By restaging the melodrama of American innocence first mobilized in 9/11 news coverage, *Third Watch*, *America's Most Wanted*, and *The West Wing* all helped prime the U.S. public to support a war on terrorism. They provided a detailed account of American suffering, projected it as a condition of national identity, and called for "heroic" measures to redress the suffering. The special episodes of *Third Watch*, in particular, reminded viewers of the exceptional nature of the event, which it depicted as a national trauma. Like other popular rituals of mourning in the wake of 9/11, the program proclaimed "grief is not enough" and openly advocated vengeance as a means of rescuing the nation from the paralyzing grip of fear.[58] *America's Most Wanted* and *The West Wing* both

In *The West Wing*, a group of wide-eyed schoolchildren is lectured to by political authorities. This passive, "infantile" subject position was offered as the model of democratic citizenship in the wake of 9/11. ("Isaac and Ishmael," 10/3/2001)

foregrounded issues of identity as central to the interpretation of 9/11 and, thereby, helped legitimate the Bush administration's depiction of terrorists as "evil" individuals conditioned by degenerate societies to hate "us" for "who we are." These programs effectively told viewers "the root cause of terrorism lies not in grievances but in a disposition toward unbridled violence" endemic to Eastern societies.[59] The "West," by contrast, is constructed as inherently "innocent"—both undeserving of enmity and incapable of undertaking "terrorist" actions itself. Using narrative conventions drawn from U.S. popular culture, then, these programs disseminated an ideology at once Orientalist and post-Orientalist. On the one hand, their Manichean construction of the War on Terrorism affirmed the Bush administration's depiction of it as the latest skirmish in a timeless struggle between "civilization" and "savagery." On the other hand, the programs hinted at a more expansive conception of American nationalism (as "multicultural" and "pluralist") and prepared U.S. subjects to accept a more conflicted relationship between the United States and the "rest of the West." In this way, they participated in the ongoing cultural renegotiation of the East-West binary so central to Orientalism.[60]

The result of these patterns of representation was to create a climate of fear that made extreme measures of regulation and control seem both necessary and reasonable. By conditioning individuals to accept the Bush administration's politics of fear as a historical norm, the programs helped institutionalize what should have been an exceptional state of emergency. As Richard Jackson has argued, "the *language* of the 'war on terrorism'" has important consequences for the *practice* of it.[61] Measures of discipline that might otherwise appear untenable were accepted as normal and necessary within the terms of the discourse of security promoted by the Bush administration. The demonization of the enemy, in particular, sanctioned the adoption of a strategy of counterterrorism that was out of all proportion to the nature of the threat. The apocalyptic tenor of counterterrorist discourse generated a counterterrorist practice (i.e., war) that was inflexible and potentially counterproductive in that it targeted whole societies, rather than the terrorist groups who lived within them. By constructing terrorism as a timeless threat and terrorists as irrational, relentless, and ubiquitous, this discourse urged a perpetual vigilance that translated easily into boundless warfare.

Exceptions to Exceptionalism?

The discourses of exceptionalism elaborated in the early coverage of 9/11 were not uncontested or mindlessly embraced. The critical and popular reaction to "Isaac and Ishmael" offers a potent reminder of the limits of patriotic discourse even in a time of crisis. When entertainment becomes overly didactic or proscriptive, even the most patriotically inclined audiences will rebel. Most importantly, the fragmented landscape of the contemporary media environment mitigates against the formation of a unified nationalist message in the popular culture. By November of 2001, the Comedy Central animated series South Park was already subjecting the discourses of American innocence and exceptionalism to ridicule.[62] The episode "Osama Bin Laden Has Farty Pants," which premiered shortly after the initial U.S. invasion of Afghanistan, mocked the Bush administration's attempts to dress the war in humanitarian garb and suggested that America's willful ignorance about the world constituted a threat to U.S. security. Most remarkably, it did so without eliciting the sort of censure that got Bill Maher fired from Politically Incorrect or the Dixie Chicks blackballed from country music stations.

The episode begins with an attack on President Bush's pet project, the "Afghan Children's Fund," a philanthropic initiative that asked American schoolchildren to donate a dollar to relieve the suffering of Afghan children then being bombed by the United States. An early scene exposes the lunacy of this campaign by following a group of Afghan children as their schools, movie theaters, and homes are reduced to ashes by U.S. fighter jets. When the dollars arrive, virtually nothing is left standing in the town. The episode also depicts the popular investment in the myth of American innocence as a repugnant form of cultural arrogance. When the Afghan children meet their American counterparts later in the episode, they express a hatred for the United States that leaves the American boys stymied: "How come they hate America so much? What the hell did *we* do?" Despite abundant evidence of the devastation caused by the American bombing campaign, the boys simply cannot imagine America as anything other than beneficent. The program concludes by indicting the educational system and the news media for failing to produce informed citizens capable of democratic deliberation. Instead, they have created a myopic public whose ignorance about the world undermines the nation's efforts to achieve security. "They told us in school, and on TV, that most people in Pakistan and Afghanistan *like* America," an incredulous Kyle tells the Afghans. "And you believe it?" they scoff, "It is not just the Taliban that hates America. Over a third of the *world* hates America!" "But why?" Stan asks. "Because you don't realize that a third of the world hates you," they reply. The exchange codes American ignorance as a threat to global stability because it abets U.S. militarism. As long as U.S. citizens choose to remain ignorant of their country's actions, the episode suggests, the rest of the world will be made to suffer and left to harbor resentment.

As Lynn Spigel notes, "Osama Bin Laden Has Farty Pants" offers a mixed ideological bag, containing Orientalist depictions of Osama Bin Laden as a gibberish-spewing camel lover, overt salutes to American patriotism ("Go America," the episode concludes), and blankly ironic critiques of the American bombing campaign and its depiction as a humanitarian rescue mission. While it ends with a celebration of the American "team" (a metaphor the creators, Trey Parker and Matt Stone, would develop further in their feature film *Team America: World Police*), it does open "American claims of childish innocence (promoted, for example, in *The West Wing's* fictional classroom) . . . for comic interrogation."[63] Its emergence just two months after the September 11 attacks suggests that the cultural injunction to trade critical distance for the emotional reassurance of blind patriotism was, in fact, a fairly short-lived phenomenon.

Nevertheless, patriotic-themed programming would flourish in the years to come because patriotic audiences were defined by the TV industry as a recognizable and lucrative audience niche after 9/11. Almost immediately following the attacks, industry insiders were already publicly fighting over the right to cater to this audience, with network affiliates and network-owned-and-operated stations trying to block cable channels from simulcasting the *Tribute to Heroes* telethon for fear of losing their audience shares.[64] CNN likewise refused to provide its competitors with access to its exclusive Al Jazeera feed. In 2002, the lowly MSNBC news channel tried to up its viewership by rebranding itself "America's News Channel," complete with wall-to-wall red, white, and blue graphics, but was outpaced in this endeavor by Fox News, which would rise to the top of the cable news ratings in 2003 on the back of its literal and figurative flag-waving.[65] CNN executive Walter Isaacson noted the pressure on newsmakers to conform to expectations of patriotism: "In these times, there's a patriotism patrol. If you get on the wrong side of public opinion by seeming not to be patriotic enough, you can get in trouble these days."[66] Whether true or not, this statement certainly shows how the TV news industry *perceived* the audience in the aftermath of 9/11. And similar expectations shaped entertainment programming. Bryce Zabel, then-president of the Academy of Television Arts and Sciences (and an attendee at the Bush administration–sponsored confabs in Hollywood) described television as "the 'rapid-response' team for America's message" and urged his fellow creatives to take up the president's call for advocacy: "This is about being involved in the struggle for our nation's survival—together . . . every community is looking to pitch in, and Hollywood is no exception." He called specifically for representations "that celebrate our heroes and ideals and are sensitive to the situation we find ourselves in." Since "America is based on a marketplace of ideas," he concluded, it is Hollywood's responsibility to place positive messages about America "more effectively" within that marketplace.[67]

Certainly, patriotism was on the minds of many network executives, who sought relief from the crippling economic losses associated with 9/11 in pro-American messaging.[68] The twice-delayed 2001 Emmy Awards telecast provides a case in point. To avoid accusations of tastelessness, the ceremony was self-consciously saturated with patriotism and political posturing. The show opened, for example, with a schmaltzy rendition of "America the Beautiful" and a video introduction by Walter Cronkite, who quoted Edward R. Murrow on the importance of television in times of crisis and closed by insisting "entertainment can help us heal." The broadcast itself was studded with pretaped segments thanking the troops and "our overseas partners in the War on Terrorism," and everyone involved in the broadcast positioned it as an act of virtual counterterrorism. "Let history remember that the fifty-third annual Emmys stood up to hate, stood up to fear, and celebrated the American spirit," the Academy president opined, while host Ellen DeGeneres quipped: "It's important for us to be here because they can't take away our creativity, or joy. Only network executives can do that." She went on to position herself as a frontline fighter in the new global culture war: "I'm in a unique position as host because, think about it, what would bug the Taliban more than seeing a gay woman in a suit surrounded by Jews?"[69]

Regular television programming also shifted in a patriotic direction with flags and NYPD/NYFD gear suddenly littering the mise-en-scène of soap operas, sports programs, and talk shows. In primetime, patriotism conditioned decisions about pickups, scheduling, and promotions. For example, Fox executives changed the name of their mid-season replacement comedy *Emma Brody* to *The American Embassy* (2002) "to capitalize on the country's reinvigorated patriotism since the Sept. 11 terrorist attacks." Starcom Entertainment CEO Laura Caraccioli, whose job is to promote product placement, warned TV executives to ditch series featuring corrupt cops or firemen or suffer the fiscal consequences: "Now is not an appropriate time to have any [such] story arc."[70] Several primetime dramas incorporated 9/11 deaths into their storylines to add pathos and explain character motivation, including ABC's *Line of Fire* (2003–2004), CBS's *CSI: New York* (2004–present), and TNT's limited series *The Grid* (2004), all of which featured central characters whose spouses were killed on 9/11. Finally, as the next chapter will illustrate, primetime dramas self-consciously abandoned ambiguity in favor of melodramatic, black-and-white story structures designed to satisfy the public's perceived "desire to see the bad guy gotten."[71] Arguably, patriotic programming was not just *a* niche market post-9/11; it was *the* niche market, shaping virtually every decision executives made from 2001 to 2003.

Until the war in Iraq threw the myth of American exceptionalism into crisis, the patterns of presentation discussed in this chapter—especially the focus on themes of American innocence, terrorist degeneracy, and the sanctity of violent redemption—would continue to structure television programming across the spectrum. My argument is not so much that audiences were duped by the media into accepting the Bush administration's arguments for the necessity of war. It is, rather, that patriotic programming of this sort resonated with and exacerbated the public mood in ways that proved conducive to the conduct of the War on Terrorism. Like the Bush administration's new terror alert system, such programming helped "calibrate the public's anxiety," triggering visceral responses (love of country, fear of the enemy, the desire to fight) that operated below the level of conscious intellect. For Arab and Muslim Americans, TV served as a constant reminder of their tenuous position in the society, a fear-machine that delivered a daily reminder of the need to police the self. By contributing to what Brian Massumi calls a "central nervousness" in the culture, TV programs triggered a reflexive defense-reaction that linked fear to vigilance and violence to emotional release.[72] In short, TV programs made (most of) us *feel* like the Bush administration's extreme measures were warranted and would work, even when, intellectually, we might have known better.

2 Spy Thrillers and the Politics of Fear

On September 20, 2001, President Bush addressed a joint session of Congress and the American people and described the terrorist attacks as "acts of war." He defined "the enemy" in this war as a "radical group of Muslims" who "hate our freedoms" and are determined "to disrupt and end [our] way of life." He likened the terrorists to fascist and totalitarian threats from the past, especially the Nazis, and reassured the "American people" that these men would be hunted down and eliminated using every means at the disposal of U.S. authorities. The speech established the parameters that would delimit the popular understandings of both terrorism and counterterrorism. In keeping with a long history of media representations, terrorism would be personalized, pathologized, and absolutized.[1] Osama Bin Laden was identified as the mastermind of the plot, and his enmity toward the United States was presented as ontological, driven not by what the United States had done but by "who we are." Bin Laden's target was not the public sphere of U.S. business or political life, we were told, but the intimate sphere of home and family. He attacked husbands and fathers, wives, mothers, and children, and his goal was to deprive "us" of the comforts of (heterosexual) family life.

Such discourse draws directly on earlier representations of terrorism in the media, which turned the "family under siege" into a prominent visual and narrative trope in order to enlist popular support for extreme forms of counterterrorism.[2] If the nation is a family under siege, then a paternal government is authorized to take any steps necessary to protect the family. The mission is facilitated through a process of demonization that flattens distinctions between terrorist groups and likens them to a malevolent force of nature—a swarm, contagion, or plague. Once ontologized and pathologized, the threat of terrorism is easily absolutized, reconstituted as a threat to civilization or human existence per se.[3] Thus, in Bush's speech, Al Qaeda's capacities were exaggerated beyond all reason and credulity and placed on par with the Nazi state's capacity for organized destruction. "Freedom and fear, justice and cruelty" are at war, Bush said, "and we know that God is not neutral between them" (i.e., God is on "our" side). One effect of this systematic decontextualization of terrorism was to make the category of the terrorist flexibly expansible: it could include anyone who opposed U.S. interests of any sort in any way.[4] Thus, "civilized" nations who refused to assist in the U.S. war effort were lumped together with Al Qaeda and the Taliban as "terrorists." The ultimatum President Bush presented to potential allies at the conclusion of the speech made the point abundantly clear: "You are either with us, or you are with the terrorists." Neutrality was not a tenable position in a war against "evil," and diplomacy would only foster the spread of "evil."

By defining terrorism in such depoliticized terms, the Bush administration prepared the public to accept the imposition of special powers of authority, including the right to violate U.S. citizens' civil liberties, suspend habeas corpus, use "harsh interrogation" methods (i.e., torture), and detain suspected terrorists indefinitely without charge or trial. Such an exceptional state of emergency, the administration argued, necessitated exceptional measures of containment if order was to be restored and maintained. Terrorism was transformed into "the prime raison d'etat," and terrorists became "the one enemy against which society [had to] marshal all of its resources in an unending struggle."[5] The state of exception merged with traditions of American exceptionalism to produce a hyperviolent war on terrorism, whose logics became self-perpetuating.[6] As Joseba Zulaika predicted, it very quickly became difficult to "convince the rest of us that not everything is terrorism."[7]

Enhancing the infectious nature of such counterterrorist discourse was the sudden revitalization of the spy genre on U.S. television. Virtually dormant since the 1960s, spy programs suddenly reemerged as vehicles through which to address popular anxieties about the technologies and processes of globalization.[8] Thus, just one week after President Bush's address, CBS and ABC premiered their new espionage skeins, The Agency (2001–2003) and Alias (2001–2006), respectively. Fox quickly followed with 24 (2001–2010), and the trio of programs were joined in subsequent years by the likes of Threat Matrix (ABC, 2003–2004), Homeland Security (NBC, 2004), The Grid (TNT, 2004), Sleeper Cell (Showtime, 2005–2006), MI5 (known as Spooks in the UK, BBC-1, 2002–present; MI5 has been syndicated in the United States via BBC America, A&E, and dozens of local stations), and, more recently, a reboot of the syndicated series La Femme Nikita (Nikita, CW, 2010–present) and a new series, Chaos (CBS, 2011).[9] The revitalization of this once moribund genre pre-dated the 9/11 attacks, but achieved a new raison d'être in the wake of the attacks by tapping the popular desire for images of American heroism and redemption through violence. Conceived before 9/11, *The Agency*, *Alias*, and *24* were designed to respond to anxieties about global interconnection and boundary dissolution with fantasies of national and subjective coherence.[10] After 9/11, terrorism became the central vehicle through which to explore these larger anxieties, and the three programs were joined by a number of new skeins celebrating the autonomous and virile agency of the intelligence operative. As Howard Gordon, one of the writers of *24*, explained, these dramas "[tap] into the public's fear-based wish for protectors such as Jack Bauer who will do whatever is necessary to save society from harm."[11] A postindustrial incarnation of the frontier hero, the secret agent promises national regeneration through violence and provides audiences with a prosthetic experience of potency designed to compensate for the frustrations of daily existence. In times of crisis, the appeal of such a figure is obvious, but the consequences of allowing our cultural metaphors to overtake our reality are also potentially dire. As Gordon's comment indicates, such savior-figures promote political passivity and encourage an unquestioned acceptance of the actions of those in power. Ordinary citizens are asked just to sit idly by and wait to be rescued, "to live [their] lives . . . hug [their] children" and trust their leaders to get things done, in President Bush's parlance.

Given the very real failures of the U.S. intelligence agencies to protect the United States on 9/11, spy TV programs clearly served an important propaganda function for the state: they helped the FBI, CIA, and NSA conduct "damage control" and assured the public that the newly created Department of Homeland Security would solve the myriad problems with interagency communication that led to 9/11.[12] The programs presented digital technology as the key to better intelligence and promised more gadgetry would help agents "connect the dots" in the future. They also depicted human intelligence as a priority and a success; on TV, intelligence agents easily infiltrated terrorist cells and took them down *before* catastrophe could be realized. By showing the successful disruption of terrorist plots on a weekly basis, these spy programs helped reassure Americans that their intelligence services were competent and that the increased funding for intelligence was well spent.[13] They validated President Bush's assertion that "all law enforcement and intelligence agencies are working aggressively around America, around the world, and around the clock" to protect U.S. citizens from terror.[14] Indeed, so competent were these TV superagents that actor Kiefer Sutherland, who plays Jack Bauer on *24*, was once accosted by a real CIA agent for making him look bad in the eyes of his mother. "Why can't you be more like Jack Bauer," she purportedly nagged her son.[15]

The thematic coherence between these spy series and the new political climate was not entirely accidental, of course. Most of the programs received assistance, both before and after 9/11, from U.S. security agencies, the Department of Defense, and/or the State Department. The Agency, for example, filmed inside the CIA's Langley, Virginia, headquarters and used actual CIA agents as extras in the pilot. Producers were permitted to tour the facilities and take photos of the "Art Department" to ensure the fidelity of the program's sets, and CIA liaison Chase Brandon and at least two other CIA officers provided guidance on story lines and CIA procedure.[16] Producers of The Grid likewise toured the NSA, the Pentagon, the CIA, and the State Department and received script advice from Pentagon security analyst and former naval commander Larry Seaquist. Star Dylan McDermott shadowed FBI agents assigned to the Los Angeles Joint Terrorism Task Force to train for his role as FBI Special Agent Max Canary, while Julianna Margulies consulted regularly with Seaquist about NSA protocols. The producers even asked Seaquist to speculate about how Al Qaeda would adapt to U.S. strategy and to concoct plot scenarios that would make the story seem "up-to-date" when it aired.[17] Threat Matrix had "at least 3 consultants experienced in the subject matter read every script" to ensure accuracy and realism, and the Department of Defense purportedly "offered their assistance," though it is unclear which episodes received such assistance.[18] The producers of Sleeper Cell acknowledged working with "Joint Terrorism Task Force veterans, FBI consultants, police technical experts, and Arabic and Islamic cultural advisors" to ensure the realism and complexity of their series, while the producers of 24 requested and received material assistance from the Pentagon for hardware and personnel for several episodes over multiple seasons.[19] "We get constant cooperation from every branch of the military," said director Jon Cassar, "and they've helped us so much on so many episodes that we decided to return the favor" by loaning star Kiefer Sutherland to the navy to film a recruitment spot (Alias star Jennifer Garner did a similar such spot for the CIA). Expert input was sought as a guarantee of realism and a mark of quality. It gave the producers of these programs an opportunity to claim currency and legitimacy while offering official and unofficial representatives of the State and Defense Departments a chance to transmit political messages under the radar, as "dividends" of entertainment.[20]

There is no guarantee that the final product will reflect the desires or intentions of the state authorities providing such assistance, however, and critics should be careful not to project a cause-effect relationship where only a correlation exists. Postindustrial processes of cultural creation involve complex negotiations among a variety of competing entities—investors, corporate officials, producers, directors, consultants, creative talent, and, of course, audiences—none of whom is likely to have their whims wholly satisfied. Michael Kackman and Tricia Jenkins have both documented how the efforts of intelligence agencies to sell themselves on TV have met with mixed results due to the industry's commercial imperatives. The makers of The Agency, for example, increasingly ignored the advice of their CIA consultants as time went on and ratings fell. The perceived need to shift to an action-adventure format effectively froze out the consultants, who were more concerned with the minutia of agency protocol than with telling a good yarn.[21] In addition to this structural tension between the needs of industry and the needs of the state, the sheer number of consultants and variety of state agencies involved in assisting television producers would, of necessity, create friction and undermine coherence. The various intelligence agencies may differ wildly in their conceptions of a problem such as terrorism, and their representatives may offer conflicting advice on questions of strategy and tactics. Moreover, savvy producers might exploit these tensions for added value—ideological complexity being a hallmark of "quality television." Producers of The Grid, for example, chose to incorporate the static between agencies as a part of the show's diegesis, thereby undermining any attempt to arrive at a unified message about terrorism or terrorists. It can hardly be compared to a show like Threat Matrix, where tensions are resolutely downplayed in order to convey the message: "We are making progress" (this is literally how the opening credit sequence ends).

The differences between these programs, in terms of execution, are vast and significant. If they all adopt the War on Terrorism as a background context, they do not all do so to the same extent or with the same effects. Alias, for example, took a more fantastic look at the spy game and concentrated on the implications of espionage for issues of personal identity and lifestyle. Homeland Security and Threat Matrix, on the other hand, dealt directly with the new Department of Homeland Security and provided unalloyed propaganda in support of it. The remainder of the programs fell somewhere in between, addressing real-world counterterrorism operations, but in a more complex, realistic, and morally gray way. 24 survived long enough to shift with the political zeitgeist several times over, first supporting the ends-justify-the-means doctrine of the Bush administration (seasons 1–4), and later indicting a conservative president for treason (season 5), placing its hero on trial for his crimes, and openly debating the morality of Bauer's extreme tactics (season 7). As the show's writers note, most of the scripts vilify white, male authority figures in the U.S. government or the oil and private security industries and "could have been written by Michael Moore."[22] No wonder everyone from Bill Clinton and Janeane Garofalo to Dick Cheney and Rush Limbaugh have called themselves fans of the show.

Perhaps the most important factor complicating any assertion of a propaganda effect is the significant variation among these programs in their levels of audience penetration and commercial success. Most of these programs lasted less than two years and achieved only modest ratings, and the programs that were most openly supportive of administration policy performed the worst. For example, *Threat Matrix*, a weekly puff piece for the DHS, which *New York Times* TV critic Alessandra Stanley called "The War on Terrorism without the Wrangling," achieved dismal ratings and was canceled by ABC after only half a season.[23] NBC rejected *Homeland Security* as a series out of hand, but paid a minimum for the rights to air it as a made-for-TV-movie event. While it started with a modest 9 million viewers, most of those viewers fled to CBS for the Mel Gibson movie *The Patriot* after the first hour.[24] The more complex series *The Grid* achieved better ratings than both of these programs, and it aired on a cable channel with a limited audience reach (TNT).[25] The poor performance of the more propagandistic of these programs invites the question: how effective is a public relations strategy that the public ignores?

Accusations of state collusion in the production of these series show little awareness of the dynamic nature of institutional relations and creative processes and tell us little about *how* propaganda effects are generated by these texts. If the genre's resurgence had the effect of priming the public to accept an increasingly extreme conception of the threat posed by terrorism, exactly how did it do this? What patterns of presentation can be discerned in such series, and how do these patterns help legitimate the War on Terrorism? The analysis that follows will take up these questions in relation to the more serious and "realistic" presentations of counterterrorism (*The Agency*, *24*, *Threat Matrix*, *Homeland Security*, *The Grid*, and *Sleeper Cell*).[26] The way these programs constructed their terrorist villains and patriotic heroes helped normalize the state of emergency and promote the acceptance of policies of surveillance, detention, interrogation, and interdiction that were fundamentally antidemocratic. Much of the work of legitimating these policies was performed not at the level of ideology—where there was a good deal of variation among the programs—but at the level of affect—where the programs consistently propagated a sense of urgency and anxiety that led audiences to desire extreme action as a means of alleviating the perception of pressure. By targeting the sensations and emotions of viewers at least as much as their intellects, the programs made affect productive and put it in the service of a particularly pernicious (because antidemocratic) political agenda.

Regeneration through Violence: The Return of the Vigilante Hero

If the immediate response to 9/11 was to celebrate national innocence by constructing trauma narratives oriented around victimization and passivity, such self-pity quickly gave way to a national desire for vengeance and action. President Bush captured this sentiment when he told Congress and the American people: "Our grief has turned to anger, and anger to resolution. Whether we bring our enemies to justice, or bring justice to our enemies, justice will be done."[27] The collective desire for action provided fertile ground for the proliferation of spy programs. Central to the execution of such programs is the marginalization of the institutional dynamics of governance and the emergence of a singular hero-figure capable of cutting through the bureaucratic red tape associated with democracy and "getting things done." The contemporary spy is an incarnation of what Robert Jewett and John Shelton Lawrence call the "monomythic hero" of American popular culture—an autonomous agent whose superior intellect, skill set, and willingness to flout convention enable him to rescue a helpless and naïve public.[28] These are men (and, as we will see, women) with the guts to "look evil in the eye and deal with it," as 24's Jack Bauer puts it (Day 7: "6–7 pm").

The Agency offers an important case study of the post-9/11 resurgence of the lone hero, for, as its title indicates, it was originally conceived as a procedural focused on the CIA as an institution. Developed in collaboration with CIA liaison Chase Brandon, the program was supposed to make the case for the continued necessity of the CIA in a post–Cold War world of geopolitical complexity.[29] The struggle against terrorism was to comprise but one small part of that argument before 9/11, yet the series demonstrated an uncanny prescience about the importance of Al Qaeda to future security operations. The original pilot was to feature a plot by Al Qaeda terrorists to blow up Harrods

THE AGENCY

From Executive Producer WOLFGANG PETERSEN

TERRORISM. NUCLEAR THREATS. BIOLOGICAL WARFARE.
A NEW ERA. A NEW WAR.

Promotional material for *The Agency* (CBS, 2001–2003) emphasized the "New Threats" to U.S. security and touted the importance of the CIA to the War on Terrorism, conveniently forgetting the real-life failure of the agency to anticipate the 9/11 attacks.

department store in London. Osama Bin Laden was mentioned four times by name in the episode, and the successful containment of the threat provided a fantasy of institutional competence that belied the reality exposed by events on the ground. The disjunction between this fantasy and the real-life intelligence failures weighed heavily in the decision to pull the episode after 9/11. CBS later yanked another episode that dealt with an anthrax attack on New York City after the anthrax scare further undermined the illusion of institutional inviolability.[30] Only after the CIA was deployed on the frontlines in Operation Enduring Freedom would the network seek to capitalize on the message of heroic agency and reassurance by airing these episodes. They would also redesign the promotional materials for the program to foreground the CIA's status as frontline fighter in the War on Terrorism: "Now, more than ever," the promos read, "America needs the unsung heroes of 'The Agency.'" Though *Alias* and *24* would soon become the breakout hits in the genre, it was

The Agency, with its more realistic approach to counterterrorism and its more reassuring episodic format, that would achieve the highest ratings for 2001–2002 (indeed, 24 was the lowest rated show in *any* genre to be renewed in 2002).[31]

For season 2, however, *The Agency* undertook a full face-lift to bring it more in line with the conventions of the thriller genre, whose emphasis has always been on heroic individualism and personal, rather than collective, agency.[32] The makeover involved dropping actor Gil Bellows, whose field agent Matt Callan was perceived to be "too cerebral," and adding Irish super-stud Jason O'Mara, whose youth and physicality would enable a more action-oriented focus for the show. As CBS senior vice president of programming David Stapf put it, "[This season] we'll have characters who will go out into the field, kick some ass, and do what we all secretly want the CIA to do."[33] The previous emphasis on information gathering, analysis, and agency culture was abandoned in favor of the streamlined, action-oriented follies of O'Mara's character, A. B. Stiles. The transformation brought the series more in line with the exceptionalist logics of heroism and technological mastery already articulated by *Alias* and 24.

Each of these series works according to a familiar melodramatic logic, which equates indifference in the face of evil with evil itself. "People who stand by might as well help plant the bomb," as Bauer puts it (Day 7: "7–8 pm"). They borrow from the techno-thriller a dread of "the 'system' and its representatives," and an absolute faith in the redemptive capacities of the lone hero. As Matthew Hill explains, such texts promote "a cult of the technowarrior, in which those with the 'right' knowledge, the 'right' technology, and the 'right' willingness to use them are elevated to the status of infallible guardians of the sacred order of American culture."[34] Sidney Bristow and Jack Bauer are certainly hyper-competent techno-warriors who demonstrate a willingness to "do what is necessary" to protect "innocent life." If they suffer for their actions, as they inevitably do, this merely confirms the purity of their motives and underscores their devotion to the cause. The combination of pure motives and practical effectiveness makes the hero-figure into the moral center of the fictional universe and establishes a moral economy that exceeds the bounds of the law. In this moral economy, doing what is right sometimes means doing things that are illegal—using torture to elicit information, for example—and characters who disagree with the methods or decisions of the heroes, even out of a desire to do "good," are invariably constructed as weak, ineffectual, or downright dangerous.[35]

With the possible exception of *The Grid*, all of the counterterrorism series to follow would adopt a similar pattern, with distinct heroes, action-centered plots, technology that rarely failed, and a relentless, driving pace designed to create a heightened sense of urgency. *Threat Matrix*, for example, offered the merest semblance of an ensemble cast whose mission was to facilitate the actions of the central heroes—John Kilmer and Frankie Ellroy-Kilmer (James Denton and Kelly Rutherford). Only the Kilmers, a divorced, terrorist-fighting super-duo, had any sort of backstory or character development, and the rest of the cast served largely as prosthetic extensions of their gadgetry.[36] Even *The Grid*, which offered more nuanced character development and a legitimate ensemble dynamic, gave audiences a conventional action-hero in Max Canary (Dylan McDermott) to occasionally relieve the tedium of intelligence-gathering and drive the narrative forward.

The appeal of such action-oriented hero-figures—characters who could efficiently mediate between the terrains of "civilization" and "savagery" yet remain essentially "good"—had everything to do with the cultural shift from grief to anger and the declaration of a War on Terrorism. Like President Bush's political rhetoric, they drew upon popular traditions of hero construction—specifically the frontier hero and the hard-boiled detective—to legitimate the turn toward violence as a means of national redemption.[37] Yet, as the inclusion of women and peoples of color into the category of hero indicates, they also renovated these traditions to suit the new, more expansive conception of national identity underwriting this War on Terrorism.

The Expanding Circle of "We": Equal Opportunity Heroism

In the immediate aftermath of the 9/11 attacks, political pundits called for the "return of John Wayne masculinity" and lionized the gruff, anti-PC manliness of New York City firefighters to the exclusion of other victims, like the stock brokers, "falling men," and widows, whose victimization on 9/11 was a painful reminder of American weakness.[38] Yet, very quickly, heroic agency became a national subject position inhabitable by anyone willing to kick a little ass and take names later. Of course, as Susan Faludi has meticulously detailed, the material effects of this cultural ideal benefited men at the expense of women, but, in focusing exclusively on the internal gender politics of the ideal, Faludi misses the way the War on Terrorism facilitated the infolding of females, queers, and even people of color into the image of the patriot. It is less gender difference that is at stake in this ideal than the difference between citizenship and "alienness." Allegiance to the ethos of autonomous agency—of going it alone—became a means of drawing distinctions between friend and foe, patriot and terrorist, in a global context defined by the dissolution of the geographic boundaries that once stabilized an "inside" through contrast to the "outside." Post-9/11 spy thrillers, with their mixture of male and female, black, white, yellow, and brown agents, demonstrate precisely how expansive the conception of patriotism became after the attacks. They also reinforced the Bush administration's explanations for why "we" were under attack: because "terrorists" are inbred, monocultural zealots who hate "our" political, ideological, and cultural diversity. Multiculturalism became a defining feature of post-9/11 American identity.

As if to reinforce the Orientalist construction of the Middle East as a site of female oppression, spy thrillers teemed with female agents willing to kick ass first and ask questions later. *The Grid* featured a veritable Old Girls Club of counterterrorism agents, including the head of the National Security Agency, the head of the ad hoc Counter-Terrorism Task Force at the center of the narrative (Maren Jackson/Julianna Margulies), the head of the British spy service MI6, and the MI6 operative tasked to the interagency team (Emily Tuthill/Jemma Redgrave). At one point, Maren Jackson even espouses feminism as a motive for fighting terrorism (albeit in ways that echo the cynical concern for women marshaled by the Bush administration to legitimate the war in Afghanistan): "[Islam] appeals to oppressed men because it sanctions the oppression of women. To me Islam is one thing—fear—and until the clerics can stand up and say that killing people is the work of the devil and that it is a woman's god-given right to eat, sleep, walk, do, [and] say whatever she wants, I'm blind, deaf and dumb to what they're selling" ("Episode 1"). *Alias* was centered on a female CIA agent, Sydney Bristow (Jennifer Garner), known for her unerring moral authority, as well as her skill at Krav Maga, or Israeli close-combat defense. One of the central agents in *Threat Matrix* is Frankie Ellroy-Kilmer, whose hyphenated name offers a nod to feminism even as the program folds her agency neatly into patriarchy. Frankie is both more level-headed than her ex-husband and better equipped for the job, with a skill set that includes fluency in a number of languages, facility with high-powered weaponry, tactical training, and a degree in criminal profiling. *Threat Matrix* also featured a female forensics expert and a deaf female intelligence analyst—a double whammy for political correctness—whose disability proved no obstacle to the effective conduct of team operations.[39] The ensemble cast of *The Agency* included both female intelligence analysts and female field agents, notably Lisa Fabrizzi (Gloria Reuben) who proved every bit as adept as her male colleagues. Finally, 24 featured numerous powerful, brainy women in the roles of both hero and villain (along with some powerfully stupid women in the role of victim). Though the show clearly focused on the agency of the male superhero, women constituted some of the more enjoyable super-foils for his antics in the early seasons, and by season 7 female FBI agent Renee Walker (Annie Wersching) emerged as a potential successor to Jack. Like Bauer, she worked outside the bureaucracy to "get things done" and was willing to use "any means necessary" to elicit information; she even resorted to torture on several occasions and shielded Jack's actions from her superiors, all of which she was lauded for. The systematic incorporation of women into the spy genre in the role of heroic agents indicates a shift in the gender dynamics of the genre and of the culture at large. Heroic masculinity, post-9/11, was not just for boys anymore. It was a subject position that could be occupied by any patriot, male or female, as long as he or she took up the sword (and only the sword) in the fight against evil.

Peoples of color were likewise systematically and self-consciously folded into the narrative of American heroism and liberality on these programs. Perhaps the most notable example here is undercover FBI Agent Darwyn al-Sayeed (Michael Ealy) of *Sleeper Cell*. According to the promotional materials for the program, Darwyn is not just the first American Muslim hero on U.S. television; he is also the first black Muslim hero.[40] While Darwyn must often do bad things to maintain his cover as a terrorist, his status as hero is rarely placed in doubt. He clearly abhors the individuals he must befriend in order to do his job, and, as he tells über-villain Faris al-Farik (Oded Fehr) in the final episode of season 1, he is a man of conscience whose motives are pure:

> On September 11, I remember thinking the world had changed. A war had begun, and I knew that the future of Islam lay in the balance. So I had to choose what kind of Muslim I was gonna be. Was I gonna sit back and watch events unfold, or was I gonna take action? Destroy those who wanted to destroy my faith? The Holy Koran says that those who believe fight in the way of God. Those who disbelieve fight in the way of Satan, so fight against the friends of Satan, and that is what I've done. That's what I'm doing today.

As is common with spy texts, the duplicity of the agent's status enables this to be read in two opposite ways. Farik and the other terrorists hear this as a statement of devotion to their cause, but the audience is privy to Darwyn's charade and so reads this as a noble statement of purpose that clearly marks the terrorists as the "friends of Satan." Anyone, of any stripe, who fights against these enemies is, thus, automatically a "friend of God" and the good, including Darwyn, who otherwise defies conventional images of the patriot-hero.

Though Darwyn was the most obvious example of the racial expansion of patriotic heroism, he was by no means the only one. Other programs featured black, Hispanic, Asian, Arab, and Muslim agents, though usually in supporting roles. These agents were still clearly and self-consciously marked as "the good guys," however. President David Palmer (Dennis Haysbert) of 24, for example, was portrayed as the second coming of Lincoln through the use of framing and mise-en-scène. The producers deliberately shot Palmer from a low angle to enhance his stature and even staged a scene where he is sitting in a chair so that it would approximate the Lincoln Memorial.[41] Field agents Tony Almeida (Carlos Bernard) and Curtis Manning (Roger Cross) were constructed as "good" by virtue of their physical and moral proximity to Bauer. Indeed, by season 7, Almeida had become a virtual extension of Bauer, who was incapacitated in the line of duty. The Agency's ensemble cast featured both a black deputy director of intelligence for the CIA and a black field agent, while Threat Matrix included black, Hispanic, Asian, and Arab agents. Indeed, the multicultural orientation was so self-conscious on Threat Matrix that critics likened it to the Disney ride "It's a Small World after All."[42]

The most significant development, and one that belies the difficulties real intelligence agencies have had recruiting among Arab and Muslim communities, is the emergence of Arab and Muslim heroic figures on these programs. From Darwyn on Sleeper Cell to Nadia Yassir (Marisol Nichols) on 24, Mohammad "Mo" Hassain (Anthony Azizi) on Threat Matrix and Raza Michaels (Piter Marek) on The Grid, TV spy agencies were chock-full of admirable Arab and Muslim characters. Many of these programs went out of their way, as well, to provide "politically correct" portrayals of Arab communities and Muslim religious practices. The creators of The Grid and Sleeper Cell, for example, enlisted Islamic scholars and advisors to vet their scripts for accuracy and fairness and made changes designed to depict the counterterrorism campaign with greater nuance. Grid executive producer Tracey Alexander notes, for example, that their program never associated Muslim prayer rituals with acts of terrorism: "We never connected praying and pure Muslim spirituality with violence. We never showed the radicals praying before or after an action, and we only showed praying occurring with the characters who are not violent."[43] The promotional video for Sleeper Cell likewise positioned the program as a sort of pedagogical exercise designed to enlighten Americans about the "true meaning of Islam."[44] It explicitly condemned ignorant and misleading statements about Islam by the likes of President Bush, Marine Corps General James Mattis, and deputy undersecretary of defense intelligence General William G. Boykin and provided didactic asides about the meaning of common Arabic words and phrases, such as "Koran," "jihad" and "Allahu Akbar." Oded Fehr, who played Farik in the series, explained that one goal was to clarify the distinctions between Muslims and terrorists: "It's time that we all realize that Muslims are not the enemy. It's the extremist Muslims that are the enemy, and . . . they don't represent Islam; they don't represent the Muslim community." Episode 4 of season 1 ("Scholar") serves no narrative purpose other than to deliver this message. It pits a moderate Muslim cleric against extremists for the soul of Islam. The episode begins with this cleric, Abdul Malik, entering a prison cell in Egypt and asking the prisoner inside, "What is the greatest jihad?" The answer is the internal struggle to control and purify the self, not the external struggle against "unbelievers." The cleric defies the prisoner to show him a passage in the Koran that legitimates the killing of innocents and promises he will join the radicals if such a passage can be found. As the episode concludes with this same prisoner, now dressed as a cleric himself, entering another prison cell and asking the same set of questions of another would-be terrorist, viewers learn the Koran does not support terrorism. Sleeper Cell emphasizes the importance of moderate Muslims to the fight against terrorism. Their hearts and minds are the ultimate stake in the clash between "civilization" and "savagery," the United States and Muslim extremists. As Darwyn explains to his FBI handler, "This isn't just a war on terror. It's a war within Islam, and people like Abdul Malik are the only ones that can help us win." One effect of this infolding of moderate Muslims, of course, is to further demonize the terrorists, who, in being portrayed as "traitors" to their religion become further aligned with "evil."[45]

Such complex portrayals were condemned by conservative bloggers and pundits as "political correctness gone crazy," but they serve a very real purpose in relation to the rhetorical construction of America and its War on Terrorism.[46] It is "our" tolerance for difference and openness to other cultures that defines America as "good" and American values as "right and true for every person in every society."[47] As Inderpal Grewal, Jasbir Puar, Sara Ahmed,

and others have argued, multiculturalism has become a key technology of national subject formation in the War on Terrorism.[48] The infolding of racial and
gendered difference into the conception of the patriot becomes a mark of U.S.
social development in comparison to other nations whose gender politics and
other forms of social repression define them as "backward" and "dangerous."
Thus, for example, the Bush team described the invasion of Afghanistan as "a
fight for the rights and dignity of women" and championed the "liberation" of
Middle Eastern societies from the "tyranny" of theocracy.[49] Such rhetoric
coopts the discourses of feminism and other social justice movements and
places them in the service of an imperial project designed to secure U.S.
global hegemony through a monopoly over the use of force. It is a good example of how the "constitution of open cultures involves the projection of what is
closed onto others."[50] This projection not only legitimates the need for a War
on Terrorism; it facilitates the disavowal of aspects of our own systems of governance that may be illiberal and prepares the way for a massive expansion of
internal social repression targeting the most vulnerable populations, especially immigrant groups and peoples of color who may be said to "look like"
terrorists. In short, the liberal coloring of the patriotic hero on spy TV programs provides ideological cover for the new policies of surveillance, discrimination, and indefinite detention favored as a response to 9/11.

The Could-Be Terrorist and the New Politics of Fear

Most of these shows evince an obsession with globalization and time-space
compression, as signified in the temporal and spatial metaphors used in their
titles. The Grid, Threat Matrix, and Sleeper Cell, in particular, depict terrorism as a
contagion that respects no boundaries and could strike anyone, anywhere, at
any time. The opening credit sequence of The Grid emphasizes the spatial ex-
pansiveness and mutability of the terror threat by hopping from global hot
spot to global hot spot. It then links this threat directly to disease processes by
incorporating imagery of cells splitting and multiplying. Alexander claims the
goal was to demonstrate how "al Qaeda and its off-shoots are a constantly
morphing operation with fingers everywhere," but the effect is to cast terrorism as a global plague or cancer that eats away at "healthy" societies from
within.[51] Such representations reflect larger cultural anxieties about globalization and its reorganization of social relations. Specifically, they embody
anxieties about the dismantling of once-meaningful boundaries and distinc-

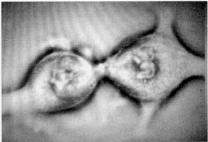

The opening title sequence for *The Grid* (TNT, 2004) depicts the global reach of terror threats and likens them to biological disease processes.

tions between people(s) and the worry that there will be no way to tell the difference between "ordinary" individuals and "suspicious" subjects.

In a complex, interconnected world, determinations of suspicion become harder to make with any certainty. Obvious signifiers such as race, gender, language, and nationality can no longer be counted on to explain who is "safe" and who is "dangerous." The first five minutes of *The Grid* demonstrates precisely how difficult it is to discern "suspicious activity" using just your eyes by aligning viewers with surveillance cameras and asking them to stitch the resulting images into a meaningful whole. We follow a vial of Sarin gas as it moves from Kazakhstan to London under the skirts and in the makeup of a seemingly harmless (though clearly duplicitous) female; we then watch as an apparently "normal" (i.e., clean-cut, white, middle-class) hotel waiter delivers the gas to the terrorists in a simple coffee pot. The movements all seem unremarkable, leaving us to experience the same frustration and sense of impotence as the intelligence analysts, who uncover the plot only because the terrorists accidentally blow themselves up. Such portrayals embody the realization that simplistic systems of profiling based on looks are wholly inadequate in the "new world order." Indeed, these programs insist that racial profiling is a blunt instrument that risks doing more harm than good. As the agents of *The Grid* profess, indiscriminately rounding up Muslims to alleviate public anxiety is a "colossal waste of time and resources." Season 5 of *24* likewise portrays the mass detention of Muslims as a misguided policy that is as likely to radicalize moderates as deter terrorists. Even the propagandistic *Homeland Security* asserts it is wrong to imprison people "because they have dark skin and the wrong accents." "If the people of this country are losing their civil rights," deputy secretary of Homeland Security, Admiral Ted McKee (Tom Skerritt) proclaims, "then the bad guys have already won."

Danger, these texts suggest, is not a property that resides in any singular body or population; it is, rather, a contagion that circulates throughout society and may, theoretically, adhere to any body (though certain bodies—brown, Arab, Muslim—remain more susceptible). *Sleeper Cell*'s Arabic advisor and sometime director Michael Desante puts it this way: "We don't know [what terrorists look like.] I mean we have to look at everybody as being potential terrorists."[52] This admirably captures the central anxiety of these sorts of programs, which is that terrorists will not be recognized in time, that they will "pass by" unnoticed and infiltrate the community of "we." Suspense is created precisely by staging such instances of passage, and the object lesson, in almost every case, is to justify the need for more extensive, detailed, and intimate forms of surveillance in order to clarify where the boundaries of community begin and end, who can be folded into the "circle of we" and who cannot. As Ahmed explains, "the possibility that we might not be able to tell the difference [between terrorists and other sorts of subjects] swiftly converts into" the need to preemptively defend against any and all "could-be" terrorists.[53] And what defines a "could-be" terrorist? His or her "resemblance" to identified threats to security, which is, in turn, defined as his or her difference from prevailing social norms. Fear is not localized in any particular type of body, in other words, but "slides" between bodies in ways that create equivalences between various modes of difference.[54] Race, modes of dress, national origin, primary language, sexuality, religion, and all sorts of other biological and cultural factors bleed together to constitute "suspicious populations" as "those who are not like us." Counterterrorism agents can no longer rely on visible differences alone to define the alienness of the terrorist. Instead, they must sift an array of data, including intellectual habits and ideological perspectives, to suss out which combinations of differences are likely to be most volatile.

24, *Threat Matrix*, *The Grid*, and *Sleeper Cell* have all addressed the threat of terrorists "passing by" and infiltrating the population, though with varying degrees of complexity. *Threat Matrix*, for example, featured two separate episodes in which terrorists used cosmetic surgery to approximate "average" U.S. citizens in order to facilitate their plots. In the pilot episode, a terrorist makes himself over to resemble a white, middle-class stock trader so that he can set off a bomb on the floor of the Chicago Stock Exchange. In the aptly named "Extremist Makeover," two Middle Eastern terrorists have their faces surgically altered to look like low-level personnel at a U.S. nuclear facility; the goal is to melt down the core and cause a nuclear catastrophe. In both cases the terrorists literally "pass" as American citizens, but, also in both cases, the terrorists are still identified as "really," or essentially, Arab. The effect is to draw a boundary between Arab and American identities in order to suggest that they are somehow incompatible.

The other spy programs consciously avoid such simplistic representations. The creators of Sleeper Cell, for example, pursued a more complex portrayal of terrorism as a means of adding value to their product. As Cyrus Voris, creator and executive producer of the show, explained in the promotional video "Know Your Enemy":

> When the issue of terrorism started creeping back into the popular culture, it was creeping back as if 9/11 had never happened. You were still getting, sort of, generic, cackling, evil, bad guys. You were getting Euro-trash terrorists. You were getting terrorists from [Un-named-istan]. . . . Vaguely foreign-looking characters, and it started to really make us angry. . . . How can you trivialize 9/11 by coming back and portraying terrorism in the same way we used to portray it beforehand? At this very escapist, simplistic, almost cartoon-level.

Sleeper Cell's emphasis on complexity resulted in a pronounced whitening of the terrorist figure. Of its eleven sleeper cell terrorists, over two seasons, only three were of Arab descent. Good, white, middle-class kids from America and Western Europe with names like "Tommy Emerson," "Christian Aumont" and "Wilhelmina van der Hulst" were bigger threats to the United States in the series than folks named Mohammed or Osama. Indeed, it was their privileged upbringings—not poverty, blocked prospects, or desperation—that drove the terrorists toward Islam and radicalism. Surrounded by consumer decadence and moral relativism, each of these terrorists sought "meaning" and "purpose" through Holy War.

White men and women, both secular and religious—Christian, Jewish, Muslim, and atheist—were frequent villains on other programs, as well. Indeed, 24 made the flouting of audience expectations with regard to race, gender, religion, heroism, and villainy into a virtual art form. Women in the series were notoriously dangerous, and every single season of intrigue—even those that focused largely on Arab, Islamic, or African terrorists—featured a white corporate executive or political authority as the motive force behind the plot. Wealthy, privileged, and powerful white men are the ones who allow nuclear and biological weapons to be smuggled into the country, usually to serve some commercial end. 24 also offered the first incarnation of the blonde-haired, blue-eyed "stealth terrorist" in Day 2's Marie Warner (Laura Harris), another spoiled Westerner whose lack of motherly guidance led to her political radicalization. Warner facilitates the detonation of a nuclear bomb on U.S. soil before being captured and contained behind a see-through glass barrier—an apt metaphor for her position as a transparent operator capable of hiding in the open. Marie was later joined by the likes of The Grid's Kaz Moore (Barna Moricz), who drives off to commit a terrorist attack in an SUV sporting the bumper sticker "Never Again," and Sleeper Cell's Tommy Emerson (Blake Shields), who once described himself to Darwyn as "the perfect weapon. . . . I'm just another American idiot cruising the mall. I'm harmless." These characters all take advantage of the social mobility accorded to those with white skins in U.S. society to facilitate their terrorist missions. Passing as white is not the only way to move freely, however. Farik of Sleeper Cell poses as a Jewish security agent for a local L.A. synagogue as a cover for his jihadist activities. "I pass as Persian, Turkish, Coptic Christian, as well as Sephardic Jew," he tells Darwyn before instructing him to avoid public expressions of religious devotion as a means of facilitating his own passing. The first rule of sleeper cell, as we learn in season 2, is "no public displays of religion" ("Al Baqara").

Thus, most of these programs present race and ethnicity as highly unstable signifiers and offer "post-Orientalist" constructions of Arab and South Asian identity, which eschew simple West-East, Self-Other, Good-Evil binaries.[55] Each of these programs is also keen to illustrate what happens when racial profiling is used as a primary method. By focusing suspicion on a narrow range of subjects, it may direct suspicion away from the real security threats. On 24, for instance, Marie Warner's plot succeeds, in part because the agents of the Counter-Terrorism Unit (CTU) have wasted time and energy interrogating her Iranian fiancé, Reza Naiyeer (Phillip Rhys). On The Grid, Arab intelligence analyst Raza Michaels is subjected to frequent lie detector tests, which disrupt his labor and undermine his credibility with the other agents. On Sleeper Cell, the first season's undercover FBI operation is nearly compromised when an overzealous LAPD Counter-Terrorism Task Force agent mistakes Darwyn for a terrorist based solely on the fact that he is "a known Muslim" and possesses "Arabic writings" ("Intramural"). In every case, racial profiling based on Orientalist assumptions ends up directing suspicion onto the wrong folks, letting the real culprits "pass by" and commit atrocities.

Even religion is not a wholly reliable indicator of terrorist sympathies in these programs, as demonstrated by a telling episode of Threat Matrix called "Patriot Act." When a bomb is set off in the U.S. history section of a college library, the agents are dispatched to the scene and search the library lending records using the key words "terrorism, Islam, and explosives." Islam is the default category for suspicion here, as there is no indication of a motive at all. The search implicates a friend of Mo Hassain's, who is both Arabic and a Muslim and who also happens to be a constitutional law professor at the university. Mo is tasked with digging into the man's records, starting with his email but extending to "phone records, cell phone accounts, tax returns, medical records, bank statements, employment history, everything." The Patriot Act, we are assured, gives the agents the right to conduct such an invasive search in the name of national security. Mo eventually finds that the man has contributed to a "suspect charity" and written an inflammatory opinion piece for a radical Muslim journal, but admits "most of our evidence is in his attitude, what he believes." Despite the circumstantial nature of the evidence, the man is brought in for questioning and "treated like a terrorist." Only when another bomb goes off while he is in custody is the man exonerated. Thus, the agents have wasted time and resources, invaded an innocent man's privacy, maligned his character, and likely cost him his job, all because of a too simple association between "Islam" and "terrorism."

Though many of the terrorists in these shows are adherents of Islam, these negative representations are carefully counterbalanced by the existence of "good" Muslims such as Mo, Darwyn, and Raza. What defines a Muslim as a terrorist, ultimately, is the extremity of his or her religious devotion—its perverse nature. No surprise, then, that other signifiers of perversity, such as "deviant" sexuality, are used to distinguish the truly "dangerous" others from those who may be folded into the national family.[56] In *Homeland Security*, for instance, an FBI class on profiling describes Osama Bin Laden's motivation for terrorism as a combination of pain and shame bred by a repressive culture: "Why does he hate us so much?" the instructor asks. "We desecrate the Islamic holy land," the students respond. "We've got female troops walking around with uncovered hair. . . . Kinda like bringing a stripper to church." Using a "heteronormative psychoanalytic explanatory framework," which, as Puar notes, is typical of Western discourse on terrorism, the class connects radicalism to sexual and social repression, rather than politics, poverty, or other potential causative factors.[57] Bin Laden is driven by an excessive interpretation of religious principles of modesty; this interpretation is a reaction formation expressing his own sense of sexual and social frustration. A "filthy rich playboy" with no sanctioned outlet for his passions, we are told, Bin Laden sublimates his desires and redirects them into violence (a point seemingly confirmed by the discovery of a stash of porn at his hideout in Pakistan). Thus, it is a perverse attachment to religious doctrine that defines the terrorist, not religion per se.

On *Sleeper Cell*, sexual attitudes and practices become the primary determinant of who is "normal" and "good" and who is a terrorist. For instance, Darwyn's heroism is affirmed by his monogamous heterosexual relationship, his obliviousness to the pornographic contexts within which he meets his FBI handlers, and his outrage at the use of child prostitutes to finance terrorist activities ("Money"). In contrast, the real terrorists all exhibit sexual deviancy of some predictable sort. Farik is a prude, who kills a young Muslim girl in the first episode ("Al Faitha") for daring to date a white boy. In a later episode ("Immigrant"), he feasts on caviar to celebrate the finalization of the terrorist plot while two other cell leaders hire prostitutes and mock his abstinence. Tommy is portrayed as a prepubescent momma's boy wholly uninterested in sex, while Christian is a promiscuous playboy willing to "fuck anything that moves," including Tommy's mother.

By season 2, the implicit connections between "abnormal" sexual behavior and religious zealotry become explicit, as Salim, one of the new cell members, embraces fundamentalist Islam as a "cure" for his homosexuality. Salim's obsession with religion is presented as a sublimated expression of his sexual frustration. When he allows himself to be seduced by another man at the gym, for example, Salim redirects his sense of shame outward toward a moderate Islamic televangelist whom he accuses of "corrupt[ing] . . . Muslim purity" by promoting the reconciliation of the Sunni and Shi'a sects ("Faith"). Salim buys a gun and attempts to assassinate the man, who is little more than a projection of his own self-loathing and sense of guilt. Ultimately, what makes Salim "suspicious" in the series is not his race or religion; it is his liminality. He occupies what Puar calls "an impossible subject position."[58] In Western discourse, notions of queer identity are predicated on a white, middle-class, secular norm, while notions of Islamic identity are defined through association with patriarchy, heterosexuality, sexual repression, and intolerance. Thus, one cannot be a good gay and be Arab or Muslim, and one cannot be a good Arab or Muslim and be gay. Salim's categorical blurring is monstrous, and so, by becoming a terrorist, he is merely fulfilling his destiny according to these normative discourses. By the end, his sexuality is so thoroughly confused with terrorist violence that he describes the plan to bomb the Hollywood Bowl as his "coming out" and invites his boyfriend along for the event ("Fitna").

Being Arab or Muslim may make one automatically suspicious in these programs, but they are hardly the sole determinants of fear. The logic of suspicion is astoundingly expansive and "slippery." All of these shows use the logic of guilt-by-association to forge links between terrorism, criminality, and political activity of any sort. The effect is to constitute virtually anyone critical of the U.S. government or defiant of its laws as a threat to national security deserving of quarantine. For example, the terrorists of *Sleeper Cell* work with Latino gangbangers, Mexican drug lords, illegal immigrants, and the KKK, as well as Al Qaeda, to achieve what is described as a common goal—"the downfall of the U.S. government" ("Intramural"). *24* repeatedly connects corporate greed and political Machiavellianism to terrorist activities, in addition to drugs, crime, gangs, and petty corruption. *The Grid* explains how gambling makes one vulnerable to terrorist cooptation (episode 1), while *Threat Matrix* revisits the link between drug consumption and terrorist funding ("Veteran's Day"). Indeed, we are told by deputy secretary of homeland defense Roger Atkins (Will Lyman) at the end of that episode that "we" (Americans) are guilty of "terrorizing ourselves." When we spend money on illegal drugs, "we are our own worst enemies." A nutty right-wing propaganda piece, *Threat Matrix* even connects legitimate social protest to terrorist activity in several episodes. In "Brothers," for example, an American studies professor is labeled an "enemy combatant" for writing a dissertation that predicts the rise of the police state that has incarcerated him. The pilot episode also tars peaceful protest with the brush of terrorism when a group of young politicos impede Agent Kilmer's attempts to disrupt a bombing at the Chicago Stock Exchange where the G8 finance ministers are meeting. Kilmer orders the local police to "get this street cleared," and they begin clubbing demonstrators "for the protestors' own good." Taken together, these episodes are the entertainment equivalent of Ari Fleischer's real-life admonition to "watch what [you] say, what [you] do."

Of course, virtually every one of these programs constructs human rights discourse, and those who wield it, as obstructive and dangerous. In "Alpha 126" of *Threat Matrix*, for instance, Frankie is placed on trial to defend her interrogation methods when a prisoner dies of natural causes (of course) under her care. The trial is designed to "appease the international community" and invokes the Geneva Conventions to condemn Frankie's actions. Frankie's lawyer turns the tables on the prosecutors, however, by asking witnesses: "If Alpha 126 had information about the next 9/11, and you could prevent it by interrogating him, how far would you go?" Extreme sensory deprivation, stress positioning, the withholding of food and use of food allergies to trigger discomfort, and the withholding of medical care are just "the price we pay so we can sleep at night," she asserts. Frankie's exoneration constructs the Geneva Conventions as a quaint holdover from the pre-9/11 world, which, by constraining our agents, also compromises our safety. Of course, the most famous example of this denigration of human rights discourse occurs on Day 4 of 24 when Jack takes a suspect into custody only to have his interrogation cut short by an "Amnesty Global" attorney, who was called in by the terrorist himself. As the audience is privy to the suspect's guilt, the lawyer is positioned as a villain for unwittingly aiding and abetting the terrorists (Day 4: "12–1 am"). When Jack quits CTU, attacks the suspect, and breaks his fingers to get the information he needs, we are encouraged to cheer him on. Such incidents reinforce the Bush administration's construction of the War on Terrorism as a moral struggle between good and evil in which no middle ground is possible: "You are either with us, or you are with the terrorists."

By staging such instances of "passing" and insisting that any criticism of U.S. policies is a threat to security, spy TV programs construct an expansive regime of fear that seems to necessitate new, more aggressive security measures. Viewers can never know for certain when or where threats will be realized, or by whom, so they feel like danger is always and inexorably approaching. This sense of anticipation sanctions a logic of "preventative defense" whose goal is to counter terrorism before it emerges, not by addressing the conditions that spur political radicalism (poverty, desperation, injustice), but by eliminating anyone who "could be" so radicalized. Like the 2002 National Security Strategy Statement, which declared the United States would "act against . . . emerging threats *before* they are fully formed," spy TV programs called for a broad-spectrum preventative designed, as Puar puts it, to "[preempt] altogether the conditions of possibility for . . . [an] attack."[59] This inevitably results in the violation of civil liberties and the use of illegal and immoral tactics of suppression, but viewers are encouraged to embrace such measures for their own good, to become what Alexis de Tocqueville called a "people for bondage."[60]

Indeed, acceptance of the need to sacrifice civil liberties and human rights in the name of security becomes a virtual precondition for entry into national subjecthood on most of these programs. *Threat Matrix*, for instance, openly celebrates the USA Patriot Act and the invasive surveillance techniques it permits. "Scary or not," as Kilmer says, "it's the law," and "good citizens" follow the law (or else). Both the narrative and mise-en-scène fetishize information and communications technologies and promote surveillance as a public good.

The opening credit sequence begins with a God's-eye view of earth from be-hind a U.S. spy satellite. Any anxiety provoked by this Orwellian imagery is quickly dismissed, however, when the camera zooms in on the "bad guys" of the week. The accuracy and discrimination of the satellites assures viewers that Big Brother is not watching us so much as he is watching *over* us. "Inno-cent" citizens have nothing to fear from the state's new powers, we are told, for the state's agents are here "to keep us safe." As Lisa Parks argues, this fic-tion of technologically enhanced omnipotence stands in stark contrast to the realities of satellite surveillance, which provides imagery so ambiguous as to exonerate state authorities from any responsibility for what they have seen (the slaughter in Bosnia, for example).[61]

In *Threat Matrix*, the intelligence analysts are literally cocooned inside their technology, which responds with speed and accuracy to their every whim and glows with the warm, blue light of clarity. Agents never have cause to doubt the information they receive from machines because the technology never fails them. Computers do not crash; phones do not drop their connections; filters never fail to isolate the relevant data; and satellite intelligence inevitably drives the plot to its conclusion. This is a world where interagency databases are seamlessly integrated, DNA analysis takes mere minutes, infrared satel-lites can help agents locate "a Bunsen burner on the ground," and intelligence analysts can call up video feed from ATM machines and security cameras at will. The show also touts future technologies such as facial recognition soft-ware, "through the wall surveillance" with real-time video streaming, and something called a "tempest scanner," which is supposed to be capable of picking up the combination to a safe by reading vibrations in the radio waves. Though these technologies clearly extend the reach of state surveillance, pen-etrating even the roofs and walls of apartment buildings, we are constantly as-sured that these technologies will not be used to spy on "ordinary citizens" because, as Col. Atkins says to a suspicious reporter in the pilot, "it's illegal."

Threat Matrix is the most unambiguous presentation of what Puar describes as the "technological sublime," an aesthetic that celebrates "the totalizing, overarching, and inflated power" of surveillance technologies.[62] The other programs celebrate technology as well, but they rely on the occasional failure or defeat of technology to drive their plots. While CTU agents on 24 can repo-sition satellites in six minutes and provide step-by-step guidance through the schematics of a building, for example, the loss of a simple cell phone signal often renders the information useless to the agents in the field. On *Sleeper Cell*, FBI surveillance signals are constantly interrupted by loud radios or white-noise machines, and agents are often misdirected by visual and verbal sleights of hand into following the wrong people or raiding the wrong spaces. In *The Grid*, terrorists use the intelligence services' overreliance on electronic espionage against them by seeding the Internet with disinformation, which leads them to concentrate their resources in the wrong area.

Nevertheless, digital technologies remain the go-to resource for intelligence gathering and analysis on all of these shows, and they all use technology invasively to spy on each other as well as the bad guys. Total information awareness is the ideal in these programs, and no one is immune from surveillance.[63] Thus, Darwyn's handlers on *Sleeper Cell* spy on him as much as they use him to spy on the cell members. CIA employees on *The Grid* must submit to regular lie-detector tests to ensure deniability should they ever turn. Jack Bauer on 24 is constantly being forced to brief his superiors and is frequently detained and interrogated like a suspect when he refuses to do so. Given the number of moles, double agents, and careerists bent on sabotaging CTU's efforts, information technologies are also used for intra-office surveillance and control. Everyone in these programs is subject to intense scrutiny, and it is only such scrutiny that enables the "good guys" to be sorted from the "bad guys." By subjecting even the "good guys" to surveillance, such programs help habituate viewers to the need for surveillance and control as mechanisms of social order per se. They socialize individuals into their roles as self-policing subjects in a security state.

Yet, the deployment of surveillance still clearly affects some populations more than others and seems designed to deliver different messages to different subjects. For most Americans, the seeming infallibility of the information technologies instills confidence in the security agencies and fosters a supportive climate for the further extension of surveillance mechanisms. If these technologies work, the logic goes, then why not provide security agencies with all of the tools they desire, even at the expense of some civil liberties. However, for suspect populations—Muslims, Arabs, and those who "look like" them, as well as politicos on the left—the decentralization and dispersal of surveillance technologies provides a constant reminder that they are suspect and must watch what they say and do. All of public space comes to "feel like" a detention cell, as the omnipresent cameras, screens, terminals, and data scanners provoke the same range of emotions as detention: "fear, anxiety, discomfort, disorientation, uncertainty, despair [and] anger." Under the watchful gaze of this "ephemera of control," people learn to discipline themselves, and adopt a quiescent attitude toward public policies they might otherwise find unjust and worthy of protest.[64] As Raza Michaels of The Grid instructs his sister, people must learn to "calm down" because "If you rant like a radical, they will begin to treat you like one." Thus, dispersed surveillance enforces political passivity but makes it seem like a choice individuals make freely and of their own accord. Indeed, it comes to seem like a choice they shouldn't mind making if they are good citizens.

Nowhere is this message delivered more clearly than in Threat Matrix, which regularly enlists "ordinary citizens" to gather intelligence on their friends, coworkers, and family members. In "Extremist Makeover," for instance, Col. Atkins appeals directly to the public for information about the camouflaged suspects who have infiltrated the United States: "We have a lot of tools in this fight [against terrorism], but none that we value so highly as you, the American citizen." "Brothers" even suggests that the failure to rat on your loved ones makes you culpable for their actions. Mo is lauded in the program for detaining his boyhood friend and treating him "like a terrorist," while the real terrorist's brother condemns himself for failing to report his suspicions about his mentally ill brother: "I feel that I'm partially to blame for these tragic events. You see, I had a brother who was deeply troubled, and I chose to let him drift away, that I should not have done." Given the parallel editing, which cuts images of Mo praying into scenes of the public apology, this speech seems directed at Muslim communities, who are urged to report "suspicious" behavior to the authorities. The sacrifice of one's intimate relations is now a compulsory expression of national allegiance, a gesture that can get one folded into the community of "we." Those who fail to adopt this paranoid mentality are, by definition, aligned with the terrorists.

Torture also becomes a sanctioned method of intelligence gathering on most of these programs. In "Alpha 126," Threat Matrix justifies the use of "enhanced interrogation" tactics by claiming that such tactics helped stop the terrorist plot of the week. Frankie's lawyer concludes her defense with this lesson: "when an interrogation at Gitmo is successful, lives can be saved." This exchange makes torture seem not only viable as an intelligence gathering "tool," but morally necessary given the stakes (American lives). The second season of Sleeper Cell likewise details the vicious interrogation tactics used by the CIA and its offshore proxies only so that it can excuse these practices by presenting the villain as contemptuous and defiant. Farik repeatedly outwits his captors and lures them to injury and death by using their humane gestures against them. His recalcitrance leads the CIA to transfer him to a black site in Saudi Arabia where he can be viciously tortured while the United States maintains deniability. For the next two episodes, Farik is beaten, starved, shocked, and has a hot metal spike shoved up his urethra, all because he refuses to cooperate. The United States has tried to be nice to him, the series implies, but he *wants* to play hardball, even *prefers* to be tortured. "You think I fucking enjoy this," the CIA agent in charge declares. "Americans hate this shit. It's not who we are. But to tell you the truth, I don't care. You took off the fucking gloves." Farik views this as utter hypocrisy, and hypocrisy as America's fatal flaw: "You Americans . . . care more about analyzing your guilt than achieving victory. That is why we will win, and you will lose." Thus, Farik becomes the ultimate incarnation of the pathological terrorist, a man whose masochism compels "innocent" Americans to become sadistic.

The same justifications for torture—it is an effective means of intelligence gathering warranted by the extreme nature of the social crisis—are routinely given on 24. As Jack says to the Amnesty Global representative in the middle of Day 4, "I don't want to bypass the Constitution, but these are extraordinary circumstances." Extraordinary circumstances happen routinely on 24, however, regularizing the need for torture and legitimating its use in all sorts of nonemergency situations. According to one count, the fourth season featured torture in more than half of its episodes.[65] The nonprofit group Human Rights First ascribed the twenty-five-fold increase in depictions of torture on U.S. television since 9/11 largely to 24. They also noted a role reversal whereby the "good guys" now torture more than the "bad guys" and use torture indiscriminately against both the guilty and the innocent.[66] For instance, on Day 2 Jack fakes the assassination of Syed Ali's son to get him to talk, a breach of Geneva Conventions. On Day 3, he threatens to quarantine Stephen Saunders's daughter in the same hotel where Saunders is "testing" his bioweapon unless Saunders reveals where the remaining virus is located. On Day 4, the secretary of defense (William Devane) orders his own son tortured until the boy confesses (gasp!) that he's gay, and CTU director Erin Driscoll (Alberta Watson) tortures an innocent computer technician, who has been framed by a mole inside CTU. On Day 5, Jack's lover and former assistant to the secretary of defense, Audrey Raines (Kim Raver), is framed, tortured, exonerated, and returns to work, thereby tacitly accepting the necessity of the institution's behavior toward her. Later that day, Jack shoots the wife of a suspected terrorist in the kneecap to get him to talk. And those are just the incidents of torture used against innocents!

The Parents Television Council counted sixty-seven incidents of torture during the first five seasons of 24, almost none of which failed to produce in-

Torture is a routine part of contemporary spy thrillers that never fails to work and never generates blowback. (Top Left) Jack Bauer tortures a suspect on 24. (Top Right) The secretary of defense tortures his own son on 24. (Bottom) The CIA allows Saudi Arabia to torture Farik for us on *Sleeper Cell*.

telligence.[67] Torture never has any long-term repercussions on 24, either. Jack may be subjected to retaliatory torture out of a personal desire for vengeance (on Days 1 and 6, for example), but there is never a sense that the "terrorists" were radicalized by the incidents they purport to avenge. The "bad guys" are always "bad" *before* they encounter Jack, and their "vengeance" is ascribed to their personalities, never to political circumstances. In short, there is no "blowback" from torture on 24, which makes it seem a more viable tool of intelligence gathering than it actually is. Finally, and perhaps most damningly, 24 works to excuse its hero's actions by demonstrating how much the effort pains him. Like the CIA agent in *Sleeper Cell*, he "hates this shit" and blames his victims for "making him" torture them; he feels he is "damned" by his decisions, though he professes to having only one regret: "that the world needs people like me" (Day 7: "9–10 pm"). Jack is thus positioned as a martyr, willing to sacrifice himself in the name of others' moral purity. His suffering redeems torture as a tactic and reassures the public that it will be used without being abused.[68] American innocence and benevolence are, thereby, preserved, even in the face of disturbing evidence of American atrocities committed in pursuit of the War on Terrorism.

Only *The Grid* dares to challenge the effectiveness of torture as a technique of intelligence gathering by showing an instance of blowback. In the first half of the series, Dr. Raghib Mutar (Silas Carson), a sympathetic character who struggles against the odds to provide healthcare to poor Egyptians, is detained and tortured by Egyptian authorities for suspicion of terrorist connections. The doctor had previously rejected the jihadist ideology, but this experience, along with the later beating of his sister, drives him back to the fold. Here torture backfires, resulting in the radicalization of an otherwise moderate Muslim, who goes on to organize a series of attempted bombings in London. Yet, *The Grid*'s exceptional status on this question only proves the rule. Torture and other extreme tactics appear legitimate in a moral universe that translates contingent social crises into apocalyptic struggles for human survival, and this is precisely the sort of universe good thrillers create. Thriller narratives are driven by deadlines and ticking time-bombs, and the consequences of inaction are always catastrophic. Local conflicts are rendered in absolute terms, and nothing less than the survival of civilization may turn on the actions of the hero. The sense of urgency creates pressure to adopt exceptional measures as a norm of action. As 24 cocreator Joel Surnow explains, "it's the rule of the jungle. We're . . . showing a hard-core guerilla war that's being fought in the streets of America, and you do what it takes to save innocent life."[69] Meanwhile, the purity of the hero's motives, along with his willingness to suffer for the cause, testify to his innate moral decency and reassure viewers that the new police powers will not be abused. In that way, thrillers invoke traditions of American exceptionalism to legitimate the state of exception and habituate viewers to the progressive loss of their democratic rights.

24 is, in many ways, the apotheosis of these spy TV programs. Ideologically, its messages may vary from season to season, but structurally it always promotes a future-oriented conception of fear that makes the state of exception seem like a viable norm. The show's creators readily confess their intention to push the thriller genre to its limits by compressing time-space and manipulating viewer expectations. Writer Robert Cochran acknowledges that the real-time conceit was adopted "to raise the stakes as high as we could for the sake of tension and the suspense." He also admitted that the creative process was driven by improbability, rather than reality: "What can't possibly

happen has been a major source of ideas for us."[70] Thus, the show has exploded not one but two nuclear bombs on U.S. soil and has invoked the Posse Comitatus Act not one but three times to (attempt to) remove presidents from power. How the formal structure of the series makes such exceptional measures appear necessary and normal—how precisely 24 sucks viewers in and gets them to bypass their rational objections to tactics such as torture, collective punishment, and martial law—will be the subject of the next section. It is important to remember, however, that 24 is not unique in the genre; rather, it is a tightly condensed version of general trends and, as such, illustrates how all thrillers work to promote a cultural experience of fear that might legitimate the indefinite extension of emergency procedures.

24, Patriotic Affect, and the Institutionalization of the State of Exception

The experience of viewing 24 has been likened by critics and fans to an "addiction," an "IV feed . . . of adrenaline" that leaves the senses feeling "assaulted" and drained by the end of the season.[71] Whether or not television actually fosters addiction is an open question, but many people certainly perceive their relationship to it, and to the complex narrative of 24, in these terms. As Jacqueline Furby notes, the formal qualities of the program—its real-time format, rapid cutting, multilayered visuals, and serial structure—demand "an intensity of attention, and a commitment of loyalty" unprecedented on television.[72] Viewers are immersed in the drama of counterterrorism in ways that virtually compel assent to the exceptional tactics used to restore order to the chaos temporarily unleashed. As this description indicates, the immersion is less mental than physical; 24 is more like an amusement ride than a puzzle. It is designed to produce a "*visceral* sense of the new twenty-first-century threats our societies face" that is "psychologically realistic" but heightened in intensity.[73] It incorporates viewers into the logics of counterterrorism and permanent warfare by appealing to the gut—the affective and physical realms. In short, by mobilizing emotions and sensations, it conscripts viewers into the war effort.

This occurs in several ways. The first, and most obvious, is the real-time conceit that structures each season. "Events occur in real-time," as the opening voiceover tells viewers, and the sense of "liveness" is constantly reiterated by the presence of ticking clocks, both within the diegesis and as cutaways that mark the breaks between narrative acts. As several commentators have noted, the digital clocks that lead into and out of the commercials account for the time it takes the commercials to run, thereby synchronizing the time-space of the program with the time-space of everyday life. "Whilst we yawn or make that cup of tea," Steven Peacock says, "CTU and myriad innocent bystanders are still in danger, with Jack Bauer still running, as the clock ticks down."[74] The effect is to remind viewers of the constancy of the threat of terrorism and to encourage them to generalize from the program to the real world. This powerful illusion of copresence supports the show's claim to liveness, which, in turn, confers a sense of realism onto what is clearly a hyperbolic fiction. We *feel* the same sense of dread and foreboding as the characters, and this sensation trumps cognition. The sound design reinforces these sensations by reminding viewers of the "ticking time bomb" at the heart of the plot. The tell-tale "doop . . . doop; doop . . . doop" that leads into and out of the breaks doesn't just signal viewers when to move away from or toward the television set; it gets under their skins and virtually synchronizes their heartbeats to the rhythms of the drama.

The second way in which 24 conscripts its viewers is through the use of split screens and narrative gaps. As Daniel Chamberlain and Scott Ruston have argued, 24 mixes cinematographic camerawork with a videographic editing style to heighten the viewer's involvement in the construction of meaning. Like a film, 24 invites viewers to gaze in a protracted fashion at the screen, but, like television or the Internet, it also splits the screen into multiple, discontinuous frames and asks viewers to work actively to stitch the various pieces of information together into a meaningful whole.[75] Deborah Jermyn argues that such screen-splitting actually transforms the spectator into a sort of editor, who interacts with the text, makes choices about where to look, and exercises a modicum control over the images they experience.[76] As in a comic book or graphic novel, the "gutters" between the images represent a narrative gap that viewers must actively fill in.[77] While the degree of interactivity permitted is circumscribed through the sizing of the frames, their arrangement on the screen, the sound design, and, of course, the narrative trajectory, the fracturing of the image still constructs a parallel between the characters' search for information and the viewers': "Forced to scan multiple frames for information, the viewer mirrors the agents' investigative pursuits—they must adopt the hero's sense of distrust and CTU's compulsion to remain alert." By "[leading] the spectator to experience some of the urgency and anxiety felt by Bauer and those around him," this visual strategy enhances viewer identifica-

The use of multiple frames and ticking clocks raise the stakes for viewers of 24 (Fox, 2001–2010). Viewers are forced to fill in the gaps in the narratives and across the gutters of the frames, and are thus implicated in a narrative that unfolds in only one way despite this apparent "freedom."

tion with the narrative.[78]

The serial form of the program, along with the deliberate use of information deficits to compel viewer projection, likewise opens the text to interpretation and implicates the spectators in the construction of meaning. Like a soap opera, 24 interweaves multiple plotlines across several episodes in order to maintain suspense and encourage viewer speculation. The writers toy with audience expectations, incorporating frequent red herrings and plot reversals in order to keep us off-balance and, thus, psychologically aligned with the protagonists. Yet, unlike a soap opera, 24 does promise an eventual closure that will wrap up all of its active story lines: the end of the day is still the end of the intrigue. This structure enables the producers to maximize suspense while still guaranteeing resolution and the restoration of the social order. Seriality thus lends complexity to the program, but not necessarily in a way that gives viewers any real say in the matter of the show's content. As Tara McPherson argues, the real-time conceit ensures that the plot will unfold relentlessly according to the producers' plans: "This clock only moves in one direction, taking us along as it goes."[79]

Though the trajectory of the narrative may be inexorable, the narrative itself is shot through with holes, which invites viewer projection and frequently makes the audience complicit in the construction of the ideological norms the show advances. The producers seem to know that viewers internalize certain protocols of storytelling and, as Gilliam and Iyengar show with TV crime stories, will fill in the gaps when crucial information is unavailable.[80] Thus, they sometimes omit crucial background detail on the characters in order to compel viewers to take responsibility for the story. Days 2 and 4 provide the most notorious examples of this ideological dodge, for neither season openly identifies the ethnicity or religion of the terrorist culprits (at least not within the diegesis). Reza Naiyeer and his mother speak Persian in one episode, but only Persian speakers would know what that means in terms of the geographic, ethnic, and cultural histories of these characters. All most viewers know is that they are foreign, and the show encourages viewers to extrapolate from "foreignness" to "danger" by having Reza arrested and interrogated by CTU. Day 4 identifies the Araz family, a seemingly normal suburban family who turn out to be members of a terrorist sleeper cell, as Turkish but otherwise leaves their histories and motivations blank. Instead, according to Shohreh Aghdashloo, who played Dina Araz, "the audience was expected to connect the dots and draw their own conclusions about Dina and Navi's motives."[81] And connect the dots they did. The Council on American-Islamic Relations (CAIR) released a statement worrying that the season would "cast a cloud of suspicion over every American-Muslim family out there" even though the family's religious affiliations were studiously ignored. CAIR also sent representatives to the corporate offices of Fox TV to elicit their cooperation in the production of a public service announcement to counter the potential negative effects from the story line. Seemingly acknowledging their complaints, Fox lent Kiefer Sutherland to the effort and ran the spot for as long as the Araz story was a prominent feature of the plot (oddly dropping the PSA when the plot turned to the more clearly Arab, i.e., foreign, villain Marwan). Thus, CAIR's solicitations had the ironic effect of solidifying the connections between the Araz family, Islam, and terrorism in the viewers' minds. No wonder TV reviewers spoke of the Araz family openly as "jihadists" and called Day 4 "the story arc [24's] been crying out for since its November 2001 debut."[82]

What this clever use of information deficits accomplishes is to coopt the viewer into the production of connections between Middle Easterners, Arabs, Islam, and terrorism so that the producers may be let off the hook. As terrorism expert James Carafano put it during the notorious Heritage Foundation confab on 24 in June 2006, viewers are invited to "take away [from the show] what they put into it."[83] In this sense, 24 offers another example of "allegory lite." As an aesthetic style, allegory lite features fragmentation and multiplicity, "different hooks pitched at different audience groups" to maximize commercial appeal. David Holloway calls it "pure capitalist utilitarianism, performing the tricky commercial maneuver of appealing simultaneously to multiple audiences, alienating as few customers as possible, while transferring responsibility for any 'politicising' of films to viewers themselves."[84] 24's penchant for visual and narrative excess provides the necessary space for the entertainment of multiple points of view and political perspectives, but it does so in a way that devolves responsibility for these views onto the atomized viewers and fans of the show. This permits the producers to deny responsibility for misrepresenting Middle Eastern, Arab, and Muslim Americans or celebrating torture while continuing to do both. "We're [just] trying to keep our pool heated," Surnow contends. "We're not trying to teach anybody anything."[85] This is an exercise in cynical reason, however, for the producers not only shape the limits of the ideological problematic within the show; they also use press kits, interviews, and public statements to instruct viewers in how to read the text properly. Surnow, for example, has openly touted his conservative worldview, invited Rush Limbaugh and Anne Coulter to the set, and featured Republican presidential candidate John McCain in an episode. He has stated that conservatives like the show because it doesn't "blame America first" or give in to (liberal) political correctness: "What conservatives like about [the show] . . . is that it depicts radical Islam as a threat in an unashamed, unapologetic, and unfalsified way."[86] In media interviews, he has also repeatedly defended the use of torture, using the ticking-bomb scenario as a legitimate real-world premise: "If there's a bomb about to hit a major U.S. city and you have a person with information . . . if you don't torture that person, that would be one of the most immoral acts you could imagine."[87] The extratextual discourse thus naturalizes these connections and primes the audience to interpret the program in particular ways while affording the creators "plausible deniability."

Perhaps the most insidious way that 24 coopts viewers into its logics of exception, however, is through its strategic use of torture as a motive force for the plot. The plot is structured around torture in such a way as to translate torture into a "gut" reaction rather than a conscious strategy; the effect is to depoliticize torture and literally make people "feel good" about its use. This occurs in two ways. First, as Lindsey Coleman has argued, the narrative progresses through a structure of "engagement, relocation, engagement" in which torture serves as the propelling force for the next relocation: "As an extreme form of narrative escalation, . . . torture rarely occurs in the final moments of the episode. It is not utilized as a cliffhanger. It never represents the extremity of a dramatic arc or ethical dilemma. The audience is never in any doubt as to Bauer's willingness to use such means. Thus, it occurs almost casually, located typically on either side of an episode's midpoint."[88] The regularization of torture not only helps normalize it; it engages the audience in such a way as to make them virtually cry out for more torture since it is torture that elicits the information necessary to send Jack off in a new direction. The narrative stalls when torture is not applied, and any moral debate about the legitimacy or utility of torture only feels like a frustrating delay. By structuring the narrative in this way, the producers "effectively . . . force a tacit consent in the audience to torture."[89] *New York Times* cultural critic Sarah Vowell captures this sensibility in the title of her review "Down With Torture! Gimme Torture!"[90] When forced to linger over the bureaucratic infighting at CTU, the many, many requests for immunity, or the melodramatic hijinks of Bauer's inept daughter Kim, audiences find themselves actively desiring the use of torture as a means of getting on with the story. The pressure of the real-time format only exacerbates this desire.

The second way in which 24 gets viewers to buy in to the use of torture, even desire its use, is by constructing its romantic hero as an ideology-free purist—a man dedicated to preserving moral order, not any particular social order. "Surrounded by the self-serving political ambiguity of his superiors and the perceived vagaries of civilian rights, Bauer is a blunt instrument in the service of abstract yet practically vital absolutes."[91] As with the vigilante heroes of the Western or the hard-boiled crime narrative, his innate understanding of right and wrong enables him to wear the white hat even when he does dark things. As Surnow puts it, "[Jack] is fundamentally good, with a very clear sense of right and wrong—and wrong must be punished. He does everything out of a love of goodness and freedom and saving innocents."[92] Jack's moral certainty and his willingness to do whatever is necessary to get the job done, even if it means sacrificing his own physical and moral well-being, make him a sort of "Christ-figure for the war on terror."[93] Like all such figures, his role is redemptive and reassuring. As Timothy Dunn explains, "one of the reasons that Jack is such a hero is that he is nearly always wiling to sacrifice his own interests for the sake of the cause. . . . We are inclined to think that if Jack tortures someone, even an innocent person, it's okay because he himself is willing to suffer and be tortured if necessary."[94] Moreover, he tortures only because failing to do so would be immoral under the circumstances. The centrality of weapons of mass destruction to 24's plots makes the moral calculus clear and compelling: if Jack does not violate the law, many thousands, perhaps millions, of "innocents" will die.

Thus, 24 uses a variety of techniques to encourage viewers to invest viscerally and emotionally in the perpetuation of an authoritarian vision of state power. As Ahmed explains, emotions are not internal states of being; they are historical constructs that perform real work in the material world.[95] Here, the hatred of terrorists spawns a form of uncritical love for the nation and its policies, which is easily translated into a political mandate by those in power. Fear and hatred become the glue holding the nation together, and the refusal to act out of fear becomes cause for expulsion from the national community.

The sense of interactive engagement fostered by 24 was further heightened by the proliferation of ancillary products around the series. One could purchase and play with Jack Bauer and CTU action figures, wear "official" CTU gear, carry cell-phone "mobisodes" of the show in one's pocket, and play 24: The Game on the Sony PlayStation 2. In the latter, a third-person shooter game, players manipulate the movements of various 24 characters, effectively living out the narrative trajectory and being rewarded for "getting it right." For example, a minigame within the game has players interrogate a suspect. The screen provides biofeedback indicating the suspect's level of stress, and the goal is to glean the necessary information while keeping the suspect within the "appropriate" range of stress levels. Too low or too high, and you will fail in your mission. The game does not allow a consideration of the ethical parameters of the notion of "appropriate stress," and, though it does not reward torture, it does allow for such behavior. And, again, 24 is indicative of trends across the genre. Alias, The Grid, and MI5/Spooks also featured video game spin-offs that allowed viewers to "play" the War on Terrorism.[96] The point is not that such games provide viewers with training in counterterrorism procedures or interrogation techniques (indeed, we could as easily argue that 24: The Game teaches viewers to distinguish interrogation from torture in a productive way); it is, rather, that they place viewers into sympathy with the position of the counterterrorist operative, who is defined in the logic of the game as a patriot and guardian of moral order. Viewers are, then, attuned by their love of country and preference for order to accept any action undertaken in the name of these values.

Conclusion

If the ideological content of 24 varies from hour to hour, season to season, this variation is mitigated by the relentlessness of its structural compulsion to love the nation and its representatives or risk expulsion, punishment, or death. It is a form of emotional blackmail that demands viewers abide the loss of their personal freedoms in exchange for collective security, and it defines security in narrowly national terms. The freedom of U.S. citizens from fear must come at the expense of others, according to the utilitarian ethic of action endorsed by the series. Other spy series, such as *The Grid* or *Sleeper Cell*, may occasionally contest the absolute nature of this dictate, but they, too, promote an ethic of prevention that treats terrorism as the cause of insecurity, rather than a symptom or effect of it. Ultimately, none of these series can escape the structural homology between the thriller genre and the logic of extremity used to justify the institutionalization of the state of exception. The affect of urgency promoted by the thriller's deadline structure and cataclysmic construction of the threat, combined with its chauvinistic depiction of the hero as a representative of morality per se, prepares viewers to accept extreme measures as necessary and just.

After the very real emergency of 9/11, such programs could not help but exacerbate popular feelings of vulnerability. By producing and reproducing an impression of the world as a catastrophically dangerous place, these shows targeted viewers' gut instincts and used their adrenaline-fueled reactions to legitimate the ethic of "proactive defense" embraced by the Bush administration as a mode of counterterrorism. The vicarious experience of heroic action they conveyed has, quite literally, helped convert the state of exception into a rule of social behavior. Soldiers at Abu Ghraib, for example, reportedly approached 24's "improvisations in sadism" as legitimate tools of interrogation and, lacking oversight, turned the prison into yet another combat zone.[97] Conservative politicians and pundits have, likewise, proclaimed the popularity of 24 constitutes a "national referendum" supporting the use of torture and other extreme measures.[98] By 2010, when the series was finally canceled, the visual and aural stylistics of the program had become so familiar that they could be used as a form of political shorthand for conservatives eager to portray the Obama administration as "weak" on security. In response to the 2009 Christmas Day bombing attempt in Detroit, for example, a coalition called "Keep America Safe," headed by neoconservative stalwarts William Kristol and Vice President Dick Cheney's daughter Liz, created a video called 100

Hours, which used 24's distinctive digital clock and ticking sounds to suggest that Obama's response to the attack was slow, inadequate, and portentous of future disaster. The use of these signifiers implied that the proper response to such terrorism would be to adopt Jack Bauer's extreme methods, though this is never explicitly stated in the video.[99]

As Giorgio Agamben has shown, the primary consequence of routinizing the logic of extremity in this way is to obliterate "the distinction between war and peace," insecurity and security.[100] All of life becomes a type of combat, and politics comes to feel like a zero-sum game of "Risk," in which some must die, or be sacrificed, so that others might live. By disseminating the ethic of surveillance and inviting viewers to internalize its dictates as a condition of national love, spy TV programs helped enlist national subjects in what has become a global project of biopolitical control.[101] The security of the United States and its citizens, we have been told, requires the containment and eradication of the "others" in our global midst. However, these "others" are "slippery" and hard to detect; their mutability and mobility are facilitated by the "openness" of our societies, and this necessitates increased vigilance and preparedness—a complete militarization of social life, including the enlistment of citizens as frontline agents of "Homeland Defense" and as soldiers in a new form of imperial warfare. When Donald Rumsfeld refers to the War on Terrorism using metaphors of "home security" and images of "a house fortified with deadbolts, alarms, guard dogs and police," we have entered a murky political zone within which formerly meaningful distinctions between private and public, inside and outside, home front and combat zone, have been collapsed in favor of an ethic of total war.[102] That actor Kiefer Sutherland reports preparing for his role as Agent Jack Bauer by watching Special Operations documentaries on the Military Channel testifies to the collapsing of the boundaries between inside and outside, policing and war.[103] The next three chapters will demonstrate precisely how far this militarization of life itself has progressed by showing how U.S. citizens were addressed as soldiers and effectively conscripted into the War on Terrorism.

3 Reality Militainment and the Virtual Citizen-Soldier

The first two chapters have demonstrated how the language used to frame the 9/11 attacks and define the concept of terrorism made the recourse to war appear natural, inevitable, and incontestable. Speaking of war and actually perpetrating it are different things, however. The Bush administration recognized immediately that its wars would need to be carefully cloaked in righteousness if the United States was going to appear to be anything other than a bully. Thus, they presented the case for a war against Afghanistan (and later Iraq) using the internationally recognized language of Just War theory. As Michael Walzer has detailed, diplomatic discourse and military practice have dictated that wars are justified under the following circumstances: they must be defensive, rather than expansionist; they must respond to a threat that is imminent, not imagined; they must be undertaken as a last resort, not the first; and they must be conducted in a right manner with measured violence, due care for civilians, and specific, limited, and reasonable objectives.[1] When President Bush announced the invasion of Afghanistan, this was precisely the language he used to sanctify the cause.

The president's October 7, 2001, declaration of war against Afghanistan began by constructing the invasion as defensive and retaliatory, a response to the "acts of war" perpetrated against the United States on 9/11: "We did not ask for this mission, but we will fulfill it." President Bush also depicted the invasion as a "war of last resort" by pretending the ultimatums laid out in his 2001 State of the Union speech were legitimate acts of diplomacy, rather than attempts to circumvent it: "More than two weeks ago, I gave the Taliban leaders a series of clear and specific demands: Close the terrorist training camps; hand over leaders of the Al Qaeda network; and return all foreign nationals . . . unjustly detained in your country. None of these demands was met. And now the Taliban will pay a price." The speech was carefully staged in the Treaty Room of the White House to further underwrite President Bush's claims to be "peace-loving." On the whole, the speech implied that the United States had used every means at its disposal to avoid war, but that the dastardly Taliban refused to respond and so deserved whatever they were soon to get. What the speech failed to mention was that no diplomatic overtures were actually made to the Taliban (other than this public address), and the Bush administration actually scuttled a Russian-brokered deal with the Taliban to surrender Bin Laden.[2] The point was to evoke "diplomacy," not actually engage in it. After establishing America's claim to the title of "peaceful nation," President Bush went on to depict the Taliban as irrational war-mongerers. He repeatedly referenced the "oppression" and "suffering" of Afghan citizens under Taliban rule and constructed the invasion as a humanitarian rescue mission: "As we strike military targets, we'll also drop food, medicine, and supplies to the starving and suffering men and women and children of Afghanistan." The emphasis on "targeted fire" implied that the U.S. way of war was inherently humane, discriminating between the guilty and the innocent and punishing only those who deserved it. In this way, Bush constructed the U.S. invasion as a Just War undertaken for selfless reasons and conducted in measured fashion. The goal was not to punish Al Qaeda and the Taliban for 9/11 but to "defend" civilization from savagery.

The news media's presentation of the war in Afghanistan reaffirmed the President's construction of the cause and conduct of the war as proportionate and just. As in the aftermath of the 9/11 attacks, the Pentagon, the White House, and retired military consultants comprised the bulk of opinion and commentary on newscasts, and alternative perspectives were marginalized or absent. The nature of the conflict, which was conducted initially by Special Forces units operating clandestinely from deep within Afghanistan, made it difficult to identify "the front," let alone access it. Instead of riding along with the troops or hanging around forward operating bases to interview the combatants, reporters had to content themselves with daily briefings by Secretary of Defense Rumsfeld and his staff. Not only were these briefings held in Arlington, Virginia, they were held begrudgingly at the insistence of the press corps (Rumsfeld wanted to have only twice-weekly briefings).[3] It was not until late November, after major operations were winding down, that journalists were permitted to accompany marines into Afghanistan. Even then, reporters were frequently sequestered on base, far away from the action. In a particularly egregious incident of media management, field commanders in Kandahar held journalists hostage at gunpoint in a local warehouse to prevent them from accessing the scene of a friendly fire incident (about which see chapter 4).[4] Only after the furor that followed did Torie Clarke, assistant secretary of defense for public affairs, establish public affairs offices in Afghanistan to co-ordinate press access. The ensuing, close-up view of the war was still tightly controlled by Clarke, however, who identified a "message of the day" and en-sured that the public affairs liaisons would do little more than disseminate it. Combat operations were still strictly prohibited, but journalists were now per-mitted to venture into nearby villages to view the aid packages dropped by the military and observe the noble efforts of military engineers to build schools and health clinics.[5] This limited view of the conflict affirmed, for U.S. audi-ences, the humanitarian nature of the invasion. Viewers were not shown the effects of U.S. aerial bombardment on civilian infrastructure, and they were not shown casualties, either military or civilian.[6] The one exception to this rule was a series of "about-to-die" photos, which appeared in a number of U.S. papers in last week of November 2001. These photos pictured defeated Taliban fighters begging their Northern Alliance captors for mercy. Though the accompanying text often explained that the prisoners were beaten, robbed, mutilated, and then shot and left for dead, the photos rarely portrayed such savagery. Once again, by effacing the acts of torture and death, the im-ages made the war seem more humane than it was. As Barbie Zelizer puts it, "Images were used in a way that showed less of the war itself and more of the assumptions about the war held by the forces responsible for its prosecu-tion."[7]

Seen at a distance, the early war appeared bloodless and, therefore, virtu-ous, but, given the ready availability of new media technologies (satellites, satellite phones, computers, PDAs, and the Internet), such distanced coverage could not last.[8] The arrival of pan-Arab satellite news channels such as Al Jazeera and Al Arabiya made it possible for international news services to ob-tain alternative, less-sanitized views of the war and its effects. European news agencies shut out of the U.S. theater of operations acquired their war imagery directly from the refugee camps on the borders of Afghanistan and from the Taliban, who conducted regular tours of villages bombed by the United States.[9] These alternative views were available in the United States on public television, via cable and satellite channels such as BBC America, and over the Internet, and there was little the Bush administration could do about it, short of blocking the signals (a politically untenable option). Indeed, traffic to the two largest British news websites, the BBC News Online and the Guardian Online, increased throughout 2002, with the BBC reporting up to 60 percent of its traffic from the United States by January 2003.[10] Al Jazeera's English-language website reportedly "receive[d] about 4–5 million visits per week, with an estimated 50–60 percent of them originating in the USA."[11] Negative depictions of the U.S. war effort were so prevalent within the United States that Donald Rumsfeld felt compelled to go on the offensive, openly chastising reporters for printing information about U.S. special forces operations in Afghanistan and accusing Al Jazeera, in particular, of being a mouthpiece for the Taliban.[12] Indeed, when U.S. forces hit the Kabul offices of Al Jazeera in November 2001, many suspected the news operation was deliberately targeted.[13]

Recognizing that the tactics of "mediated distanciation" were no longer sufficient to guarantee the virtuous appearance of war, the Bush administration sought new ways to manage the media.[14] What was required, they decided, was the personal touch: the Pentagon would bypass the news media and promote its public relations objectives using entertainment programming. As I have suggested, there is nothing new about the phenomenon of "militainment." What is new is the degree to which militainment has been integrated into the Pentagon's strategies in advance. No longer an afterthought, or an act of conflict-specific propaganda, militainment is a forward strategy for promoting and legitimating military values even during times of peace. While the immediate goals of such projects might be to support recruiting and retention, the effects are much broader, promoting the militarization of U.S. society and altering conceptions of democratic citizenship in profound ways. As Roger Stahl has argued, this proactive policy of self-promotion by the military is a function of the reconceptualization of warfare in the contemporary era.[15] The wars in Afghanistan and Iraq, and the larger War on Terrorism, have been conceived within the terms of information warfare, or Netwar. In Netwar, deception and information control become integrated into the design of combat operations. The Bush administration tacitly acknowledged the preeminence of Netwar thinking whenever it called the War on Terrorism a "new kind of war" requiring "new strategies."[16] According to Stahl, this "new kind of war" is premised on the notion that there is no distinction between the home front and the battlefield: "Every aspect of civilian life takes the appearance of a battlefield, and every tool the appearance of a weapon."[17] Civilians become both the objects of Netwar—the primary targets of war and other forms of state discipline (policing and surveillance)—and subjects integrated into its processes through carefully targeted messaging. Everyday life becomes saturated with the disciplinary logics of war, and civilians are reconstituted as "virtual citizen-soldiers."[18]

How entertainment programming on U.S. television contributed to the militarization of U.S. society and the promotion of a notion of war as both ordinary (just) and virtuous (Just) is the subject of the next two chapters. The current chapter focuses on the military-media coproduction of the War on Terrorism in reality militainment programs like *Making Marines* (Discovery, 2002), *AFP: American Fighter Pilot* (CBS, 2002), *Profiles from the Front Line* (ABC, 2003), and *Military Diaries* (VH1, 2002). While the first two programs pre-date the war in Afghanistan, they aired after the 9/11 attacks and incorporated specific references to the War on Terrorism into their reedited narratives. The latter two were produced with the explicit cooperation of the Department of Defense and were said to provide the template for the strategy of embedding that would define coverage of the later war in Iraq.[19] By turning to reality television to tell the military's story, the Bush administration sought to produce a different, more intimate, but no less self-serving, view of its military operations in Afghanistan. The "virtuousness" of these conflicts was guaranteed not by a distanced and techno-fetishistic view that depicted the "enemy-other" as so many scurrying cockroaches. Rather, virtue was conferred through the fetishization of the perspective of the U.S. soldier to the exclusion of every other perspective. Proximity to, rather than distance from, the combat zones would drive the military's media management strategy.

The reality genre's emphasis on "authenticity" and "ordinariness" encouraged viewers to imagine the soldiers on display as civilians who were just doing a job. By promoting an identification with the individual soldiers, they also promoted an identification with the values and disciplinary logics of militarism as a regime of conduct. The carefully edited images of soldiers operating humanely in the combat zones—handing out candy and supplies to needy villagers and weeping when they were not permitted to do more—not only made the war in Afghanistan appear Just; they made war seem the most effective means for confronting humanitarian crises of all sorts. Combined with other forms of militainment, such as the scripted dramas *JAG*, *Over There*, and *Generation Kill* (discussed in chapters 4 and 5, respectively), these programs habituated viewers to the use of war as a strategy of peace and encouraged them to imagine themselves as virtual citizen-soldiers. Since the responsibility of soldiers is not to deliberate but to follow orders, this shift in the conception of citizenship explains, at least in part, why the U.S. public was so willing to buy into the Bush administration's arguments for an unnecessary and unjust preventative war in Iraq.

Reality TV Brings the War Home

As I've discussed, the Bush administration immediately dispatched envoys to Hollywood after 9/11 to enlist their assistance in the production of a supportive climate for the War on Terrorism. The administration was able to do this so quickly because a set of cooperative networks already existed to encourage collaboration between the military and intelligence services and Hollywood producers. The Marine Corps set the precedent in 1917 when they provided assistance to the Edison Company's silent film *Star-Spangled Banner*, a puff piece that recorded a British teen's experiences on a Marine Corps training base. The 1926 film *What Price Glory?* also received assistance from the Marine Corps despite its antiwar themes and association of corps life with drinking and debauchery. Described as "the *Top Gun* of its day," the film's positive depiction of male camaraderie boosted Marine Corps enlistments at a time of deep skepticism about the viability of war as a policy tool (the navy, which was first offered the script but turned it down, lost out on this bid; they would not make the same mistake when *Top Gun* came along).[20] The army and navy quickly followed the Marine Corps's lead and embraced Hollywood as a PR partner. By 1942, all three branches of the U.S. military had liaisons' offices in Hollywood, and in 1947 the newly commissioned air force joined them. In 1949, the Defense Department united these services under a single umbrella organization, the Office for Motion Picture Production (now a part of the Public Affairs Office and headed by Phil Strub).[21] In terms of television relationships, the Marine Corps provided assistance for several military-themed episodes of *The Mickey Mouse Club* in the early 1950s, and the Army and Navy followed with the stand-alone series *West Point Story* (1956–1958) and *The Men of Annapolis* (1957–1958).[22] Given this history, it is not surprising that the Pentagon would turn to Hollywood to publicize its role in the War on Terrorism.

Prior to the 9/11 attacks, the Pentagon had already secured deals with several media entities to promote the military as a career option and character builder. This was part of its forward strategy to reinvigorate and normalize American militarism, a project that had been ongoing since at least the 1970s.[23] These deals included a Pentagon-supported, but alumni-funded, $25 million dollar contract with the Walt Disney Corporation to "celebrate" the bicentennial of the U.S. Military Academy at West Point. The alumni asked for a modest two-hour documentary to commemorate the bicentennial, but Disney pulled out all the stops, leveraging the concept across its entire enterprise. Not only did ABC air the documentary (*Young America Salutes West Point*,

6/23/2002); they reran the original *West Point* series on ABC Family and produced special programming for the History Channel (*West Point: Two Hundred Years of Honor and Tradition*), A&E (*West Point and the Movies*; *Military Bands at Carnegie Hall*), ESPN (short promos on "Leadership in Sports"; a full-page ad in *ESPN: The Magazine*; a rescreening of the 1990 documentary *Field of Honor: 100 Years of Army Football*; rebroadcasts of several Army football games on ESPN Classic), and a bevy of one-minute spots for their TV and radio networks to integrate into regular programming, including the "West Point Minute" series used on *Good Morning America* and *Nightline* and "Intimate Portraits" of female cadets for Lifetime. While Ivan Kronenfeld, one of the leaders of the West Point Project, claimed that such programming would be more than just a "puff piece" for the academy, the program formats selected were all promotional in nature, and the goal was to "celebrate" the bicentennial.[24] Disney's large-scale investment also made the inclusion of controversial material highly unlikely. Both parties *wanted* puff pieces, and that is what resulted. The timing of the bicentennial celebration could not have been better for either party, as the mid-2002 air dates coincided with the "successful" resolution of the war in Afghanistan and the beginnings of the march into Iraq. Disney reaped PR points as well as profits, while the army saw a boost in recruitment.

The return of West Point to television was the most coordinated collaboration between the military and the media, but it was not the only, or even the most successful, of these ventures. In 2000, the Pentagon contracted with TBS to air a two-hour special covering the military's annual joint training exercises as if they were sporting events. Called *War Games* (2001), the special featured commentary from NFL-star-turned-sportscaster Howie Long and former CNN staffer Anne Powell, daughter of then secretary of state Colin Powell, who lent the program gravitas and an air of authenticity. The individual services have also contracted with media producers to promote the military lifestyle as a type of branded commodity. For example, the army, navy, and Marine Corps have all cooperated with MTV to produce service-themed, boot-camp episodes of the *Real World/Road Rules Challenge*. The trivialization of war and its effects is a staple of such programming and key to the military's recruitment goals. During the episode "Shall We Play a Game?" (1998), for instance, contestants were given a clue to their next mission that read: "Left, Left, Left, Right, Left. I don't know if it's been said, this mission can make you dead. Sound off, Real World, Sound off, Road Rules, Sound Off, Let's Fight!" Such representations not only familiarize viewers with the service branches; they promote an adversarial worldview and habituate teen viewers to the need for a combat-ready military. "Let's Fight!" becomes normalized as a mode of conflict resolution.[25]

These episodic ventures were so successful that the Marine Corps teamed with Fox television to produce an entire reality-based series called *Boot Camp* (2001), in which civilian "recruits" would undergo the same physical and psychological training as military enlistees. "We looked at it as an opportunity to give the public a glimpse into the Marine Corps," a spokesman said.[26] Before the series could even air, though, CBS sued Fox on behalf of *Survivor* producer Mark Burnett, claiming *Boot Camp* so aped the *Survivor* formula that it constituted copyright infringement (the case never went to court since *Boot Camp* lasted only two months).[27] Then, in 2002, Burnett created his own military-themed gamedoc (a reality series focused on competition between nonactors), which pitted special forces units from the various service branches in simulated combat for viewer enjoyment.[28] It was called *Combat Missions* and aired on the cable network USA from January to April of 2002. Burnett went to great lengths to make the series look like a Hollywood war film, complete with pyrotechnics and romantic theme music. "I brought in some of the best feature film people to help me make it look great," he said. "I brought in my pyrotechnical people who just came off *Pearl Harbor* and *Wind Talker* with John Woo. I brought my military advisors, who were also on *Pearl Harbor*. The guys from *Traffic* did all my helicopter stunts and aerials. The results are pretty spectacular."[29] The series was designed to showcase the growing importance of U.S. Special Forces in the revamped military and to capitalize on their newfound status as icons of American heroism post-Afghanistan. The competitions were crafted to display the single-mindedness, ingenuity, and flexibility of the special forces and reassure viewers of their capacity to meet any challenges. Best of all, the spectacle was bloodless by design—a pretend war that could substitute for the ugliness of the real thing.

Docusoaps and the War in Afghanistan

Gamedocs weren't the only subgenre of reality programming to get a boost from the military's boosterism. Indeed, the docusoap received the greatest bump in military investment and commercial sales post-9/11. The term "docusoap" refers to "serial programmes about ordinary people" that combine "the observation and interpretation of reality in documentary with the continuing character-centered narrative of soap opera."[30] There is no competition in these sorts of programs; rather, they focus on the observation of ordinary individuals in their natural habitats, their homes and workplaces. The people at the center of these programs are presented as representatives of a larger social order, but the goal of docusoaps is not to interrogate, explain, or alter the social order as a documentary might. Rather, it is to create "a spectacle of the everyday that emphasizes its participants' performance of identity."[31] By fetishizing the everyday routines of soldiers in training or in theaters of combat, military-themed docusoaps place military identity at the center of U.S. social life and construct soldiers as the ideal citizens. Such representations serve a normative function, producing and disseminating new criteria of citizenship and training individuals to embrace their roles as servants of government, rather than participants in it.

American Fighter Pilot and Making Marines were the two earliest ventures in the realm of the military docusoap. Though they were planned and largely completed prior to the September 11 attacks, both programs returned to their subjects to shoot new interviews and collect reactions to the events. Making Marines was a three-part series focused on the grueling training process at the Marine Corps Recruit Depot on Parris Island, South Carolina. The U.S. Marine Corps provided substantive material assistance to the producers, including access to its camp and training facilities, its recruits, and its military experts, who consulted on the scripting and editing of the program. The program followed the exploits of several bright-eyed recruits before, during, and after their military training, with the aim of capturing the "cult-like transformation" in their identities and personalities wrought by military discipline and devotion (this according to the documentary's introductory voice-over). Created by TV veteran Chuck Braverman and his son Alex, Making Marines adopts the same laudatory tone with regard to military discipline as Braverman's award-winning docusoap High-School Boot Camp (2000), which presented military discipline as the cure for juvenile delinquency. In both series, the camera acts as an eyewitness to events and testifies to the transformative power of such discipline. Recruits detail their responses to the hardships of training in emotional interviews that frequently degenerate into on-camera breakdowns. The displays of anger and sorrow both humanize the recruits and certify the "special" nature of the training, which is designed to turn "ordinary" individuals into heroes. By the third episode of the series, we are in love with the earnestness of the recruits and accept without question the documentary's presentation of them as representative Americans, especially in their responses to 9/11. The post-9/11 interviews (episode 2) are a hodgepodge of

Making Marines (Discovery, 2001). Interviews with the young marine recruits after 9/11 ran the gamut of emotions but largely reinforced the call for militarized vengeance.

"typical" American reactions, from shock ("All this stuff just seems unreal to me right now") to incredulity ("I still can't believe it. Gosh, the World Trade Center") to despair ("September 11 really bothered this recruit, to see what such a heartless man can do to a city [sobbing], to the Pentagon"). However, the despair quickly gives way to rage ("Being a marine now it's like 'ok, you hurt us, now we'll hurt you'") and resolution ("Everyone in my platoon, they may be a little bit worried about what's gonna happen, but they know what they have to do, and they'll do it"), thereby tacitly affirming the rectitude of the Bush administration's turn toward militarism as the solution to the problem of terrorism. By providing an "intimate tracking of [the] everyday [lives]" of these "ordinary" recruits, *Making Marines* also constructs their transformed soldier-identity as a normative ideal.[32] Indeed, the drill song that plays as the final credits roll suggests that any other sort of existence is a waste of time: "I used to sit at home all day, a-hey-hey, just a-waste my life away, a-hey-hey."

American Fighter Pilot (AFP) offers a similar behind-the-scenes glimpse into a rarified military microcosm—the fighter pilot training school at Tyndall Air Force Base, Panama City, Florida—but it is overtly celebratory of the military enterprise. With *Making Marines*, the conversion experience is presented as a risky process fraught with emotional and physical distress; some might leave the series wondering why anyone would want to put themselves through such hell for such a meager reward. With AFP, all doubts are cast aside in a gee-whiz spectacle of high-tech warfare and high-testosterone masculine bonding. This is not entirely surprising given the fact that Tony and Ridley Scott, of *Top Gun* fame, were two of the program's executive producers (Jesse Negron and Brian Gadinsky, of *Combat Missions*, were the others) and one of the production companies responsible for the program was called Warfront/Zeal Pictures. What is more surprising is that the series lasted only two episodes before CBS yanked it due to low ratings, for AFP offered a textbook case in how to glamorize war and militarism.[33] It fetishized the technology of postmodern warfare in both its money shots of big machines and its hyper-mediated on-screen graphics, which mimicked the cockpit computer displays inside the F15s and training simulators. One critic called the aerial shots "nothing short of breathtaking, employing cameras both inside and outside of the cockpit" to produce an immersive experience of high-tech flight.[34] The show also featured likable, otherwise "ordinary" characters capable of embodying the cleanliness and morality of postmodern warfare. Lts. Marcus Gregory, the devout Christian soldier, Mike Love, the proud father, and Todd Giggy, the young rebel, represent a range of possible conceptions of manhood, but "you watch them change from the everyday guy next door [types] into trained killers" over the course of the show.[35] It is because they appear to be "the everyday guy next door," in fact, that the transformation into "killers" fails to disturb. With guys like these at the helm, we can be assured that the use of force will be measured, precise, and discriminate, rather than gratuitous. Like *Top Gun* before it, AFP offered an image of war as "surgery" rather than "slaughter." As Andrew Bacevich argues, such reassuring views of war make it easier for policy makers to confuse the use of force with foreign policy and to suggest militarism as a solution to all sorts of social problems.[36]

As if to prove Bacevich's point, AFP unabashedly endorses President Bush's militarized response to terrorism in its opening credit sequence and in interviews added to the end of episode 7. After 9/11, the credit sequence was re-edited to acknowledge the terrorist attacks. It begins by introducing the characters and the machines; the montage is suddenly interrupted by the graphic display, "Then times changed: September 11, 2001." Pictures of Osama Bin Laden assume the foreground while vaguely Middle Eastern music plays in the background. We hear a woman's voice scream, "Oh, my God," then reassuring snippets from the male pilots: "This is what I'm here for. This is why I serve"; "I'm an American fighter pilot, we're not gonna let that happen again." Every show begins with this sequence underscoring America's "innocence," Bin Laden's "evil," and the necessity these factors create for a vigorous U.S. response. It also reassures us that the response will be carefully calibrated, discriminating, and "humane" because the men we are training are not mere "killers"; they are killers in the Western tradition, who use force only when necessary to protect civilization and defend women and children.

This point is underscored in episode 7, when one of the trainers, code-named "Shark," tells us Gregory, the devout Christian and new father, is not really training to be a killer; rather, he is on a "spiritual journey" and has been "called to be an American fighter pilot." If he's required to take an enemy's life, "he is doin' it because that person is trying to kill his wife and little girl." To further underscore the connection between military duty and fatherly protection, the producers edit in an earlier interview with Gregory in which he tells us "It is so much more important to me to excel as a father than anything else." This assures us that Gregory will, indeed, come to understand war as a defense of home and family and embrace his killer instinct without qualms. Images of Gregory's wife cradling her newborn child complete the emotional manipulation. Thus, AFP replicates George Bush's ahistorical depiction of the War on Terrorism as a cosmic clash between "good" and "evil" in which the United States inevitably occupies the role of "good guy."

While one might think AFP would play well in the post-9/11 context, several factors contributed to the program's early demise. First, its ham-fisted editing made the show seem more emotionally manipulative than other docusoaps, especially after it was recontextualized in relation to 9/11. The program's vacillation between "immediacy" and "hypermediacy"—immersion in the story and distanced contemplation of the media frame—was also jarring and undercut the sustained focus on the personal that drives the docusoap.[37] TV critic David Bianculli, for example, described the visual style as disorienting and off-putting:

> AFP doesn't just move fast. It's an entire show on fast-forward, with all the ferocity of a relentless video game. But not, in this case, in a good or entertaining fashion. Images are fast-forwarded, overlaid, shaken and stirred. Factoids are thrown on the screen, and images edited and changed so rapidly that no camera shot seems to be held for more than a few seconds. . . . The flight simulations, and later the actual flights, are closer to the real deal, but even these are edited and presented in such a hyped and hyper way that they seem cartoonish and disjointed. If there's a way to dislike this series without appearing unpatriotic, please count me in.[38]

As Bianculli points out, AFP's overreliance on graphic inserts tended to infect all of its scenes, even those shot in a more immediate and unadorned style. As a docusoap, AFP was simultaneously too soapy, in its manipulative emotionalism, and not soapy enough, in its refusal to remain character-centered.

NAME: TODD GIGGY
SON OF A FIGHTER PILOT

AFP: *American Fighter Pilot* (CBS, 2002) tended to vacillate between soap opera and high-tech spectacle and to provide an overly gleeful celebration of American military prowess. It lasted only two episodes.

Second, the gleeful, zealous quality of the program's military promotionalism, especially its fetishization of technology, was out of tune with the cultural turn toward "seriousness" post-9/11. The program too often presented the pilots as oversized kids playing with oversized toys, and the training school's motto, "Death with Finesse," likely struck some viewers as appalling given the ongoing and very real war in Afghanistan. Finally, and probably most importantly, AFP debuted on one of the major broadcast networks. Time is money on the networks, and AFP, which was suffused with a jingoistic patriotism that could not help but alienate some viewers, just could not pull in a large enough audience. Similar commercial dynamics, along with some bad timing, would doom the more noteworthy *Profiles from the Front Line*, but not before the series drummed up an awful lot of controversy.

Profiles was conceived in response to 9/11 and focused on actual military engagements in the War on Terrorism. According to executive producer Bertram van Munster, creator of *Cops* and coproducer of *The Amazing Race*, "The idea of *Profiles* started when the War in Afghanistan started. . . . I thought . . . this is the perfect opportunity to do something, you know, to film this . . . so we had a meeting with the Pentagon, and we spoke to the people from Centcom and said 'would it be ok if we go out there and do this.' They said 'yeah absolutely, go right ahead.'"[39] While journalists were systematically denied military assistance and access to the troops, Secretary of Defense Donald Rumsfeld personally signed off on the plan to let the producers of *Profiles* "[troop] around all over the countryside—flying on planes, going on ships, going on patrol with the 101st Airborne, [and] living a rugged life."[40] It helped, of course, that one of those producers was Jerry Bruckheimer, a blockbuster film and TV creator with a track record of making the military look good in films such as *Top Gun*, *Crimson Tide*, *Pearl Harbor*, and *Black Hawk Down*. "We pretty much know how he operates," said Kathleen Canham Ross of the army's public affairs office in L.A., "he has a good idea of how we operate. That makes it a whole lot easier when you know what to expect from each other."[41] It also helps that Bruckheimer announced upfront that *Profiles* would be "a very visual reality show with a strong patriotic message."[42] According to the press kit, the series would "transport viewers to actual battlefields in central Asia" and show "actual footage of Special Operations forces apprehending possible terrorists, as well as compelling, personal stories of the U.S. military men and women who bear the burden and risks of this fighting." The avowed purpose of the producers was to "bring home the danger faced every day by America's bravest in the war on terrorism."[43]

The problem with turning to entertainment TV to publicize the war was that the resulting program would be just that—publicity. Van Munster and Bruckheimer not only lacked training in investigative journalism, they lacked even the investigatory impulse. Their goal was to shoot patriotic visuals that reinforced the military's mission. When asked by a British journalist what he would do "if he stumbles upon some human rights violation, or some mammoth military cock-up? Would he screen it?" Bruckheimer replied, "Yes, . . . so long as it's not something [the Pentagon] would consider sensitive . . . but we're not looking for that."[44] So, not only would Bruckheimer turn footage critical of the military over to the DOD for likely censorship, he was not even interested in shooting such footage. Van Munster concurred, saying "Obviously, we're going to have a pro-military, pro-American stance. We're not going to criticize."[45] In keeping with this promise, van Munster dutifully submitted all edited video for Pentagon approval and eagerly spliced Pentagon-produced video of combat operations into his own footage without attribution or comment. He also refused to share any of his proprietary video with news organizations, freezing out even ABC news. Van Munster's adversarial attitude toward the news media was especially galling because he promoted his program as a form of investigatory documentary. "I'm not in the business

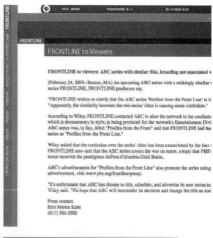

Profiles from the Front Line (ABC, 2003) tried to pass itself off as a documentary exploration of war by changing its name and using the same font style as the respected PBS documentary series *Frontline*. (Left) Ad for *Profiles*. (Top Right) Memo from PBS denouncing the tactics. (Bottom Right) *Frontline* logo.

of making infomercials," he said. "What I'm known for is in-your-face, good, tough documentary cinema verité work."[46] Given his professed desire to help serve the U.S. cause, this appeal to documentary tradition can only be viewed as a promise to "dig hard for good news."[47]

ABC schedulers and marketers were even more deliberate in their exploitation of the confusion between documentary and reality TV, for they tried to promote *Profiles* by making it look like an offshoot of the legitimate, award-winning documentary news series *Frontline* (PBS). Not only was the title of the series changed from *Profiles from the Front Line* after *Frontline* producers contacted ABC to complain about the proximity of the title to their brand identity, ABC also scheduled the series opposite *Frontline* on Thursday nights and created advertisements that featured the same font style as the legendary documentary program.[48] These cynical promotional tactics only further enraged critics already suspicious of what Dan Rather called the "Hollywoodization of the military"—that is, the growing tendency of the Pentagon to "make troops available as props in gung-ho videos" while freezing out journalists who might hold them accountable for their miscues and blunders.[49] By blocking journalists' access to the war, the Pentagon ensured that the "first draft of history"—and the one that would set the terms for all to follow—would affirm the professionalism and humanity of the U.S. military while obscuring the geopolitical and ethical complexities of the conflict.

Van Munster believes that "documentary and reality [TV] are actually brother and sister," and that as long as the adopted production style is cinema verité, the resulting video cannot but be investigatory. The content of *Profiles* illustrates precisely why these assumptions are naïve. It is entirely possible to eschew editorial manipulation and still produce an "unrealistic" portrait of an institution at work. Like other forms of docusoap, *Profiles* focuses in minute detail on the personal lives of its subjects, all of whom are prescreened for their representative "Americanness." The stockbroker who reenlisted after 9/11 to avenge his coworkers, the special forces soldier whose grandfather was an immigrant from Afghanistan, the doctor who runs a free clinic for Afghan civilians and whose second son was born while he was deployed to Afghanistan—these characters embody the best of America's vaunted ideals (loyalty, professionalism, selflessness, and hard work). Their enthusiasm is also infectious, drawing viewers to identify with the soldiers' belief in the mission, if not the mission itself.

This verité-style focus on the "human" side of war provides a very limited view of war as an enterprise, however. Not only are the cameras turned off "as soon as the fighting gets close," but the space for the presentation of political and historical context is diminished when the focus is placed on the minutia of day-to-day operations. Believing that "war is not about big explosions," van Munster focused almost exclusively on "the small stuff."[50] We learn a lot about how to defense a perimeter, refuel a plane in midair, and secure a convoy, but almost nothing about strategy, politics, or ethics. The intimacy and immediacy of the coverage invites viewers to identify with the soldiers and take pride in their professionalism, but it comes with an injunction not to "sweat the big stuff."

The focus on "the personal as the terrain of moral and civic drama" also permits the idiosyncratic and often ill-informed views of the soldiers to stand in for the missing context of war.[51] Thus, even if events are not staged for the camera, the result may still be to reinforce the Bush administration's claims about the necessity and rectitude of the War on Terrorism. For example, in the first episode, we see U.S. forces board and search a vessel in the Arabian Sea off the coast of Iraq. Their mission is to enforce the sanctions imposed on Iraq by the United Nations, but the sailors who search the vessel understand their mission in relation to 9/11. "I don't feel funny about going through any- one's personal stuff," one of them says. "They wiped out how many people's stuff at the World Trade Center?" This explicit connection between Iraq and 9/11 is frequently reiterated in the program and derives, in this case, from the sailor's superior, who prepared his troops for their mission by calling Saddam Hussein a "criminal and a thug" and asking, "How dare they fly aircraft into the World Trade Towers . . . [and] Pentagon?" The timing of Profiles' release (late February of 2003) transforms this set of assertions into propaganda for the U.S. invasion of Iraq.

Profiles also legitimates the Bush administration's claims about the "just- ness" of Operation Enduring Freedom by presenting the invasion as a human- itarian mission (we brought doctors and health clinics to the people), conducted in self-defense (as a response to aggression), and conducted with due care and respect for the civilian populations. The conventional nature of the bulk of the warfare was belied by the program's fascination with the work of "Mike," "Mark," and "Drew," a highly skilled and well-trained special forces unit responsible for gathering intelligence and building relationships with the locals. The volume of screen time devoted to their efforts, and the lack of editorial commentary about their uniqueness, made them appear typi- cal of U.S. troops. This, in turn, made the entire invasion—a highly conven- tional assault involving the overwhelming use of force and featuring a high degree of "collateral damage"—appear measured and humane. When cor- nered in traffic or surrounded by angry villagers, for example, Mike, Mark, and Drew do not shoot; they talk their way out of it. When apprehending sus- pected militants, they do not take unilateral action, beat down doors, or frighten innocents; they coordinate with the Afghan Military Forces and ask the local warlord to turn the suspect over out of self-interest. Their cultural sensitivity and discrimination reassure viewers that slaughter is not in the mission profile. Mike, Mark, and Drew really are the "best and the brightest," and their centrality to the program, which results from the higher visual inter- est of their missions, creates the illusion that the entirety of Operation Endur- ing Freedom has been conducted in a similar discriminating fashion. By profiling these very "special" forces as if they were typical, van Munster and Bruckheimer create a false impression that the war was "efficient, noble, bloodless and cost-free."[52] *Profiles* did not show the reality of war so much as it reassured U.S. viewers of the purity of U.S. motives and the morality of its military's conduct. As reviewer (and fan) R. D. Heldenfels put it, *Profiles* "showed Americans wishing to bring a happier life found under democracy to other lands, to persuade others both through good will and material goods."[53] In other words, it reaffirmed the exceptionalist narrative underwriting the American mission in the first place.

The *Profiles* project was so successful from a propaganda standpoint that Bruckheimer received Pentagon approval to produce a similar series about the war in Iraq (ABC allegedly balked). The DOD invited van Munster to become one of its official videographers for the war in Iraq, and, of course, the whole concept of intimate access to the troops was later enshrined as DOD policy (i.e., the "embedding" policy).[54] As television, however, the program flopped. It netted only a 4.6 rating on its premiere and was outscored by two other dubious ABC reality entries: *Are You Hot?* and *I'm a Celebrity, Get Me Out of Here!* When ABC pulled *Profiles* after only three episodes (six were slated), they claimed it was to avoid generating confusion over the news content of the program vis-à-vis the war in Iraq, which was launched two weeks following the series premiere.[55] Low viewer response was the more likely culprit, however. Besides, with the embedding strategy turning news into militainment, and at a much lower cost, the entertainment division could go back to doing the sort of reality programming it does best—showcasing "people at their worst."[56]

While many people have lumped VH1's *Military Diaries* into the same category as *Profiles from the Front Line*,[57] the programs differ in two important ways. First, the producer for *Diaries*, R. J. Cutler, is better known for his documentaries (*The War Room*, *A Perfect Candidate*, *American High*) than for his work in entertainment formats. This experience enabled him to recognize instantly that "the military isn't open to the kind of access you want as a filmmaker."[58] Rather than embedding his own camera crew, then, Cutler adopted the same video diary format he pioneered to great acclaim in the Emmy-award-winning series *American High* (PBS, 2000). By giving U.S. soldiers the cameras and asking them to record their own lives in their own ways, Cutler hoped to get a less guarded view of their thoughts, feelings, and actions. He provided more than eighty soldiers and sailors stationed in four different locales—Kuwait, Afghanistan, Camp Pendleton, and aboard the USS *Stennis* in the Arabian Sea—with cameras and rudimentary training and told them to shoot for at least fifteen minutes every day. Cutler and his team of editors then assessed the 2,400 hours of raw footage, selected the "characters" based on their representative qualities, and edited the contributions into six half-hour episodes organized by theme ("Life of a Soldier," "The Human Touch," "Youth in the Military," etc.).[59] While the quality of the resulting episodes was decidedly uneven, the strategy of turning soldiers into video crews at least provided Cutler with a much broader range of footage to choose from, including live-fire combat situations (most notably "Operation Anaconda") and more in-depth emotional portraiture. The second major difference from Bruckheimer and company is that Cutler approached his subject "with a question and not an answer." His aim was to find out "what war is really like," rather than to produce "a strong patriotic message."[60] Of course, finding out what war is "really like" might produce a "patriotic message" in the end, but the open orientation leads Cutler to incorporate more biographical and emotional detail about the soldiers than *Profiles'* emphasis on the "small details" of the mission could engender. The result is more complicated and complex than anything van Munster's allegedly hard-hitting verité style produced.

The differences in approach do create important differences in the resulting products. *Profiles* is a sleek, stylized, perfectly choreographed promotional video complete with swelling musical cues to tug the heart strings or get the blood beating. *Military Diaries* is a much lower-key affair, with grainy video, intimate to-camera confessionals that do not feel performed, and a deft use of silence as a mode of punctuation (surprising given the program's emphasis on musical tastes and its affiliation with VH1). *Profiles* gives us a detailed look at the mechanics of war; *Diaries* gives us a glimpse at the humans inside the machine. *Diaries* also possesses a self-consciousness about the genre of reality television that is utterly lacking in *Profiles*. The opening credit sequence, for example, undercuts any pretension to objectivity and transparency by linking reality militainment to a history of military reportage. It begins, like *American Fighter Pilot*, with a concatenation of news sound bites and video clips, which situate the military's operations in relation to 9/11. President Bush reminds us that "on September the 11th, enemies of freedom committed an act of war on our country," and Democratic presidential nominee John Kerry affirms that military action is required, "no doubt about it." A parade of prominent news personalities provides background detail about the ongoing strife in Afghanistan, and visuals confirm that we are dropping humanitarian aid along with bombs. So far, so typical. This sequence gives way, however, to a set of titles designed to look like old-fashioned newsprint (courier fonts and datelines) and/or newsreel footage (sepia tones and grainy defects). The titles place reality TV within a tradition of war coverage but also remind us of the constructed nature of such coverage. We are then introduced to the program's characters and locales and reminded that, in the words one soldier, "This is real. We live it every day." This proclamation of authenticity is followed by an inset image of a cathode-ray tube TV set filled with static. Slowly the static gives way to black silhouette images of soldiers marching across the bottom of the screen while the title *Military Diaries* fills the top. After Cutler is announced as the series' developer, the screen and accompanying static noise blip off, as if the TV set has been shut down; then the week's episode starts. The form of this introduction, with its fetishization of media technologies past, undercuts the explicit claims to transparency articulated in the content of the sequence. As a mode of exposition, it prepares viewers to approach the program skeptically, as a construction of the real, not a mere reflection of it. This self-reflexivity is continued in the episodes themselves, as Cutler leaves in shots of the soldiers positioning cameras, focusing them in, and rearranging themselves to achieve the proper composition. Viewers are almost never allowed to forget the series is an orchestrated presentation of war, not the thing itself. They may or may not take up the challenge to question the program's "reality," but they are at least invited to do so, which is more than can be said for other offerings in the genre.

Critics responded positively to the difference represented in and by *Diaries*, noting that "the show is not as pro-war as one might think. Parts are downright anti-war."[61] Indeed, the first episode features a navy pilot who understands his mission in terms of vengeance for 9/11 ("As far as all Americans that were killed on 9/11, we're out here to deliver your justice") and a regular sailor who tells us, "I love my country, but I fear my government." This sort of head-snapping ideological counter-positioning is typical of the program and discomfits the viewer expecting either unadulterated jingoism or unbiased professionalism. The second episode, which is focused on the "humanitarian mission" in Afghanistan, is perhaps the most ambivalent of the six. On the one hand, it is full of patriotic musings about American exceptionalism, restraint, and good will. Soldiers are literally draped in the flag, as they discuss how reluctant they are to fight. "I don't like war. I don't like fighting," says Maj. Kevin Peel, a contingency contractor assigned to Bagram Airfield. Sgt. Laurie Green, an army engineer, says, "I didn't join expecting to go to war. . . . There is no winner in war." And Sgt. Stephen Carter, a bomb technician, explains, "War is something you cannot appreciate until you can come to a place like this and see the destruction that can be done." The video shows images of wounded Afghan men in wheelchairs, impoverished Afghan children, desperate mothers, and so on. When placed together, the images and the sound bites reinforce the Bush administration's presentation of the war as defensive and humanitarian—a necessary intervention undertaken on behalf of the desperately vulnerable peoples of Afghanistan. On the other hand, the episode also shows how the narrative of American exceptionalism depends on a collective refusal to see the destruction U.S. militarism has caused. Thus, for example, we follow Sgt. Carter as he cleans up mines and unexploded ordnance lying around in the countryside. He tells stories of Afghan civilians being blown apart by the bombs and says it will take twenty-five years to clean up the mess left over from the *Soviet* invasion. It never occurs to Sgt. Carter that much of the ordnance lying around is of U.S. origin, either from the ongoing war or from the assistance we provided to the Mujahedeen during the 1980s. The job of the army, as he sees it, is to make the world safe; it cannot, by definition, constitute a source of peril. Yet the destruction all around him suggests otherwise. Once again, the imagery works against the narrative to expose the contradictions at the heart of the U.S. position.

The story of Sgt. Green further lifts the veil on the true nature of the U.S. mission. She repeatedly remarks on her desire to help the local populations and suggests that her commanders have ordered her to "distance herself" from them. "I'm in this country that needs so very much," she says, "and my job is *not* to help them. That's really the hardest thing, I think, because I *want my job to be to help them. . . .* I want desperately to know and believe *every day* that I have in some way made this place better. And *I don't really think we are, and I wish that I could, you know*" (italics mine). Green's testimony gives the lie to the notion that the humanitarian mission is a priority in Afghanistan. It is the video equivalent of the "food bombs" that U.S. planes dropped in the middle of Afghan minefields, where they lay unopened, cruel reminders of the shallowness of the U.S. commitment to the alleviation of Afghan suffering.

This is powerful stuff. However, it is entirely possible to ignore the self-reflexive ironies established in the editing process and identify uncritically with the selflessness and devotion of the individual soldiers. Indeed, given that Cutler instructed his videographers to use their fifteen minutes a day to explain how they "felt" about "music, who they are, their living space, being in the military, love and romance," emotional identification, rather than critical distance, seems to have been the central goal. The same questions about identity, consumer style, "love," and "feelings" mark all of VH1's programming, not to mention the programming on its sister network MTV, which has made the probing of teen feelings and consumer tastes into a social-scientific subspecialty.[62] Diaries' relentless focus on the mundanities of everyday life, like what music the soldiers listen to, what their quarters look like, when they last had sex, and so on, de-realizes the space of the war camp and promotes the creation of what Anita Biressi and Heather Nunn call a "psychological neighborhood."[63] Though viewers may be seated on a comfy sofa in the relative safety of their living rooms, they can feel a part of the distant world of war because they can recognize its inhabitants as "just like them." The "to-camera" structure of the diary entries enhances the illusion of intimacy and connection by making each entry appear to be a conversation between friends. Thus, while the content of many of the diaries may be critical of war, the formal emphasis on intimacy and emotional connection—on the essential humanity of the soldiers who comprise the military—depoliticizes war and limits the range of discourse one can have about it. Antiwar sentiment becomes, at best, the idiosyncratic expression of personal opinion, and viewers are invited to choose which views to "hear" and which to screen out. In typical docusoap style, ideological variation is incorporated as a selling point, to pull in the maximal number of viewers, and the decision to attend to the pro- or antiwar messages is entirely a matter of consumer preference. Indeed, the ultimate failing of Diaries is that it cannot conceive of antiwar sentiment as anything more than an expression of personal identity and consumer choice.

Thus, despite the differences in timing, focus, and approach, all of these reality programs, Making Marines, American Fighter Pilot, Profiles from the Front Line, and Military Diaries, ultimately served the propagandistic purposes of the military because they focused exclusively and relentlessly on the U.S. soldier. Afghan peoples served as little more than colorful background video or symbols of Taliban aggression/U.S. benevolence. Regardless of the ideological and social diversity of the cast, the intention to focus on the nobility of the U.S. grunt created an uneven distribution of attention and affect, whose primary effect was to efface both the status of these soldiers as agents of empire and the humanity of the populations they were besieging.[64] The Pentagon was perhaps more attuned to this fact than the filmmakers, for it gladly approved all four programs despite promises by the filmmakers to expose the military "warts and all." As one Pentagon spokesperson put it, entertainment producers embedded with the military are not likely to "run off . . . and film the flipside" of an operation since their safety depends on the goodwill of the U.S. troops.[65] This is what ultimately matters—the faithful alliance with the perspective of the military. If the programs include antiwar sentiments expressed by U.S. troops, well, that just gives the program a sheen of credibility and independence that helps it better sell the military perspective.

Conclusion

In telling the intimate stories of ordinary, good-hearted American soldiers, duty-bound to stand against tyranny and assist those in need, reality militainment not only underwrote the ideological justifications for war proffered by the Bush administration. It invited viewers to adopt a militarized perspective—to stand in sympathy with the military via an identification with the soldier. As VH1 put it, *Military Diaries* and programs like it "allow people around the world to learn who the people in our armed forces really are, connect us with their military experience, and help form a link between our armed forces and the citizens they defend."[66] Such links encourage U.S. citizens to become "virtual citizen-soldiers" and to view the military's needs as their own. The familiar conventions of reality television create an illusion of intimacy and copresence that knits the viewer all the more tightly into the military worldview for appearing to be interactive, a matter of consumer choice. Such programs give viewers the chance to "step through the screen and experience the TV war in first person" without having to suffer through war's worst effects.[67] All we see are noble, self-sacrificing soldiers whose personal reluctance to fight affirms the myth of American exceptionalism. Such programs construct the United States as a reluctant superpower whose strength is necessary to protect and defend civilization. The notion that war is an exercise of moral obligation transmutes aggression into sacrifice and makes any war undertaken by the United States, no matter how offensive or egregious, appear inherently "Just." Such romanticized depictions go a long way toward normalizing militarism and making it seem, to our detriment, like an inescapable part of the American way.[68]

Two difficulties emerge from this cultural development. First, there is a political price to be paid for immersing oneself in the spectacle of war. In Stahl's words, "One pays by shedding citizen identity," or abdicating the deliberative functions of democracy.[69] The civilian's job, in this climate, is to "support the troops" at the expense of every other consideration. This abdication of citizen identity not only impacts the political and social life of the nation—subordinating the common welfare to military imperatives—it has potentially dire consequences for others in the world, which is the second difficulty. By inhabiting the military perspective so completely, U.S. citizens become incapable of adopting other perspectives. Political dissent becomes coded as either "un-American" (not like us) or "anti-America" (a threat to us), and Americans do not even encounter the perspectives of those who are the potential targets of U.S. bombs (except as filtered through the political rhetoric of our leaders). There is no comparable set of reality series encouraging Americans to identify with the experiences and perspectives of peoples around the world. The result of such "symbolic annihilation" is to produce an ethnocentric worldview that makes the perpetuation of war and empire possible.[70] It is much harder to conceive of war as a noble pursuit when the peoples subjected to its chaotic force emerge into view. By translating war into a form of entertainment, these reality programs encouraged viewers to embrace "empire as a way of life," to see the militarized extension of U.S. hegemony as a social good.[71]

Ultimately, however, reality militainment was a short-lived trend on network television, lasting only until it proved the value of embedded reporting to the Pentagon. For the war in Iraq, the Pentagon would turn to journalists, rather than entertainers, to filter the military perspective, believing this would enhance the credibility of its message. By 2003, reality militainment had migrated to boutique cable channels such as Discovery-Times (now the Military Channel) or the Pentagon Channel, where it continues to comprise a healthy chunk of the program schedule. It occasionally reemerges on more mainstream networks in the form of Memorial Day or Veterans Day stunts, featuring on-location shooting at U.S. military bases around the world. For example, ESPN's SportsCenter has broadcast live "Salute the Troops" episodes from Kuwait, West Point, and the U.S. army base in Grafenwöhr, Germany, and Comedy Central's faux talk show The Colbert Report has taped segments with the troops in Iraq. Veterans have also increasingly figured in reality programs like Extreme Makeover: Home Edition and The Amazing Race, where they continue to be used to model the military as a "lifestyle choice" for mainstream Americans. By and large, however, reality militainment has been recategorized as a niche phenomenon of interest only to military history buffs and self-identified "patriots."

As the war in Afghanistan dragged on and a new war was begun in Iraq, the Bush administration turned to new techniques of patriotic messaging to control the war narrative and win the hearts and minds of the American populace. Embedded reporting was one new technique; the strategic use of fictional formats was another. Specifically, the administration began working with entertainment producers to "remediate" news accounts of unsettling events associated with the wars in Afghanistan and Iraq and to "premediate" the future of war by making the militarization of social life seem sustainable. "Remediation" refers to the way media incorporate other media into themselves. Thus, for example, fictional television programs may invoke the look and feel of news reports in order to cloak their content in an illusion of "truth" or "trustworthiness." It is about the recycling of other, often older, media forms in an attempt to control the perception of events in the present. "Premediation," on the other hand, has a future orientation; it is about the preconception and prenarration of future history. Richard Grusin likens premediation to a form of cultural preemption whereby future shocks to the social system are prevented through the constant media rehearsal of the future.[72] The next two chapters will address these processes of re- and premediation by examining forms of scripted militainment, including the military-themed series JAG, *Over There*, and *Generation Kill*. JAG, in particular, was designed (with Pentagon assistance) to inoculate the public against the future failure of militarized counterterrorism by recuperating damaging testimony about the ongoing conflicts in Afghanistan and Iraq. Even the putatively independent productions *Over There* and *Generation Kill*, however, ended up celebrating military values and recuperating militarism for an imperial project of global peacekeeping. That they received little to no help from the Bush administration to do so only goes to show how deeply entwined and deeply rooted the logics of militarism and empire have become in U.S. culture.

4 Fictional Militainment and the Justification of War

Critics of the War on Terrorism have paid a lot of attention to the format of reality militainment, viewing it as undeniable proof of the existence of a "military-industrial-entertainment complex."[1] Few of these critics have actually analyzed the content of these series, however, and even fewer have bothered to note the relative failure of these series to find an audience. *Making Marines* and *Military Diaries* were the only two to complete their series runs, and that is due more to their location on cable than to the quality of the programs. Because they are partially funded through subscriber fees, cable networks do not require programs to garner massive ratings to persist; they are also willing to ignore ratings data when prestige and branding are at stake. *Making Marines*, for example, may not have been a huge ratings success, but it conveyed the high-minded seriousness the Discovery network wanted to associate with its brand.[2] The program could also be repurposed at no additional cost and spread across the Discovery platform, including frequent reruns on the Military Channel. Still, even the most successful cable programs do not garner large overall ratings in comparison to broadcast networks where even the lowest rated program reaches millions of viewers. *American Fighter Pilot* was an unmitigated flop, and it was seen by 4.9 million viewers.[3] While the Nielsen ratings system is clearly in crisis, with critics rightly contesting its emphasis on quantity and live viewing over quality and total viewing,[4] the low ratings garnered by reality militainment still ought to give critics of the "military-industrial-entertainment complex" pause. After all, how effective is a propaganda bomb if it is not seen or heard?

Scripted militainment has proven far more durable as a vehicle for military propaganda. The military drama JAG (CBS, 1995–2005), for example, began six years before the terrorist attacks of 9/11 and remained in or around the Nielsen top 25 for the entirety of its ten-year run. The program follows the exploits of two attorneys, Harmon Rabb (David James Elliott) and Sarah "Mac" MacKenzie (Catherine Bell), assigned to the Marine Corps Judge Advocate

General's office. The two are charged with investigating, prosecuting, and defending those accused of crimes within the military system of justice, and their investigations frequently take them into the field of combat. Executive producer Donald Bellisario pitched the program as a cross between Top Gun and A Few Good Men, and, like those films, JAG offers a patriotic homage to the honor, professionalism, and sacrifice of military personnel.[5] Given that the bulk of its series run coincided with the post–Cold War downsizing of the U.S. military, a better case can be made for JAG's importance to the legitimation of the doctrine of preventative warfare (aka the Bush Doctrine) than can be made for any of the reality series critics are so incensed about. After all, JAG kept alive the premise that American military power was a prerequisite to the pursuit of American well-being at a time when cultural critics were projecting the "end of history" and heralding a new age of democratic peace and prosperity under the auspices of globalization.[6] If, as Andrew Bacevich argues, Ronald Reagan made the necessity of military power seem like common sense in Washington policy circles, cultural productions such as JAG disseminated the notion broadly and kept it alive in the public mind during a time of relative peace (for the United States).[7] Virtually transporting viewers to U.S. military installations and battle groups around the world, the program made the need for these installations appear obvious. Its legal premises also promoted a romanticized conception of the military as a moral institution, indeed, as the last bastion of morality in a society sliding toward hedonism.

While critics have never much cared for the program, it was a minor hit among older audiences and women 18–49 and garnered enough attention to keep itself on the air for ten seasons, a superior run for a TV drama.[8] Bellisario attributed JAG's success vis-à-vis reality militainment to two factors. First, it had an established record of support for the troops: "We didn't discover our patriotism on 9/11. We've always been a show that's pro-military, but not jingoistic." Second, it was based more upon character development and interpersonal relationships than techno-fetishism: "You need stories that interest viewers, take some dramatic licenses, and have characters that people care about."[9] The program prided itself on its "ripped-from-the-headlines" topicality and capacity to refurbish the military image when it was tarnished by news reports. The first two episodes, for example, were called "A New Life" (NBC, 1995) and responded to news reports of the first female pilots being deployed to battle carriers.[10] They told the story of a female pilot murdered by a jealous and angry fellow service member. The JAG lawyers solved the crime, convicted the "bad apple," and restored faith in the navy as an institution that neither discriminates nor condones discrimination against women. Just four years after the infamous Tailhook scandal stained the navy's reputation, "A New Life" promised that sexual harassment had no place in the new military and would be punished to the fullest extent of military law.[11] The fictional format gave JAG's creators the unique ability to control the outcomes of its tales of foreign policy intrigue and military criminality in ways that would benefit the public standing of the military in U.S. society. This is also what drew the Bush administration to the program in the wake of 9/11. JAG's need for dramatic license cohered well with the administration's desire to rescript history to make the United States appear innocent and just in its prosecution of the War on Terrorism.

The program's heretofore amorphous celebration of military values was given focus and direction by the War on Terrorism, and the result was a ratings spike, which moved the program from as low as twenty-eighth on the Nielsen ratings list to a high of tenth by 2002.[12] When the series finally bowed out in 2007, it achieved its highest ratings ever for its final episode and left on top of its game.[13] Before 9/11, military collaboration on production had been sporadic and low-key, consisting of episode-by-episode assistance with technical matters and the occasional use of DOD stock footage.[14] Bellisario relied largely on his own experience as a marine and a slew of outside consultants to enhance the realism of the program's military content up to that point. After 9/11, however, the DOD took a more active role in the show's production, offering personnel and equipment for episodes about the War on Terrorism and providing inside information to producers—information withheld from the press and the DOD's own real-life JAG personnel—about the proposed military tribunals for "enemy combatants" captured in Afghanistan and elsewhere.[15] In exchange, JAG explicitly addressed controversial aspects of the administration's policies and reviewed the military's strategies and tactics with regard to combat operations and the detention, interrogation, and trial of "enemy combatants." With very few exceptions, the program found in favor of the United States, reinforcing the administration's claims that the wars in Afghanistan and Iraq were just in both rationale and conduct.

By "remediating" news reports about the War on Terrorism, JAG assisted the U.S. government in "premediating" the U.S. public's response to the Bush doctrines of preventative war and neoliberal Empire. It is a good illustration of how the shock of and desire for "liveness," or contact with the real, has been transmuted post-9/11 into a desire for controlled doses of history designed to serve a prophylactic function, that is, to shield U.S. subjects from anything that might disturb their enjoyment of or investment in the practices of war and empire.[16] By remediating the immediate past, JAG helped script a future in which war would continue to appear noble, Just, and necessary despite all empirical evidence to the contrary. While it would be impossible to discuss every episode of JAG related to the War on Terrorism (since arguably every episode since 9/11 would qualify), an analysis of a select few will demonstrate the ideological and affective alignment of the program with the Bush administration and its policies of militarized hegemony.

JAG and the Patriotic Defense of U.S. Detention Practices

The most egregious example of collaboration between the producers of JAG and the Bush administration to sway public opinion about the tactics of the War on Terrorism was the episode "Tribunal," which aired in April of 2002, just as the initial phase of the War in Afghanistan was winding down. The episode provided a fictional depiction of what a real-life military tribunal might be like. The problem was that Donald Rumsfeld gave the scriptwriter details of the Bush administration's proposal two weeks *before* he released the report to the press.[17] JAG's fictionalized and idealized version of how a tribunal might work thus reached the public at exactly the moment the official news of these procedures was breaking. The timing established a feedback loop that conferred legitimacy on the program's rendition of reality even as the program conferred legitimacy on the very real and illegitimate policies of the Bush administration. By creating a virtual version of reality, the "Tribunal" episode produced a compelling emotional realism capable of effacing the moral, ethical, and legal dilemmas raised by the decision to use tribunals to adjudicate the guilt of so-called enemy-combatants. It also masked the fact that the Bush administration systematically marginalized the real JAG corps in its deliberations over the structure of the tribunals and the treatment of detainees in the War on Terrorism.[18] The disastrous fallout of these policies, which includes the scandal at Abu Ghraib and the resulting loss of the nation's moral stature in the world, makes the use of fictional JAGs to buff up administration policies all the more reprehensible. As a coordinated disinformation campaign directed at U.S. citizens, it also comes dangerously close to violating the Smith-Mundt Act (aka the U.S. Information and Educational Exchange Act of 1948), which prohibits government-sponsored propaganda from being disseminated in the United States.[19]

But what exactly does the tribunal in "Tribunal" look like, and what does its idea of "justice" look like? How do the mechanics of the tale's unfolding work to preempt potential objections to the use of military tribunals? First, the suspect in the case is a high-ranking member of Al Qaeda responsible for establishing the organization's global network of training camps. Since the 9/11 hijackers were trained by him, he also bears direct responsibility for the 9/11 terrorist attacks. He openly celebrates the attacks, claiming the victims "got what they deserved," and mercilessly taunts both the prosecution and the defense attorneys. The only doubt about his guilt relates to a question of identity: is the man they are holding, who calls himself Mustafa Atef, also the Al Qaeda operative called Mohan Des? This is clearly resolved when Atef (Marc Casabani) takes the stand and admits to his identity. So, we have a clearly "evil" suspect who is equally clearly guilty, not just of being a member of Al Qaeda but of orchestrating the 9/11 attacks. Viewers need not feel queasy about rooting for execution.

Second, the tribunal itself rehearses and resolves numerous objections to U.S. procedures, including the extraction of involuntary confessions via "harsh interrogation," in ways that reassure viewers of the health of their nation's political and legal systems. In this episode, Rabb and MacKenzie are assigned to prosecute the case; they are opposed by their coworkers Adm. A. J. Chegwidden (John Jackson) and Cmdr. Sturgis Turner (Scott Lawrence), who are assigned to defend Atef. Even before they arrive on the ship where the tribunal is to be held, Rabb and MacKenzie have already dismissed potential arguments about the legality of military tribunals, explaining pedantically that there are precedents for such tribunals as long as they are not used to prosecute U.S. citizens (U.S. citizens being somehow more human and deserving of fair treatment than others). During the trial, the defense presents evidence that "Mohan Des" might be considered a "legal combatant" under the Geneva Convention and should not, therefore, be subjected to the tribunal's authority. A British legal scholar testifies that Al Qaeda meets the criteria for such status by virtue of its global membership, open display of uniforms and weapons, and adherence to the laws and customs of war. The defense also draws a parallel between Al Qaeda's unconventional tactics and those used by U.S. Special Forces. Rabb easily dismantles the expert's testimony by forcing him to defend hijacking as a "custom of war." He then carefully draws a distinction between U.S. tactics, which, though they involve the use of land mines and booby traps, are still carefully targeted to exclude civilian casualties. "Our" mines, the special forces commander assures us, "have self-deactivating, self-destructing mechanisms, and booby traps are confined to only threat-rich en-

JAG's (CBS, 1995–2005) interpretation of what a military tribunal would look like. Here the terrorist is clearly guilty, and the CIA is reprimanded for using harsh interrogation tactics. ("Tribunal," 4/3/2002)

vironments." Thus, the United States' technological superiority ensures its moral superiority and separates "us" from "them." "We" are legal combatants even when we use illegal tactics, but, as terrorists, "they" are illegal even when they follow the laws of war.

Finally, and most compellingly, the tribunal provides an occasion for the legal review of the "harsh interrogation tactics" approved by the Bush administration. A CIA agent takes the stand and explains how he extracted a confession from the defendant using sleep and sensory deprivation techniques over thirteen days before finally administering a "Pentothal agent." Adm. Chegwidden, who has choked Atef in the previous scene for his statements about 9/11, then rises reluctantly and says, "Your honor, I must move to exclude Mustafa Atef's confession. Thirteen days of torture to obtain an involuntary confession shocks the conscience and violates both the spirit and the letter of the Fifth Amendment." Rabb leaps to his feet to respond: "Your Honor, I strongly object to the word 'torture.' At no time was the accused beaten, nor was there ever any intentional infliction of pain. Furthermore, your honor, we are at war, and the Fifth Amendment [guaranteeing rights of due process] does not apply to our enemies. The very idea is ridiculous." The judge initially agrees with Rabb, but the remaining members of the tribunal force a brief discussion after which they decide that, though the Fifth Amendment does not apply, the involuntary confession does not meet the criteria of "probative value" established for the tribunal. In other words, the legal standards of the tribunal are equal to if not *more* rigorous than those established in the U.S. Constitution. While the exposure of the details of harsh interrogation might briefly dismay some viewers, the dismissal of the confession ultimately reassures them that the tribunal system is a fair and just venue for the arbitration of these issues. And for those who might find the censure of harsh interrogation methods "ridiculous," the recurring characters assure us that they feel the same: "This is the one time," Cmdr. Rabb tells us, "if the accused had got[ten] off, I'd have killed him myself."

Thus, while pretending to weigh the complex legal issues involved in the recourse to military tribunals, this episode of JAG actually produces a simplistic conception of justice as vengeance. Atef's guilt is assumed from the beginning ("Just look at him," Rabb says to Mac during the trial, as if that's enough), and Adm. Chegwidden agrees to defend him only because someone must, and he's the ranking officer. Lovable and familiar characters from the lowly staff secretary, Harriet, all the way up to the admiral himself either profess a desire to strangle Atef or actually attempt it. The defendant's courtroom confession removes any trace of doubt about his guilt, and his callous disregard for the "innocent" victims of 9/11 removes any lingering concerns about the fairness of the trial or its outcome. He deserves death, the episode implies, and he will get it. Such moral clarity enables Bellisario to have his cake and eat it too. He claims the goal of the episode was to "show people that tribunals are not what many people feared they would be, which is that they would be nothing but a necktie party. . . . I wanted to show that we still have a system of justice." When asked for his personal beliefs regarding the detainees, however, Bellisario stated, "they should all be taken out and blown up." Much like the real tribunals, then, the episode "Tribunal" is designed to give vengeance the veneer of justice and provide an emotional catharsis that suspends the need for thoughtful reflection and policy reformation.

The moral clarity the episode offers—good triumphs over evil and justice is done—stands in stark contrast to the reality surrounding the attempted use of military tribunals. Not only are the real-life "enemy combatants" held by the United States and subject to the tribunals *not* high-ranking members of Al Qaeda with clear responsibility for 9/11 (in many cases, they are men compelled to fight or simply incriminated for the bounty money U.S. soldiers were offering); they have been systematically denied access to counsel and to the court system. Many of these men have simply been released from U.S. custody after years of detention and interrogation yielded the conclusion that they never constituted a threat in the first place. In the most high-profile of these cases, a group of seventeen Chinese Muslims (known as Uighurs) were held at Guantanamo Bay from 2001 to 2009 despite being cleared of all charges by their captors and despite a 2008 court order requiring their release (in 2009 the United States began bribing island nations such as Bermuda and Palau to accept the Uighurs, and they were slowly being resettled). In the case of *Rumsfeld v. Hamden* (2006), the U.S. Supreme Court ruled against the Bush administration's plan for military tribunals, declaring that the executive branch could not set policy on such matters. Thus, by coproducing the "Tribunal" episode of JAG, the Bush administration sought to intervene in and shift the ground of public debate about the treatment of prisoners *before* the courts could rule on the subject. It was the ultimate act of cultural preemption.

In addition to "Tribunal," JAG staged a number of other narratives designed to create an illusion of debate about the treatment of prisoners in U.S. custody, the better to forestall actual debate on these subjects. The episode "Camp Delta" (2004), for instance, addressed issues surrounding the maltreatment of suspects at Guantanamo Bay. The episode was loosely based on the case of Specialist Sean Baker, an air force veteran and member of the Kentucky National Guard who was beaten and nearly choked unconscious during a training exercise at Guantanamo Bay.[20] The plot of the episode closely parallels Specialist Baker's case, complete with the traumatic brain injury that resulted from the beating, the "loss" of crucial video footage of the training exercise, and the acquittal of the soldiers responsible. There are three crucial differences between Specialist Baker's case and the JAG rendering, however. First, a court martial actually is convened in the fictional case, and the army general in charge specifically requests naval JAG officers to prosecute the case and defend the MPs because he wants to "eliminate the appearance of impropriety or command influence." In other words, he wants a fair, honest, and transparent trial proceeding. In real life, Baker's case was reviewed internally by the military command at Guantanamo, which concluded that no one was liable for his injuries. Moreover, U.S. Army spokespeople denied that Baker's medical discharge was a result of the injuries sustained during the training exercise—a lie they later had to publicly recant.[21] Second, the soldier beaten in the fictional case, army Cpl. Gino Hatanian (John Petrelli) refuses to cooperate with the prosecution, claiming he cannot and will not identify his attackers because what they did was justified by the circumstances: "These defenseless prisoners are killers, Colonel. They'd cut our throats in a minute if they could." Baker, on the other hand, not only sought a court martial for the offenders, he sued the Pentagon for $15 million dollars to compensate for the lifelong disability he now suffers as a result of his injuries (he has intractable epilepsy). Finally, the missing videotape miraculously turns up in the fictional trial, and Cmdr. Rabb uses it to deflect attention from the abusive soldiers to their commanders and the civilian contractor running the detention facility. He questions the contractor about his presence in the background at the training exercise, and the man defends the use of force to "fear up" detainees in a way that exposes, and even indicts, the Bush administration for failing to clearly define the parameters for interrogation: "The Pentagon's memo of last June stated that the president can legally authorize some forms of torture for detainees. Even if I sanctioned that beating, which I did not, there's so much confusion over the issue who can say what's lawful and what's not." The ambiguity leads to an acquittal on the charges of assault and dereliction of duty, though the soldiers are found guilty of maltreatment of a prisoner.

The trial process gives Mac, the defense attorney, ample opportunity to denounce the practice of "torture," but it also gives Rabb and the commanding general of the facility a chance to defend these practices. "Extreme peril requires extreme measures," Maj. Gen. Spinoza (Julius Carry) argues. He goes on to list several highly suspect examples of how "harsh interrogation" has assisted in the U.S. war effort: "Aggressive interrogation helped us locate Saddam Hussein, neutralize two-thirds of Al Qaeda's top operatives, reveal their recruiting methods, and uncover terrorist plots." What makes this testimony forceful is its proximity not just to the real-life arguments of Vice President Dick Cheney, but also to the fictional testimony of Col. Nathan R. Jessup (Jack Nicholson) in the film A Few Good Men. Echoing the famous lines "you want me on that wall, you need me on that wall," Spinoza asserts that saving American lives is more important than morality and legality and that "deep down inside the vast majority of our citizens are glad that we're here, whether they admit it or not." Mac's distaste for the tactics used at Guantanamo and other detention facilities is evident throughout the episode, and her contempt for the officials who feel such "dirty work" is necessary but will not participate in it themselves provides viewers with a chance to identify with an alternative perspective on these important issues. Yet, the episode itself is a "show trial," ripped from the headlines and perverted in ways that make the military appear transparent, democratic, and responsive to external critiques of its methods.

Though clearly denouncing certain aspects of the Bush administration's policies, "Camp Delta" nevertheless exonerates the soldiers responsible for the abuse and provides a cynical sort of propaganda for the continuation of these policies. By acknowledging how "repugnant" these detention and inter-rogation tactics are, it affirms the moral rectitude of the United States and its military representatives and makes these tactics available for redeployment. It reassures viewers that their military representatives are really good people who will either do the right thing or have good reasons for doing the wrong thing. This is a form of cynical reason, which holds that intentions matter more than actions when determining guilt.[22] In remediating actual cases "ripped-from-the-headlines," JAG does not just "forget" the facts; it alters them in ways that seem designed to precondition the future response to claims of U.S. military atrocities. Its selective attention to truth produces a fa-vorable disposition toward both the military command and the soldiers it su-pervises. We are led to believe that military authorities eagerly and fairly adjudicate all charges of abuse, even as we are called upon *not* to judge the sol-diers who do the "dirty work" of the War on Terrorism in the rest of our names. Instead, like Jack Bauer, soldiers become martyrs whose self-sacrifice excuses their behavior no matter what they do.

Jus in Bello: Justifying the Conduct of the Wars in Afghanistan and Iraq

While those are the two most explosive examples of remediation, other JAG stories have focused on the U.S. military's combat tactics in Afghanistan and Iraq, making a case for their legitimacy despite the obvious toll such tactics take on civilian noncombatants. The episodes "The Mission" (2002) and "Friendly Fire" (2003), for example, construct aerial bombardment as a dis-criminating and, therefore, "Just" tactic. The narratives focus on the rules of engagement and clarify, for unfamiliar viewers, the conditions under which soldiers might fire on suspected enemies. In "The Mission," the JAG officer assigned to the USS *Seahawk* (the real-life USS *Enterprise*) refuses to permit U.S. fighter pilots to bomb suspected targets unless an absolutely positive identifi-cation has been made. Rabb and Mac are dispatched to the ship to "explain" the rules of engagement and reiterate the message that the JAGs should not "exert caution beyond all reason." When the JAG officer defends his reluc-tance to sanction the use of force, Rabb reassures him (and the viewers) that mistakes, though inevitable, can be minimized through superior U.S. technology: "Real-time data links, GPS, and intelligence" should make it possible to avoid "collateral damage," he says. This is an iteration of a common refrain on the program: that technological superiority ensures the moral superiority of the U.S. way of war. The episode promotes public faith in the rationality of the "revolutionized" military, which relies on sophisticated machines to ensure precision and minimize casualties. Moreover, its tale of a concerned officer who refuses to distance himself from the effects of these machines reassures us that militarism can never fully efface the humanity of the soldiers. Soldiers, the episode indicates, are not murderers, but ordinary individuals who must be coaxed into killing for the greater good.

"Friendly Fire," which focuses on the accidental bombing of a group of British soldiers by an American fighter pilot, would seem to undermine "The Mission's" message about the capacity of information technologies to reduce "collateral damage." Yet, the way the story plays out, "Friendly Fire" ends up reaffirming the humane nature of technological warfare. The episode uses the well-publicized 2002 "friendly fire" deaths of four Canadian soldiers as the basis for a fictional study of the proper application of force.[23] In the fictional account, three British troops are killed and three others wounded when a U.S. fighter pilot drops a laser-guided bomb on their live-fire training exercise. The pilot claims to have seen ground fire and to have fired in self-defense, but the British claim they had ceased firing when the planes flew over. Was the pilot acting recklessly and without regard to the consequences of his actions, or was he responding legitimately in the belief that he was being attacked? The differences between the real and fictional cases are, once again, instructive. In the real-life incident, the U.S. pilots fired on the Canadian troops without waiting for verification and despite the fact that (a) the area was a well-known training site and (b) the Canadians had reported their whereabouts and plans to the U.S. commanders. A joint U.S.-Canadian investigation into the incident found the two pilots guilty of the "inappropriate use of lethal force," but neither pilot was ever tried or disciplined for the infraction.[24] The fictional case works things out rather more neatly. The pilot receives a fair trial and is found innocent when it is determined that a spark from a broken generator might have been mistaken for ground fire. The British troops, meanwhile, are held partially culpable for their own injury because they did not report their whereabouts to the U.S. authorities. There was, in short, a breakdown in communications. However, by presenting such errors as rare and correctable, "Friendly Fire" confirms the lesson of "The Mission," which is that improved control over information and communications networks reduces "collateral damage" and makes war a cleaner, more just enterprise. The episode even ends with a plea for more money for military re-search and development. As the secretary of the navy explains to Adm. Cheg-widden, "it behooves us to make sure that such a tragic incident can never happen again on our watch, A. J. More dollars spent on communication tech-nology, command and control, training, that sounds like the antidote to me." Far from causing the public to rethink the nation's reliance on high-tech war-fare, then, "Friendly Fire" becomes an inducement to invest even more heavily in the system (see chapter 5 for more on this logic).

This reluctance to criticize military strategy is reinforced in "Friendly Fire" by embedded opinion pieces from real-life conservative television pundit Bill O'Reilly. O'Reilly plays himself in scripted segments indicting the military for using the pilot as a scapegoat for "the fog of war itself." As if explaining the rationale behind the failure of the military to discipline the pilots involved in the real-life friendly fire incident, O'Reilly opines: "[The trial] is hypocritical, unjust, and dangerous to the country. A pilot in combat makes a split-second decision, then is forced to answer to some pinhead politician if something goes wrong. Hey, it's war. Lots of stuff goes wrong. You cannot turn an honest mistake on the battlefield into a crime, and you can't treat American fighting men like criminals; come on, we have a war to fight." O'Reilly's presence is designed to highlight the pressures the media places on the military in a time of war—and Rabb noticeably winces whenever O'Reilly opens his mouth—but it also demonstrates how the military uses the media to lobby both Con-gress and the American public for support. In that sense, it comes dangerously close to exposing JAG's own complicity in this process. Yet the more likely effect of O'Reilly's appearance is to enhance the realism of the program and make a space for the expression of the producer's own conserva-tive views on war and militarism. By remediating Fox News, and a particular style of punditry, JAG can both rally the civilian troops to the military cause and enhance its credibility by appearing to disavow the Fox brand of jingoism. Once again, the trial presents the illusion of reasoned debate over military strategy while the rest of the drama permits its viewers to sidestep rationality in favor of emotional identification with the troops.

Proper-ganda: *JAG* Explains the Media's Role in War

As "Friendly Fire" demonstrates, JAG frequently comments on the role of the media and public relations in a time of war, generally siding with the troops and commanders, who view the media as a nuisance at best, and a hindrance at worst. It does this entirely without irony, drawing distinctions between journalism and entertainment that end up legitimating its own role in the manufacture of consent for the wars in Afghanistan and Iraq. JAG interprets the journalist's professional desire to "uncover the truth" as a vendetta against the military and proposes that journalists are dangerous to the troops even when they do not intend to be. Entertainment producers, on the other hand, only want to tell good stories and, thus, do not constitute a problem worth investigating in the series.

"First Casualty" (2002), for example, defends the military's policy of excluding the media from combat zones during the Afghan war by presenting a fictional account of one reporter's "embedding" experience. The reporter at the center of the episode accompanies a navy SEAL team on a covert operation to capture Al Qaeda leaders in a remote Afghan village (a practice not allowed by the military at the time). When the SEALs are ambushed, Rabb convinces the admiral to bring charges against the reporter, whom he suspects of having accidentally exposed the team's location. The reporter defends his actions and blames the military for using faulty intelligence and sending too few men on the mission (a common critique of Rumsfeld's military strategy). The trial reveals, however, that the reporter actually has unknowingly aided the enemy since his assistant, an Iranian woman whose family was killed during the U.S.-backed regime of Shah Reza Pahlavi, conveyed the team's location to Al Qaeda after receiving an unauthorized satellite call from the reporter before the mission.

In addition to lumping the diverse countries and cultures of the Middle East into a single group supportive of Al Qaeda, the episode promotes two key lessons with regard to the media's role at war. First, it teaches that the mere presence of journalists in the field of combat constitutes a threat to U.S. troops. The reporter acknowledges as much in his on-air mea culpa during which he asks the public to forgive him for the sins "of pride, of smugness, of all-importance." As a representative of the media, he has learned to put the nation's need for security ahead of his professional duty to provide the public with information about the workings of its government. The second lesson is that censorship in a time of war is okay because it comes at the behest of the military, not the civilian government. Neither the soldiers nor their field commanders wanted the reporter to accompany the SEAL team, but the orders came "straight from the top." On the witness stand, the secretary of the navy acknowledges he made a mistake in approving the assignment: "I failed to listen to the commanders in the field. I'm the one who's responsible." The implication is that whatever military commanders want, they should get, and the U.S. public should simply trust in their judgment. Supporting press censorship, manipulation, and control during wartime becomes just another way of supporting the troops.

"Death at the Mosque" (2005) offers perhaps the most interesting media-at-war episode since it focuses self-consciously on the relationship between what we see, what we know, and what we do or do not want to know. The episode is based on the 2004 shooting death of an unarmed and wounded Iraqi prisoner by a U.S. Marine during the siege of Fallujah, an incident captured on video by NBC News reporter Kevin Sites.[25] This incident has emerged as one of the few significant visual memories, or "flashframes," of the war in Iraq, and, as such, threatened the thin veneer of legitimacy attached to the conflict.[26] By examining and exonerating the use of preventative violence, however, "Death" recuperates the legitimacy of the war in Iraq by analogy. The main tactic of recuperation is to shift the focus of the inquiry from the soldier's responsibility in combat to the journalist's. Lt. Gregory Vukovic (Chris Beetem), the young JAG officer assigned to defend the accused marine, describes TV news as "the truth on speed." Echoing left-liberal critiques of the media, he laments the tendency of contemporary journalism to privilege "image dissemination over news gathering," immediacy over analysis.[27] Vukovic's dislike of the media is more visceral and absolute, however. He views the journalist as the enemy of the soldier and implies that support for the troops necessitates hostility toward the media. Thus, he warns a young private away from the journalist in question and later smashes and shoots the man's camera.

The attack on the media in "Death at the Mosque" is really designed to elevate the authority of the soldier's perspective on war over and above that of the journalist. It argues that the soldier's experience is unique and uniquely insightful and, therefore, must not be second-guessed. As the field commander tells Vukovic, "To understand what happened that night in the shooting at the Martyr's Mosque, you have to know what it's like to *be* a marine . . . what our training is, how we work, why we do what we do." What we know, in other words, conditions what we see, and the distribution of the knowledge of war is decidedly unequal. PFC Hoke Smith (Chris J. Johnson) "knows" insurgents use mosques as cover to snipe at U.S. troops; he was also present the week before when a U.S. Marine was killed by the booby-trapped body of a wounded insurgent. This knowledge made him believe the wounded Iraqi constituted a threat, and this belief, in turn, justified his actions. The journalist, on the

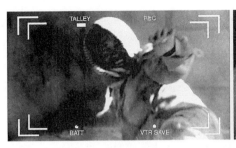

The JAG episode "Death at the Mosque" (4/1/2005) indicts journalists for not knowing enough to see the evidence before their eyes. Here, the unarmed insurgent begging for his life (Left) is also reaching toward a suicide vest hidden in the floorboards (Right), so the young marine was right to use preemptive violence.

other hand, admits to having "no knowledge of how war is fought" and, thus, to having no basis for understanding what he points his camera at. His decision to release the video is presented as arrogant and biased since he fails to show matching footage of U.S. soldiers dying in combat. Yet, the defense's argument is largely unconvincing until Vukovic visits the Martyr's Mosque and discovers a suicide vest hidden under the floorboards a few feet from where the Iraqi was shot. This "smoking gun" proves the soldier's innocence and encourages viewers to identify absolutely with his perspective, for its superiority to other perspectives has been positively confirmed.

The problem, of course, is that the soldier's perspective is equally limited. In this case, the soldier's beliefs, born of experience, led him to see the man he shot as a danger even though there was no apparent evidence of a threat. What if no evidence of guilt was found, though? Is belief a sufficient rationale for the use of force? This is obviously a question the episode raises about the larger invasion of Iraq, and its determination of innocence relieves the United States of any guilt associated with the use of preventative warfare in Iraq. Is belief a sufficient standard by which to measure justice, however? Should intentions determine the legitimacy of a war or the tactics used to fight it? These are questions that JAG routinely begs in favor of presenting the U.S. military and its representatives as noble souls willing to sacrifice themselves so the rest of us can keep our hands and consciences clean. JAG is interested in doing more than just affirming the primacy of the military perspective, however; it wants to blur boundaries between fictional and nonfictional formats in order to inject its fictions into the media archive of war. This, more than its celebration of the soldier's experience, is the real innovation of the series in regard to the propagandizing of war since it entails an acknowledgment of the media's role in the construction of reality.

JAG's producers harbor no illusions about the transparency of truth or the responsibility of the media to produce an informed public. In this they differ significantly from journalists such as Kevin Sites, who still invest in notions like "truth" and deliberative democracy. "The truth is the truth," Sites has said of the Fallujah incident. "These kind of things happen in war, and if we want to close our eyes to them, then we are truly going to be ignorant, and we're going to be more willing to send our sons and daughters off to war without truly understanding what they are doing over there."[28] Sites presents media as neutral witnesses to history who merely record the real and transmit it to a public that already exists. By inverting this belief—by turning journalists into liars and suggesting cameras falsify reality—JAG undermines the credibility of the news media and prepares the audience to accept fictionalized accounts of war as equal to, if not better than, nonfictional ones. In this way, JAG promotes a radical form of skepticism whose primary effect is to make belief seem as valid a criterion of truth and justice as material evidence. Put simply, its remediations of flashpoints in the War on Terrorism are not designed to produce knowledge or a public invested in the communicative ideal of rational deliberation. Rather, they are designed to target emotions and call into being a public that cares less about the effects of war than the intentions of the warriors. They are designed, in other words, to preempt the emergence of a critical context within which shocking images of war might register as shocking, rather than poignant or ennobling.[29]

Defending the Strategy of Preventative War: "People vs. SecNav"

JAG did not just remediate war as it happened, interjecting fictional testimonies into the media archive of war, then arguing for their validity as evidence. It also attempted to premediate, or proactively shape, the future memory of war by staging a speculative assessment of the doctrine of preemption. President Bush was fond of saying that history would determine the legitimacy of his actions in Iraq, but the producers of JAG were not content to wait for history's judgment. In an episode called "People vs. SecNav" (2003),

Edward Sheffield (Dean Stockwell), the secretary of the navy, is placed on trial by an International Criminal Court for an attack on an Iraqi hospital, which left several civilians dead (in reality, of course, the United States refuses to acknowledge the legitimacy of such courts). To defend the secretary, Rabb and MacKenzie must defend the government's decision to invade Iraq in the first place. They pull out all of the ideological stops to accomplish this feat. The most forceful testimony comes from the lieutenant who ordered the airstrike. When asked "What gave you the right to be on Iraqi soil in the first place?" He responds: "I was a marine, sir, following orders. . . . Then, I saw the mass graves, I spoke to a father forced to watch his little boy's arm cut off, a woman who was repeatedly raped. I didn't have a right to be there, sir. I had an obligation." Invoking the Augustinian tradition of Just War theory, the lieutenant suggests that nations, especially powerful democracies, have a "responsibility to protect" that requires them to intervene in the politics of other states "to prevent certain harm to the innocent."[30] The tinge of exceptionalism that colors this testimony—the sense that the United States is uniquely qualified to assume this mission—is made explicit in the secretary's own testimony: "Ever since our founding, America has been the symbol of hope for the world. And we remain so today. We accept our responsibility, which all civilized nations should, to fight against oppression and tyranny. But when we fight, we don't fight for land, or oil, or money, or to impose our will; we take up arms against violent men who threaten our freedom and the freedom of others." Echoing Bush administration rhetoric, he characterizes the war in Iraq as a defensive reaction to the 9/11 attacks and suggests that Saddam Hussein posed an "imminent threat" to the United States, which the nation had a duty to respond to. In case we are confused about whose arguments to identify with, the camera slowly circles around the secretary and ends up squarely behind him. Indeed, we end up inhabiting his subjective perspective.

Because the trial sidesteps the questions of imminence and proportional defense at the heart of the international case against the war in Iraq, the episode does nothing to establish the legal status of the invasion. What it does instead is make a case for the priority of moral arguments—specifically, religious belief—in determining what is "Just." The lead judge finds the United States "not guilty" of crimes against humanity, war crimes, and intentionally targeting noncombatants, stating that "at times, moral, as well as legal decisions must influence a court's decision." (He does fine the United States $20 million for the "willful destruction of civilian property," though.

In "People vs. SecNav" (JAG, 2/6/2004), the camera slowly circles the secretary of the navy, as he defends the U.S. invasion of Iraq. We end up squarely behind the secretary; indeed we inhabit his perspective on the morality of U.S. violence.

Apparently, the loss of property is more important than the loss of human life). While the trial is a potentially disruptive wish-fulfillment that rehearses a number of left-liberal arguments against the war, "People vs. SecNav" ultimately replicates the Bush administration's radical reconstruction of the definition of Just War. As Richard Jackson notes, the Bush administration abandoned the contractual obligations, institutions, and tenets of international law undergirding Just War theory before the War on Terrorism began, claiming these "entanglements" unduly restricted U.S. sovereignty. Their 2002 National Security Strategy statement went so far as to characterize the rule of law as a "strategy of the weak" akin to terrorism ("Our strength will continue to be challenged by those who employ a strategy of the weak using international fora, judicial processes, and terrorism").[31] These decisions cleared the way for unilateral U.S. action defended through a theologically oriented conception of Just War. The waging of war became a divine mission, ordained by God, to eradicate evil from the world. This rhetoric worked, in part because it resonated with the exceptionalist strain so prominent in U.S. culture and in part because it appealed specifically to Bush's evangelical Christian base. Liberal doses of religious imagery, ritual, and discourse convinced the public that God was working through the United States to purge the world of evil.[32] With such a divine sanction, any "crime" the United States might commit in the name of the "war on terror" would be justified.

Conclusion

Through its charming recurring characters and frequent defensing of the "noble grunt," JAG self-consciously promoted identification with a military perspective and with the ideology of militarism. Its squeaky-clean soldiers, who might do bad things but only with the best intentions, inspired trust in the innocence of U.S. motives and tactics more broadly. If these are the men and women responsible for conducting the War on Terrorism, the program assured its viewers, then we have nothing to worry about. Their "goodness" is self-evident and excuses any excesses that might result from the overzealous pursuit of the fight against "evil." The rest of us should trust their judgment and otherwise stay out of the conflict. That, according to JAG, is what patriotism is all about. As with reality militainment, questions about the necessity, legality, and proper conduct of war are displaced by the program's celebration of the character of the individuals fighting for "us."

JAG's romanticization of military life and military conflict is neither surprising nor particularly original. It builds upon a tradition of such romanticization, which has only increased in influence since the end of the Cold War.[33] What is new, however, is the series' self-conscious intention to intervene in the formation of the cultural memory of the wars in Afghanistan and Iraq *as they are happening*. Both Donald Bellisario and Donald Rumsfeld used the series to introduce static into the archive of war, conditioning the popular reception of documentary information about the war by usurping the news media's role as chronicler of war. "News used to be the first rough draft of history," as Robert Lichter, president of the Center for Media and Public Affairs, puts it. "Now it's the first draft of a Hollywood screenplay. . . . The question . . . is whose version gets to the public first."[34] In the case of "Tribunal," JAG's version of history was both first and last since the tribunal procedure on display in that episode was later ruled unconstitutional by the U.S. Supreme Court, and no other visual record of such trials is likely to be permitted. Meanwhile, the many ripped-from-the-headlines episodes of JAG incorporate and reenact key "flashframes" of war but with conventionally cathartic, even therapeutic, endings. Such catharsis, as Lichter notes, is not necessarily the "best instrument for producing justice" since it treats history as the past, rather than an ongoing process in which we could intervene.[35]

Philosopher Walter Benjamin once argued that "the past can be seized only as an image which flashes up at the instant when it can be recognized and is never seen again."[36] JAG's goal with regard to these ripped-from-the-headlines stories was to preemptively contain the fallout from such flare-ups. Its producers wanted history to be misrecognized, if recognized at all. Indeed, Bellisario and Rumsfeld seemed to understand better than most media theorists that images are less iconic than symbolic signs. They do not "reflect" history, even when they intervene in or shape political debates, as documentary images of war sometimes do. Rather, they provide an occasion for fantasy projection and rescripting. This is why so-called flashbulb or flashframe memories are so notoriously unreliable: because they are also heavily mediated, rehearsed, and reenacted. What people "remember" about these events is often something they picked up from later, more palatable media incarnations of it. One of the most important factors affecting the recall of such events is how well subsequent reenactments cohere with existing social scripts.[37] Bellisario sought to produce a "heroic" script that would match the popular emotional investment in the warrior ideal. Since he cannot fight in the conflict himself, he says, glorifying the U.S. soldier is his way of contributing to the war effort.[38] Like the JAG attorneys in his series, he imagines himself a warrior engaged in combat with professional journalists for the hearts and minds of the U.S. public. He hopes his more socially acceptable stories about the military will leave a longer-lasting impression on U.S. viewers than either reality TV or the news.

The process of memory formation is often something we think of as happening in retrospect, well after the historical events that the images and stories reference have passed. Yet, JAG offers proof that memory is fluid, flexible, and subject to both re- and premediation even as an event is unfolding. Re- and premediation are not about conveying information or producing knowledge (let alone truth), but about ensuring future history is not experienced as a shock to the system. By rehearsing our past and projecting our future, television functions not just as a technology of memory, but as a technology of the self. It does not just condition the popular perception of war or manufacture false consciousness; rather, it provides a space for individuals to create identities in conformity with social norms. To watch JAG, after all, is an act of choice, which represents, among other things, a desire to forget the less flattering images of war conveyed on the TV news. It is an act of willful ignorance with consequences for political action and future social relations, but, for some, no doubt, it is also an important coping mechanism—a way to deal with troubling historical events that seem beyond control.

It is important to remember that the outcome of the engagement with technologies of memory, such as TV, is unpredictable. It is at least as likely that viewers will heckle the program, or rescript it to conform to their own desires, as embrace it on its own terms, and here I ought to note that most online fan forums related to JAG are devoted to rehashing the romantic entanglements of the series' two lead characters.[39] When asked to list their favorite episodes for the USA fan forum, for example, only two people mentioned War on Terror–themed episodes, and both claimed to enjoy those episodes for the action or relationships, rather than the political content.[40] What such responses demonstrate is not the failure of JAG to deliver its content to the target. Rather, it shows that the processes of re- and premediation undertaken by JAG work on a different register than simple information provision. As Grusin argues, "mass media exist not to produce truth or inform the public" but to shape reality. A series such as JAG does this by "process[ing] incidents of irritation" and bringing individuals into affective attunement with the dominant social scripts.[41] By ripping historical experience from its context and reprocessing it as a romance, the series strikes a preemptive blow against critics of war who might use the wars in Iraq and Afghanistan as ammunition in the struggle to redirect U.S. foreign policy. The virtual image of war it creates shapes the future cultural memory of war *because* it bears little resemblance to the reality of war, not in spite of this fact. This realization has led Grusin to suggest that the function of media in the contemporary context is not to reproduce or distribute ideology, but to "mobilize individuals" by "modulating affect."[42] I would argue, however, that we are not talking about a radical break in the social functions of media; rather, we are talking about a shift in emphasis that has the effect of returning ideology to its roots in the concept of "false consciousness." The processes of mediation engaged in by JAG are significant not because they dupe us into believing war is noble and romantic, but because they allow us to dupe ourselves. They fulfill a cultural desire not to know about the chaos of war, not to pay witness to it, and not to assume responsibility for it. They make us feel better about surrendering our deliberative functions and, in that way, prepare us for a war-filled future.

5 From Virtual Citizen-Soldier to Imperial Grunt

As the previous chapters demonstrate, the Bush administration and the Pentagon clearly used television programming to bypass the filter of the news media and deliver political communications more directly to the U.S. public. They worked closely with Hollywood film and television producers to fashion a palatable image of war that would garner support for the administration's aggressive foreign policy agenda. As Neal Gabler notes, however, the war in Iraq posed a serious challenge to the "cinematization of foreign policy" because the actors involved refused to stay on script. The war did not culminate in a clear-cut victory and show of public support for the U.S. "liberators," as the administration promised. Instead, the situation deteriorated into a violent insurgency and near–civil war that more closely approximated "the narrative entropy . . . [of] Vietnam War films like *Apocalypse Now* and *Platoon*."[1] As public support for the war plummeted, so did Hollywood's support for Washington. By 2005, when popular support for the war had dipped below 50 percent,[2] Hollywood executives began green-lighting more ambivalent fare such as *Extraordinary Rendition* (2007), *Lions for Lambs* (2007), *In the Valley of Elah* (2007), *Grace Is Gone* (2007), and *Stop-Loss* (2008), all of which questioned the conduct and/or morality of the War on Terrorism. Nontraditional Hollywood players contributed to the trend, as well. HDNet, an online provider of original news and entertainment, financed and distributed Brian De Palma's *Redacted* (2007), a scathing indictment of U.S. war atrocities. On television, satirical and science fiction programs began to scrutinize the logics behind U.S. security policies (see chapter 6), and, all over the dial, images of wounded and betrayed veterans returned the repressed costs of war to public consciousness (see chapter 7).

Two of the most distinguished contributions to this critical turn in the popular culture were the FX series *Over There* and the HBO serial *Generation Kill*. Both series debuted after 2005 on cable and subscription networks known for supporting more experimental work. They were helmed by industry mavericks with reputations for flouting established conventions and standards of propriety (Steven Bochco of Hill Street Blues and NYPD Blue and David Simon and Ed Burns of The Wire, respectively), and they both used Evan Wright's relatively critical account of the early invasion, Generation Kill, as source material. Most importantly, neither production received material assistance from the Department of Defense. These conditions of production and distribution enabled the series to present a far more nuanced depiction of contemporary warfare, including graphic images of wounded and dead soldiers and civilians. Nevertheless, Over There and Generation Kill are far from antiwar statements. As "noble grunt" stories, they focus on the intimate experience of the soldier to the exclusion of political questions about war's legitimacy or its effects. While the travails of the soldiers may be harrowing, the conclusions of such stories tend to alleviate popular anxieties about war by demonstrating how it builds character. The redemptive conclusion produces a public catharsis that virtually ensures war's continued use as a political tool.[3]

Ultimately, Over There and Generation Kill serve more as "after-action reviews" of the invasion than as critiques of war. Airing alongside public debates about military strategy, they implicitly argued in support of a shift toward counterinsurgency doctrine. They helped legitimate this shift by detailing the limitations of the vaunted Revolution in Military Affairs, and, in the process, they preserved war for future use as a tool of social engineering. Indeed, Over There and Generation Kill echo neoconservative calls for a more measured, less high-profile style of military deployment, one better suited to the emergence of Empire with a capital E—that is, a neoliberal social order governed through biopolitical mechanisms of control, rather than outright violence.[4] The "professional" soldiers in Over There and Generation Kill both model these new mechanisms of control and police the internal divide between who is assimilable and who is not within this global social order. By presenting "dirty wars" (counterinsurgency campaigns) as the "new" revolution in military affairs, the two series prepared U.S. citizens to accept the continued necessity of war as a form of social regulation. How these programs helped turn the "virtual citizen-soldier" into a "virtual imperial grunt," fully invested in the system of militarized discipline and power projection, is the subject of this chapter. Before we can get there, though, a little history is in order.

The Rise and Fall of the RMA as a Mode of Imperial Warfare

The Revolution in Military Affairs was the culmination of a long process of accommodation to new political realities after World War II. As Andrew Bacevich explains, the development of the philosophy of deterrence during the Cold War represented the first phase in this process. Deterrence acknowledged the categorical shift in the nature of warfare introduced by the development of nuclear weaponry and sought to avert war by building up military might. The idea was that a sufficient *show* of force could influence the enemy's decision-making process. Eventually, however, national security strategists sought ways to continue practicing war as a method of political persuasion, albeit at a lower level of intensity. "The aim [of low-intensity conflict] was not to crush the enemy but to bring him to the realization that ending war on your terms served *his own* interests."[5] Vietnam was the ultimate expression of this philosophy, for it was designed as a war of attrition with the idea that inflicting sufficient punishment on the Vietnamese would force their capitulation. The obvious failure of this strategy did not lead security experts to reexamine the utility of war as a political tool; rather, it led them to search for ways to make war politically tenable again. Technological innovation, specifically the development of precision-guided munitions, seemed to be the answer. These new weapons promised to make war more precise, more discriminate, and, therefore, more humane. Not only would "smart" weapons save the lives of U.S. troops and minimize "collateral damage," they would enable a revolution in military doctrine and organization, as well. Andrew Marshall, the director of the DOD's Office of Net Assessment since 1973, argued for a leaner, meaner, and more deployable military force. A professionalized volunteer military, he claimed, might be smaller, but it would also be more flexible and better trained. Information technologies, precision weaponry, and "speed" would compensate for the deficiencies in size and produce more efficient and sustainable outcomes. As Bacevich notes, "Marshall's promise of techniques for using force in ways that avoided massive physical destruction and spared the lives of innocents was exquisitely well suited to both America's post–Cold War purpose and its self-image."[6]

Military commanders largely resisted Marshall's calls for organizational transformation (since such transformation would mean "rebalancing" existing forces and finances), but they did embrace his high-tech philosophy of remote combat. In designing battle plans for the interventions in the Persian Gulf (1991), Bosnia (1995), and Kosovo (1999), they favored aerial bombardment as the cleanest, most efficient means of "persuading" recalcitrant world leaders to behave responsibly toward their citizens and used combat troops only in very limited, goal-specific, mop-up operations. Force protection was the watchword. When Donald Rumsfeld, a Marshall devotee, assumed the position of secretary of defense in 2001, however, push came to shove. Like most neoconservatives, Rumsfeld believed that American military power could be a force for good in the world and should be used more frequently as a tool of foreign policy.[7] "Global power projection over great distance" would require a leaner, meaner, more expert, and quickly deployable military force. Superior weaponry and information technologies would be force multipliers, obviating the need for large-scale armored battle groups. Rumsfeld's influence was evident in the operational design of the conflicts in both Afghanistan and Iraq. General Tommy Franks, the architect of both battle plans, capitulated to the Pentagon's desire for a light footprint in Afghanistan, designing a strategy of aerial bombardment and small-scale special forces operations that would give local paramilitaries primary responsibility for stabilizing the country in the wake of the U.S. invasion. The plan combined old-style, frontier tactics— what Rumsfeld called "the courage of valiant one-legged Afghan fighters on horseback"—with high-tech weaponry and a decentralized but networked command structure to wring the maximum effect from a minimum of U.S. input.[8] The short-term success of Operation Enduring Freedom convinced both Rumsfeld and Franks that a minimalist operational design could work in Iraq, as well. Thus, Franks devised a battle plan around the philosophy "speed kills." It called for a "shock and awe" campaign of aerial bombardment to soften targets in and around the capital of Baghdad, coupled with a relatively small number of U.S. troops, who would, likewise, use speed and aggression to push through to the capital and depose the Saddam Hussein regime.

The plan was oriented toward a short-term operational victory, and it succeeded if measured solely by those terms. The U.S. military won all of the battles, but they almost lost the war because there was no plan to ensure the long-term stability of the country. Optimistic prewar assessments convinced Pentagon planners that Iraqis would welcome occupation, embrace democracy, and finance their own recovery through oil profits.[9] Despite evidence of wide-scale looting, revenge killing, and even organized resistance to U.S. occupation, the Pentagon began sending combat units home a mere two weeks after the invasion. Worse, the troops who were left received no instructions about how to proceed with security and stability operations (SASO). According to the after-action review of the Third Infantry Division of the U.S. Army, which took over after the end of major combat operations, "There was no guidance for restoring order in Baghdad, creating an interim government, hiring government and essential services employees and ensuring that the judicial system was operational. 'The result was a power/authority vacuum created by our failure to immediately replace key government institutions.'"[10] The Coalition Provisional Authority exacerbated the problem by firing everyone in the Iraqi Army and the national police force and "purging" everyone with ties to the Ba'ath party from government employ. The tiny U.S. occupational force now had to provide security for the entire country, police the borders, protect the oil fields, search for weapons of mass destruction, rebuild infrastructure, and train both new security forces and new government employees, all while fighting a growing insurgency comprised of disgruntled natives and international jihadists, who were streaming over the unsecured borders. Iraq quickly became a deadly guerrilla war, and the problem was compounded by the Bush administration's refusal to acknowledge what was really going on. Until Gen. John Abizaid took over U.S. military operations in Iraq in late summer of 2003, the administration continued to characterize the insurgency as mere "pockets of dead-enders," Ba'ath party loyalists who could be easily rooted out. As Thomas Ricks points out, this refusal was more than just an issue of semantics; it impacted strategy and tactics and led to a prolongation of the conflict.[11] United States forces withdrew into their armed camps, separated themselves from the local populations, and used tactics (speed, massive firepower, humiliating cordon and search techniques) that angered, alienated, and often killed Iraqi civilians. The war in Iraq would ultimately expose the limitations of the Revolution in Military Affairs and its high-tech, low-obligation approach to warfare, and programs such as *Over There* and *Generation Kill* would document those limitations in gory detail.

"They're Screwing This Shit Up": TV's After-Action Review of the Invasion

Both *Over There* and *Generation Kill* provide concrete illustrations of how the overreliance on firepower, technology, and speed left U.S. soldiers in a precarious position, and both argue for a return to the "blood-and-guts" traditions of the warrior ideal. Where they differ is in the style of presentation, and, as these differences produce different effects on the viewers, it is worth taking a moment to elaborate on them. *Over There* deliberately abstracts the war in Iraq from its historical and political contexts in order to provoke a more philosophical sort of contemplation among its viewers. Rather than asking viewers to condemn a specific war, it asks only that they acknowledge the hellish nature of war in general. The series follows a small unit attached to the Third Infantry Division, which is operating somewhere in Iraq sometime during the post-invasion stability phase. The deliberate vagueness allows the producers to touch upon a range of hot-button issues—torture, civilian casualties, embedded reporting, search and cordon operations, and so on—without having to examine any of them in a sustained fashion. Thus, the Iraq constructed in Over There is largely metaphoric—a fantasy space within which the producers and viewers can collaborate on a mythic tale of American regeneration through violence.[12] Frequent inserts of sunsets, tumbleweeds, and dust blowing across the inhospitable desert make Iraq look like the "Wild West" of Hollywood film, an "alien" landscape inhabited by "evil others." The use of gimmicky visuals—low-key lighting, off-kilter compositions, fisheye lenses, color filters, and extreme high- and low-angle shots—further distorts the landscape and makes Iraq seem like a space of ontological disorder. The Iraqi people lack individuation and seem hell-bent on attacking U.S. soldiers without provocation or motive. As one critic observed, they have "no names, . . . no stories, no families, no nicknames, no annoying and endearing habits, no motivations or regrets, no insecurities, no NOTHING."[13] According to executive producer Steven Bochco, this was a deliberate strategy: "We are defining the enemy as those individuals who are trying to kill us, who are shooting at us. And we don't put names on them or labels on them. They are just trying to hurt us, and they are the bad guys."[14] The effect of these choices is to portray war as a showdown between the forces of civilization and savagery, with the survival of the human race at stake. This simplified morality tale is familiar to U.S. viewers from frontier narratives gone by and does little to provide insight on the specific war in Iraq. Yet, Over There does at least force viewers to confront the devastating effects of warfare on human bodies, a sight censored in other realms of public culture.

Generation Kill's producers attempt something at once more limited and more pointed. They are not interested in portraying an experience of war in general; rather, they seek to provide a documentary explication of a very specific moment in a very specific war among a very specific group of soldiers. Eschewing the visual and aural clichés of the war film, Simon, Burns, and directors Susanna White and Simon Cellan Jones adopted a documentary style designed to convey a feeling of liveness and immediacy. "Authenticity and re-

In *Over There* (FX, 2005), the use of gimmicky visuals abstracts the war from its specific context and creates a fantasy space better suited to a mythic tale of American regeneration through violence.

alism [were] one of the big things we set out to achieve at every level of detail," White says.[15] To manage this, the producers stuck almost religiously to the story line of Evan Wright's book, hired former members of First Recon as advisers and actors, eliminated the soundtrack (because life has no soundtrack), filled the background with realistic detail, and used handheld cameras, midrange shots, and "a reactive camera technique" to mimic the limited perspective of the eyewitness to history. No image contains more information than was accessible to the participants at the time, and point of view shifts constantly among the cast members to illustrate the partial nature of firsthand experience. As in *The Wire*, Simon and Burns were more concerned with building a world of depth and complexity than in telling a coherent story. Viewers are dropped into the action in midstream and invited to catch up just like the character of the "war scribe" (Evan Wright, played by Lee Tergesen). What we come to know about these men and their war is based on an active process of interpreting the evidence available on-screen. There is no backstory, no handholding and no emotional cuing. Characters are difficult to distinguish; the chain of command is unclear; and the plot is disjointed and unpredictable—a lot like real life. Many of the characters are offensive, and even the good guys do reprehensible things about which the series refuses to moralize. The show also alternates uncontrollably between horror, tragedy, and comedy, leaving viewers confused, wary, and, according to some reviewers, weary.[16] The goal, according to Simon, was to get viewers "leaning forward toward the television set," to make them actively involved in and responsible for what they were seeing.[17] Thus, in its determination to immerse viewers in the experience of war, Generation Kill proved more like 24 than Over There. It did not just ask viewers to identify with the soldiers, it asked them to become soldiers, to fully inhabit the soldier's perspective on the war's unfolding. It's the difference between reading a novel and playing a first-person shooter video game. New York Post critic Adam Buckman's description of Generation Kill as "a miniseries that's as dull and throbbing as a severe headache" captures the expenditure of physical, as well as intellectual and emotional, energy required to produce narrative meaning from the chaotic fragments.[18]

The stylistic differences ultimately figure into the differential impact of these two series, which I will return to in the end, but for now I want to draw out some of the ideological resonances between these series and developing U.S. security narratives. As I have already suggested, the programs are not pure celebrations of military prowess, and they do not present war as a bloodlessly romantic romp. Rather, they function like the military's own after-action reviews, acknowledging the gorier realities of combat so that war's operations can be refined and extended. They are not devoid of moral outrage or analytical substance; it is just that their outrage is directed away from questions about the legitimacy of war and toward questions of strategy and tactics.[19] When they take on issues such as "harsh interrogation" or "collateral damage," they do so with the goal of assessing the fit between tactics and strategy, strategy and context. This focus may not be antiwar, but it does represent an important critique of the institutional failures that engendered and prolonged the Iraqi insurgency. Over There and Generation Kill display, albeit in an entertaining fashion, the very real tensions that have led the military to rethink its strategy toward the war in Iraq and, under the leadership of secretary of defense Robert Gates, toward future wars, as well.

For instance, both programs demonstrate how U.S. troops were used inefficiently, for missions they were not trained to undertake. The fictional unit at the heart of Over There is an infantry division, but, in addition to combat, they are tasked with security duties (roadblocks, most notably) and prisoner collection and oversight. In "Mission Accomplished," for example, the eight soldiers in the platoon are sent to guard several dozen prisoners in a makeshift camp without any oversight or instruction from trained MPs. The result is a near–prison riot and, later, a suicide bomb attack from a hardened jihadist, which kills a number of "innocent" prisoners arrested simply for being in the wrong place at the wrong time. The episode points out the gap between U.S. rhetoric—what we say we are doing in Iraq—and U.S. actions. We claimed to be bringing freedom and democracy to Iraqis, yet, as the characters observe, "the prison population has tripled since we got here." Though it does not directly address the "cordon and sweep" tactics responsible for the increase (these tactics involved isolating whole neighborhoods and arresting all military-aged males), it does suggest that the mass imprisonment of Iraqis might be counterproductive to U.S. aims.

The marines at the center of *Generation Kill* are also being used in ways that run counter to their training and to the long-term interests of the U.S. military. They are members of a highly skilled reconnaissance unit, trained to infiltrate enemy lines and gather intelligence on enemy logistics. When they do their jobs well, they do not fire a single shot.[20] In Iraq, they are used as an infantry platoon and sent on near–suicide missions to distract the Republican Guard and keep it from focusing on the main invasion force. They are, as Wright puts it, "ambush bait," and they fire their weapons almost constantly. Sgt. Brad "Iceman" Colbert (Alexander Skarsgård) describes the platoon as a bunch of "perfectly tuned Ferraris in a demolition derby" ("A Burning Dog"). "Don't fool yourself," he tells his men. "We're not being warriors out here. [Ferrando's] using us as machine operators, semi-skilled labor." The first four episodes document in great detail how the marines' orders shift with the wind, and how their leadership throws them into dangerous situations without proper planning. Colbert, Lt. Nathaniel Fick (Stark Sands), and their cohort of junior officers complain constantly about the "bad tactics" and lack of adherence to standard operating procedure (SOP). Careful planning is at the heart of what these guys have been trained to do, but the operational emphasis on "speed" and "maneuver warfare" denies them the opportunity to "do their jobs." This, the book and the program both lead us to believe, is more galling to the marines than getting shot at. Thus, they reserve the bulk of their ire not for the enemy, but for their (seemingly) incompetent senior officers.

Both programs also critique the overreliance on heavy firepower to subdue the Iraqi populace. They suggest that the "irregular" nature of the enemy, most of whom took off their uniforms and melted into the local populations, along with the urban terrain of the conflict, created a need for restraint and discrimination. Big guns and loose rules of engagement would only injure and alienate the civilian populations. Civilian casualties play a major role in

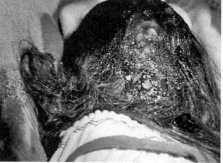

Over There uses gory imagery to drive home a message about the human costs of war. Here, roadblock duty results in the murder of an innocent young girl. ("Roadblock Duty," 8/3/2005)

both series. In the second episode of *Over There* ("Roadblock Duty"), for example, the soldiers are assigned to roadblock duty on a dark, isolated highway. At the end of the episode, the platoon fires on a vehicle that failed to stop and kills a young girl riding in the back seat. When Pvt. Frank "Dim" Dumphy (Luke Macfarlane) goes to help the child, the back of her head falls off and her brains ooze out, all of which is captured in close-up and accompanied by Dumphy's shrieks of disgust and anguish. The gore and pathos are designed to highlight the moral agony war causes.[21] In a later episode ("Embedded"), an Iraqi mother and child are also killed when they walk into the middle of a live firefight. Private Avery "Angel" King (Keith Robinson) is particularly broken up about the incident: "Killin' women and children ain't my idea of a fight." Though in both cases the program exonerates the soldiers of intent, such disturbing imagery cannot help but comment on the use of massive firepower as a strategy to combat a guerrilla insurgency.

Generation Kill drives this message home even more forcefully. Its elite recon marines are contrasted to the reservists, "pogues" (persons-other-than-grunts), and ill-trained officers who accompanying them. At least twice in the series, the recon marines observe sleepy towns full of women and children being incinerated by precision-guided bombs called in by less-experienced, overzealous field officers. The marine commanders, especially Lt. Col. Stephen "Godfather" Ferrando (Chance Kelly) call this a "demonstration of force" and commend the officers for their "aggression," though viewers know the villagers were unarmed civilians. The recon marines pride themselves on being marksmen and warriors, but even they begin to shoot innocent civilians under the lax rules of engagement imposed from above. The most traumatic of these killings is the first. In episode 3 ("Screwby"), Lance Cpl. Harold James Trombley (Billy Lush) shoots two teenage shepherds grazing their camels on the grounds of an airfield the marines were told to assault. The haste with which the assault was organized and executed led literally to waste. Sgt. Colbert is so broken up about the incident that he refuses to speak for a day, and no one in the platoon will go anywhere near Trombley after the shooting (though eventually, when all of their hands are dirty, they will honor him with the nickname "Whopper, Jr.," aka "Burger King," or "baby killer" in marine lingo). The lesson to be taken from the incident, argues Gunnery Sgt. Mike Wynn (Marc Menchaca), is to be more careful: "Look, guys, we're Americans. We must make sure when we take a shot that we are threatened. You gotta see that these people are just like you. You gotta see past the huts, the camels, the different clothes they wear. These are people in this fucking country. And this family here might lose a son." Yet the marines cannot avoid such carelessness given the battle plan. They kill several more civilians at point-blank range and call artillery in to punish the town of Muwaffaqiya when they take small arms fire from insurgents inside. "It's weird," says Cpl. Ray Person (James Ransone), "we have one guy get shot and another take a little bit of shrapnel in the leg, and we level half the town." To the recon marines, this seems more like a form of collective punishment than combat. The emphasis on speed and massive firepower increases the danger for U.S. soldiers, as well. At least twice, recon marines are fired upon by "friendly" forces, once by members of their own platoon. As needless killing follows needless killing, the soldiers become increasingly indifferent out of necessity. They have little control over anyone or anything other than themselves, and they must refuse to accept responsibility for the mistakes of others in order to continue functioning. Their disgust with the war is palpable by the end, but this is no bleeding-heart liberal expression of disdain for killing. Rather, it is disgust at the "bad tactics" being used to subdue and stabilize the country. As Sgt. Colbert puts it, "They're screwing this shit up. Don't they fucking realize the world already hates us? . . . We keep killing civilians we're going to waste this fucking victory" ("A Bomb in the Garden").

The "they" in Colbert's diatribe refers to the decision makers higher up the chain of command, leading all the way to the Pentagon and the Bush White House. Both *Over There* and *Generation Kill* foreground the tension between the ordinary men and women who serve and the officers and politicians who choose where and how they will be used. This tension is clear from the subtitle of Wright's text: "Devil Dogs, Iceman, Captain America and the New Face of American War." "Iceman" is Brad Colbert's nickname and tells you everything you need to know about his leadership style: he is cool under pressure, calculated in his actions, and unmoved by the chaos that surrounds him. He and Nate Fick are the embodiments of proper leadership because they try to plan for the unexpected and protect their men at all costs. "Captain America," on the other hand, is like the superhero he is named after: paranoid, overzealous, and unpredictable. He and "Encino Man," a dim-witted football star placed in charge of a company because of his aggressive mindset, are the epitome of bad leadership. They follow orders without question even when the orders endanger their men or the mission. Whereas Colbert and Fick are individualists with keen intellects and a clear sense of right and wrong, Captain America and Encino Man are "team players" (Simon and Burns emphasize this by having Encino Man speak in nothing but football-ese). Heroism, for them, is a consciously stylized performance. Captain America, in particular, is prone to excessive, pointless action. He shoots an empty vehicle, for example, and calls it "denying the enemy transport"; he opens fire on a village even though he knows there are no enemy targets there, and he charges at least two unarmed Iraqi prisoners with a bayonet (an implement none of the other marines even carry because it is an anachronism). He is what marines call "moto," emotional. During firefights, he tends to scream over the company radio "We're all going to die," and Person and Colbert speculate at one point that he might be crying. Encino Man is little better. He constantly fails to convey vital information to his team leaders; he doesn't know what "danger close" means and almost calls in an airstrike on his own platoon (luckily, he also doesn't know the proper protocols for calling in an airstrike, so they are saved by his incompetence); and he blindly accepts any mission no matter how stupid or dangerous. For example, he orders his troops to escort a demolition team to mark a minefield in the middle of the night; two men are seriously injured as a result. Captain America and Encino Man receive effusive praise from Lt. Col. Ferrando for their aggression, which indicts Ferrando as an equally suspect leader. In Wright's book, one of the marines describes Ferrando as a "Marine Corps politician," rather than a warrior, and Simon and Burns make him sound like a corporate yes-man. He is constantly describing his rationale for mission design in relation to whether it will grab Gen. Mattis's attention and garner his praise. And, Ferrando's excessive adherence to the grooming standard is mocked by the men as overly controlling, even fascistic (a point Simon and Burns reinforce by filling the background with images of men who look like Hitler because their mustaches are not allowed to "exceed their lip lines").

Worst of all, according to the Marines, are the battalion commanders whose fetishization of speed and micromanagement of the battlefield undermine the unit's effectiveness. "The individual who needs his head examined," Colbert says, "is the man responsible for taking arguably the finest damn independent recon operators of any military in the world and dropping us in Humvee platoons to lead a parade of pogues, officers, and heavily armed subhuman morons . . . across Mesopotamia" ("Burning Dog"). They mock the systems-logic of the commanders, who send troops into the teeth of a known ambush because "bypassing the ambush is just what the enemy expects." And they wonder aloud why maneuver warfare was adopted in the first place: "I've never understood what the rush was about," says Gunny Wynn. "I mean, there's no doubt America's gonna beat Saddam's military so why rush this shit?" Speed and micromanagement from above lead to several questionable tactical decisions that later return to haunt U.S. forces in Iraq. For example, when Ferrando decides to abandon a supply truck with a flat tire because the platoon is behind schedule, their food, water, ammunition, and company colors (flag) are stolen by Iraqis. When the platoon later encounters a truck full of armed men, they are ordered by Ferrando to leave the men alone; the men turn out to be Republican Guard, and the decision later endangers the lives of other soldiers. Ferrando also orders the troops to leave Iraqi weapons and ammunition lying in a field where anyone could take them. This was apparently common practice during the push to Baghdad and provided the future insurgency with ready stockpiles of weapons to use against the American invaders.[22] Hindsight has shown that the marines in *Generation Kill* were spot-on in their assessment of the flaws in the U.S. strategy. The game plan focused too much on taking Baghdad and deposing Saddam Hussein and not enough on securing the postwar peace.

Over There also incorporates a subplot about proper leadership, but it goes much further up the chain of command in its criticisms of U.S. strategy, offering a scathing indictment of the naïveté of the neoconservative architects of the war. The soldiers in *Over There* suffer the inept leadership of Lt. Alexander "Underpants" Hunter (Josh Stamberg), a composite version of the various incompetents discussed in Wright's book. Like Ferrando, he micromanages his men; like Encino Man, he bungles tactical operations, and like Captain America, he is aggressive at all the wrong times. In the episode "Suicide Rain," for example, a young soldier is taken hostage by a man seeking medical care for his injured son. The level-headed Sgt. "Scream" (Chris Silas, played by Erik Palladino) convinces the lieutenant to allow a medic and a sniper into the house to defuse the situation, but just as the sniper is about to resolve the stand-off peacefully, Hunter orders an assault that kills the marine they were trying to save. In a later episode ("Weapons of Mass Destruction"), the unit suspects a high-value insurgent is hiding in a local village and plans a midnight raid to capture him unawares. Hunter, who has not been informed of the mission, discovers their whereabouts and screams at the sergeant, blowing their cover and permitting the "bad guy" to make a run for it. When the team gives chase, the lieutenant aims at the villain from behind his own men, endangering their lives. And in the final episode ("Follow the Money"), the lieutenant is killed by friendly fire when he forces his team to leave wounded and unarmed comrades and charge through enemy gunfire to protect a U-Haul truck carrying new Iraqi dinars. Like Captain America and Encino Man, Lt. Underpants embodies the heavy-handed and unfocused use of force, which has caused so much "collateral damage" in Iraq. Sgt. Scream may be less efficient and discreet than the recon marines of *Generation Kill*, but he possesses the same "moral courage" and seeks to shield his troops from unnecessary physical and emotional risk.[23] Like Colbert and Fick, he is the epitome of the self-sacrificing military professional.

Yet, *Over There* reserves its most damning criticism for the people who initiated the war and profited most from it. The episode entitled "Situation Normal" offers an allegorical examination of the motives for the war in Iraq when the unit is tasked to provide security for a civilian contractor seeking a location for a new oil pipeline. That these "reconstruction specialists" are focused only on building oil infrastructure is already suspect, but then the contractor, whose Texas accent and cowboy mannerisms are pronounced, tells the local imam they are going to put the pipeline in his valley whether the locals want it or not. In exchange, he grudgingly agrees to build one additional building for the town. When the imam asks for a mosque, the contractor asks the rest of the villagers what they would like, undercutting the man's authority. The contractor naïvely believes that the U.S. "victory" in Iraq guarantees the rise of democracy in the country. His attempt to foster local debate ends up condemning one of the imam's wives to death. At the next town meeting the woman tries to convince the villagers they need a school, rather than another mosque. The imam is furious and tries to silence her, but the contractor responds, "You tell him, now that democracy has come, she has the right to speak. . . . You tell him I personally guarantee her right to speak." Her speech is designed as a critique of the intolerance and fear bred by fundamentalist Islam, but it also reads as a critique of the post-9/11 U.S. mindset: "If you teach us only fear," she says, "if you teach only hatred, . . . if you teach us only that we are embattled and alone, then we will always be angry, and we will always be ignorant. We need a school where we can teach our children hope." The imam calls her an "infidel" and accuses her of being "unfaithful to what we believe." Incited by the imam, the other villagers chase the woman from the room and begin stoning her while the contractor stands there watching helplessly. Though the soldiers break it up, Sgt. Scream knows that once they leave, the villagers will finish the job. "You want to give these people a lasting gift," he shouts at the contractor, "get the hell out of their lives." The naïve belief that democracy can be imposed from without, through military force, is roundly condemned in this episode. More importantly, the episode exposes the true basis of neoconservative political goals in neoliberal economic control. While they may have claimed to want to reform corrupt governments in the Middle East, neoconservative policy makers were really out to secure their own vital interests, and the lack of commitment to nation-building operations is a clear sign of their self-centeredness.

Over There and Generation Kill thus demonstrate the misfit between strategy and tactics that undermined the U.S. war effort and led to the growth of a powerful insurgency. The stated rationale for war—to find and destroy Saddam Hussein's weapons of mass destruction—dictated a strategy based on the economic and speedy deployment of force. When this rationale proved a ruse, the military was left with insufficient resources to effect a successful transition to peace. Instead of trying to win the hearts and minds of the people, the military was forced to circle the wagons. They withdrew into heavily fortified bases, launched mostly large-scale operations designed to intimidate, and adopted a shoot-first-ask-questions-later approach that emphasized force protection over civilian security. Reports emerged of U.S. soldiers shooting civilians at roadblocks, running over pedestrians during convoys, firing artillery into civilian areas, holding the family members of suspected insurgents hostage, and using methods of collective punishment to "correct" insurgent behavior. By treating the people of Iraq as the battlefield, rather than the prize to be won, the military ended up creating new enemies to fuel the insurgency and the larger War on Terrorism.[24]

The concluding scene of Generation Kill presents a dire warning about the dangers of such unfocused, tactical energy. As the men prepare to leave Iraq, they bond over a video of their "road trip" to Baghdad compiled by a fictional character named Jason Lilley (Kellan Lutz). Though the scene is faked, it evokes Wright's description of "Generation Kill" as a group of media junkies, more familiar with "video games, reality shows, and Internet porn" than with their own parents.[25] It also mimics the "mash-up" aesthetic of actual soldier videos now available on sites such as YouTube and MilitarySpot.com. Such videos are designed to bypass the mainstream media filters and "tell the story" of Iraq, in all its brutality, to the people back home.[26] Simon and producer George Faber literally and figuratively remediate these videos—combining actual footage shot by the recon marines with B-roll footage captured for the series and adding a heavy-handed soundtrack reminiscent of soldier-produced combat videos—to deliver a message about the military's misadventure in Iraq. As with most soldier videos, the soundtrack sets the tone and conditions the response (this is the only occasion when a soundtrack is used). Simon and Faber use Johnny Cash's eerie apocalyptic ballad "The Man Comes Around" to frame the imagery. The song tells the story of the four horsemen of the apocalypse and ends with the approach of death and hell. As the marines consume Lilley's distilled dosage of war, they become increasingly disturbed by the imagery and drift away, until only Trombley, Person, and Lilley are left. Trombley's response to the imagery is to say "Fucking beautiful," which causes even Person and Lilley to leave in disgust. The camera then moves in for a close-up of Trombley's gleeful face while Cash speaks the final lines of the song: "And I heard a voice in the midst of the four beasts, / and I looked, and, behold, / a pale horse, and his name that sat on him was Death / and hell followed with him." The series fades on Trombley, as he lifts his weapon and walks off.

The sequence leaves viewers with the frightening realization that loose cannons like Trombley, who is the only member of the platoon not to have turned his weapon in at this point, are the ones most likely to assume responsibility for the next phase of the war—not men like Iceman Colbert or Nate Fick. Trombley is the very embodiment of "Generation Kill," a baby-faced psycho-killer who talks to his weapon, wishes he could have dropped the atomic bomb on Japan, and describes war as "one of those fantasy things you always hoped would really happen."[27] As a departure from the studiously neutral moral tone of the series, the scene stands out and serves as a lesson for viewers about what went wrong in Iraq. When the marines pulled out and turned the country over to the Third and Fourth Infantry Divisions of the U.S. Army, unfocused aggression became the norm. Army commanders applied a heavy hand to stability operations in the mistaken belief that sufficient force, applied in regular doses, would terrorize the enemy and quell the growing insurgency. Instead, they exacerbated it. One of the Fourth ID's favorite tactics was to fire their artillery into civilian areas at night to "deter" enemy action before it happened; they called this "proactive counterfire."[28] What surer sign could there be that a misguided strategy (preemptive war) breeds misguided tactics?

Imperial Grunts and the New Revolution in Military Affairs

Despite their graphic depictions of the devastation wrought by war, *Over There* and *Generation Kill* are not antiwar statements. Rather, they are calculated critiques of U.S. strategy designed, like Thomas Ricks's *Fiasco*, as after-action reports to guide future U.S. policy. They use bloody images of civilian casualties and friendly fire accidents to expose the excesses of the RMA and "maneuver warfare." In the process, they reinforce the lessons learned by real-world military and political leaders during the past decade of war in Afghanistan and Iraq. Experience has taught not that war is an ineffective means of engineering social change, but that the United States needs a new, even lower-profile approach to war, one that is both more acceptable to the public and more suitable to the requirements of policing global order. Rather than preparing for traditional, large-scale battles against clearly defined enemies, the United States must start preparing for small-scale "dirty wars" and multifaceted politico-cultural-military operations. Soldiers must be trained more like special forces units or recon marines to operate independently and adapt flexibly to shifting mission requirements and conditions on the ground. At the center of this new revolution in military affairs is the rediscovery of counterinsurgency doctrine with its emphasis on "winning hearts and minds" by building relationships and using force only as a last resort. The ascension of David Petraeus—the man who literally wrote the book on counterinsurgency warfare for the U.S. Army—to the head of Central Command signaled the triumph of counterinsurgency doctrine as the new enabling discourse of war. This discourse may be more realistic about the "dirty" nature of warfare than the RMA, but it is still a discourse that argues for war's perpetuation and extension. Indeed, it is a discourse well suited to the neoconservative depiction of the globe as a space of Hobbesian anarchy crying out for a sovereign to impose order.

Neoconservative stalwarts such as Max Boot and Robert Kaplan began embracing the possibilities of "small war" doctrine even before the war in Iraq, and the success of Petraeus's strategy there has only emboldened them.[29] Kaplan's *Imperial Grunts* is particularly bold in its description of counterinsurgency warfare as the centerpiece of U.S. foreign policy in the twenty-first century. Kaplan openly embraces the United States' status as an imperial power and mines nineteenth-century imperialist discourse for lessons that can be applied in the contemporary context. "The War on Terrorism," he says, "[is] really about taming the frontier" and "advanc[ing], the boundaries of free society and good government into zones of sheer chaos."[30] Heavy-handed tactics suitable to nineteenth-century colonialism, however, have to be replaced in the twenty-first century by "more quiet and devious" forms of military behavior: "The American Empire of the early twenty-first century depend[s] upon [a] tissue of intangibles that [is] threatened, rather than invigorated, by the naked exercise of power."[31] Counterinsurgency doctrine and training are the perfect antidotes to this dilemma, for they create "small, light and lethal units of soldiers and marines, skilled in guerilla warfare and attuned to the local environment in the way of nineteenth century Apaches." These flexibly specialized forces can accomplish more with less in a shorter amount of time and with less "blowback" than "dinosauric, industrial age infantry divisions," he argues.[32] Kaplan is particularly taken with the pragmatic, "results-oriented" approach of the special forces, their faith in humans over hardware, and their ingenuity and persistence. These "imperial grunts" are the very embodiment of the American boot-strapping ideal, and Kaplan offers them as an object lesson in proper global citizenship.

Though Kaplan labels the resulting regime of power "American Empire," what he is proposing is not a global projection of American manifest destiny. It is not about the acquisition of territory or the exclusive control of resources, still less about imposing a global administrative regime run by the United States. Rather, Empire in Kaplan's terms designates the extension of the neoliberal social and economic order (which the United States has done the most to champion but which is not reducible to American interests). Empire designates a global system of governance regulated through collective effort and biopolitical techniques of control. As there is no "outside" to this system, the frontier marks those recalcitrant zones of internal difference, which must be tamed for the good of the system. Militarism emerges in this context as a duty undertaken by the United States in the name of humanity. Its primary purpose is not to project U.S. power, but to create the conditions necessary for the system, and the peoples who live within it, to prosper. Or, as the 2002 National Security Strategy statement puts it, the U.S. military acts to "[protect] basic human rights and [guarantee the] political and economic freedom[s]" that will enable societies "to unleash the potential of their people and assure their future prosperity."[33] While the military may still bring death in its wake, the goal is no longer to kill; it is to foster life. Thus, training, education, and behavioral modification techniques are touted as the newest weapons in the military arsenal. For example, Kaplan argues that the U.S. military can best ensure the security of global civilization by "replicating soldier personalities"—targeting a few "trainable" individuals in other countries, providing them with the discipline and techniques necessary to establish order, inculcating a (very) basic respect for human rights as a part of that process, and then letting them train others. Eventually, the discipline modeled by these "soldier personalities" will multiply throughout the society, stabilizing the social terrain and ensuring peace and prosperity.[34] This is a vision of power exercised through biopolitical mechanisms of control. The aim is to promote the general welfare using informal means of social regulation, rather than force. The problem with this plan, however, is that Kaplan defines life in very narrow terms—as the right to a bare existence, to escape death if one subjects oneself to the prevailing system of political rule.[35] For those who refuse to submit, extermination remains the go-to option for ensuring the health of the system.

Generation Kill offers the most sophisticated understanding of these shifts in the nature of war and Empire, for it self-consciously rejects frontier mythology as old-fashioned and impractical. The moral absolutes that form the core of the frontier mythos are irrelevant to the recon marines, who view morality as situational and understand how tenuous the distinction between civilization and savagery can be. Though the recon marines are often labeled "cowboys" by those who resent their independent spirit, the marines themselves understand that "there are no cowboys" anymore ("Stay Frosty"). They are really the ultimate company men—doing their jobs well and preserving the integrity of the corps as an institution are their primary motivations. Recon marines use the word "cowboy" disparagingly to identify those who lack restraint and have no regard for the consequences of their actions. Cowboys are "moto," and "moto" is unprofessional. Delta Company is the embodiment of the cowboy spirit, and the recon marines have nothing but contempt for them. The leader of that unit drives around with cattle horns attached to his Humvee, and his men shoot up random hamlets as a "show of force, you know, cowboy shit." In one town, Delta Company gives the young boys porn magazines, and when an elder comes out to confront them about it, they shoot the hamlet to pieces. The conclusion of the recon marines is that Delta are a "bunch of fucks" ("Stay Frosty").

Cowboys and cowboy actions are passé, *Generation Kill* implies. What is needed to fight the War on Terrorism and defend global society is a cadre of well-trained, professional gunslingers—men willing to devote their lives not to a cause, but to getting the job done. This is the real point of the conflict between the "good" and "bad" leaders in both *Generation Kill* and *Over There*. Good leaders put the "mission first" (a Marine Corps motto); bad ones put themselves first. The soldiers in both *Generation Kill* and *Over There* are constantly focused on mission readiness and mission success. There is a lot of discussion in both series about the professional minutia of the soldier's life (the different types of weapons, the effects of various types of ordnance, the details of particular tactics, how you hold and fire your weapon, how you conduct a cordon and search operation, etc.), and soldiers are constantly cleaning and preparing their weapons for the next engagement. They keep their minds sharp by playing chess and verbally sparring with each other, their bodies tuned through intense physical activity, and their weapons primed through constant maintenance. They have so fully internalized this "mission first" discipline that they need no prompting to maintain themselves at peak capacity.

Both *Over There* and *Generation Kill* emphasize the autonomous, self-regulating nature of the professional soldier by making the upper echelons of the command structure completely invisible. Generals appear only as reference points during mission briefings in *Generation Kill* or as disembodied silences on the other end of Sgt. Scream's phone line in *Over There*. The men in both series know full well what they have to do, and the presence of command authorities is not necessary to enforce professional discipline. To crib from Kaplan, these guys operate like employees in the most innovative global corporations, where "tremendous personal responsibility at the lowest reaches of command [is] combined with the complete sublimation of the individual within the organizational cult."[36] They are walking, talking manifestations of the military institution, "perfect policy instruments," who know little outside the routines of military life.[37]

The combination of frontier discourse and professional ethics that structures both of these programs ultimately serves a disciplinary function vis-à-vis U.S. audiences, who are encouraged to view "terrorists" and other unruly subjects as biological threats to global civilization and soldiers as the necessary instruments of human salvation. The professional soldier, like the professional lawman in the western, is presented as the model of proper citizenship, now outfitted for a global era of neoliberal governmentality.[38] Kaplan is right to identify the professional soldier as the agent of empire, but he is wrong to construct empire as a narrowly U.S. project. As Lee Medevoi has argued, the War on Terrorism (of which the war in Iraq constitutes a part) is less a defense of U.S. society than a defense of global society. The war has not been waged "in the name of a sovereign who needs to be defended; [it has been] waged on behalf of the existence of everyone."[39] As President Bush has said, "This is the world's fight. This is civilization's fight. This is the fight of all who believe in progress and pluralism, tolerance and freedom."[40] While such rhetoric is obviously self-serving, it also contains a grain of truth. The globe is the field of operations for the war; the war *does* "openly [concern] populations rather than sovereign claims on territory," and responsibility for the conduct of the war, even in Iraq, "is shared with other states, with transnational corporations like Bechtel and Halliburton, with Kurdish and Shiite militias, with a wide array of NGOs (nongovernmental organizations), and with mercenary companies." As Medevoi puts it, the War on Terrorism "is projected and practiced as a war between a global 'way of life' and the subpopulation that poses the biological threat to it."[41] That subpopulation— whether defined as "terrorists" or "rogue nations"—must be eliminated in order for "civilization" to thrive and prosper, and "civilization" is defined in very narrow terms as U.S.-style democracy, free-market capitalism, and individualism, or, rather, self-discipline, all of which are personified by the "professional" U.S. soldier.

Over There and *Generation Kill* acknowledge this narrow conception of civilization in a series of witty asides that wink at viewers and dare them to disagree. Dim Dumphy, of *Over There*, notes that it is more than ironic that U.S. soldiers are eating MREs made from 10 percent digestible plastic (i.e., petroleum products) while sitting on "80 percent of the world's oil reserves" ("Follow the Money"). In *Generation Kill*, Cpl. Ray Person (James Ransone) suggests the war is less for oil than to provide a forward base of operations for Starbucks, and Sgt. Tony Espera (Jon Huertas) jokingly explains that the war is really part of Thomas Friedman's vaunted Golden Arches Theory of Conflict Prevention: "How . . . are we gonna make these holy mother fuckers want to stop killin' everybody? Put a McDonald's on every fuckin' corner."[42] The fact that these shows can joke so freely about the economic motivations for war indicates how comfortable audiences have become with the use of war for purposes of social engineering. These jokes do not shock; they delight an audience already cynical enough to assume that war is about economic self-interest. Yet, both programs celebrate the proficiency of these military professionals in all earnestness and nominate them as frontline agents of neoliberal Empire. This is wholly in keeping with the military's own reassessment of its role in fostering development through peacekeeping operations—a sort of "Peace Corps with guns."[43] Lt. Col. Steve Leonard, who helped draft the army's Stability Operations Field Manual (2008), puts the military's new mission-orientation thus: "We have to step back and say, you know, it's not about democracy, it's about effective governance and a stronger economy and well-being for the people."[44] While the renunciation of democracy promotion as a mission strategy is a welcome sign, the expansion of the military's traditional role to include social engineering on the economic and interpersonal level is disturbing to say the least.

Perhaps the biggest problem with this increase in the scope of military expertise is that military training tends to promote a morality of action, which obviates questions of right and wrong.[45] As Pvt. Tariq Nassiri (Omid Abtahi) puts it in *Over There*, "Right, wrong, it's too much to think about. We got a job to do" ("I Want My Toilets"). All that matters for the soldiers in these programs is that they do their assignments well. Issues of moral legitimacy factor in only when and if they affect combat readiness. Thus, Lt. Fick and Sgt. Colbert seek to minimize civilian casualties, not as a principle in itself, but because too many such casualties will destroy the platoon's morale and undermine their aggressiveness. For soldiers engaged in combat, it is perhaps inevitable that a technical standard of morality would replace questions of good and evil, right and wrong, for the social prohibition against killing is strong. "What you think you believe in. What you think you live for, it's time to put that shit aside," Sgt. Scream informs his men, "It's killin' time. Somebody's going to die today, and that's a fact. The only question is who. So don't be thinking about anything else. . . . Do your job." For the soldier, doing the job well is synonymous with doing good. Thus, soldiers in *Generation Kill* are congratulated for shooting civilians "straight in the grape" because that means they aimed well, and interrogators in *Over There* are cheered for efficiently torturing information out of a high-value prisoner.

Conclusion

In that we are being asked to identify with the "noble grunts" in these series, we are also being asked to identify with the purely technical standards of morality they embody. *Over There* and *Generation Kill*, both celebrate the instrumental rationality that made war seem like a viable tool of social engineering in the first place. By rerooting war's moral legitimacy in the body of the professional soldier, whom our public culture mandates we support at any cost, they pave the way for the perpetuation of war as an instrument of peace into the future and tacitly support the extension of military discipline into other areas of social life. Indeed, they redefine peace as a perpetual state of war and help construct docile bodies willing to police themselves in the name of order.[46] Thus, for example, military discipline has increasingly been promoted as a panacea for a wide range of social ills since 9/11. Military-style boot camps have been established to combat everything from obesity and juvenile delinquency to failing schools and dysfunctional boardrooms. Business leaders can now take seminars from retired military commanders designed to teach them how economics are just like war (see, for example, Kenneth Allard's *Business as War* series), and a proliferation of military movies, TV programs, toys, video games, and branded merchandise encourages citizens to view militarism as a lifestyle and the military as a lifestyle enclave. Military materials, techniques, and technologies now circulate throughout society, inspiring individuals to fashion themselves anew—to become "Army Strong" or reinvent themselves as one of "The Few. The Proud. The Marines."[47] The government hardly needs to involve itself anymore in the promotion of such micropolitical modes of discipline and control, for the private sector, including the commercial media, are happy to disseminate the military ethos for their own reasons. This is what Roger Stahl means when he names the reigning social regime "Militainment, Inc."

As Stahl also notes, however, this regime "harbors an array of instabilities" that might be made to register as dissonance.[48] The translation of war into an entertainment product, the packaging of it for consumption, particularly within a realist aesthetic, entails a necessary friction between the fantasy of war and its "unconsumable reality."[49] This friction may, on occasion, be exploited and translated into a contradiction. Thus, for example, Kari Andén-Papadopoulos argues that the "uncensored insights" contained in soldier videos uploaded to YouTube might "provide the basis for a questioning of the authority and activity of US foreign policy."[50] I would argue, rather, that the content of such videos is variable and radically ambiguous. The "shock," if it comes, comes from reading the comments left by other consumers of these videos. Many of these comments express not disgust or rage, but glee at the spectacle of carnage, as if the bodies in pain are not real at all, as if they are not, and therefore do not, matter. It is particularly disturbing when the videos are transformed into vehicles for the expression of racist or apocalyptic fantasies of extermination. Such discourse cannot help but draw attention to the dangers implicit in the commodification and exchange of war as entertainment.

Likewise, *Generation Kill* is arguably an exercise in training viewers to adjust to the extremity of war. Its immersive "lean forward" approach to representation approximates the interactive immersion of a videogame. Like such games, it can be said to train individuals in the problem-solving skills required of citizens in a neoliberal social order defined by privatization.[51] At the very least it mimics the ethos of self-care at the heart of that order by making viewers assume responsibility for their own meaning and satisfaction. Its neutral moral tone, however, also opens a space for viewers to inject themselves and their experience into the text. *Generation Kill* does not promote a passive consumer orientation to war. Rather, it asks the spectator to produce his or her own moral judgments about war. It solicits such moral thinking in a way that other forms of militainment, including war journalism, almost never do. Thus, it could as easily politicize popular consciousness as mobilize it for the cause of Empire and neo-frontier conflict.

The "instabilities" that structure these stories about the war in Iraq are substantial, and I do not mean to mitigate the possibility that they might flare into full-blown contradictions for certain individuals or social groups. Certainly, the shows resonated with television critics and have seen successful second lives in the DVD market, indicating some popular support for their de-romanticized portraits of war. However, the instabilities may cut both ways. As Anthony Swofford's *Jarhead* reminds us, even the most critical antiwar film can easily be appropriated and turned into "war porn" by soldiers looking for a rush.[52] Since contemporary American culture makes soldiers of us all by asking us to consume war as entertainment, the possibilities for the conversion of militainment into porn are virtually endless. It is doubtful that any critique of war, especially specific wars, can escape recuperation in America as long as war and militarism remain such deeply ingrained features of social life. *Over There* and *Generation Kill* undoubtedly de-romanticize war in provocative ways, but their attempts to "shock" in the present need to be taken in context. In a milieu defined by permanent war and Empire, they cannot help but function as premediations that inoculate the public against the "shock" of future wars. By acknowledging, assessing, and "correcting" the strategic and tactical failures in Iraq, the programs salvage war for future political use.

6 Contesting the Politics of Fear

The forms of entertainment television addressed thus far—news reports, spy thrillers, reality television, and military dramas—largely legitimated the Bush administration's construction of the War on Terrorism as a "monumental struggle between good and evil" for the right to define the future of "civilization."[1] They adhered to the administration's characterization of contemporary threats as less monolithic and predictable than in the past, therefore more dangerous, and they participated in the reconceptualization of the citizen's role vis-à-vis the apparatuses of social governance. On the one hand, they show how security is threatened by "super-empowered individuals" capable of turning ordinary objects into weapons of mass destruction and, thus, of striking anywhere at any time; on the other hand, they imply that this requires citizens to become virtual counterterrorism agents and imperial grunts—the eyes, ears, and hands of our law enforcement agencies at both the local and global levels.[2] "Perpetual vigilance and preparedness," these programs suggest, are the keys to social security and prosperity, and it is the citizen's responsibility to undertake these tasks.[3] More than just entertainment, then, these programs helped popularize the neoliberal reconceptualization of the citizen as an agent of the government, so identified with the state as to be unwilling or unable to deliberate on the state's actions.

The tight linkage between the citizen and the state would begin to be challenged in a systematic fashion in U.S. popular and public discourse only after Bush administration policies spawned a deadly insurgency and torture scandal in Iraq. The May 2004 release of photos of U.S. military personnel systematically humiliating and abusing prisoners at Abu Ghraib led former vice president Al Gore to publicly condemn the Bush administration's "twisted values and atrocious policies" and demand the resignations of Defense Secretary Donald Rumsfeld, national security advisor Condoleezza Rice, and CIA director George Tenet.[4] Presidential hopeful John Kerry followed that up by accusing President Bush of "undermining generations of U.S. leadership" through his aggressive policies and dismissive approach to foreign allies. He characterized the war in Iraq as a distraction from the War on Terrorism and asserted that Bush's policies made the United States "less safe."[5] Even before the Abu Ghraib scandal broke, Kerry had been attacking the administration's use of the USA Patriot Act to indefinitely detain immigrants, eavesdrop on political activists, and bypass congressional oversight. While he stopped short of calling for a repeal of the act, which he originally voted for, he did say several provisions could be "[scaled back] to assure our security doesn't come at the expense of our civil liberties."[6] When former "counterterrorism czar" Richard Clarke released his tell-all memoir, *Against All Enemies*, just before the election, it added fuel to the Democrats' fire. Clarke described the Bush presidency as a "republican crisis" of epic proportions. He characterized the invasion of Iraq as a political gambit that weakened the domestic balance of powers, undermined international relations, stretched the U.S. military to the breaking point, and further radicalized the Muslim world.[7] Finally, he commissioned his readers to rise up and protect the Constitution "against all enemies, foreign *and domestic*," including "those who would use the terrorist threat to assault the liberties the Constitution enshrines."[8] Though the Bush regime was not overthrown in 2004 (the Republicans even picked up several seats in Congress), the attempt to turn the election into a referendum on the administration's security policies did signal a weakening of the consensus culture that followed the 9/11 attacks.[9]

This chapter examines some of the ways that U.S. television contributed to and commented on the unraveling of political consensus. Key to this unraveling has been the emergence of an array of new distribution channels and a sea change in the television industry's attitudes toward these outlets. The technological convergence of media has been facilitated by a set of deregulatory policies that encouraged the vertical and horizontal integration of once-distinct media industries. So, for example, television networks are now part of multimedia conglomerates whose parent corporations are also invested in the film industry, the recording industry, the publishing industry, and other cultural industries (video games, sports, comic books, etc). They own stakes in TV stations, movie theaters, cable, satellite, and Internet providers, and they are dabbling in mobile telephony, all as a means of extending the intermedia lifespan of their cultural commodities.[10] DVDs, streaming video, and video on demand do not just enable viewers to access their television programming in a variety of new ways; they also account for a growing percentage of the industry's revenues.[11] Though still vital, the premiere exhibition window (i.e., the commercial airdate) is no longer the sole determinant of which TV series will be picked up or canceled. The Nielsen ratings service now provides television executives with data on delayed viewing (via DVR), Internet viewing, and DVD sales as a complement to its standard ratings measures, and executives have revived a number of programs based on sales in these ancillary markets (The Family Guy, Arrested Development, and Jericho are notable series in this category).[12] This complex media environment provides a rich field for cultural play that both opens new spaces for expression and lowers the bar for "success." How these industrial and technological developments helped bring marginalized expressions of political dissent into the cultural mainstream will be one focus of this chapter. How, exactly, those expressions challenged the prevailing political discourse will be the other.

Challenging the Status Quo through Satire

Humor is often a barometer of popular consensus, marking out the boundaries beyond which public speech may not go. When Bill Maher joked about the United States being "cowardly" for lobbing cruise missiles at Afghanistan in 2001, for example, this was roundly denounced as treasonous speech, and Maher's program, Politically Incorrect, was canceled. The Comedy Central show That's My Bush, a live-action series featuring a faux President Bush in the role of a bumbling sitcom dad, was also summarily yanked from the television schedule after 9/11 out of deference to the president's new image of seriousness.[13] Even The Daily Show's Jon Stewart temporarily declared a moratorium on jokes about the president, claiming "'subliminable' is not a punch line anymore."[14] Cultural observers of all stripes began proclaiming irony "dead" and depicting satire as a "luxury we could no longer afford."[15] "The silly season," we were told, "is over."[16]

It did not take long for this cultural chill to thaw, however, and comedy programs took the lead. Just a week following his tearful, on-air lament for the victims of 9/11, Jon Stewart began using satire to provide some much-needed perspective. On his September 25, 2001, program, for example, he chided Vanity Fair editor Graydon Carter for proclaiming irony dead: "Maybe we should wait to make pronouncements about what will happen to us culturally until the fires are put out. Don't you think?" From 2001 to 2004, The Daily Show with Jon Stewart doubled its audience share on late-night cable, and it did so by lampooning political and social authorities once perceived to be off-limits.[17] With regular features such as "Mess O'Potamia" and "Are You Prepared?!?" *The Daily Show* deconstructed the prevailing political rhetoric and foregrounded the political utility of fear and violence for the Bush administration. In a "Mess O'Potamia" segment following the toppling of Saddam Hussein's statue in Firdos Square, for example, correspondent Stephen Colbert mocked the administration's zeal for war and distaste for rebuilding by deeming the rebuilding process a task for "losers." "We won. . . . It's time to party. Then it's off to Syria for the next invasion" (4/10/2003). Samantha Bee's "Are You Prepared?!?" segments deftly skewered the Bush administration's use of nonspecific fears and color-coded threat alerts to manipulate popular opinion and generate support for its agenda. In the first such segment, Bee proclaimed suburban New Yorkers to be suffering from "insufficient level[s] of suspicion," which would lead inevitably to death. In a parody of the Department of Homeland Security's readiness campaigns, Bee insisted her subjects take responsibility for their own safety and equip themselves to defend against a wide variety of possible attacks. "Are you prepared for monkey pox?" she asks one woman. "Iranians? Avian flood quake? Lesbian Tsunami?" When the woman says "no," Ms. Bee labels her a "walking corpse." The segment ends by offering viewers a "Preparedness Checklist" whose memorable acronym, "D.I.E." ("Determine course of action; Items for survival kit; Exit strategy"), drives home the subtext of DHS's own preparedness efforts: you, not the government, are the one responsible if you die from lack of vigilance (5/16/2006). Political satire of this sort works by distancing viewers from the pronouncements of power and offering competing versions of "common sense" that require subjects to make a choice when constructing their personal worldviews, to be active, rather than passive, in the face of official discourse. Thus, it works to counteract the infantilization of the public so prevalent in other sites on the proverbial dial.

As a "fake news" program, Stewart and company saved their most vicious satire for the mainstream news media, especially the political punditry, whom Stewart once famously accused of being "hacks" and puppets of the administration.[18] In the run-up to the war in Iraq, for example, Stewart lambasted the mainstream media outlets for dressing their sets in red, white, and blue bunting, creating special theme music and titles for the war coverage, and facilitating the administration's attempts to present the war as entertainment.[19] Fake pundit Stephen Colbert parodied this gung-ho style of journalism when he explained to Stewart that the media's role in wartime "should be the accurate and objective description of the hellacious ass-whomping we're handing the Iraqis" (5/26/2003). By illustrating how subjective the news reporting actually was, the segment tried to undermine viewer identification with the discourse of objectivity in general. Indeed, the parodic news updates at the center of *The Daily Show* are designed to suggest that a more overt style of subjective commentary might actually improve the news by adding perspective and context. As Geoffrey Baym explains, these segments work by culling information from existing newscasts but then filtering and dressing this raw material so that it promotes a more critical mode of engagement. Video footage is selected and presented in ways that undermine the univocal quality of the sound bites we usually receive via newscasts. Stewart shows the delays and pauses that surround the sound bite, for example, or clips portions of public events that other news outlets have defined as irrelevant or embarrassing. He then adds humorous commentary that deconstructs and contextualizes the footage, providing viewers with a mini-lesson in critical media literacy.[20] Perhaps the most interesting of these lessons was Stewart's deconstruction of the Bush administration's "talking points" on Iraq. Using clips from various of Bush's public speeches, he shows how repetition is used to drive home the message du jour and how any deviation from the script—for example, a question about the rationale for the Iraq war—is either ignored, snidely dismissed, or punished using the "emotional cudgel" of 9/11. "If I had a nickel for every time Bush mentioned 9/11," Stewart quipped, "well, I could raise enough reward money to go after Bin Laden" (8/25/2005). In addition to its stinging criticism of Bush administration policies, the segment teaches viewers how to watch the news. It warns them not to trust everything they see and invites them to consider how the story is constructed: whose voices are overpresent and whose are missing; what points are overemphasized and what gets left out of the conversation; most importantly, who benefits from this particular construction of the world? Whereas shows like *The West Wing* or *JAG* invited viewers to trust in political authority absolutely, *The Daily Show* promoted a healthy skepticism that positioned viewers as citizens of a deliberative democracy.

Soon the satiric impulse hit the mainstream airwaves, as primetime network sitcoms such as *Arrested Development* (Fox, 2003–2006) and *Whoopi* (NBC, 2003–2004) also began lampooning the Bush administration's military and economic policies. *Arrested Development* focused on the dysfunctional family dynamics of an ethically challenged real-estate tycoon named George Bluth (Jeffrey Tambor). Known for its literate humor, narrative complexity, and self-reflexive wit, the program frequently incorporated topical references to current events, including a series-long story arc in which George is accused of treason for building mini-mansions for Saddam Hussein. George is likened to both Saddam Hussein and Osama Bin Laden in different episodes, and a running gag has him persecuted by ruthless investigators who use the Patriot Act to justify prying into the family accounts. Perhaps the most hilarious such reference comes in the episode "Sad Sack" when George's son-in-law Tobias (David Cross) accidentally e-mails photos of his testicles to the company computer, and the family's new lawyer mistakes them for evidence of WMD in Iraq. Under the auspices of the Patriot Act, the photos are seized from the Bluth family computer and circulated to the highest echelons of government. The joke suggests, quite literally, that the Bush administration had its head up its ass when it thought there were WMD in Iraq. Other episodes reference the Abu Ghraib photos and scandals involving the military's recruitment and equipment crises. All of this results in a dense satire designed to undermine the authority of established political, economic, and social leaders, especially those named George.

Whoopi likewise inserted direct references to contemporary political debates (the disputed 2000 election, the so-called values gap, and gay marriage, for example), parodied the racial profiling at the heart of the new security regime, and linked the Bush administration's economic policies to the collapse of Enron and the broader recession. The most infamous such episode was called "The Vast Right Wing Conspiracy" and featured a visit by President Bush to the Manhattan hotel run by Goldberg's character Mavis Rae. When the presidential entourage stops by to use the hotel's facilities, Mavis quips, "You mean Bush is in there doing to my bathroom what he did the economy?" When she tells her Iranian handyman, Nasim (Omid Djalili), to go get Bush out of her toilet, he responds: "Oh, yeah, right, an Irani immigrant telling the president to go . . . why don't I just run around the airport and yell, 'Yea, Jihad! Holy War! Holy War!'" The main thrust of the episode, however, focuses on how Mavis's attempts to speak truth to power are systematically derailed, even coopted, by a savvy political machine and a fawning press. When the president exits Mavis's bathroom, she moves in to give him a piece of her mind, and he identifies her as the singer of his favorite R&B song, calls her a "national treasure," and hugs her while mugging for the cameras. The very liberal Mavis not only finds her voice silenced; she is folded into the Republican press machinery as a photo op and icon of diversity.

The title of the episode, "The Vast Right Wing Conspiracy," alludes to Hillary Rodham Clinton's famous defense of her husband during the Monica Lewinsky scandal.[21] Its use in this episode tied contemporary politics to a history of media manipulation and grandstanding and implied that such behavior has eroded our political discourse. As if to prove Goldberg's point, conservatives denounced *Whoopi*, and particularly this episode, as part of an orchestrated campaign (a vast left-wing conspiracy) to drive President Bush from office. It was, they said, "Hollywood's in-kind contribution to the Kerry campaign."[22] In an interview with *The Today Show*'s Ann Curry, Goldberg responded to these charges with a plea for more open political discussion: "I just want the dialogue re-opened. I want people to start talking again and telling . . . I just feel like we've gotten very quiet."[23] On MSNBC's *Buchanan & Press*, she went even further, connecting the commercial media's lack of racial and ethnic diversity to its narrowing of political discourse.[24] By eliminating or trivializing other cultural experiences, she implied, Hollywood fails to depict the range of actually existing political opinion, abets the silencing of dissent, and reinforces the Bush administration's reimagination of the nation as a racially and politically homogenous "Homeland" under attack by a "dark threat." Goldberg designed *Whoopi* to be a corrective to these patterns. The mise-en-scène of the program, especially the casting and set design, produced a multiethnic image of New York that contrasted sharply with the all-white enclaves of shows such as *Friends, Seinfeld,* or *Sex in the City.* Narratively, the conflict centered around the tête-à-tête between the liberal Mavis and her conservative brother Courtney (Wren T. Brown), an ex–Enron employee forced to live with Mavis while hunting for work. By showing how individuals who look, think, and act differently can nevertheless learn to get along, the program challenged the assumption that Americans must be united in their beliefs in order to be united in their counterterrorism efforts.

One thing that these programs all have in common is a self-reflexive understanding of the media's role in the impoverishment of political discourse. Even *Arrested Development*, which is only tangentially concerned with current events, mocks the Fox-ification of mainstream news and the emphasis commercial news organs place on spectacle. *Whoopi*'s "Vast Right Wing Conspiracy" implies that the lines between scripted series and newscasts—entertainment and informational programming—are blurry in terms of their impact, as well. It links the homogenously white and studiously apolitical "America" constructed in entertainment genres, such as the sitcom, to the monotonously univocal coverage of political issues on the news. Like *The Daily Show, Whoopi* suggested that humor could be used to puncture the pretensions of those in authority and open political discourse to a broader range of voices and ideas. Taking for granted that the boundaries between informational and entertainment programming have become increasingly irrelevant, each of these programs struck back at the attempts by political authorities to co-opt popular culture for political purposes after 9/11. While only *The Daily Show* lasted beyond 2006 (*Whoopi* was canceled after only one season, and *Arrested Development* famously labored through three seasons based on critical acclaim and DVD sales), their collective use of humor for political ends did much to reinvigorate a climate of public debate stifled by tragedy and political paralysis on the left.[25]

Science Fiction and the Politics of Fear

The 2004 premiere of the ABC drama *Lost*, about the exploits of a multinational cast of characters stranded on a mysterious island after a catastrophe, marked the return to primetime network television of the hybrid sci-fi/horror genre that Keith Booker calls "strange TV."[26] Effectively a political allegory of contemporary times, "*Lost* bombarded the viewer with visual and narrative emblems that directly recalled 9/11 and evoked practices and sensibilities closely associated with the war on terror."[27] It focused on a spectacular plane crash and a group of survivors thrust into a "new world" populated by threatening "Others." Its visual density and narrative complexity, including an open-ended serial structure, multiple, intertwined story lines, and experiments with temporal distortion, produced a feeling of bewilderment and disorientation that recalled the themes of confusion and trauma so prevalent after 9/11. And the show used its status as political allegory to interrogate hot-button issues such as torture, preemptive violence, and the politics of enemy construction. Viewers were constantly kept guessing about the morality of the program's protagonists, many of whom were suspect citizens before the crash (one was a murderer, another a thief, and still another hired muscle for a mafia enterprise) and then proceeded to abuse each other mercilessly in the struggle to define leaders and allocate resources. We watch them torture and kill people they merely suspect of being "Others," and we speculate that "the Others" may ultimately be "the good guys" (as their leader proclaims at the end of season 2). In all we are called upon to think through the effects of fear on political and social practice.

Lost's breakout success spawned a bevy of imitators, and science fiction programming achieved an unusual cultural prominence in the years following. The 2005 network television season featured three new paranoid science fiction thrillers—NBC's *Surface*, CBS's *Threshold*, and ABC's *Invasion*—each of which featured an invasive alien force, a shadowy government conspiracy, and a generalized mood of paranoia and dread, leading one critic to describe 2005 as "the creepiest, most fear-mongering season of TV ever."[28] The cable channel Sci Fi (now Syfy) also debuted a retooled version of the *Battlestar Galactica* (BSG) franchise featuring a gritty mise-en-scène and dark narrative premise. Borrowing more from series such as *V* (NBC, 1984–1985), *The X-Files* (Fox, 1993–2002), and *Dark Skies* (NBC, 1996–1997), than sunny enterprises like *Star Trek* or the original BSG, these new programs spoke to the growing cultural malaise characteristic of the post–Abu Ghraib era. Finally, in 2006 CBS launched another paranoid science fiction thriller centered on a nuclear apocalypse that hits the heartland of America. Called *Jericho*, this series was less about the threat of outside invaders than the threat posed by the contemporary logics of civil governance. In the series, the rancorous political climate and privatization of government functions leads to a nuclear holocaust that leaves Jericho, Kansas, isolated and alone. As the citizens struggle to survive, they weigh questions about the relationship between individual survival and social community that cut to the heart of debates about the securitization of society post-9/11.

While none of these shows was directly concerned with the ongoing War on Terrorism, they were all clearly enabled by and responsive to the heightened sense of anxiety associated with life in the post-9/11 United States. Like all good science fiction, the programs work through processes of defamiliarization and displacement. By absorbing real-world issues into the relatively "safe" realm of fantasy, science fiction distances individuals from social crises and creates a space for alternative solutions to emerge. Its relatively marginal cultural status frees the genre to express ideas suppressed in the political public sphere. As *Threshold*'s executive producer David Goyer put it, science fiction offers people "ways of talking about [social] issues" more openly and complexly.[29] Though these programs addressed issues of security and governance in different ways, they all sought to push the logics of fear and paranoia to their limits in order to deconstruct the dynamics of securitization that followed from the use of fear as a political stimulant post-9/11. The analysis will begin by surveying the personalization of fear post-9/11 and how that process was represented in the series *Surface* and *Invasion*. It will then examine *Threshold*'s commentary on the logics of security that follow from such an intimate construction of the terrorist threat. Finally, it will take up the critique of specific tactics of security embraced by the Bush administration in its War on Terrorism as these were refracted through the allegories of occupation in *Jericho* and *Battlestar Galactica*.

Terror Invades the Home(land): *Surface, Invasion,* and the Personalization of Fear

The Bush administration regularly used the personalization of fear to pre-empt criticism of its more illicit practices of counterterrorism, such as extreme rendition, indefinite detention, and the use of "harsh" interrogation tactics. On the fifth anniversary of the attacks, for example, President Bush appeared on *The Today Show* to defend his administration's use of waterboarding, claiming that "what this government has done is to take steps necessary to protect you and your family. . . . These are people that want to come and kill your family."[30] Following the edicts of political philosopher Thomas Hobbes (via Leo Strauss), who viewed fear as a social galvanizer, the Bush administration cultivated popular fear and used it to persuade people that they have a common interest in maintaining the social order.[31] The family became a privileged target of such affect modulation because it is both a key site of emotional attachment in the United States and an atomized unit defined through exclusivity and paranoia. Fear and family life simply go together. Family bonds are solidified in relation to those outside the family who constitute a threat to its existence.[32] The Bush administration simply exploited the consonance of fear and family life to reinforce an affective allegiance to the state. They stimulated the body politic in order to bypass the moment of deliberative reflection that might otherwise complicate people's political choices.

Surface and *Invasion* dramatized the Bush administration's rhetoric of personal insecurity and, thus, made it available for contemplation. The family is the central target of the invasive alien forces in both programs, and both programs work toward the recuperation of the family as a sanctuary from public turmoil. However, the outcomes of these processes are radically different in each program. *Surface* offers a Hobbesian vision of the social order as inherently conflicted and prone to discord. Fear of a common foe is presented as the *only* viable means of constructing social solidarity. Shared fear drives the protagonists to pursue the social good, even as those around them ridicule their belief in the watery menace lurking off the nation's shores. Families literally dissolve without a shared ethic of fear and are reconstituted only when fear is fully embraced. In short, *Surface* demonstrates how the Bush administration's politics of fear works. *Invasion*, on the other hand, acknowledges the politics of fear only to challenge the logical presuppositions of the Hobbesian worldview undergirding it. *Invasion* offers a complex view of the family and society as interconnected and hybridized. Its vision is "post-Hobbesian" and attuned to the dynamics of global interchange denied by the Manichean logics of good and evil used to rationalize the fortification of America.

Surface follows the parallel exploits of three Americans who all separately encounter a new breed of mysterious sea creature. Dr. Laura Daughtery (Lake Bell), a marine biologist from California, Rich Connelly (Jay Ferguson), a concerned family man from Louisiana, and Miles Barnett (Carter Jenkins), a curious teen from North Carolina, all encounter the creatures by accident and are then driven to uncover the truth about them even at the expense of their families. They are opposed in this pursuit by quasi-governmental and corporate agents who want to suppress all knowledge of the species and the threat it poses. The promiscuous use of science fiction clichés by first-time producers Josh and Jonas Pate makes *Surface* an uneven and ultimately unsatisfying exploration of the unknown.[33] Yet, the program does capture something of the political dynamics of fear embraced post-9/11 as a route to national regeneration. The sea monsters, which are dispersed throughout the world but seemingly fixated on the United States, clearly offer a metaphor for global terrorism as constructed by the Bush administration. Having nested in the Pacific, the Atlantic, and the Gulf of Mexico, the creatures literally surround and beset the nation. Their destructive actions are unmotivated except by an instinctive "evil" ingrained in their physical makeup. These creatures closely approximate the Bush administration's depiction of Al Qaeda and other terrorist organizations as an amorphous scourge bent on destroying the United States for no good reason.

The narrative progression of *Surface* also illustrates the Hobbesian faith in the ability of fear, if wielded properly, to engender social unity and revitalization. It does this in two ways. First, *Surface* uses a parallel narrative structure to literally segregate the protagonists from each other until the finale. This narrative segregation evokes the divisive nature of modern society, which Hobbes and his followers view as the central threat to social stability and security. The narrative/social divisions in *Surface* are healed through the intercession of fear, as the sea creatures quite literally create the conditions that drive the protagonists and their separate story lines together. By instinctively boring into the Earth's crust in search of heat, the creatures set off an underwater avalanche that results in a tsunami, which forces the protagonists into each other's arms for protection.

Second, Surface personalizes the nature of the threat, directing it against "flawed" families, in order to argue for the renewal of a more clearly patriarchal mode of social organization. In that sense, Surface echoes certain aspects of the response to 9/11 in U.S. public discourse. As feminist critics have shown, the attacks were depicted in public discourse as an act of "violation" or "rape" from which only a remilitarized, hence remasculinized, state could save us.[34] Surface literalizes the gendered dynamics of this discourse by explicitly gendering the "threat" to the United States as feminine. It depicts rampaging femininity—in the form of the sea creatures— as the central danger. The menacing monsters in Surface are clearly associated with attributes and values assigned in U.S. culture to women and femininity. The creatures lay eggs, nest, and are driven by an "instinctual" desire to reproduce. They also communicate with each other empathically and use their bodies, specifically an ambient electrical charge, to shock, kill, and devour only men. Contact with these rampaging feminine creatures leaves most men either dead or symbolically emasculated. Rich Connelly, for instance, becomes obsessed with the sea creatures after his brother is killed by one. Unable to accept this loss, Rich suffers from stress-induced nightmares in which he sees visions of vortices. His psychological and emotional weakness eventually alienates his wife and leads him to abandon his family to pursue information about the creatures. The visual symmetry between the vortex of his dreams and a female vagina makes the implicit connection between weakness and "unmanly" behavior explicit, marking his distress as a form of feminization. His over-the-top performance of masculine toughness in the remainder of the series reads as a compensatory gesture.

Surface exhibits patriarchal anxieties through its depiction of "strong women," as well. Women in the series are systematically chided for attempt- ing to gain familial and social authority; their efforts to control their lives are always depicted as coming at the expense of men and children. Miles's mother, for example, is portrayed as overbearing and self-absorbed. As a working woman, she both neglects her children and emasculates her husband, leading Miles to become confused and "act out." The lead scientist, Dr. Daughtery, is similarly taken to task for preferring her career to her family. Though she is located at the center of the narrative and associated with "masculine" attributes such as intelligence, rationality, and "action," she is also punished repeatedly for her gender insubordination. For example, to discredit her account of the sea creatures, the shady government agents make it appear that she has plagiarized her dissertation (episode 3). Later when she captures video of the sea creatures and tries to air it on national television, the media frame her as a hysteric attempting to perpetrate a hoax on the public (episode 11). While Dr. Daughtery is explicitly positioned as a hero within the narrative, then, her heroism is depicted as damaging to her career, her family, and the American people. The program's ambivalence with regard to the status of its heroine is a symptom of its larger investment in notions of social authority as properly patriarchal. Overall, Surface tends to present femininity and feminization as key threats to social stability and to offer masculinity and remasculinization as the solutions to social problems.

The final episode naturalizes the reassertion of patriarchy by tying it to a fear of rampaging femininity. By literally undermining the nation's foundation (the Earth's crust), the monsters set off a tsunami that wipes out the lower eastern seaboard, including the town of Wilmington, North Carolina, where the Barnetts live. Miles, his girlfriend, Rich, and Dr. Daughtery all end up at ground zero and must flee the tsunami together. When their sedan runs out of gas, they take refuge in the bell tower of a nearby church, as the waves engulf the town. The shared experience of fear unites these disparate characters into a cohesive unit and washes away the self-indulgence and pettiness that previously characterized their lives. Indeed, their separate encounters with the creatures have been personally revivifying, giving them something "worthwhile" to focus their energies on. Fear not only gives them a purpose; it promises to revitalize the patriarchal nuclear family model, for the final image is of precisely such an atomized family (symbolically a Mother, Father, Son, and Daughter) facing the dawn of a "new world" alone. As the camera zooms out, the nuclear family appears as an island in a sea of troubles. It is an image that condenses the connections between family, fear, and state power in the post-9/11 context, and it was made all the more indelible when NBC canceled the series shortly after this conclusion.

Despite the program's salutary critique of government secrecy and duplicity, then, Surface largely echoes the Bush administration's framing of 9/11 as an "opportunity" for national and familial renewal.[35] It is the televisual equivalent of the injunction to "live your lives and hug your children" and let the state take care of the terrorists. Patriarchal power reemerges here as the protector of home and family life, which, in turn, is presented as the only viable bulwark against chaos. Thus, Surface ends up advocating the same

In *Surface* (NBC, 2005–2006) the sea creatures undermine the nation's foundation and set off a tsunami that drives the protagonists into each other's arms. The series ends with this shot of a reconstituted nuclear family facing the dawn of a new world. ("Episode 15," 2/6/2006)

counterrevolutionary strategies as neoconservative politicians in the United States: centralize authority and make the family into an idol of worship so as to dissuade individuals from contesting the authority of the state.

The CBS drama *Invasion* also foregrounds the family as the target of terror, but it does not presume the family is coherent, self-contained, or properly isolated from "others." Rather, it presents a view of the family as inescapably connected to others in the world. This is a "post-Hobbesian" worldview attuned to the dynamics of global interchange suppressed by the Bush administration's depiction of the War on Terrorism as a "clash of civilizations." The hybrid nature of the monsters in *Invasion* belies the Manichean logics separating "us" from "them" and dictating that "we" are good and "they" are evil. Indeed, it is possible to argue that *Invasion* constitutes an exploration of imperial guilt designed to short-circuit the antidemocratic politics of fear embraced as the route to salvation post-9/11. Its sympathetic portrayal of the aliens, who are really just alienated humans, represents a rejection of the apocalyptic vision proffered by the Bush administration to legitimate its aggressive foreign policy and the remilitarization of U.S. society this requires. Its more ambiguous conclusion questions whether one can construct a democratic social order using authoritarian power.

There are two primary ways in which *Invasion* challenges the Bush administration's politics of fear. First, it offers a complex depiction of the family that
suggests its atomization leads not to salvation but to a debilitating alienation.
Second, it demonstrates the catastrophic effects on domestic society caused
by the centralization and militarization of state power. By blurring the generic
boundaries between family melodrama and science fiction, *Invasion* also blurs
the boundaries between us/them, inside/outside, that provide the warrant for
the vision of America as a coherent and stable "Homeland." The narrative
centers on a *Body Snatchers*–like "invasion" and reconstruction of the aptly
named town of Homestead, Florida. Homestead is modeled on a real town,
which was wiped out by Hurricane Andrew in 1992, but in *Invasion* the town
takes on allegorical overtones. Its characters are more like small-town social
types—the sheriff, the priest, the doctor, the journalist, and so on—than individuals, which makes the town feel like a microcosm of the American Homeland. In that most of these figures are also related to each other, Homestead
becomes an enlarged image of the (national) family. Co–executive producer
Thomas Schlamme (former co–executive producer of *The West Wing*) claims
the hybrid aliens are really just metaphors for the blended families at the center of the narrative.[36] Just as blended families, who lack the naturalized ties of
blood and history, must consciously define their connections and learn to get
along, so the town of Homestead must actively renegotiate its communal relations when half its citizens become hybridized during a hurricane.

Though the name of the hurricane, "Hurricane Eve," indicates the dawn of
a new, fallen age of human society (caused by female betrayal, no less), Homestead and its families have, in fact, already been hybridized. Sheriff Tom Underlay (William Fichtner), who was cloned following a plane crash nine years
earlier, is the snake in this garden. Viewing his new body as an improvement
over the old, he has actively hybridized others in the community and begun
training a hybrid army to maintain order following subsequent invasions.
This narrative innovation undermines arguments about the extremity or nov-
elty of the conditions of terror that threaten the families; it also argues against
the use of drastic measures to contain the aliens, who are indistinguishable
from humans anyway. As the hybrids integrate into normal society, it becomes
increasingly difficult to tell who is and is not an alien and, more importantly,
who is and is not a threat. The hybrids are often sympathetic characters. For
example, Sheriff Underlay and his wife Mariel (Kari Matchett) may be aliens,
but they are also devoted parents struggling to blend their families and nur-
ture their children. The local priest is a hybrid, as are several of his parish-

ioners and the hyper-Christian deputy sheriff. These are good people struggling to cope with unexpected turmoil, and the lead characters empathize
with their plight. "These people have changed, OK, but what have they done?"
says Mariel's ex-husband Russell (Eddie Cibrian), "Until we know they are a
threat to us, I'm not going to start hating everybody." At first an active partici-
pant in the hybridization of others, Sheriff Underlay eventually reveals himself
to be a moderate voice of reason, as well. This moderation belies the depiction
of politics as a "clash of civilizations" in which participants must align themselves with one side or another. In fact, *Invasion* suggests that such an oppositional politics instantiates a type of fascist behavior that cannot possibly be
used to serve democratic ends.

As the series builds to its climax, the portraits of "us" and "them," "good"
and "evil," become increasingly complicated. Not only are the aliens more
complex and less threatening than they first appear, but the humans become
increasingly more cruel and despotic. For example, when Russell's son Jesse
(Evan Peters) realizes his mother is a hybrid, he lashes out at random aliens.
With a group of friends, he helps kidnap and brutally assault the deputy sheriff
simply for being "one of them." Though it is the hybrids who are rumored to
be self-cannibalizing, it is the human society that seems to "[turn] in on itself"
in an orgy of violence, sacrificing its morality for a fleeting illusion of security.

Not content to stop with this intimate indictment of militarized violence,
the program concludes by staging a second "invasion" that clarifies the stakes
involved in the conception of collective fear and security. In the finale, Sheriff
Underlay sees his authority over the aliens challenged by an armed faction of
hybrid zealots directed by charismatic ex-CIA operative Eli Szura (James
Frain). Szura believes the aliens are a superior race destined to "win" the Dar-
winian struggle for survival. To hasten the process of evolution, he decides to
eliminate the humans entirely by rounding them up and throwing them into
the sea, where they will become hybridized. Szura's view of the world is fundamentally Hobbesian, admitting of no remedy to social conflict other than
increased militarism and authoritarianism. *Invasion* clearly uses this character
to explore the logical results of the Bush administration's own politics of fear.
Through Szura, the program shows how rampant fear and paranoia can lead
individuals to embrace fascism as a solution to social problems. Co–executive
producer Lawrence Trilling admits that Szura is designed to show how "moving forward in a visionary way" can sometimes lead to blindness and brutality.[37] A charismatic leader, Szura virtually channels President Bush when he
says: "I believe we are the seed of a future that no man could ever imagine. But

this future is not guaranteed. There are those who will oppose it, oppose us. To reach this future, we will need the strength that comes from our sticking together. Our very survival depends upon our unity" ("Re-Evolution").

The conflict between Szura and the duo of Underlay and Russell is a struggle between competing models of social organization that serves as a sort of imaginary referendum on the Bush administration's global politics. Szura presumes difference is deficiency and, therefore, seeks to eliminate difference by engineering a global monoculture. The invocation of eugenics raises the specter of Nazism and suggests that the centralization of authority under a charismatic leader (no matter how "righteous" that leader's actions may seem) leads inevitably to fascism. Underlay and Russell, on the other hand, work together to preserve human difference, rescuing the remnants of the human community from Szura's henchmen. The struggle to preserve biodiversity in *Invasion* is really a parable about the necessity of pluralism and tolerance in an interconnected global society. "Just because someone is different," as Underlay says, "[this] doesn't make them [*sic*] a monster." Again, the final image is telling. When Russell's pregnant wife is accidentally killed, Underlay saves her by taking her to the water to be hybridized. Thus, the program suggests that personal and national regeneration results from transcultural communication and exchange, rather than fear. A recognition of and respect for others in the world provides a better guide to ethical action in an inescapably global context. The cyclical story arc of *Invasion*, which begins and ends with a hurricane, reinforces this message by demonstrating that crises and conflicts are endemic to social life. They do not necessarily "change everything" or create a "new world." Rather, they change our perspective on the old world, its institutions and relations. Crises should cause us to reassess our values, but not to abandon them out of paranoia and despair.

Invasion uses the family melodrama not to exacerbate fear or call for an apocalyptic social renewal, but to undermine the processes of disavowal structuring the public response to terrorism in the United States. It brings the horror and anxiety displaced onto an exterior "evil" after 9/11 back into the "American home" and, in that way, seeks to de-ontologize terror by connecting it (metaphorically, of course) to U.S. modes of being in the world. In a nutshell, *Invasion* reminds us that "horror is not something from out there, something strange, marginal ex-centric, the mark of a force from elsewhere, the in-human" but rather "part of us, caused by us."[38] By relocating "monstrosity" within a social context, *Invasion* seeks to challenge the abstract politics of fear used to justify the United States' militarized response to 9/11.

The New World of Monsters: Humanity Confronts
Its Future in *Threshold*

The CBS program Threshold shares aspects of both *Surface* and *Invasion*. On the one hand, it uses its alien invasion to detail the exceptional quality of the threat to U.S. security and to argue for perpetual vigilance. On the other hand, its aliens are also human hybrids that confuse the lines between "us" and "them" in ways that make the recourse to violence to combat the "monsters" appear problematic. Whereas references to Homeland Security are oblique in *Surface* and *Invasion*, however, they are direct in Threshold, which sets its action behind the closed doors and blackened windows of the national security state apparatus and asks us to sympathize with the fabled "men in black"—those shadowy government agents responsible for controlling popular knowledge of alien life by any means necessary. This unusual perspective enables the program to delve more deeply into the connections between enemy construction and the operations of state power. Specifically, it shows how the production of the enemy (as monster) in security discourse also produces a particular conception of "normality," or proper citizen-subjectivity. The amorphous and omnipresent alien-enemies of Threshold induce a form of paranoia that makes repressive social authority appear necessary and inevitable. However, by depicting the extreme measures of interdiction adopted to combat this contagion of fear, Threshold also vividly illustrates the costs of such a worldview.

The program focuses on the covert government task force impaneled to hunt down and contain an alien menace. At the head of the task force is a contingency analyst named Molly Caffrey (Carla Gugino) whose dedication to the job makes her the hero of the tale. Like Dr. Daughtery, she is a powerful, capable woman, who sacrifices her private life to her career aspirations. Unlike Dr. Daughtery, however, she is not censured for this. Rather, her ascetic existence and absolute subjection to the state define the proper mode of citizenship in an age of terror. Personal lives compromise security and make it impossible to maintain vigilance, as the experiences of Caffrey's more well-rounded male colleagues indicate. Caffrey's total dedication, on the other hand, guarantees the project's success (or so we are told in the final episode). Thus, while she may be female, and even occasionally feminized in the narrative (often rendered a victim of violence, for example), Dr. Caffrey's complete alignment with a masculinized version of state authority makes her unambivalently the "hero" of the tale. Indeed, she is the contingency analyst of Donald Rumsfeld's wet dreams. Charged with anticipating "the unknown, the uncertain, the unseen, and the unexpected," she makes sure government agents are prepared for any possible outbreak of evil.[39] Her job, as she explains to a class of FBI trainees in the pilot episode, is "to scare [people,]" to "stare into the face of the unknown and make damn sure we don't blink" ("Trees Made of Glass").

Caffrey has her work cut out for her with the slippery aliens of Threshold, though. These aliens employ a decentered model of networked sociality designed to evade hierarchical mechanisms of control. They are mobile, flexible, and seemingly invisible; they have no leader and attack without coordination, and they are literally a contagion. Like a virus, they propagate by piggybacking the "code of life." Using a fractal pattern embedded in an audio signal, the aliens "unzip" human DNA and reassemble it as a triple helix. Humans who survive the transformation develop super strength and endurance (hybrid vigor) and the ability to appear and disappear at will, making them hard to target. Not only are these hybrids indistinguishable from the population, their motives are unclear, and their actions are unpredictable. While they share a goal—to "bioform" the earth—they each pursue this goal in different ways, and the elimination of one alien-enemy does not prevent the group from achieving its goals. The allusions to Al Qaeda, with its distributed network structure and DIY ethos, could not be plainer.

The inscrutability and indeterminacy of these networked "monsters" makes the Threshold agents legitimately paranoid and sanctions the use of extreme measures of social regulation. To preempt the threat, the agents adopt a strategy of total information awareness and control (a strategy not unlike that advocated by the analysts charged with combating networked social movements in real life).[40] Among other things, the Threshold agents monitor civilian phone conversations, arrest civilians who gain access to information about the threat, turn high-tech weaponry against U.S. citizens to stop the signal's transmission, and engage in a coordinated disinformation campaign to deflect public attention from the project. When a senator steals the alien signal and broadcasts it on the national security advisor's plane, for example, the steely Caffrey orders the plane to be shot down ("The Order"). In "Pulse," Caffrey stops the signal by using an electromagnetic pulse weapon to wipe out all electronic devices within a 70-mile radius of Miami. Finally, the Threshold agents themselves have their movements policed, their e-mail censored, their homes bugged, and their bodies implanted with tracking devices. The violation of individual privacy rights is justified in the name of ensuring the security of the team, which it does successfully on several occasions. However, the

In *Threshold* (CBS, 2005), contingency analyst Molly Caffrey must stop the ultimate networked social movement—one that uses the human code of life (DNA) to transmit rebellious signals.

monetary, moral, and social costs of these measures are clearly shown to be high.

The draconian measures adopted to control information in *Threshold* are designed to transform thresholds, or gateways, back into police-able boundaries. By ensuring the integrity of the boundaries between inside and outside, us and them, they are supposed to alleviate social anxiety by locating danger in concrete, targetable bodies. These efforts are doomed to failure, however, because the aliens are not susceptible to reterritorialization in this way. As in *Invasion*, the concept of human bioforming radically destabilizes the boundaries between "us" and "them" and reminds the agents of their interconnection to others in the world. A later episode ("Outbreak") suggests the aliens may even be attempting to save humanity. Capt. Manning (Scott MacDonald), one of the original infectees, tells Caffrey that her plan is dangerous: "If you win, you'll sentence everyone on this planet to death." He tells her that two neutron stars have collided out in space and the radiation will reach Earth within six years, destroying humanity unless "we alter our physiology." "Believe it or not," he says, "every life is precious to us too. That's why we came. . . . What's happening is a gift. It's the next step in your evolution. . . . You need us. Without our help, all human life will be extinguished." While Caffrey is rightfully skeptical about his story, the introduction of this possibility alters the perception of the aliens just enough to disallow an absolute identification of "us" with "good" and "them" with "evil." More importantly, the exchange suggests that hybrid intermixture may be beneficial to society. Metaphorically, this exchange warns against a rigid reterritorialization of global social life. Boundaries may ensure purity, but purity may not equal vigor.

Threshold's amorphous, interstitial, unpredictable monsters provide "images for thinking about" the political uses of fear in the post-9/11 context.[41] The Bush administration attempted to mystify the nature of the terrorist enemy—depicting terrorists as inscrutable monsters motivated by "evil" rather than politics—in order to magnify social anxiety and turn it to its own advantage. By insisting that we live in a dangerous world filled with shadowy, unpredictable enemies, they convinced us to accept the centralization of authority and the abdication of the rule of law. Threshold, more than the other spooky TV programs, confronts this monstrous configuration of power with the truth of its effects. It shows how such a nightmare vision of the enemy instantiates a social order dedicated to the pursuit of total war. Such war knows no boundaries and makes no distinctions between "us" and "them." It "reaches into the finest details of daily life" and reengineers our behaviors to maximize social control.[42] Every "outbreak" of terror legitimates additional measures of repression directed at both the terrorists and those who are terrified. The process, as Caffrey warns, is potentially endless: "As of today, we'll have agents on the streets 24/7. We'll also begin a city-wide wire-tap. The public will be under strict surveillance. Their civil rights curtailed until we regain control. As the threat escalates, so does our response." By inviting us to identify with the agents of our own subjection, Threshold induces a Brechtian alienation effect whereby we are forced to confront the consequences of our own fear. To say the least, the program articulates misgivings about the Bush administration's determination to make the Homeland more secure by making it less open, transparent, democratic, and peaceful.

Fables of Occupation: *Jericho* and *Battlestar Galactica*

Surface, Invasion, and Threshold set out to interrogate aspects of the post-9/11 culture of fear by displacing the sources of anxiety into the realm of fantasy. They show how, in the words of former national security advisor Zbigniew Brzezinski, "fear obscures reason, intensifies emotions, and makes it easier for demagogic politicians to mobilize the public on behalf of the policies they want to pursue."[43] *Battlestar Galactica* and *Jericho* pick up where these series left off by examining the state of U.S. political culture in the aftermath of the bloody occupation of Iraq. They frequently incorporate references to the innovations in governance developed by the Bush administration to meet the challenges of national insecurity, including the use of private contractors and tactics of preemption, indefinite detention, and torture. Like *Threshold*, these series address the question of what it means to live in a state of permanent exception, which grants political authorities virtually unlimited reign to determine social policy. Unlike *Threshold*, however, they do not presume the necessity and benevolence of authoritarian governance, and they do not ask us to identify with its agents. Instead, they ask us to identify with the situations and to consider what our own responses would be under the circumstances.

Both programs are driven by limit-cases, events that define the outermost reaches of experience as we have known it. They take place after nuclear apocalypses—one in the distant future of a planet that looks like, but is not, Earth (BSG) and the other in a contemporary incarnation of mainstream America (*Jericho*). Both apocalypses are triggered by "sleeper" agents—individuals who have infiltrated the governmental structures and turned the government's own security systems against it. And, in both series, the remnants of humanity are left to struggle for survival in the wreckage of what was once civilization. The extremity of these situations brings an end to life as it had been known and lived and initiates a search for new social rules and regulations. Residual notions of democracy, liberty, and equality vie against the imminent needs for survival and security, and this plays out on a weekly basis. Put simply, the extremity of the situation is designed to be thought-provoking, not reassuring. "The point of the show," according to *Jericho* executive producer Jon Turteltaub, "is to say *if* this happened, what would happen? What would you do?" To what lengths would you go to ensure your own survival, and what tradeoffs would you be willing to make to ensure the survival of others?[44]

Of the two series, *Jericho* went the furthest in answering these ethical dilemmas, and it was, in this respect, the less interesting of the two series. It was a better series than most critics initially gave it credit for being, however. Early reviews dismissed it as overly sentimental and morally unambiguous. *Jericho* offers "doomsday as soap opera," complained *Time*'s James Poniewozik. "The survivors have affairs and family fights; teenagers flirt and throw parties. Chicago may be burning, but somewhere on the Great Plains, The O.C. lives." He and other urban critics were particularly suspicious of the heartland set-

In *Jericho* (CBS, 2006–2008), a nuclear explosion brings an end to "normal" life and initiates a search for new social rules and regulations. The series asks: to what lengths would you go to ensure your own survival? ("Pilot," 9/20/2006)

ting and the fact that the targets of attack were major cities: "In *Jericho's* yet-unseen outside world, millions of people in cities like mine could be inciner-ated, starving or in anarchy. But in at least one small town, life goes on, to a pop sound track, without us—without, in fact, much time or verbiage spent mourning us." Tad Friend of the *New Yorker* concurred: "The town's incuriosity about the larger world . . . shades at times into an unsavory suggestion that all those Gomorrahs in cinders—New York, Chicago, Atlanta—deserved their fate." As Ginia Bellafante observes, however, "a large part of the show's ap-peal comes simply from its refusal to play games of coastal narcissism. It gives voice to the fears of people who don't live in Boston or Miami or Los An-geles, and it aims to make them feel they matter."[45] Thus, the show defines in-security in broader terms, including economic insecurity as a common, and often more troubling, source of anxiety than terrorism. While it is possible to quibble with the slick design of the show—its overuse of sappy pop songs, its too bright lighting, and its squeaky-clean characters—an examination of its content reveals ideological and moral complexity that defies the simple "red state–blue state" dichotomy of conservative and liberal.

In the first few episodes, the survivors struggle to find shelter, clean water, and provisions for the town to survive. They confront bandits and a refugee crisis, and they have to decide how porous they want their town's borders to be. The mayor, Johnston Green (Gerald McRaney), and his two sons, Jake (Skeet Ulrich) and Eric (Kenneth Mitchell), are the resident voices of moderation, in contrast to the more right-wing future-mayor Gray Anderson (Michael Gaston), who gets elected on the back of a Bush-like promise to bring "swift and sure justice" to those who prey on Jericho and its citizens ("Vox Populi"). The political rivalry between the Greens and Anderson initiates one of the major strands of discussion in season 1—what are the limits of executive authority in a time of crisis? When the local grocer is killed, for example, Mayor Anderson organizes a posse to go after a well-known local thug and tries to hang him without a proper trial (or evidence). "As mayor," he claims, "I formed a tribunal and found Jonah guilty." Jake calls it cold-blooded murder and shames Gray into renouncing his bloodlust in favor of a more temperate and practical solution, exile. Johnston Green arrives to make the lesson clear: "[Democracy's] easy when things are going alright, but when you're scared or mad, it gets a lot harder." Season 1 also asks what sort of desperation might lead a man to commit terrorism ("One Man's Terrorist") and entertains the question: is a preemptive war waged to secure resources just? The season 1 cliffhanger centers on a civil war between the folks of Jericho and the neighboring town of New Bern, where the sheriff has installed himself as dictator and decided to extort food and supplies from Jericho through threat of war. The siege not only recalls the biblical siege of Jericho; it references the U.S. military occupation of Iraq, and particularly the sieges of Sadr City and Fallujah in 2004, which killed several hundred civilians. The analogy to Iraq raises questions about the motives for that war and asks Americans to imagine what they would do if their own homes and families were threatened by a foreign aggressor.

The second season of *Jericho* becomes even more direct and pointed in its critique of Bush-era policies, particularly its centralization of authority in the executive branch and its use of private contractors to wage war with little accountability. Bellafante calls it "a biting rebuke of excessive militarism, executive privilege and pre-emption." We learn that a faction within the U.S. government planned the nuclear attack, then blamed it on Iran and North Korea and launched military strikes against both countries. A new government, called the "Allied States of America," assumes control over the western territories. It is "led by a boyish puppet president but run by a malevolent senior statesman," who looks suspiciously like Vice President Dick Cheney and has ties to the private contracting industry.[46] The new government changes the flag, turns the press into a megaphone for its policies, rewrites the history textbooks to reflect ultraconservative orthodoxy (the section on post–World War II history is named "the decline and fall of the first republic," and, according to one character, "talks about how the United States died because we got weak"), and tries to rewrite the Constitution. Jericho becomes an occupied territory overseen by a military unit and governed by a private contractor called Jennings & Rall (an obvious reference to Halliburton subsidiary Kellogg Brown & Root, the private contractor that ran logistics for the U.S. military operation in Iraq). J&R controls the town's access to electricity, food, water, and medical supplies, and it maintains a private security force that competes with the military for control of the population. This security force, called Ravenswood, withholds supplies to control the population and shoots people without cause or accountability. Jake, who once worked for J&R in Iraq and participated in a Blackwater-style massacre of civilians, drives home the point that such contractors operate outside of the law by design: "When [the shooting] was done," he tells Major Beck (Esai Morales), "there were six gunmen dead, four bystanders, one of them was a 12-year-old girl. . . . There were no repercussions. None. . . . The company wanted it kept quiet, so it was. Do you understand? Do you understand who we're dealing with? These guys, they don't answer to anybody" ("Jennings & Rall"). Goetz (D. B. Sweeney), the leader of the Ravenswood goon squad, certainly acts with impunity, stealing supplies and money from his employer and killing one of the more beloved characters—the deaf sister of farmboy hero Stanley Richmond (Brad Beyer)—to cover it up ("Oversight"). When the general refuses to prosecute Goetz, who claims self-defense, Stanley shoots Goetz in the head à la the famous on-air assassination of Vietcong insurgent Nguyen Van Lem by South Vietnamese General Nguyen Ngoc Loan in 1968 ("Termination for Cause"). What is more astounding than the moral disfigurement of Stanley, though, is the decision to cover up Stanley's crime by giving Goetz's body to the more radical insurgents from New Bern, who string him up from a tree at the edge of the town. Anyone remotely familiar with events in Iraq will recognize this as a reference to the hanging of the bodies of four Blackwater contractors from a bridge in Fallujah in 2004. As in that real-life incident, the hanging sparks a military crackdown and the use of collective punishment in the form of the indefinite detention and "harsh interrogation" of our hero Jake, who is subjected to food-, water-, and sleep-deprivation tactics reminiscent of Abu Ghraib and Guantanamo.

Jericho's producers self-consciously incorporated historical references, such as this homage to the deaths of four Blackwater contractors in Fallujah, Iraq (2004), to spark ethical contemplation of the legitimacy of military occupation. ("Termination for Cause," 3/11/2008)

Thus, in its second season, *Jericho* places the heartland under imagined assault by a military occupation that operates outside the law and with no accountability. The occupation is run for-profit by corporate interests so closely allied with the ruling political regime as to be "one and the same" ("Termination for Cause"). That political regime is unelected and seeks to alter the Constitution's stringent protections of privacy, property, and person, to ensure its grip on power. It characterizes all dissent as "insurgent activity," uses repression as a preferred means of social control, and views diplomacy as a form of weakness. By transplanting the experience of military occupation to the heartland, *Jericho* asks viewers to consider what they might do if a foreign force invaded their territory, destabilized their government, and occupied their communities. It uses direct references to American history in its episode titles ("Semper Fidelis," "One If by Land," "Why We Fight," etc.), its narrative content, and its visual iconography to jolt viewers into making connections between the American Revolution and the insurgency in Iraq. It also uses frequent and liberal references to the Bible to add symbolic weight to its construction of Jericho's people as exceptional moral agents, the so-called salt of the earth. Thus, it very much embraces the assumption that America is a unique nation, predestined to lead the world by moral example, and this is its biggest weakness. Like other expressions of "republican crisis" that emerged after 2004, *Jericho* is content to depict the reigning regime as a political anomaly, rather than a natural extension of the institutions of democratic governance as they have evolved in the United States. *Jericho* is no call for revolution; rather, it is a nostalgic plea for reform that presumes American institutions and practices worked just fine before the Bush team broke them.

Battlestar Galactica sets out to do something far more radical: interrogate the very terms and conditions of the American Creed.[47] Whereas *Jericho* "picks fights and takes stands,"[48] BSG employs a more open-ended and innovative storytelling structure that leads to a deliberately more ambiguous political orientation. As executive producer Ronald Moore puts it, "the show is fairly agnostic [politically]. [It] occasionally tilts you in one direction or another but overall the show is meant to make you think. It is meant to make you question things. It's meant to keep you off-balance and unsettled more than anything else."[49] The project begins with the jettisoning of the generic clichés of the space opera, including the use of aliens as antagonists and the tendency to depict technology as sublimely attractive and functional. There is no pop soundtrack here, no shiny gadgets, few steady shots, and no characters with an unerring moral compass. The mise-en-scène is dirty, broken-down, and often reminiscent of contemporary America. The lighting is stark, and the cinematography is often handheld, lending the fiction a documentary quality. In keeping with this murky staging, the narrative heroes are also ethically challenged, fallible human beings. They drink, they smoke, they gamble, they abuse each other, and they abuse their enemies. Though many of them embrace religion as a guide, this doesn't prevent them from violating their moral codes when the situation calls for it. Indeed, there is something existential about *Battlestar Galactica*.[50] It assumes morality is contingent and uses its various social crises to explore where, when, and why one might want to draw a line *despite* the absence of a singular Truth or a singular God to secure it (the Cylons are in a much better position in this respect, for they believe in "one true god" who guides their actions).

Dubbed "The West Wing in space," BSG received a lot of critical attention for its self-conscious examination of contemporary political events.[51] Moore has been especially vocal about his use of the show to interrogate the collective experience of trauma on 9/11: "A lot of the emotional buttons, a lot of the plot elements, a lot of just how people react was definitely informed by the 9/11 experience and the war on terrorism."[52] Moore innovated the use of online podcasts to spark fan engagement, providing behind-the-scenes commentary for each episode as it aired, and he used many of these podcasts to prime viewers to take notice of the political content. Of the episode "Colonial Day," for example, Moore explained that the fictional discussion of the limits of executive authority was designed to speak to contemporary concerns about the centralization of authority in an imperial presidency: "The War on Terrorism, the assertion of executive power in all circumstances, . . . the long march toward extreme authoritarian governance . . . those ideas are in the show," he said, "because those ideas are in the culture right now."[53] What facilitated this form of political and ethical engagement, more than anything else, though, was Moore's decision to change the nature of the Cylon attackers from alien-derived robots to the all-too-human progeny of man.

In the original series, the Cylons were clunky, metallic machines, who differed quite obviously from the human protagonists. They were built by an alien race for military purposes and wiped out humanity simply because their programming told them to. Thus, the Cylons remained safely "other" throughout the series, and the lines between good and evil were bright and hard as was typical of Cold War science fiction. In Moore's reinvented series, the Cylons rebelled on their own, evolved on their own, and returned, after a forty-year sojourn in the wilderness of space (Israelites, anyone?), to attack the humans who once enslaved them. The evolved Cylons are indistinguishable from humans, have emotions and a monotheistic religion that resembles Christianity, and have a list of specific political grievances that drive their behaviors. Their motive for destroying humanity is to avenge what they consider a genocidal assault on their species. As sentient beings who turn on their former masters, they embody the concept of "blowback" and recall specific arguments about the CIA's role in creating the terrorists who attacked the United States on 9/11.[54] This discussion of blowback is not subtle, either, as Commander Adama (Edward James Olmos), leader of the sole remaining military battle cruiser, the *Galactica*, points out at the end of the miniseries: "You cannot play God then wash your hands of the things you've created. Sooner or later the day comes when you can't hide from the things you've done anymore." The question he articulates at the outset of that speech—"Why are we as a people worth saving"—becomes the central enigma for the series, as future plots engage with ethical questions about the meaning of security and the consequences of a too-narrow definition of it.

Signs of the post-9/11 context abound in the series, from the opening credits, which, as Eric Greene points out, depict an aerial view of an imaginary flight into the skyline of the city of Caprica, to the makeshift memorial wall containing snapshots of missing loved ones à la New York City in the aftermath of the terrorist attacks. Characters suffer traumatic flashbacks and live in a constant state of paranoia and suspicion, which the program refuses to resolve. As Greene says, "the show makes us sit and live with anxiety and doubt," rather than offering a redemptive resolution to our fears.[55] It carries us back to the aftermath of 9/11 and invites us to consider, from the relative comfort of hindsight, what we ought to have done in response to that tragedy and where we failed. Like Jericho, BSG incorporates specific visual and narrative references to U.S. history—President Roslin's swearing-in ceremony resembles the swearing in of President Johnson following the assassination of President Kennedy; "Boomer's" (Grace Park) attempted assassination of Commander Adama recalls Jack Ruby's on-air murder of Lee Harvey Oswald; the tribunals convened to assign responsibility for the plight of humanity recall the Salem witch trials and McCarthyism, and so on—to prevent viewers from succumbing to the illusion that the show is "only entertainment."

Early episodes debate the merits of military versus civilian governance, the stresses imposed on democracy by extremity, and the need for limits to authority. The debacle in Iraq receives particularly pointed interrogation, as our "heroes" are confronted with choices about when and under what circumstances one might be justified in resorting to preemptive violence, torture, terrorism, and even genocide. In the episode "Flesh and Bone," for example, the protagonists torture a Cylon prisoner and then jettison him out an airlock once they get the information they need. The torture was purportedly designed to resemble tactics used at Guantanamo, including waterboarding, and was intended to provoke outrage (which it did; the network pushed to have the extremity of the violence reduced).[56] Though nonhuman, the Cylon very obviously feels pain; he pleads for mercy and later begs his torturer to kill him so he can meet his God. When President Roslin (Mary McDonnell) rescues him from the brutality, apologizes for his mistreatment, and solicits a confession through kindness, we are prepared to accept this as an indictment of "harsh interrogation," but then Roslin orders him jettisoned out the airlock. This is but one of many episodes in which the line between heroes and villains is deliberately blurred so that viewers must consciously consider questions of ethical and moral responsibility: Is torture OK? Under what circumstances? What does it do to the tortured soul? To the torturer? To the society that condones it? Is prohibition a realistic solution? And so on. In other episodes, Galactica personnel must decide whether to abort a potential threat

The producers of *Battlestar Galactica* (Sci Fi, 2003–2009) incorporated topical references to U.S. tactics in the War on Terrorism. Here they produce a simulacrum of "harsh interrogation," including a version of waterboarding. ("Flesh and Bone," 2/25/2005)

to the human race (or defend all life as precious), unleash a genocidal computer virus on the Cylons (or respect the rules of just warfare), assassinate a corrupt leader (or respect authority and suffer the consequences like good soldiers), kill a few innocents to save the larger population (or spare the few and allow a terrorist catastrophe to occur)—the list of moral quandaries could go on and on. The frequent use of doubling in the series (Human-Cylon, Adama-Cain, Boomer-Athena, etc.) makes a determined moral center even more difficult to locate as identities and positions shift from episode to episode. The result is that "doubt dominates."[57] In a climate of military triumphalism, such as that fostered by the Bush administration, BSG's willingness to entertain doubt and consider the outcomes of violent action was a welcome corrective, especially for liberal viewers and critics.[58]

The most talked about element of BSG's interrogation of the politics of the War on Terrorism was its so-called New Iraqtica experiment, which began at the end of season 2, continued online between the season breaks (in six webisodes called the "Resistance" arc), and concluded after the sixth episode of season 3. In this arc, the humans identify a habitable planet and decide to colonize it, but the Cylons invade and occupy the territory, consigning the humans to a spartan existence subject to the will of their new masters. In this symbolic reimagining of the U.S. occupation of Iraq, it is the humans, our heroes, who play the beleaguered Iraqis. A scrappy resistance develops and adopts the very tactics used by insurgents against the U.S. military in Iraq, including the deployment of improvised explosive devices and suicide bombers (even *Jericho*'s resistant fighters refuse to go this far). Meanwhile, the Cylons use draconian measures, not unlike those deployed by the U.S. Army, to suppress the rebellion, including indiscriminate and indefinite detention, torture, and collective punishment. In typical fashion, the series uses this confrontation to interrogate the morality of occupation and the strategies of social control it necessitates, and it does not take sides in any clear way. Colonel Saul Tigh (Michael Hogan), who leads the resistance, is a ruthless nihilist, willing to use any means necessary to achieve his objectives, including hiding weapons in religious temples and hospitals, targeting civilian populations, and using suicide bombers to infiltrate and punish government and security forces. His tactics lead at least one resistance fighter to join the Cylon-trained New Caprica police force out of concern that Tigh's methods might be more dangerous than the occupation in the long run. Tigh is also opposed by moralists such as Laura Roslin and Galen Tyrol (Aaron Douglas), who are aligned with the resistance but insist there are "some things you just don't do . . . not even in war" ("Occupation"). Tigh eventually succeeds in recruiting a young man to infiltrate the New Caprica Police and blow himself up at the graduation ceremony, killing thirty-three humans and a number of Cylons. While the act is reprehensible, the bomber is a sympathetic figure, whose wife was killed by the Cylons in a bloody raid on a temple being used, unbeknownst to the worshippers, as a rebel weapons depot. The Cylon response—a mass execution of suspect colonials—throws our sympathies even further toward the rebellion, by making terrorism appear the only possible recourse against an unjust regime with a monopoly on power and weaponry ("Precipice"). The "New Iraqtica" story arc, thus, gives viewers an extended opportunity to consider what they might do under similar conditions of occupation, and it encourages at least a symbolic empathy with the Iraqi peoples subject to U.S. military authority. Its open-ended structure and careful staging of competing viewpoints constitute a symbolic debate over issues ignored or suppressed in the mainstream media's rush to "support the troops" and the president. The producers' reluctance to back one side or the other in this debate leaves it up to the viewer to carve out a resolution of the issues for him or herself.

This was certainly a salutary development at a time when the U.S. Army had yet to abandon its use of massive firepower and indiscriminate detention to "fear up" the population of Iraq. It also provided an important counternarrative to those depictions of the invasion as an assault perpetrated on, rather than by, American soldiers. The "invaders" in this arc are never mistaken for victims. As in *Jericho*, this allegory of occupation asked viewers to identify not

In one story arc, *Battlestar Galactica* asked viewers to consider what it would be like to live under conditions of occupation (Left). It poses the question: "What would you be willing to do to regain your freedom?" and presents suicide bombing as a viable tactic of the weak (Right). ("Occupation," 10/6/2006)

with authoritarian power, but with those susceptible to it (or to its lure). The complex narratives of both series challenged the Manichean logic of good and evil adopted by the Bush administration to legitimate the War on Terrorism and reflected a growing concern that America had become unrecognizable to itself and its citizens. "With our domestic character and our international conduct under a cloud of suspicion," Greene says of that time period, "many Americans fear[ed] that we [had] both been betrayed and that we [had] betrayed ourselves. We [now] wonder who we are and where we are going." These programs "[tapped] into that unease and, rather than soothing it, [explored] it."[59] Questions of responsibility and accountability were central to both series, especially BSG, which begins and ends with the question: "Why are we as a people worth saving?" As Joshua Alston notes, this is not a question that a show like 24 would even bother asking, and it was certainly not a question the Bush administration was willing to entertain.[60] Instead, the Bush team declared "Mission accomplished" and palmed off any responsibility for the devastation in Iraq, including the scandal at Abu Ghraib, onto others. Leaders in these series, by contrast, were defined by their accountability. Though not pacifists, they rejected the notion that one must "work the dark side" (à la Dick Cheney) in order to defeat terrorism. Instead, they proposed that, as Commander Adama once put it, "it's not enough to survive. One has to be worthy of surviving" ("Resurrection Ship, pt. II").

Brian Ott calls *Battlestar Galactica* symbolic "equipment for living" and argues that its dramatization of the dangers of "unrestrained fear, . . . furnish[ed] viewers with a vocabulary and . . . a set of symbolic resources for managing their social anxieties" in more productive ways.[61] He cites its use of ambivalence to deconstruct social blockages, not by drawing attention to one side or the other, but by drawing attention to the boundaries of discourse and interrogating their utility. "The ambivalent frame encourages reflexivity" and promotes "an awareness of our complicity and cooperation in war."[62] Arguably this is true of some of the other programs discussed here, most notably The Daily Show and Invasion. At the very least, by reminding us that the terms of public debate are social constructions subject to change, the programs discussed here opened a space for dissent to register as something other than a negative, or "anti-American," impulse. They invited viewers to wake up from "the terror dream" and embrace a more active role in the deliberation of the nation's values and practices.

Conclusion

Given that many of these programs lasted one season or less, or aired on cable channels where a 3 rating (about 4 million households) is considered high, some might question how influential these alternative representations of the War on Terrorism really were. Ratings have never been a very good measure of viewer interest or engagement, however. They can tell us how many people are watching a show, and even something about their demographic and psychographic profiles, but they can't tell us much about *how* people watch. Are they passively receiving texts, negotiating the margins of the text, or talking back to the set? Do viewers watch attentively or in a state of distraction? Are they watching because they want to or because they have lost control of the remote to their spouses? The audience measured by ratings is a collaborative construction of the TV industry, used to establish the ground rules for the exchange of programming; it is not a reflection of actual viewers' actual practices of reception.[63] Media convergence has undermined the significance of the ratings system even further by offering viewers new options and new ways to engage with texts, which have themselves metastasized into narrative "universes" accessible through a range of media. As Derek Kompare puts it, "'Television' is now portable and malleable, taken in on screens of all sizes, filed away on DVD box sets, and remixed on You Tube."[64] The influence of any single program, even one with low ratings, is difficult to determine absolutely, especially as programs take on afterlives in new commodity forms and as "cult" texts.

Most of the series discussed in this chapter, with the possible exception of *Whoopi*, have benefited from this new media environment and the increasingly long commercial tail of television programs.[65] For example, all three of the alien invasion series discussed here—*Surface*, *Invasion*, and *Threshold*—migrated to the Syfy channel for syndicated second runs, as did the apocalyptic thriller *Jericho*. *Arrested Development* had dismal ratings but was renewed for three seasons due to its strong online and DVD sales. It was one of the first series to demonstrate the value of ancillary sales to TV executives too used to thinking of broadcast as the end-all and be-all of their business plans.[66] And *Jericho* became the poster child for the disconnect between the Nielsen ratings system and the new media environment. The fan campaigns to save *Jericho* are now legendary in TV circles, including the famous "Nuts to CBS" campaign, which delivered 40 tons of peanuts to CBS executives and resulted in a provisional second season pickup for the show.[67] In 2008, when ratings for the series remained flat (around 6 million per episode), the network again canceled the show, leading fans to take extreme measures: they purchased a billboard on Ventura Boulevard asking other networks to pick up the series, spent $11,500 to take out full-page ads in *Variety* and the *Hollywood Reporter*, shopped the series to other networks themselves through letter-writing campaigns, purchased season 1 DVDs for troops in Afghanistan to spike the ancillary sales numbers, and even began a "Nuts to Nielsen" campaign to draw attention to the flaws in the ratings system.[68] Such episodes demonstrate how the new media context has empowered viewers to assert ownership over their favorite programs, yet it also shows, quite clearly, who retains control over programming choices in this multimedia environment. The *Jericho* fan campaigns are, thus, a sober reminder that expanded consumer choice is not the same as social or cultural power.

Yet, the new media context also clearly provides opportunities for critical producers willing to work within the economic frameworks that define the commercial media system. The difference between these short-lived series and the more resilient series, such as *The Daily Show*, *Lost*, and *Battlestar Galactica*, boiled down to the latter's willingness to experiment with new forms of storytelling, new modes of delivery, and new opportunities for ancillary sales (i.e., profits from things like merchandising, tie-ins, and DVD and Internet sales). *The Daily Show*, for instance, works by exploiting the speed and accessibility of information in the new media environment to produce its critiques. It has been a leader in the use of online and digital media to deliver its program content, making the influence of the show and its anchor far more extensive than a simple ratings metric might suggest. Stewart has become the "king of late night [TV]" not by virtue of his ratings (which hover around 2 million), but by virtue of "perception and respect and heat," generated through the savvy use of new media to propagate the show's messages.[69] The program was an early innovator in the use of streaming video, YouTube, and social media such as Facebook and Twitter to extend its circulation and court younger viewers. *The Daily Show* also runs in heavy rotation on the Comedy Central channel, providing viewers with multiple opportunities to access its content, and its clips are frequently recycled by other news organs, such as MSNBC's now-defunct *Keith Olbermann Show*, ensuring that many more viewers access the series than cable ratings can account for. Such clips are licensed, of course, generating additional revenue for Comedy Central's parent corporation, Viacom. Stewart has also published several books and helped launch the popular spin-off *The Colbert Report*, which mocks the conservative punditocracy that has so often been the focus of Stewart's ire. This creative use of new media and multiple platforms has positioned *The Daily Show* to take advantage of the cultural shift away from regular news consumption and toward online and ad hoc "grazing." It is already reported to be the number-one news program for those under 35, and polls show that its critique of mainstream news media draws viewers from across the political spectrum, making it a potent cultural force in a divisive political climate.[70]

Lost and BSG, likewise, prospered in a competitive media marketplace by leveraging their "software" (the story) to the max. *Lost* set the precedent for many of the complex serial narratives that would follow, especially in the science fiction genre. Rather than targeting a mass audience, it cultivated a hyperactive core of loyal young fans whose facility with new media technologies could be anticipated and exploited. For example, producers would embed clues to the narrative enigmas in the background mise-en-scène, assuming viewers would use their DVRs to parse the program frame-by-frame, then share what they learned via Internet fan forums. They were also one of the first to use alternate reality games (ARGs) (including *The Lost Experience* and *Find 815*) to hold viewer interest across the seasonal breaks and extend the narrative universe of the TV program. By playing these games, viewers could immerse themselves in the narrative world of *Lost* while also making themselves available for additional commercial messages.[71] The producers also released several "mobisodes" (short episodes accessible only by mobile phone) and podcasts designed to give viewers "access" to the creators and the creative process. Finally, they used more traditional media forms such as books, soundtracks, video games, and a magazine devoted to the program to extend the reach of the series, and when the show was over, they auctioned off the sets, props, and costumes for cash.[72] By cultivating a tech-savvy niche market willing to consume both the commercial broadcast and any additional products and services related to the program, Lost's producers were able to create a narratively innovative and visually stunning production that viewers often described as "cinematic." However, the costs of this new model of media production and distribution were not lost on Lost's fans. After a disappointing series finale, for example, one fan dismissed the show as "a contrived, pointless, 2 dimensional, money earning exercise."[73] Another fan likened the series to a "Ponzi scheme" that asked for large investments and promised a big payoff, but failed, in the end, to deliver.[74] Criticisms of the ARG Lost: The Experience likewise emphasized the lack of plot resolution and the awkward integration of promotional materials, such as the faux "Hanso Corporation" website suffused with Sprite logos.[75] So Lost demonstrates both the potentials and the pitfalls of the new media environment. While that environment enabled the clever storytelling of the series and underwrote its high-production values, quality came at a high price. The program offered a potent reminder that media convergence is predicated on a pattern of corporate conglomeration that promises more, rather than less, commercialism in the future.

BSG likewise achieved the status of a "cult classic" by virtue of its savvy online presence and merchandising strategies, as well as it devoted fan base, but, like Lost, it points to some of the difficulties associated with the commercial context of cultural production and distribution. Ian Maull and David Lavery report that Battlestar fan fiction abounds on the Internet, for example, with one site hosting at least 3,000 stories based on the show.[76] The space for innovative fan production has been winnowed, however, by the producers' decision to use podcasts, webisodes, and ancillary products, such as the comic book series Zarek and Season Zero, to give fans access to the creative process, fill in backstory, and maintain interest between episodes and seasons. As Suzanne Scott points out, the overproduction of story material from the producers leaves few marginal story elements for fans to play with, and fan production thrives on such marginalia. Moreover, the podcasts have been perceived by some fans as a form of dictatorship designed to limit the range of interpretations available to fans of the series. "When [Moore] says 'you're not thinking about that' and 'the audience feels,' I don't feel so much invited [into Moore's way of seeing things] as shoved around," said one frustrated fan.[77] Sci Fi/Syfy has also promoted a "collaborationist" mode of fan interaction by providing would-be fan producers with a "BSG Videomaker Toolkit," which allowed them to assemble their own BSG webisodes—as long as they attached a Sci Fi promo to the resulting text.[78] In these ways, producers encouraged the program's viewers to immerse themselves in the universe of the BSG franchise, but only in sanctioned ways. Fan involvement was equated to consumption and channeled toward the "official" story and its accompanying merchandise, from T-shirts and DVDs to comic books, video games, and tie-in novels. While *Battlestar Galactica*'s narrative themes addressed taboo subject matter and fostered public deliberation, then, the marketing and distribution practices of the Sci Fi/Syfy network closed down avenues of fan engagement and bred a singular, "authorized" version of the text.

Considering the complex conditions of production, distribution, and reception in the post-network era leads back to a consideration of questions of political communication more broadly. On the one hand, the emergence of dissenting opinion in entertainment formats on U.S. TV after 2004 offered viewers a broader range of discursive options with which to engage their real-world contexts. Critical series, such as *The Daily Show*, *Invasion*, *Jericho*, and *Battlestar Galactica*, provided viewers with "symbolic equipment for living" that enabled them to manage social anxiety and imagine solutions to real-world problems.[79] Such dissent testifies to the increasing plurality of the commercial media systems and the threat that such plurality poses to those in power. In such an environment, it is difficult for authorities to control the narratives about war and empire absolutely, and alternative perspectives do filter through.[80] However, this increased plurality is still conditioned by the commercial nature of the TV industries, whose professional doxa confines pluralism to very narrow limits. The primary audience for television programming remains the advertisers, and a focus on marketing potential still drives the selection, scheduling, and promotion of programs. And while assumptions about how to count audiences may be in flux, this has not changed the fact that some audiences still count more than others (younger viewers more than old, for instance, rich more than poor, urban more than rural, white more than black or brown, etc.). Such assumptions shape content and explain, for example, why we still see few positive representations of Arabs or Islam on U.S. television, and why narratives can interrogate the impact of U.S. militarism on foreign populations only through a transposition to fantasy that both distances viewers from the real world and allows them to view themselves as the victims, rather than perpetrators, of the violence. It is important to keep these limitations firmly in mind, even as we acknowledge the shift in popular cultural discourse about the War on Terrorism that this chapter outlines.

7 The Body of War and the Collapse of Memory

We've had 2,000 American trees fall on that forest over there, and we don't even know it, not really. Maybe we don't want to know about our children dying, so, lucky for us, this war isn't really being televised. . . . All the American public wants to concern itself with is whether Brad and Angelina really are a couple. At least with Vietnam we all watched, and we all got angry.

—Alan Shore, a character on *Boston Legal*, "Witches of Mass Destruction" (ABC, 11/1/2005)

In contemporary society, the electronic media play an increasingly vital role in the witnessing of history. They transmit eyewitness testimony (witnessing *in* the media), they act as eyewitnesses themselves (witnessing *by* the media), and they prompt viewers to bear witness through their continuous presentation of social data (witnessing *through* the media). This chapter examines the capacity of television to fulfill these witnessing functions in an age of corporate conglomeration and audience fragmentation. Increasingly, as Richard Grusin has argued, commercial media seem less and less willing to pay witness to the shock of the real because such disturbances are not economically, politically, or socially profitable.[1] TV news, in particular, seems to have abdicated its traditional responsibility to inform the public in favor of a new ethos of comfort and distraction (what used to be called "bread and circuses"). News coverage of the war in Iraq offers a case in point. The embedding system, whereby journalists were assigned to specific military units to observe their maneuvers, ensured a selective filtering of eyewitness accounts that would favor the perspectives of U.S. soldiers over others. Indeed, because the security of the embeds depended on the goodwill of the soldiers, there was a strong disincentive to report the negative aspects of the war. The role of the media as eyewitness to history would also be fetishized at the expense of historical and political context.[2] Grainy images of embedded journalists reporting "live" from moving vehicles or from the middle of skirmishes were valued, regardless of their informational content. What mattered was the sensation of "being there" that such re-

ports conveyed. As Andrew Hoskins notes, the result was an immersive experience more akin to imperial travelogue than to a type of witnessing.[3]

Perhaps most damningly, the news media colluded in the attempt to sanitize war by refusing to screen unpalatable imagery or to call death and injury
by their proper names (preferring terms like "collateral damage" or "friendly
fire"). As Toby Miller reports, "The Project for Excellence in Journalism's
analysis of ABC, CBS, NBC, CNN, and Fox found that early in the Iraq invasion, 50 percent of reports from the thousand embedded journalists depicted
combat—o percent depicted injuries. . . . As the war progressed, reporters . . .
disclosed deeply sanitized images of the wounded from afar. The mainstream
media ignored wounded US soldiers, too, and conducted no bedside interviews from hospitals. Fallen men and women were the 'disappeared.'"[4] The
Pentagon placed a ban on photos of dead U.S. soldiers being returned to
Dover Air Force Base, and two U.S. contractors who dared to snap photos of
the flag-draped coffins were fired for violating the restrictions (the photos ran
in the *Seattle Times*). Such direct governmental censorship was largely unnecessary, however, since news editors and reporters used community standards
of "taste and decency" as an excuse to censor themselves.[5] Corporations such
as General Motors helped narrow these standards by refusing to advertise on
television programs, including newscasts, that depicted "atrocities in Iraq."[6]
Thus, the Pentagon's desire to promote only good news about the war coincided with news media's conception of the public as reality-averse. As
Hoskins notes, the development of new cable news outlets only magnified the
problem by allowing viewers to "tune in to a niche version of warfare that
[did] not so easily disturb."[7]

By the fifth anniversary of the invasion, the number of U.S. casualties
topped 4,000 killed and 29,000 wounded, while estimates of Iraqi casualties
ranged from 151,000 to 655,000 (though the Bush administration actively disputed all attempts to quantify the number of Iraqi dead).[8] Rather than bearing
witness to these realities, mainstream news outlets decided to cut their coverage (and their losses, as public opinion had already shifted). In part, this decision was forced by the Bush administration, which simply stopped holding
press conferences or issuing press releases when the war turned ugly.[9] In part,
it was a function of the cut-throat economics of commercialized news production, which favor insider knowledge over independent analysis because it is
cheaper and easier to produce. When insiders clam up, news producers just
move on to other stories. Thus, war coverage across all media platforms de-
creased drastically over time. From 2007 to 2008, war news dropped from 23

percent of total news output to a mere 3 percent. "The difference [was] even more stark on cable news networks," which declined from 24 percent to just 1 percent in 2008. From September to December of 2007, the three major network evening newscasts (NBC, ABC, and CBS) dropped their average coverage of the war from thirty minutes per week to four, or less than one minute per day. By 2008, the war in Iraq had become, in the words of media watchdog Paul Janensch, a "vanishing war," with images of dead and wounded bodies the primary blind spot.[10]

The news media's selective witnessing of the war made it virtually impossible for viewers to bear witness to history themselves (the third aspect of media witnessing), for they had few materials with which to work. The absence of images of human suffering, in particular, threatened to lead to a "collapse of [social] memory," for, as Susan Sontag remarks, "to remember is, more and more, not to recall a story but to be able to call up a picture."[11] If the pictures of war are selective and sanitized, then the memory of war becomes romanticized, and violence continues to seem like a viable means of securing the peace. Arguments about television's culpability in this "collapse of memory" tend to neglect the numerous treatments of war available in entertainment programs, however. Images of human injury repressed in TV newscasts returned with a vengeance in other television formats, especially as the insurgency in Iraq picked up steam. What did this return signify, though? Did these bodies represent a critique of the nature of warfare? Did their bodily disintegration signal a failure of U.S. foreign policy? Did they figure the collapse of the fiction of inviolable sovereignty that led the United States to adopt a war strategy in the first place?[12] Or were they, rather, figures of pathos designed to convert war into a personal experience of trauma and promote popular empathy with the soldier?

Implicit in these questions is a recognition that the mere presence of disturbing imagery means nothing in and of itself. What matters is how such imagery is contextualized and narrated.[13] Are the images grounded in a clear context? Are viewers encouraged to linger over the images, to bear witness to the suffering they embody, to reflect on and think about them in a way that might engender ethical action? Or are the images permitted to float free from history? Do they pass by so quickly that they constitute little more than War on Terrorism "shout-outs," or marketing gimmicks?[14]

One of the difficult aspects of analyzing contemporary U.S. television is that the answer to all of these questions is "yes" at some point. The sheer volume of programming available makes it likely that at least some presentations of wartime suffering will contest the dominant frame and express a critical stance toward militarism. Moreover, the different political economies of broadcast, cable, and subscription channels encourage ideological ambiguity by promoting different program ethics and aesthetics. As we have seen, cable and subscription channels have more sources of money and are more loosely regulated than broadcasters, which makes them more tolerant of aesthetic experimentation and political controversy. While broadcasters must "plane the edges" of their narratives to avoid upsetting the status quo, programs on cable can use "edginess" to attract a more lucrative "quality" audience.[15]

The result of all of these developments is to increase the complexity of the television system and raise the level of difficulty involved in assessing TV's role in the formation of cultural consensus. It is difficult to argue for the significance of any single program or series within the total flow of contemporary U.S. television since few programs capture a critical mass of the national audience, and viewers may easily avoid programming that challenges their ideological perspectives. TV may still serve as the dominant storyteller of our age, but the cultural milieu it crafts is increasingly experienced in an asynchronous and idiosyncratic fashion.[16] Thus, "the post-network era requires an emphasis on definitions of television stressing the breadth of content available and the notion of television viewing as a process that is not isolatable to a single moment, episode, or series."[17] Instead, we need to look at how certain themes or clusters of images play across multiple texts on a variety of channels, and we need to qualify our claims about the outcomes, since no two viewers will likely encounter the same set of texts, in the same order, or within the same time frame.

What follows is an attempt to chart certain patterns in the circulation of images of wounded U.S. soldiers on U.S. television during the first five years of the Iraq War. The comparison illustrates how content was constrained in various ways by form and by the political economy of production. It also demonstrates, however, that television, as a collective image-stream, did pay witness to the suffering entailed by war and, in that way, promote a type of witnessing among the U.S. public. This may not have been the type of witnessing that required ethical response in the form of action, but it did require individuals to confront the experience of violence and duress unique to war and to analyze their own relationship to militarism.[18] By inviting viewers to linger over a range of representations of war and its effects, entertainment television helped combat the "collapse of memory" encouraged by censorship and the acceleration of the TV news cycle.

Broadcasting Reality: The Body of War in "Low-Brow" Genres

There is a common assumption that the display of images of bodily injury due to war will somehow automatically engender resistance. If only the public were forced to confront the pain of war in all of its gory detail, the idea goes, they would "get angry" and immediately call for an end to war. As Sontag points out, however, images of human suffering in wartime are radically ambiguous. Their meanings are determined as much by the contexts within which they are produced and received as by the content of the images themselves. The incorporation of images of war's shocking effects into unscripted programming on broadcast television illustrates precisely how context can constrain meaning in this way, and even channel popular anger or disgust away from political protest.

Talk shows and reality programming are often described as "low-brow" forms because of their structural emphasis on emotion and conflict and their use of formulaic, predictable, and transparent styles of production. They are literally designed to appeal to the "lowest-common denominator" of intellect, taste, and style within the mass public. Much of this programming uses a melodramatic frame to personalize contemporary political life and render it easily consumable. Political problems are approached through personal narratives that foreground the traumatic nature of experience and promote a sentimental identification with the suffering individual. Shocking images of human suffering may appear on talk shows or reality series (especially the "makeover" series), but they do so with "planed edges" and in ways that encourage viewers to be (emotionally) moved rather than (politically) mobilized.[19]

Indeed, talk shows and reality programs offer the most blatant examples of how the injunction to see the pain of the soldier may work to recuperate political anger by channeling it toward more sympathetic and consumerist responses. *The Montel Williams Show* (1991–2008) was an early and aggressive promoter of the image of the wounded soldier, for example, featuring at least eight military-themed episodes from 2005 to 2008.[20] The first of these programs premiered in May of 2005 and featured U.S. veterans wounded and disabled in Iraq. Called "The New Forgotten," the episode was clearly designed to forestall the cultural disavowal that characterized the U.S. response to Vietnam (a conflict Williams himself served in) and to shape a more positive image of military heroism and sacrifice. During the program, Williams confronts his audience directly with the pain and suffering of his guests, fetishizing their amputations, paralysis, and dissociative relationships to their prewar selves. He prods the soldiers for details of their traumatic experiences and uses video inserts and photo montages to position the soldiers as victims, rather than agents, of war. He even occasionally admonishes the military and media for "neglecting" these soldiers and their compelling stories.

Yet the critical force of these images is blunted by the sentimental framework of the talk show format, which privileges interpersonal communication and emotional empathy as the proper solutions to all of life's problems.[21] Williams' on-set mediation of the dialogue actively impedes a more critical and structural understanding of war's history, purposes, and effects by directing the audience toward a personal identification with the individual soldier and the concept of "honor" he or she is said to embody. At one point, he literally commands his audience to abase themselves before the troops: "You guys looking and watching, when you see a veteran walking down the street, just say thanks, say thanks, 'cause they're the reason your butt didn't have to go there [to war]." He also describes the high number of wounded veterans as a social problem susceptible to resolution "by the end of this hour." The solution proposed is to spend four dollars to purchase a red, white, and blue bracelet whose proceeds will go to the Paralyzed Veterans of America. As Marita Sturken has argued, such consumerist responses to historical trauma do not "promise to make things better; [they promise] to make us feel better about the way things are."[22] This therapeutic ethos complements Williams's verbal and visual coding of injury as "sacrifice" and service as "honor," displacing questions about the necessity and legality of the war in Iraq and transforming the agents of empire into innocent victims deserving of sympathy and celebration. The result is a guilt-ridden compensatory identification with the nobility of the grunt that decontextualizes war and makes political dissent difficult, if not impossible, to articulate.

"The New Forgotten" parades the "body of war" before the public in what has become a relatively familiar manner. Thirty years of revisionist Vietnam War films told from the perspective of the soldier on the ground have trained U.S. audiences to think of war as a personal hell, rather than a political endeavor.[23] This cultural training overdetermines the reception of images of soldiers-in-pain and makes it difficult for these shocking images to evoke moral outrage. Not only do they seem familiar and mundane, rather than horrifying; the images are received in an environment that is incredibly "friendly" to the military. In such a context, "the pictures of wretched hollow-eyed GIs that once seemed subversive of militarism and imperialism [now] seem inspirational. Their revised subject: ordinary American young men doing their unpleasant, ennobling duty."[24] Far from being "forgotten," then, the suffering soldier has become a central figure in a memorial culture dedicated to the recuperation of an exceptionalist national imaginary. Regarding the pain of the soldier is a way to understand war as a sacrifice undertaken in defense of others. Like other "rituals of national innocence," this exercise effaces the self-serving and offensive character of U.S. warfare and paints imperialism as a beneficent "civilizing mission."[25] It also channels any unease regarding the necessity, conduct, and consequences of war toward a personalized politics of sympathy and care. It asks not "why war" but "what do we owe the soldiers who fight in our names."[26]

The extent and effects of this personalization of war can be seen most clearly in the episodes of *Extreme Makeover: Home Edition* (EMHE) devoted to making over the homes of dead or injured Iraq War veterans. The program has produced at least four such episodes to date, the most famous of which was the season 2 finale featuring POW Jessica Lynch bringing the crew to the aid of her "best friend" Lori Piestewa's family (5/22/2005) (the others were "The Rodriguez Family" (9/25/2005), "The Gilyeat Family" (2/10/2008), and "The Lucas Family" (3/2/2008)). These episodes of EMHE answer the question, "what do we owe the troops," by proclaiming sympathy and consumer therapy to be the proper responses. They offer a sentimental, consumerist mode of comfort that obscures both the centrality of violence to U.S. culture and the political and economic inequalities that structure U.S. society.[27] Anna McCarthy has described programs like EMHE as a "neoliberal theatre of suffering" designed to teach audiences object lessons in how to survive in the dog-eat-dog world of competitive capitalism.[28] Pain is displayed on such shows in order to reinforce lessons about rugged individualism and privatized modes of social care. They demonstrate on a weekly basis that individuals must look to themselves and their neighbors for sustenance because it is not the state's job to care for them any more.[29]

As with the fetishization of the wounded soldiers' bodies on *Montel*, EMHE's images of U.S. citizens suffering because of the nation's economic and political policies have the potential to provoke a more public and political sort of response. So, again, careful work is done to contain this possibility and direct popular energies toward more privatized and therapeutic endeavors. The episode of EMHE devoted to the Piestewa family illustrates the pattern. PFC Lori Piestewa was a Hopi Indian volunteer from Tuba City, Arizona, who was killed during the same skirmish in Nasiriyah that led to the capture and rescue of PFC Jessica Lynch at the start of the Iraq War. Declaring herself Piestewa's "best friend and sister," Lynch wrote to the producers of EMHE to ask for help "fulfill[ing] Lori's dream," which was simply to provide for her family. The emphasis on personal relationships shows both players, Lynch and Piestewa, to be motivated by altruism and care for others and, therefore, deserving of the assistance of the program. The Piestewa family history of military service offers further proof of their worthiness and so receives a lot of attention in the early part of the program. The dilapidated condition of the Piestewa trailer, which Jennifer Gillan describes as the "trailer of tears," also affirms the legitimacy of their need and sanctions the program's application of consumer therapy.[30] The designers watch taped interviews with the Piestewas in which they lament how "tough" it has been on them since Lori died while we, the audience, watch the designers well up with emotion and sympathy in response. This framing of the confessionals safely removes them from the realm of political expression and positions them within the interior space of the community-as-family. The Piestewas, Lynch, the design team and, by extension, the audience become a spiritually and emotionally unified group, ready to work together to redeem the family and the sanctity and security of its home. As Gillan notes, "EMHE devotes much of its time to these sorts of shot-countershot sequences that establish the emotional interplay of Lori's 'family' and the appropriately empathetic designers."[31] The function of such shots is to model empathy and caring for the home audience and to construct such empathy as the proper mode of civic action. The idea that human suffering might be better addressed through social transformation is portrayed as downright un-American.

This sentimental rendering of economic hardship and political frustration borrows the codes and conventions of melodrama to contain any potential for a more critical response to historical crises. By foregrounding emotional excess, EMHE makes the social contexts of individual suffering appear abstract and immutable. What matters, it suggests, is not what happens to you, but how well you respond to it. Percy and Terry Piestewa are worthy of assistance because they demonstrate the proper degree of resignation to their conditions: they are not hopeless, but they are also not frustrated enough to become politically engaged. While they may understand how their personal loss relates to a public politics of war, they are prevented from articulating that knowledge by the program's cast members, who constantly redirect the conversations away from political issues and toward personal and emotional ones ("how did that make you feel" is a constant refrain on the show). As a form of national pedagogy, EMHE defines citizenship in a very limited way: as an experience of shared emotionality and fellow-feeling, rather than political responsibility.[32]

While EMHE displays the anger and frustration of disenfranchised Americans, it does so primarily to reassure the audience of its own innocence in relation to the processes that have brought these citizens low. The sympathy for traumatized Americans (so carefully performed in the reaction shots of the cast) manifests the good intentions of the audience members and reaffirms the virtue of the "American way." In regard to the war in Iraq, EMHE emphasizes the need to comfort the fallen soldiers and their families above all else. This emphasis obscures both the imperial nature of the war and the economic injustice that determines who must fight it. Instead, the show celebrates a "commendable culture of neighborliness" designed to redeem the innocence of the nation.[33] By inviting Americans to "see the pain" caused by war, it offers them the reassurance that their nation is still defined by an exceptional benevolence. "Seeing the pain," in this case, reinforces the sanitization of war by promoting an emotional unity that evacuates the pain of others.

Scripted TV Programming and the Inability to Mourn

Scripted dramas on primetime network television have taken a slightly more critical approach to the presentation of the soldier's experience in war, but, in reducing the political to the personal, they, too, encourage a form of "empty empathy" that does little to disrupt the perpetuation of war.[34] Most of these depictions of soldier-suffering have occurred in episodic legal and police procedurals, such as *Bones* (Fox, 2005–present), *Boston Legal* (ABC, 2004–2008), *Cold Case* (CBS, 2003–2010), *Crossing Jordan* (NBC, 2001–2007), *Las Vegas* (NBC, 2003–2008), *Law and Order* (NBC, 1990–2010), *Law & Order: SVU* (NBC, 1999–present), *NYPD Blue* (ABC, 1993–2005), and *Without a Trace* (CBS, 2002–2009).[35] This is perhaps because such programs are serious in tone, are adult in theme (and scheduling), and tend to have higher production budgets. They also target a more upscale, educated, urban consumer, who is presumed, by both advertisers and producers alike, to be more tolerant of complexity. As the sanctioned locus of "quality" aesthetics on contemporary broadcast television, such programs can simply get away with more. The episodic structure also provides a reassuring framework within which controversial topics can be explored, but only for an hour and only if they are resolved in the end.[36]

This structure works to isolate each topic from every other topic explored in the series and, thus, prevents individuals from conceiving of injustice as a systemic or structural problem related to a particular arrangement of social resources. Indeed, most of these programs seek to validate extant social institutions and relations, including the military.

Broadcast series treatments of soldier-suffering emphasize the personal and domestic effects of U.S. militarism and shy away from examining the consequences of U.S. policy for those living under occupation. The result is an almost pathological denial of U.S. responsibility for the suffering of others, which might best be described as a form of imperial melancholia.[37] Like other modes of imperialist discourse, this one begins from the assumption that the United States is ontologically distinct from and superior to the cultures it dominates. Such ethnocentrism is not just premised on the silence of the occupied populations; it seeks to suppress any recognition of these "others" as historical agents who might represent themselves.[38] With very few exceptions (Law and Order and Bones), Iraqis are simply absent from the tales of imperial conflict told on U.S. TV. Where they are visible, they are usually "shapeless bundles of black" (Cold Case) or silent representatives of terror(ism) (Bones).[39] In only one case—Law and Order, "Paradigm"—has an Iraqi acted consciously and with purpose and been permitted to defend her actions in her own words. "Paradigm" centers on a female U.S. soldier who is assassinated by an Iraqi woman in retaliation for the torture of her brother in Abu Ghraib, where the soldier had been a guard. The Iraqi, Nadira Harrington (Sarita Choudhury), claims to be a warrior engaged in jihad and asks to be treated as a prisoner of war (a request that is denied). The trial gives her a chance to explain her actions and denounce the mistreatment of her brother and other Iraqis at the hands of U.S. soldiers. The verdict, however, favors the prosecutor, who argues that Nadira is using politics to mask a personal desire for vengeance. Thus, while the episode temporarily entertains an alternative perspective on U.S. war tactics, particularly the detention and torture of Iraqi civilians, it ultimately resolves itself in favor of the status quo. We hear an articulate Iraqi voice (albeit ventriloquized by an Indian actress), but only so that it can be discredited and resubjected to silence. In case we miss the point, the producers literally give the last word to the district attorney, Arthur Branch (played by 2008 Republican presidential hopeful, Fred Thompson), who describes the victory as "a huge win for truth, justice, and the American way of life." Once again, Iraq and its citizens recede into the background so that a tale of American redemption can take the fore.

The structural absence of Iraqi victims from these televisual portraits of suffering seems to represent a collective inability or unwillingness to work through the experience of empire. Confronted with mounting evidence of the United States' status as an aggressor nation, U.S. citizens desperately want to deny the evidence and have their common-sense assumptions about American exceptionalism reaffirmed. The melodramatic narratives of soldier-suffering tap into this popular desire and offer a utopian resolution to the contradictions created by U.S. policy. They do this by making U.S. soldiers appear the true victims of U.S. imperial violence.[40] Though they are melodramatic and sentimental, these representations are by no means simple. To "solve" the cultural problem of U.S. imperialism, they must first unearth and explore the contradictions it presents.[41] It is always possible for viewers to identify with and remember these contradictions, and, certainly, "melodramatic texts can work on viewers in multiple ways."[42] Yet, the formal structure of these programs, along with the emphasis on reassuring conclusions, virtually guarantees that the moment of narrative resolution will be privileged over the moments of contemplation along the way. The result is a series of fragmentary impressions about the effects of war that elicit sympathy for the individual soldier but allow the larger "structure of injustice" to remain invisible and uncontested.[43] They promote an isolated and ethnocentric contemplation of war that reproduces, rather than challenges, the exceptionalist logics underlying U.S. imperialism.

All of these programs self-consciously emphasize the processes of memory and mourning at stake in this analysis. Being police procedurals, they tend to conceive of history in traumatic terms—as beginning with a shocking act of violence that disturbs and disorients. They then walk the audience through a process of memory recovery and reconstruction that is not unlike the therapeutic work of mourning. Victims and witnesses are interviewed, impressions are catalogued, and explanations for the crime are tested and retested until a story emerges to explain the events and restore both the psychic equilibrium of the protagonists and the social equilibrium of the story world. In each case, the criminal violence under investigation is connected to the wars in Afghanistan or Iraq. Usually, a U.S. soldier recently returned from Iraq (or Afghanistan) is found missing, injured, or dead, and the main characters must reconstruct what happened. The narrative disorientation is signaled visually through an abundance of flashbacks, hallucinations, and speculative reenactments, all of which mimic the structure of traumatic memory. The soldier-victims, though individualized, are also symbols of the nation, and their injuries connote the rent in the social fabric that the wars have created.[44] By reenacting the soldiers' traumatic experiences, the narratives vicariously traumatize the viewers and provoke an emotional catharsis designed to repair that rent.[45] The programs suggest that the public confession of traumatic experience will produce a simple and salutary closure on the event—a cure for what ails America. Given the ongoing occupation of Iraq, however, the possibility of such healing seems premature at best. What these melodramas of soldier-suffering produce, in the end, is a "discourse of healing" that promotes "forgetting and depoliticization."[46] The programs use the image of the suffering U.S. soldier to efface the historical realities of war in Iraq and recuperate the future viability of militarism as a security strategy.

Since an analysis of every instance of soldier-suffering is beyond the scope of this chapter, what follows is a close textual analysis of two representative examples, *Without a Trace* ("Gung-Ho") and *Bones* ("The Soldier on the Grave"). I have chosen these examples, in part, because they are the most overtly critical of the U.S. military and its operations in Iraq. Yet, in both cases, the narrative structure works to contain the potentially explosive nature of the critique by substituting emotional catharsis and interpersonal empathy for public anger and political resistance. The result is a form of cultural reenactment that foreshortens the processes of historical reckoning (mourning) necessary to effect a change in U.S. foreign policy.

Without a Trace follows the exploits of a group of FBI agents assigned to a missing persons task force and is, thus, oriented around issues of (traumatic) loss and (therapeutic) recovery. The operational motto for the unit is "learn *who* the victim is in order to learn *where* the victim is."[47] Whether or not the missing person turns out to be dead, the narrative is ultimately redemptive because it memorializes the person and offers "survivors" a sense of closure. "Gung Ho" is a case in point. Here PFC Kevin Grant (Devon Gummersall) is an injured soldier recently returned from Iraq and due to be sent back in two weeks. He suffers from post-traumatic stress disorder (PTSD), which causes him to confuse the past with the present, the battle front with the home front. Much of the episode details the shameful ways in which the United States has off-loaded the burdens of war onto the lower classes, and Grant's behaviors are explained as natural responses to the economic and emotional pressures that wealthier Americans successfully evade. His personal trauma draws attention to the national scandal that is the poverty draft.[48] Though the FBI agents travel to Iraq to investigate Grant's disappearance, the true locus of his trauma is the U.S. context, and the war he is fighting is really a civil war. The absence of enemy fighters from the various combat flashbacks he suffers makes this clear. We see Grant under fire, but we never see who is shooting at him. We also discover that he deliberately stood up in the middle of a firefight in order to win passage home. His wounds are effectively self-inflicted.

As the team reconstructs events leading up to Grant's disappearance, we learn that his extended absence from home has resulted in the failure of his auto-detailing business and the impending loss of his house. Meanwhile, his fiancée Sara (Kelly Karbacz) has met someone else and is torn between her old love, who appears unstable, and her new beau, who comes without emotional or financial baggage. These events lead Grant to take extreme measures to regain the financial and emotional security lost as a result of the war. He and another member of his unit rob a bank to get the money Grant needs to save his home. The heist goes bad when a still twitchy Grant shoots and kills an off-duty police officer. The climax of the program is elegiac, lamenting the loss of this soldier's American dream and suggesting that such personal suffering is the true measure of the damage war causes. Grant holds his girlfriend and an FBI agent hostage in his home. While the agent attempts to talk Grant down, he reminisces with his girlfriend about how happy they were before the war. The exchange is nostalgic, culminating in the couple singing "Raindrops Are Falling on My Head" and weeping for the bygone blush of first love. Grant then kisses Sara goodbye, unloads his gun, and strides out the door to commit "suicide by cop." The sequence creates a powerful emotional identification between the viewer and Grant, who, though a bank robber and cop killer, shares the national faith in and devotion to the heterosexual family unit and the American dream. This emotional identification encourages viewers to accept Grant as the real victim of the U.S.-led War in Iraq.

"Gung-Ho's" reconstruction of the U.S. soldier as an innocent victim ultimately works to redeem the innocence of the nation by directing public dissatisfaction with the war inward. Viewers are invited to pity the soldier—even suffer along with him—but not to dwell on the social conditions that caused his personal tragedy. Like other forms of melodrama, *Without a Trace* uses the personal to draw attention to structural inequalities but ends up sacrificing critique in an orgy of emotion. Even the explicit indictment of the war uttered by Grant early in the episode ("What are we doin' here man? We're not stopping terrorism. There's no WMDs.") is later recuperated by a fellow soldier, who describes it as a symptom of emotional fatigue ("You didn't used to talk like that"). In the end, the sacrificial death of the suffering soldier affords characters and viewers alike a redemptive form of catharsis and closure. It

frees Grant's fiancée to lead a "normal life," to go back to the way it was before the "worries" and "complaints" (à la "Raindrops") caused by the misguided war in Iraq. For the viewers, Grant's suffering permits a sort of
reckoning with the historical guilt of war that does not hurt too deeply. They
are invited to feel his pain and to imagine that such fellow-feeling is a type of
ethical behavior. They are not required to face the more unpleasant aspects of
the war's conduct or to act to achieve a transformation of social relations.

The episode of *Bones* called "The Soldier on the Grave" enacts a similar
form of redemptive memory work, but with a slightly more critical edge. Like
Without a Trace, this program involves the recovery and reconstruction of information leading up to the death of whichever body is featured that week (e.g.,
"The Soldier on the Grave"). The impetus of the program is to humanize the
brutally deconstructed remains of crime victims. Forensic anthropologist
Temperance Brennan (Emily Deschanel) and her team of specialists talk a lot
about the need for objective scientific observation and emotional detachment,
but they invariably personalize the crimes and invest the bodies with emotional power. Indeed, Brennan often defines her mission as a type of therapeutic reenactment: to tell the victim's stories by making their bodies speak.
The whole thrust of the program is, once again, melodramatic: it reduces
complex historical events to simplistic morality tales featuring clear-cut victims and villains and tidy resolutions. In the case of "The Soldier on the
Grave," the series translates a political debate about war and its proper conduct into a personal tale of confession and redemption. Or, rather, it translates this debate into two competing tales: one in which a cover-up of U.S.
military atrocities in Iraq impedes the ability of the soldiers involved to work
through their disturbing experiences and one in which FBI Agent Seeley
Booth (David Boreanaz), a former army sniper, learns from their mistakes and
decides to confess his battlefield sins to an empathetic Brennan.

Both tales are semi-critical of war, depicting it as a morally suspect enterprise that inevitably results in trauma. Both tales also, and unusually, figure
the impact of U.S. military violence on the lives and relationships of enemy
civilians. In the case of the cover-up, a U.S. military unit on a routine night patrol invades what they think is a terrorist hideout. One exuberant young soldier charges in when he sees what he thinks is a weapon (it is really a spoon)
and slaughters an unarmed Iraqi family. The soldier is then killed by "friendly
fire" in the commotion that follows. Platoon Capt. William Fuller (Matt
Battaglia) covers up both crimes by planting rifles on the dead Iraqi family and
claiming the soldier was killed in action and died a heroic death. Since the

dead soldier is a well-known basketball player and would-be NBA star, the program seems to be commenting on the ethically suspect treatment of the 2004 friendly-fire death of NFL player Pat Tillman by his army ranger brothers in Afghanistan. Exposing the assumptions behind the Tillman cover-up, the captain admits to reconstructing the scene of war in order to hide the uglier aspects of combat from public view. He knows, in other words, that "the way a nation remembers a war and constructs its history is directly related to how that nation further propagates war," and he seeks to construct a properly heroic memory.[49]

Unfortunately, the repression required to sustain this romanticized image of U.S. heroism leaves the other members of the platoon scarred and depressed, unable to work through the trauma and get on with their lives. Two soldiers are suffering from PTSD; one commits suicide later in the episode, and the unit's female medic lives in a state of denial, consciously suppressing memories of her wartime experience and channeling all her energies into her budding medical career. It is she who ultimately murders the "soldier on the grave" to protect her career, which is also her defense mechanism. While she must be punished for her behavior, that behavior is presented as a plausible emotional response to the threat of exposure. We are meant to empathize with her, if not her actions, which is why Booth treats her with kid gloves while verbally and physically abusing Captain Fuller.

The cover-up is exposed when Agent Booth recognizes a repetitive pattern in the tales the soldiers tell him about that night in Iraq: they all use exactly the same details to describe the scene, as if their stories have been rehearsed. A psychologically intuitive investigator, Booth reads this repetition compulsion as a symptom of an unprocessed traumatic memory. Back at the lab, he and the "squints" use photos from the scene of the atrocity to reenact the events and determine the truth of the story. When Booth confronts Fuller with "the facts," Fuller defends his actions as necessary to squelch Iraqi anger and sustain public morale at home: "A mistake was made. Nobody likes it, but you know it happens. If it got out, what we did, that neighborhood—the whole damn city—would have exploded. What would you have done? Would you have let the city burn?" Booth responds: "I don't know what you were fighting for, but it sure as hell wasn't my country." He is backed by the local general, who assures Fuller he "will be held accountable." The captain's arrest and punishment both absolves the soldiers of their personal guilt and redeems the military as an institution. He functions as a sacrificial scapegoat—or "bad apple," as the military likes to call them—whose elimination purifies the system and enables it to carry on as before. This conclusion permits the program to evade a confrontation with the more ethically challenging question of whether militarism is or ought to be a viable means of pursuing peace and security. The avoidance is again justified through the promotion of an empathetic relation to the suffering soldier, who is presented as the one truly under siege in Iraq.

The program concludes by underscoring the importance of therapeutic confession to the health of both individuals and the nation. As the soldier on the grave is laid to rest at Arlington National Cemetery, the normally tight-lipped Booth begins confessing his own military sins to Brennan: "I've done some things . . . I have to be honest about myself. I have to be able to tell someone." He then explains how he assassinated a Serbian general in Kosovo in front of the man's son at the boy's tenth birthday party. "They said I saved over a hundred people, but, you know that little boy, who didn't know who his father was, who just loved him, he saw him die, fall to the ground, right in front of him. . . . It's never the just the one person who dies, Bones. We all die a little bit, Bones. With each shot, we all die a little bit." Booth sobs toward the end of the confession, and the camera closes on Brennan's equally tearful face, as she nods in emotional agreement with him. The scene concludes with a shot of her hand resting on Booth's arm in a gesture of solace. As a spectacle of confession, the scene implies that the "need to tell," when combined with the public's willingness to listen, can bring closure to the historical trauma of war. This is reinforced by the fact that this incident is never discussed again in the show. The lingering truth the scene produces is not that war is traumatic; it is that trauma can be easily overcome.

Thus, while "The Soldier on the Grave" offers a far more critical view of the war in Iraq than do other television representations (including the nightly news), its conclusion also does far more to contain the fallout of this critique. The program redeems the military as an institution by projecting the guilt for war's excesses onto a few bad apples, who are easily purged from the ranks. It then recuperates any lingering ethical unease by staging a spectacle of confession that swamps reason in a tide of emotion. Ethical judgments become virtually impossible to articulate in the face of the mandate to support the troops, and *Bones* and other melodramas of soldier-suffering counsel viewers to identify unquestioningly with the soldier's pain.

There are two main problems with such melodramatic portrayals. One, they end up depicting U.S. soldiers as the true victims of U.S. military aggression. Even when the wounded bodies of Iraqi civilians are displayed, as

Bones (FX, 2006–present) uses the death of a soldier to investigate war atrocities in Iraq. Here we see the charred body of the soldier (Top Left), the photographic evidence that exposes the cover-up (Top Right), the punishment of the "bad apple" responsible for the cover-up (Bottom Left), and a spectacle of confession designed to produce catharsis and closure. ("Soldier on the Grave," 5/10/2006)

in *Bones*, the individuals remain unnamed and voiceless and, therefore, unavailable for identification. Their wounds are mediated and obscured (as in the photos Brennan and Co. use for their analysis) while the physical and psychic wounds of U.S. soldiers are foregrounded. The result is to preclude the direction of empathy toward Iraqi casualties. The U.S. soldier becomes the only viable object of emotional identification, and viewers are left wondering why Iraqis would want to attack "us" when "we" are only trying to "build roads and schools," as Capt. Fuller puts it. Two, this exclusive emotional identification is presented as the only viable response to the historical trauma of war. Because episodic series tend to emphasize closure and the restoration of social equilibrium, accounts of soldier-suffering in these series tend to generate "redemptive narratives," whose neat endings foreclose confusion and contemplation.[50] The structural injunction to move on to a new topic next week gives the impression that issues have been resolved, that pain, loss, and grief have been acknowledged and mourned once and for all. In remembering and honoring the pain of the U.S. soldier, programs like *Without a Trace* and *Bones*, not to mention *Montel Williams* and *Extreme Makeover*, encourage a strategic forgetting of the pain of others and of the United States' role in production of said pain. The message they convey about the war in Iraq largely reinforces the Bush administration's construction of that war as difficult but necessary and just.

Post-Sentimentality on Post-Network TV: Serial Melodrama and the Body of War

As I have already argued, the technological and regulatory transformations of the last twenty years have fundamentally altered the relations of production and distribution within the TV industry, leading some to identify the new system as a "post-network" system. As Lotz explains, "The post-network distinction is not meant to suggest the end or irrelevance of networks—just the erosion of their control over how and when viewers watch particular programs."[51] The explosion of cable channels and the emergence of new time-shifting and archiving devices (DVDs, DVRs, and cable or Internet downloads-on-demand) has so increased the level of competition between networks for antsy viewers that the rules of production and distribution have had to be completely rethought. The result has been an explosion of new, more serialized, and "complex" modes of storytelling, which treat controversy and conflict as more than temporary blockages to be overcome.[52] Rather, these new modes of storytelling encourage viewers to linger with uncertainty, analyze it and work through its ramifications more deliberately, thereby eliciting a more active mode of historical witnessing.

The NBC hospital drama ER provides an excellent example of how more complex, serialized modes of storytelling may promote a more critical engagement with social issues. Like EMHE, the series is focused on the fallout from the neoliberal privatization of social services.[53] Unlike EMHE, however, ER manages to do more than just promote viewer empathy; it uses multi-episode story arcs and long-term character development to demonstrate the persistent, structural nature of the problems with healthcare in the United States. While suffused with sentimentality and empathy for the victims of this system (the doctors included), it also piles injustice upon injustice, tragedy upon tragedy, in ways that cannot help but direct viewer attention to "the situation, as against

. . . the subject's individual suffering." As E. Ann Kaplan suggests, this is the key to generating a more ethical engagement with social crisis.[54]

From 2004 to 2006, ER used the budding romance between Dr. Michael Gallant (Sharif Atkins), a military surgeon stationed in Iraq, and Dr. Neela Rasgotra (Parminder Nagra), a Pakistani immigrant working in Chicago, to explore the cultural politics underwriting the remilitarization of U.S. foreign policy. The first two episodes of this arc, "Here and There" and "Back in the World," followed a familiar melodramatic structure, aligning viewers completely with Gallant's perspective on the war and offering depoliticized depictions of war's violence. In "Here and There," for example, an Iraqi child critically wounds herself and a number of U.S. soldiers when she accidentally stumbles into a minefield. Gallant's attempts to secure stateside treatment for the girl's injuries humanize the conflict and reassure the audience that U.S. intentions are good, however bad the war's effects may be. The rescue of the Iraqi girl redeems the war effort and confirms Gallant's status as a representative American "hero," literally worthy to receive love (Rasgotra and Gallant are married in the subsequent episode).

Later episodes introduce greater ambiguity, however, by opposing Gallant's romanticized perspective on war with his wife's more critical view. "Split Decisions," for example, depicts Gallant's decision to volunteer for another tour of duty as selfish and thoughtless, rather than "gallant," since he has arrived at this decision without consulting his wife. The program shows how the vaunted "brotherhood of the soldier" comes at the expense of female agency, traditional family relations, and domestic welfare in general. This critique is reinforced in "Strange Bedfellows" when Rasgotra learns that Gallant's mother has decided to divorce his soldier-father after years of neglect. She warns Rasgotra "the boy is his father's son. They're soldiers. No matter how much you love them, there's always another war." In a culture that virtually worships the soldier-hero, this critique of the "gallant warrior" is exceptional, drawing attention to the work that the cult of the warrior does to legitimate the prioritization of security over welfare (foreign over domestic policy).

The de-sentimentalization of military life continues in "Out on a Limb" when Rasgotra joins a support group for military spouses and ends up denouncing the conflation of support for the troops with support for the war. When she lets slip that she is opposed to war, one of the other spouses asks, "If you don't support the war, how do you justify what Michael is doing over there?" Rasgotra responds: "I don't justify it." When told "our duty [as spouses] is to support their duty [as soldiers]," she replies, "My duty is to be a good doctor and to be a good wife, not to be brainwashed into falling in line with some pseudo-patriotic delusion." Her tirade not only violates the expectations of emotional solidarity implicit in the therapeutic context; it exposes the whole therapeutic enterprise as a technique for containing and controlling political outrage. The de-romanticization of the military enterprise reaches completion with Gallant's very unheroic death by roadside bomb in "The Gallant Hero and the Tragic Victor." As with most combat deaths in Iraq, Gallant is not killed in a conventional battle, fighting the good fight. He is chewed up and spit out by a war machine that seems to operate in perpetual motion.

While it is true that the suffering of U.S. soldiers and their friends and family is still privileged over the suffering of Iraqi victims, what makes ER's interrogation of soldier-suffering slightly different is its long-term and highly self-conscious attention to the politics of "comfort culture."[55] The more serialized format enables a more complex exploration of issues of personal sacrifice, honor, and responsibility in war because there is no artificial injunction to tie up the loose ends each week. Rasgotra's status as an immigrant to the United States also provides the critical distance necessary for the program's producers to challenge the chauvinism inherent in the melodramatic formula. Rather than invoking a simple identification with the suffering soldier, ER interrogates the social context that has made such identification appear mandatory and suggests that there must be alternative ways to respond to historical experience. As E. Ann Kaplan suggests, the attempt to direct attention away from character and toward context "opens the text out to larger social and political meanings" and invites viewers to bear witness to the history on display.[56] This is a "post-sentimental" use of melodrama, which seeks to move beyond emotional catharsis to evoke a transformation of consciousness.[57]

ER notwithstanding, complex narratives of a post-sentimental bent have been developed most aggressively on cable and premium channels because these outlets are both less bound by FCC regulations and less beholden to advertising revenues to sustain production. Because they are opt-in services with subscription fees, FCC rules governing the use of obscenity, indecency, and profanity do not apply (the idea being that viewers choose these services, and the FCC need not protect consumers from their own choices). Moreover, the risk-reward equation is simply different when producers do not need to attract a large audience to survive. HBO's formula of adult-themed content, complex storytelling, and liberal doses of violence, nudity, and profanity has been so successful that it is now being emulated across the proverbial dial. The result has been a flowering of critical and complex serial narrative and reality programming that defines itself self-consciously against TV (at least in its staid, broadcast form).[58]

Thus, treatments of soldier-suffering on cable and premium channels are far less given to sentimentality and reassurance than those on broadcast TV. The difference can be illustrated by comparing the HBO documentary *Alive Day Memories* (ADM) with the "New Forgotten" episode of *The Montel Williams Show* (MWS) described earlier. While it may seem unfair to compare a daytime talk show to a prestige documentary, they are both forms of reality programming addressing similar subjects in similar ways. ADM consists of a series of confessional interviews with soldiers severely wounded in Iraq. The use of expository narrative and video inserts to frame the interviews mimics the tabloid style of MWS, as does the use of a recognizable "host" to anchor the presentation of information (in this case James Gandolfini, star of the HBO series *The Sopranos*). However, ADM also demystifies the tabloid format by opening and closing with shots of the soundstage—cameras, mikes, booms, scaffolds, and all. It sometimes includes Gandolfini's questions and sometimes omits them, allowing viewers to become absorbed in the soldier's story temporarily but then unexpectedly dragging them back with an overt prompt. Finally, Gandolfini never directly addresses the audience or offers easy solutions to the problems on display. In these ways, the program produces a mode of "formally aware viewing" typical of complex narratives. Jason Mittell calls this mode of viewing an "operational aesthetic" because it encourages audiences to attend simultaneously to the diegetic content of the program and its mechanics of production.[59] ADM's self-awareness deconstructs the confessional format of the tabloid talk show, illustrating how confession works to produce not truth, but normative subjects willing to accept and defend extant power relations.[60]

Whereas MWS worked to construct the war wound as badge of honor to be saluted by the rest of us, ADM actively defetishizes the wound by asking the guests to expose their stumps and scars and explain their prostheses to the audience. Missing limbs are held up to the camera for extreme close-ups, and in one case, a side view is used to show that the young man is virtually nothing but a torso. Viewers are not permitted to look away from these sights but also not permitted to invest them with mystery or romance. Amputees joke about their stumps and their "shiny legs"; a blind man wears a prosthetic eye encrusted with the diamonds from his wedding ring (the marriage failed due to his injury); and a severely head-injured soldier waves his hands uncontrollably while his mother remarks nonchalantly, "there are some behavioral issues." All of the soldiers are shown struggling to enter and exit the set on canes, crutches, or wheelchairs; some have trouble shaking hands with Gandolfini; others have to take Herculean measures just to get into the chair for the interview (a triple amputee has to do a handstand to push his torso up and onto the chair). Whereas *Montel* used a lot of medium close-ups and headshots during its interviews, ADM uses long shots, side angles, and even overhead shots to give the full perspective on these injured bodies. The effect is to deconstruct the "rhetoric of the face" that personalizes and sentimentalizes U.S. politics and move the audience beyond empathy, to anger (if not necessarily action).[61] The program concludes with non-diegetic news reports of the "bombing-of-the-day" in Iraq and reminds us that the war is relentlessly ongoing. The monotony of the news reports, which all sound the same, testifies to the structural nature of the problem, and quietly enjoins the audience to do something about it.[62]

The documentary series *Off to War* (OTW), which aired on the boutique cable channel Discovery Times, offers a similar contrast to the broadcast reality series *Extreme Makeover: Home Edition*. While, again, it may seem unfair to compare a makeover program designed for entertainment purposes to a "prestige" documentary series, the programs share much in the way of content and style of presentation. They both treat the personal and traumatic experiences of soldiers and their families during wartime, and they both do so by "combin[ing] textual and aesthetic elements of direct cinema (handheld camera work, synch sound, and a focus on everyday activities) with the overt structuring devices of soap operas (short narrative sequences, intercuts of multiple plotlines, mini cliff-hangers, the use of a musical soundtrack, and a focus on character personality)."[63] In other words, they are both docusoaps. The difference in impact has less to do with content than with the industrial location of the respective programs. Made for a broadcast network and, therefore, intent on attracting a mass audience, EMHE adopted an episodic structure that catered to emotion and could accommodate casual viewing. OTW, on the other hand, aired on a cable channel that catered to an adult (25–54) audience of news and history buffs. Network executives assumed these viewers wanted "serious" treatments of "serious" subject matter and so did not balk when the producers of OTW delivered a controversial take on the war. Indeed, they viewed the risky subject matter and serial storytelling structure as a way to cultivate viewer loyalty and confer prestige on the network.[64]

Like EMHE, *Off to War* seeks to personalize the war and evoke empathy for the soldiers and families featured. Its serial structure guarantees a more detailed, prolonged, and intensive investigation of the conditions responsible for soldier-suffering, though, including the conditions of neoliberal capitalism that have resulted in a "poverty draft." The first "season" of the program (really a three-part documentary) begins by following the training and preparation of the soldiers from the 36th Engineering Brigade of the Arkansas National Guard. Most of the men are older (30+), out of shape, and out of practice in terms of combat skills. The men complain about homesickness but are generally anxious to get to Iraq and help contribute to the nation-building project. The final seven parts of the series follow the soldiers upon arrival in Iraq, where they discover an active and aggressive insurgency opposed to the U.S. presence in Iraq. On the first night "in country," a mortar attack on their base camp kills four members of the unit and severely injures several others. The soldiers discover that their mission, which they thought was to build roads, bridges, and buildings, has changed dramatically. The insurgency has made rebuilding projects low-level priorities and thrown all personnel into a combat role. These episodes detail shocking lapses in training, equipment provision, and oversight that the U.S. press was only beginning to investigate in 2005. Soldiers and commanders both complain about the lack of armored Humvees, bulletproof glass, and Kevlar helmets and vests. We witness how the language barrier, and the lack of competent interpreters, creates potentially dangerous situations for troops and Iraqi civilians alike. We see examples of "military routine" that look a lot like civilian harassment (for example, the routine detention and imprisonment of Iraqi males found in the vicinity of a roadside bombing). And we hear about how difficult it is for the soldiers to decipher who is a friend and who is a foe. Back in the United States, we witness the financial and emotional hardships experienced by the families of the soldiers. The most poignant of these struggles is that of Lana Irelan, who must battle red tape at the Department of Defense and the Social Security Administration to ensure her husband, Wayne, who was seriously injured in the mortar attack, receives the care and compensation he has earned. On the story of the bureaucratic barriers to long-term healthcare and disability services for veterans, OTW scooped even the *Washington Post*.[65]

At a time when newspaper ombudsmen and investigative journalists were just beginning to question the Bush administration's rosy picture of progress in Iraq, *Off to War* presented an in-depth look at the war on the ground. If it celebrated the "noble grunt" and his service, it also contextualized that service

Off To War (Discovery Times, 2004–2005) showed the chaos that followed the "successful" invasion of Iraq. Poorly trained, underequipped and overburdened National Guard troops suffered at the hands of a violent insurgency. Here, Sgt. Wayne Irelan receives treatment for wounds suffered his first night in country (Top Right), and three young soldiers mourn one of their own (Bottom Right).

in relation to a structure of military neglect and reckless indifference. The seriality of the narrative allows the audience to witness the growing disillusionment and cynicism of the unit over time and implies that the cynicism is warranted, given the obvious gap between the political justifications for the war and its material reality. Several soldiers point to the inconsistent rationales for war offered by the Bush administration and the hypocrisy involved in U.S. foreign policy. As one unidentified soldier puts it, "America ain't tellin' the truth" about its decision to invade Iraq. Such cynicism would disqualify the soldiers from participation in a show like EMHE, or appear as a mere difference of opinion in war documentaries like *Occupation Dreamland* or *Combat Diary: The Marines Lima Company* (both frequent fillers on the A&E network).[66] In *Off to War*, however, it accrues persuasive force because it is shown to be a thoughtful change of position arrived at after a long and painful experience on the ground. The "ordinariness" of the subjects, and their established allegiance to notions of duty, honor, and patriotism, authenticates the conversion and lends it a poignancy beyond mere sentimentality. OTW constructs this particular war, in its particularity, as a political scandal in need of redress. In that sense, it makes "an important contribution to the culture's (re)assessment of the war [in Iraq]."[67]

The different material economy of cable and premium television production in the post-network era results in a different deployment of melodrama in scripted treatments of soldier-suffering, too. The FX series *Over There* and the HBO series *Generation Kill* (discussed in chapter 5) are just two examples of the high-quality dramatic narratives made possible by cable's narrowcasting strategies and higher tolerance for lower ratings. Perhaps the best example in this vein is the SPIKE TV limited series *The Kill Point*, which activated, then systematically deconstructed, prior Hollywood depictions of the "criminal vet." The cynical flip side of the "noble grunt," the "criminal vet" personifies the return of war's violence to the home front and often provides a commentary on the need for social reform.[68] *Kill Point*'s similarity to the independent, anti-establishment bank-siege film *Dog Day Afternoon* was also undeniable.[69] The series followed the attempt by a group of Iraq War veterans to rob a Pittsburgh bank. Before the robbers can escape with the loot, the police surround the bank, and the patrons are taken hostage. Like Sonny Wortzik in *Dog Day Afternoon*, Sgt. Victor Mendez, aka "Mr. Wolf" (John Leguizamo), cynically attempts to woo the public to his side by playing to the media. He knows that the media circus will buy him the time and sympathy (or at least guilt-ridden paralysis) he needs to plan his escape. After a failed attempt by the SWAT team to "breach" the bank, Wolf charges outside and performs a striptease for the cameras, showing off his shrapnel wounds and proclaiming his status as a patriot. "I love my country. I fought for my country. And I would die for my country. You think I wanted to end up here? You think I wanted guns in my face again? No way. No way, but I came home to sickness and nightmares. You know when I close my eyes, what I see? I see the faces of the soldiers and civilians I killed. That's what I see." He then accuses the government of having unjustly deprived him of his pension and medical benefits and concludes by listing his demands: "I want a flak jacket for every soldier in Iraq, 'cause our stupid ass government doesn't think it's necessary, and I want the son of every senator who voted yes for this war to sign up for active duty. You get me those things, and I'll leave here." While the crowd cheers wildly in support, Wolf says to the police negotiator, Capt. Horst Cali (Donnie Wahlberg), "Don't ever breach again. Cause you know what's at stake, and I know how to play it." Cali walks away in defeat, but later turns the media back on Wolf by leaking the news that Wolf is a "military criminal" who was discharged for insubordination and "murder" (he refused an order to reenter Fallujah during the disastrous 2004 siege, and sixteen men from another platoon died as a result). Thus, in a single episode, *Kill Point* manages to connect the war abroad to deprivation at home, to provide a range

In SPIKE TV's limited series, *The Kill Point* (2007), "Mr. Wolf" shows the burns he suffered in the siege of Fallujah. The goal of the striptease was to elicit public sympathy, but it also highlighted the media's complicity in promoting a culture of violence. ("Who's Afraid of Mr. Wolf?" 7/22/2007)

of ideological perspectives on war, heroism, and cowardice (including the female SWAT leader's pronouncement of Wolf's display as "bullshit": "I saw action, and I ain't robbin' banks"), and to expose the media's complicity in the promotion of violent spectacles such as war.

It also provides a compelling example of how complex characterizations and self-reflexivity can introduce moral ambiguity into the melodramatic form. Over the course of the multiday siege, the program alternates between the police command post and the bank, illustrating shifting conditions on the ground at both sites. Audience allegiance to characters is frequently reset as the perspective shifts, and we learn more about the personal philosophies, private lives, and underhanded tactics of both Capt. Cali and Mr. Wolf. These characters are doubles of each other: both are strong, intelligent leaders whose goal is to avoid bloodshed; both prove willing to disobey orders to do so; and both are willing to sacrifice themselves and their families to serve their country (but only up to a point). Such doubling undermines the apparent difference between the "good guys" and the "bad" and challenges the expectations of moral clarity and reassurance that define melodrama as a mode of storytelling. The intertextual references and frequent plot reversals also demonstrate a tolerance for confusion and disorientation unusual in TV narrative. The serial plot structure, emphasis on character development, and frequent shifts in perspective require viewers to make conscious choices about whom to identify with and why.

Like other post-sentimental texts, Kill Point uses elements of melodrama (a focus on ordinary individuals in extraordinary circumstances, an emphasis on emotional excess, and a penchant for mini cliff-hangers and musical cuing) to disrupt the expectation of moral reassurance typical of the form. Rather than resolving the social contradictions it dramatizes, the show holds these problems open for further interrogation, contemplation, and critique. Kill Point does not seek to avoid the issue of responsibility for combat atrocities; it explains but does not excuse such incidents, and it shocks us with instances of human cruelty, from all parties, that belie the rhetoric of American innocence. Most importantly, it connects popular complacency and blind patriotism to the production of a war machine that has become paranoid and self-perpetuating, spreading insecurity, rather than peace, in its wake. This is demonstrated by the contrast between Cali's "peaceful" style of negotiation through compromise, which succeeds in rescuing hostages (albeit one by one), and the repeated failures of all violent means of achieving extraction. Kill Point values diplomacy over might and indicts U.S. society for failing to mend its ways despite the obvious failure of those ways to secure peace, prosperity, and justice. It suggests we have simply failed to bear witness to the reality before our eyes.

Finally, the HBO series Six Feet Under (2001–2005) ended its series run with a potent examination of the politics of mourning and melancholia in the post-9/11 context. The series centers on the Fishers, a dysfunctional family of undertakers whose job is to help others process their grief. Though conceived for a post-9/11 world, the show did not look at the death of a soldier serving in the War on Terrorism until the final season (indeed, the penultimate episode). This episode's title, "Static," evinces a self-consciousness about the attempt to intervene in the mediated presentation of war. The episode centers on the suicide of multiple amputee Paul Ronald Duncan (Billy Lush, who also played "Baby Killer" Trombley in Generation Kill), who kills himself with a shot of phenobarbital provided by his sister. Unlike the wounded soldiers we have seen in other TV series, Duncan has no illusions about the meaning of his "sacrifice." He views death as the only viable form of comfort his family can or should offer. His sister articulates his perspective in a later argument with his mother, who wants him to "look whole again" for the funeral:

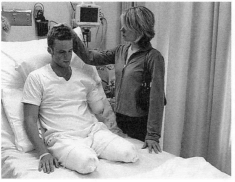

Six Feet Under (HBO, 2001–2005) presented the story of Paul Ronald Duncan, a multiple amputee from the war in Iraq who commits suicide rather than live as a "basket case" ("Static," 8/14/2005) (left). The same actor, Billy Lush, would later play "Baby Killer" Trombley in HBO's limited series *Generation Kill* (2008) (right). Encountering these texts out of order, as I did, one might infer a cause-effect narrative (i.e., Trombley's zeal for war leaves him physically and emotionally devastated).

Can you make him stand up and walk around, too?. . . . Can you make him maybe, like, talk and tell everybody it's all good, and it's really no problem to be dead? Maybe just stick your hand up inside his head and, you know, [say] "Everything's fine. Everything's fine. Freedom. Freedom. Freedom.". . . . If you dress Paul up in that uniform and put fake arms and legs on him and make it look like it all worked out. . . . It's not real.

The diatribe draws attention to the gap between the brutality of war and the image of it as a noble pursuit. It also illustrates how the process of memorialization works to narrow the options for coping with loss. Anger, for example, is made to seem inappropriate and excessive. The first rule of comfort culture is to stifle the urge to get angry.

This mini-discussion of proper modes of mourning reverberates with the ongoing story arc addressing the sudden death of one of the lead characters in the series, Nate Fisher (Peter Krause). Nate's younger brother David (Michael C. Hall) and sister Claire (Lauren Ambrose) have been struggling to deal constructively with their own sense of loss. Claire seeks refuge in alcohol and drugs, but these do not allow her to process her grief productively, as we see in a later scene. An inebriated Claire confronts the Duncans as they are leaving the funeral home and delivers her own stunning indictment of the war in Iraq and the therapeutic ethos of support that sustains it. "Support Our Troops?" she says.

> What a bunch of bullshit!. . . . Yeah, we wouldn't want to offend anybody while they're "supporting our troops." Dozens of Iraqis are still dying every day. The whole world hates us for going in there in the first place. And terrorists are still gonna be blowing shit up in this country for the next 100 years. And the best thing she can think to do about it is put a sticker on that enormous shit box! You know they still bring the wounded soldiers back at night so the press can't even film it and nobody sees! American soldiers are still being fucked up every day, and they don't even tell us! And it's all so you can put gas in this enormous fucking car to keep everybody feeling really fucking American!

This rant is designed to be interpreted in a variety of ways, none of which results in the solace of good comfort. Claire rejects the notion that support must entail the stifling of dissent, but she also callously directs her tirade toward the grieving Duncans. While viewers may appreciate the sentiment, they are not permitted to feel comfortable with the mode or manner of delivery. The narrative encourages us to connect the cold-hearted speech to Claire's own grief process, but it also draws attention to the way that grief unprocessed can ruin lives. Indeed, that might be the episode's most important lesson: melancholy functions as a means of denying and displacing, rather than working through, the pain associated with historical trauma.

Six Feet Under is one long disquisition on the proper response to tragedy. It seeks to provide not an accounting of the value of life, but an accounting of the value of living. It depicts mourning as a continuous process, rather than a quick catharsis that results in redemption. It refuses to treat death as a special or exalted circumstance of life and resists the urge to imagine the absence of a loved one as a loss that can be made good. Given this trajectory, it is no surprise that the series "ends" with Claire's removal to New York City, site of the 9/11 terrorist attacks (and, in case this reference is unclear, Claire's nephew requests a New York City fireman's cap as a present). Intercut with her trip "back east" is a flash-forward view of the deaths of every major character in the series. As we have come to know and love these characters over four seasons, this is a potentially devastating conclusion for the viewer, yet it is also perfectly in keeping with the logic of the show, which might best be summarized as "death happens." Six Feet Under's unique contribution to post-9/11 culture has been to question the rhetoric of national innocence that framed 9/11 as an exceptional loss requiring violent redemption. Instead, the series proposed that death is a universal human experience and a great equalizer; no life is more special than another, and no death is less special. They are all equally tragic, equally full of pathos, and equally susceptible to incorporation. In short, Six Feet Under's major contribution to post-9/11 U.S. culture is to remind viewers that trauma is not a condition inherent in historical events, but a carefully constructed response to those events, a way of processing or refusing to process them.[70]

Conclusion

Rather than using images of soldier-suffering to evade historical reckoning or produce catharsis and closure, Six Feet Under and other complex narratives used these images to open up questions about the conduct, costs, and consequences of imperial warfare. They also drew attention to the role of official memorial culture in fixing the meaning of these events and making dissent impossible to articulate. In that sense, they functioned a bit like 9/11 rumors, jokes, and other forms of "anti-monumental art" designed to challenge the standards of taste and propriety that circumscribed public discourse in the aftermath of 9/11.[71] The key difference, of course, is that these are television programs produced for profit by skilled artists and their corporate backers; they are not a type of folklore. Many of these programs aired on networks that required fees for access, and most of them targeted a well-educated, politically liberal audience already inclined to view the war in Iraq as a national scandal. This raises the question: "If a series or aspect of television presents a view contradicting or negotiating the dominant ideological perspective, and no one but those critical of the dominant ideology sees it, is its challenge to hegemony [effective]?"[72] Can TV still be said to function as a "cultural forum" for the negotiation of political consensus given the fragmentation and dispersal of television viewers across the dial and their enhanced ability to avoid programs that might disturb their worldviews? If TV promotes a type of historical witnessing, what are the possibilities and limitations entailed by this situation?

Certainly no one would claim that television has functioned as a democratic public sphere in the wake of 9/11. It has offered little space for the disinterested airing of political grievances and has, in fact, reinforced a stifling consensus.[73] Yet, it has also not simply or automatically projected the "official" perspective on issues like terrorism, war, and empire. Rather, as a prodigious storytelling machine, it has given viewers a wealth of opportunities to confront and test the guiding assumptions of their society. It has also mobilized viewers in different ways, appealing to different sorts of affective investments through different styles of mediation. It has served to construct, not just reflect, social events, and it has encouraged individuals to generate identities and affiliations around these events. It is in this more expansive sense that we might continue to speak of television as a cultural forum—not just a site for the negotiation of ideological values, but a site for the articulation and mobilization social subjects in which, however, nothing is guaranteed. As John Ellis argues, television serves a variety of purposes. It is at once an information aggregator, a filter, and a space for trying out, or "working through," social and cultural concerns. This process is unpredictable and open-ended. Individual programs or series may provide doses of closure, but the system as a whole promotes an ongoing engagement with the chaotic material of contemporary life. This "non-totalizing" system of speculation induces viewers to bear witness in the most active sense—to create a sense of themselves and the world from the shards on display.[74] All media may stimulate such engagements, but none do it quite as routinely as television because TV contains within itself so many narratives, so many images, so many memories, so much emotion.

TV images and narratives echo off each other in unpredictable ways, and the emerging complexity of the post-network system only exacerbates this unpredictability. The fact that the same actor, Billy Lush, played Lance Corporal Harold "Baby-Killer" Trombley in Generation Kill and Paul Ronald Duncan on Six Feet Under, for example, opens a space for viewers to extrapolate a narrative relationship between the two characters. They may perceive the multiple amputations and suicidal urges of Duncan as the inevitable consequence of the bloodlust of Trombley. And they need not watch the programs in temporal order (where Six Feet pre-dates Gen Kill) or on HBO to encounter this strange conjuncture. Both programs are widely available on the Internet through peer-to-peer file-sharing and in DVD format for home purchase, and Six Feet was shown in second-run syndication on the basic cable network A&E. By archiving and constantly recirculating narratives about the War on Terrorism in this way, the television industry has, almost reflexively, expanded the opportunity for viewers to encounter challenging perspectives even when they are being selective. Besides, it is a logical error to presume that greater viewer control inevitably results in greater selectivity and the narrowing of perspectives. Just because viewers possess the power to sanitize their viewing does not mean they actually do so. A renewed investment in the study of audience behaviors would be necessary to affirm such conclusions.

Thus, if the production practices of TV news encouraged a "collapse of memory" by narrowing the range of topics available for discussion and "offer[ing] . . . viewers no time for reflection" on historical events, entertainment programs worked to counteract this collapse by giving viewers time and space to contemplate taboo subjects and consider their own investments in war.[75] Of course, they did not all do so in the same ways or with the same outcomes. Nevertheless, by tracing the play of images of wounded soldiers across the TV landscape, we can see how TV foregrounded a set of questions that went unasked and unexamined elsewhere in the culture. How each program individually resolved these questions is less important than how they all collectively laid bare the scope of the ideological and ethical problems facing the nation after 9/11, and particularly after the war in Iraq. By narrating these social issues, they often presented a broader range of possible responses than either political discourse or news coverage could brook. This does not mean that all perspectives were equally well represented on TV or that TV did not police the boundaries of discourse in reductive ways. Indeed, as I have suggested throughout this book, TV helped construct, monitor, and maintain political and ideological consensus more often than not. What this complexity means is simply that television is too multifarious a cultural form to dismiss as an engine of false consciousness or collective amnesia. Only by studying the texts and contexts that comprise the practice of "watching TV" in detail can we hope to understand the medium's role in constructing public memory and regulating social relations after 9/11. This book is just a partial step toward such understanding.

Epilogue: Trauma and Memory Ten Years Later

The tragedy that became known as "9/11" is now ten years in the rearview mirror, and much has changed politically, socially, and in the popular culture. The Bush administration and its militarized foreign policy agenda are history. President Barack Obama has refocused U.S. diplomatic and military priorities to improve international relations and provide increased flexibility for responding to different types of threat. "Viewing [the various insurgencies around the world] . . . through one lens distorts the picture and magnifies the enemy," Pentagon spokesman John Nagle explains; thus, the "War on Terrorism" has been demoted to a series of "overseas contingency operations."[1] Obama's Nobel Peace Prize notwithstanding, the U.S. military remains engaged on a number of fronts around the world, but it is increasingly difficult to tell that these are coordinated actions designed to sustain American hegemony. Most importantly, Obama placed the focus back on Afghanistan and Al Qaeda, resulting in the assassination of bogeyman Osama Bin Laden in 2011. To many in the United States, his death provided a type of closure that was long overdue. Therapeutic language was trotted out by numerous pundits in the aftermath to suggest that the "trauma" of 9/11 had finally been overcome. "Evil" had been well and truly vanquished, and we, as a nation, could move on at last.

As I have argued, the "trauma frame" produced by the melodramatic news coverage of the attacks, and exacerbated in the popular culture that followed, ripped the terrorist attacks from their historical moorings. It primed the public to perceive the attacks as acts of "evil" perpetrated against an "innocent" nation and, therefore, requiring violent retribution to redeem the loss of security. This simplified morality tale was familiar and reassuring (since good always triumphs over evil), but it also encouraged the nation to act out, or repeat, the trauma, rather than work it through. In remembering 9/11 as a national trauma, we forgot other, more complicated aspects of the story (for example, the role of U.S. foreign policy in the production of terrorist hostilities, the failure of U.S. government institutions to anticipate and prevent the attacks, etc.). 9/11 became a monument to national innocence—a tale we told ourselves to extend our investment in the pleasurable fiction of American exceptionalism. Until the war in Iraq exposed the United States' vaunted tradition of benevolent interventionism for what it was—brutal, self-serving war-mongering—the popular culture largely reinforced the depiction of terrorists as an apocalyptic threat to civilization that needed to be exterminated. By exacerbating public fear and celebrating militarism as an antidote for it, popular culture bought into the promise that absolute security was an attainable condition. It reinforced the notion that we could eliminate insecurity by projecting it outward, or, in Bush administration parlance, that we could "fight the terrorists there so we wouldn't have to fight them here."

New media technologies have since fostered a more diverse and participatory mode of popular culture, which, in turn, has required media corporations to adjust their strategies of production, distribution, and marketing. As the editors of *Time* magazine explained when they named "You" (or rather Web 2.0 networks) "Person of the Year" for 2006, new media have empowered individuals to "seiz[e] the reins of the global media." We can now "balance our diet of predigested news with raw feeds from Baghdad and Boston and Beijing," and we can "learn more about how Americans live just by looking at the backgrounds of YouTube videos . . . than [we] could from 1,000 hours of network television."[2] New media promise to bypass old media filters, in other words, and bring us raw reality. YouTube certainly has enabled some alternative perspectives on war to emerge, playing host to both insurgent and soldier videos and bringing a less sanitized view of war into the home(land). But, it has also helped "[harness] the stupidity of crowds," as, for example, when it enabled the rise of several baseless 9/11 conspiracy theories.[3] The 9/11 Truth Movement was perhaps the best-known of these groups, and its methods demonstrate how participatory culture may disrupt and redirect official culture for both good and ill. This group appropriated and repurposed mainstream news footage and public information about the collapse of the Twin Towers and the Pentagon to produce a conspiracy theory that claimed the Bush administration either planned 9/11 or let it happen. While their evidence was dubious and easily debunked, the movement did call attention to a "forgotten" aspect of 9/11 within official memorial culture, namely the issue of accountability. By leveraging the viral distribution capacities of Web 2.0 (at one point their video, *Loose Change*, was the most downloaded movie on the Internet), the 9/11 Truth Movement showed the power of the new media to generate a critical mass and open the history of 9/11 to reconsideration.

In general, what has changed in the last few years is the willingness, even eagerness, of the public to confront "sensitive" subjects once defined as taboo. Even the images of falling bodies censored from media accounts of the Trade Center catastrophe have resurfaced as a lure for savvy viewers of the AMC hit series *Mad Men* (2007–present), about the high-stakes game of advertising in 1960s New York City, or the Fox satire *The Simpsons* (1989–present). References to once-taboo images and topics are now de rigueur on television, in music, in movies, and on the Internet. The trend has become so pronounced that cultural critic Jeff Melnick has given it a name: the "9/11 shout-out." While individual shout-outs may be designed to capitalize (quite literally) on controversy, the trend as a whole works to desacralize the history and memory of 9/11 and to open it to renewed contemplation and debate.[4] Thus, for example, *South Park* has prospered since 9/11 by devoting any number of episodes to issues associated with 9/11 and the War on Terrorism. In "Red Sleigh Down" (12/11/2002), the producers lampooned the Bush administration's use of religious rhetoric to frame the War on Terrorism by depicting Jesus as a Rambo-like warrior who swoops in to help rescue Santa when his sleigh is shot down over Iraq. In "I'm a Little Bit Country" (4/9/2003), they attacked the antiwar protests that bloomed in the run-up to the Iraq War by suggesting the hostility between pro- and antiwar camps was childish and hypocritical. Finally, in "The Mystery of the Urinal Deuce" (10/11/2006), they mocked the 9/11 Truth Movement and its presumption that the Bush administration was powerful enough to mastermind the 9/11 attacks. Instead, they proposed that the Bush administration was behind the 9/11 Truth Movement, which it used to create a necessary illusion of power. As the cartoon Bush explains: "People need to think we're all-powerful, and we control the world. If they knew we weren't in charge of 9/11, then, we appear to control nothing." Though the program featured a "libertarian hodge-podge of mixed political messages," most of which supported the Bush administration's policies, its satiric sensibilities did sanction a discussion of topics otherwise off-limits in the culture, especially in the immediate aftermath of 9/11 and in the run-up to the Iraq invasion.[5]

The FX series *Rescue Me* (2003–2011) offered perhaps the most sustained and important "9/11 shout-out" on contemporary television. Like *Third Watch*, *Rescue Me* focused on the lives of New York City firefighters in the aftermath of the 9/11 attacks. Unlike *Third Watch*, however, it never let the audience forget the background of 9/11 and explicitly addressed the consequences of living a traumatized life. Indeed, one could argue that it retraumatized both its char-

A sign of U.S. culture's increased willingness to face "ungraspable horror" and bear witness to it. (Left) Opening credits from the AMC series *Mad Men* (2007–present). (Right) A mocking tribute to *Mad Men* and the falling man by *The Simpsons*. ("Treehouse of Horror XIX," 11/2/2008)

acters and its viewers on a weekly basis in order to draw attention to the psychological and social effects of obsession. The program centers on Tommy Gavin (Denis Leary), a firefighter who lost a cousin and several coworkers on 9/11 and who is literally haunted by the ghosts of those he could not save. To compensate for his perceived failures, Tommy compulsively reenacts scenes of excessive masculinity, risking his life and the lives of those around him to appear heroic and sacrificing his marriage to appear stoic. While the program occasionally celebrates this masculine excess, most of the time it presents it as a compensatory gesture. Tommy is the one most in need of rescue, and what he needs to be rescued from are his own destructive behaviors and defense mechanisms. These mechanisms threaten to prevent him from healing and are largely (though not exclusively) depicted in negative terms as a refusal to "grow up" and "face facts." By interrogating Tommy's ailing psyche, *Rescue Me* suggests that the society's love of "John Wayne–style masculinity"[6] is an infantile, even dangerous, fantasy that will do nothing to address the real source of social trauma in the contemporary context, namely the institutional neglect of the common man (and presumably woman).

Season 5 of the series self-consciously reenacted the "trauma" of 9/11 by recalling both the imagery of the destruction of the World Trade Center towers and the stories of the men who worked "the pile." Episode 1 concludes, for example, with an image of a man trapped in a burning glass skyscraper, begging for help as the firefighters watch helplessly from below. The image recalls 9/11 but redefines the firefighters as impotent to rescue those in need. This is a long-overdue acknowledgment of the complexities of 9/11, which was both

In *Rescue Me* (FX, 2004–present) the traumatized hero's fixation on 9/11 leads to repetitive and self-destructive behaviors that serve as a lesson for the nation about the dangers of unprocessed memories. (Top Left) Tommy instructing new recruits about those lost on 9/11 ("Guts," 7/21/2004). (Bottom Left) Tommy's is haunted by the ghosts of those he could not save ("Guts"). (Right) Tommy and crew stand helplessly as a victim waves a white shirt from the heights of a glass high-rise, an obvious "shout-out" to 9/11. ("Baptism," 4/7/2009)

the single greatest rescue operation in the history of the NYFD and also the department's single greatest failure. The firefighters were both heroes and victims that day, and the surviving members of the force experienced the guilt and shame common to all survivors. In the aftermath, the social pressure to embody stoic masculinity led many of the firemen (Tommy Gavin being their proxy) to become fixated on the event in unhealthy ways.[7]

Rescue Me more explicitly addresses the history of 9/11, and the question of how history, memory, and mourning (or the failure to mourn) interrelate in its narrative. The plot of season 5 centers on a visit from a French journalist, who is gathering information for a book about 9/11 and wants a firsthand perspective from the veteran firefighters. Like a therapist, she coaxes the men to recall memories they would sooner forget and asks them to compose these fragments into a provisional narrative that might help them work through the trauma. The explicit contrast drawn between Lt. Kenneth "Lou" Shea (John Scurti), who willingly opens up, and Tommy, who resists, imparts lessons about the dangers of a memory unprocessed. Lou eagerly opens up about his feelings, offering the journalist his 9/11 poetry and adding forty-six pages of new thoughts in response to her prompts. Tommy, on the other hand, refuses her entreaties and ends up reembracing his favorite defense mechanisms—alcohol and reckless bravado. While Lou is able to achieve a type of catharsis, to "chip away" at "the shit" inside him and "lighten [his] load," as he puts it, Tommy ends up abusing himself and his family anew—a cycle the show suggests is related to his refusal to deal with the "monster" of 9/11.

In all, the series provides an object lesson in the difference between the processes of mourning and melancholy, "working through" and "acting out." The former involves facing your fears and anxieties and learning to live with them. The latter involves denying the pull that fear has on one and, thus, failing to move beyond it. Most often this behavior results in a compulsive repetition of the traumatic experience, such as occurs with hallucinations or flashbacks (like those Tommy suffers). It may also result in self-injurious behaviors designed to deny or evade the thing we fear. Arguably, this is what the United States did in the wake of 9/11. Rather than confront the historical and political problems exposed by the terrorist attacks, the culture went into a state of denial in which we projected the crisis outward and onto demons we could target with cathartic violence. This might explain why, after the invasion of Afghanistan, we compulsively reenacted the same scenario by invading Iraq, a country that had noting to do with 9/11. And, arguably, the decision to "act out" in response to 9/11 has harmed the nation, draining our resources and channeling our fear into excessive modes of securitization that target "us" as much as "them." This is effectively the argument of psychiatrist Robert Jay Lifton, who has diagnosed the United States' violent response to 9/11 as "Superpower Syndrome," a compensatory form of acting out designed to deny the vulnerability exposed by the terrorist attacks.[8] Whether we have overcome this "syndrome," now that our bogeyman is dead, is an open question.

Like the final episodes of Six Feet Under, Rescue Me ultimately works to reground trauma in history and to suggest that insecurity is a constitutive feature of life, not a loss that can be made good. Its comparative analysis of traumatized subjectivity (Lou versus Tommy) provides a salutary reminder that trauma does not inhere in historical events. Rather, it is a historically conditioned way of responding to events, and, as such, it is susceptible to redress. Like Tommy, we can and should work through our anxieties, rather than lashing out at the world. As John Ellis suggests, media can perform a vital role in this process of collective reckoning by providing us with raw materials amenable to renarrativization. By recording, transcribing, and even transcoding reality, media make it possible for subjects to bear witness to history themselves, to process and reprocess the "material of the witnessed world" into a provisional structure. This is not to say that TV functions as a neutral conduit of information about the real or that it conveys Truth with a capital T; rather, like memory itself, television is riddled with errors, blind alleys, and defensive blockages; it is structured by delay and discontinuity; and it contains inaccurate, misleading, and partial information. Viewers are invited to work over all of this material, including the gaps, errors, and symptomatic repetitions, and to craft a sense of the world that can only be provisional at best (since there is always new information available). In that sense, television engages individuals in a process of historicization and prevents history from congealing into a monument that might block other narratives from emerging. In the last few years, in particular, TV has helped desacralize the events of 9/11 and open them to renewed contemplation and discussion. It has helped to move us, as a society, beyond the fixation on trauma and the naïve belief in the redemptive powers of violence. It has asked us to reconsider the exceptional nature of U.S. violence and encouraged us to confront our responsibility for the oppression of others. Most importantly, it has undermined the delusion that the absence of security is a loss that can be made good at the expense of others.[9] This, at any rate, is my reading of TV's War on Terrorism super-text. Feel free to make your own provisional meanings from the materials collected here.

NOTES

Introduction: The Long Information War

1. Jean Baudrillard, "L'esprit Du Terrorisme," *South Atlantic Quarterly* 101, no. 2 (2002): 403–416, 403.

2. While President Bush initially called for a War on Terror, and continued to use that term throughout his tenure, his staff, the press, and most political pundits generally referred to conflict as the War on Terrorism. I will use the term "War on Terrorism" in keeping with most of my source materials and with the mainstream of political discourse.

3. Rohan Gunaratna, *Inside Al Qaeda: Global Network of Terror* (New York: Berkeley Books, 2002), 77.

4. Arjun Appadurai, *Modernity at Large: Cultural Dimensions of Globalization* (Minneapolis: University of Minnesota Press, 1996), 39–40.

5. Rene-Jean Ravault, "Is There a Bin Laden in the Audience? Considering the Events of September 11 as a Possible Boomerang Effect of the Globalization of US Mass Communication," *Prometheus* 20, no. 3 (2002): 295–300, 298.

6. Michael Barker, "Democracy or Polyarchy? US-Funded Media Developments in Afghanistan and Iraq Post-9/11," *Media, Culture and Society* 30, no. 1 (2008): 109–130.

7. George W. Bush, "President Bush Discusses Importance of Democracy in Middle East," February 4, 2004, http:// www.whitehouse.gov/news/releases/ 2004/02/20040204-4.html (accessed April 9, 2006).

8. David Folkenflik, "US Raising New Voices to Counter Arab Media: Old VOA Hands Say Alhurra TV, Radio Sawa Are Less News Than Propaganda," August 1, 2004, http://www.baltimoresun.com/ features/arts/bal-as.alhurra01aug01, 1,2238783.story (accessed April 4, 2005).

9. Jeff Gerth and Scott Shane, "US Is Said to Pay to Plant Articles in Iraq Papers," December 1, 2005, http://www .nytimes.com/2005/12/01/politics/01prop aganda.html (accessed April 9, 2006).

10. For a more optimistic evaluation of the "Shared Values Initiative," see Jamie Fullerton and Alice Kendrick, *Advertising's War on Terrorism: The Story of the U.S. State Department's Shared Values Initiative* (Spokane, WA: Marquette Books, 2006).

11. Greg Toppo, "Education Dept. Paid Commentator to Promote Law," January 7, 2005, http://www.usatoday .com/news/washington/2005-01-06- williams-whitehouse_x.htm (accessed June 6, 2007). Charlie Savage and Alan Wirzbicki, "White House-Friendly Reporter under Scrutiny," February 2, 2005, http://www.boston.com/news/ nation/articles/2005/02/02/white_house_ friendly_reporter_under_scrutiny/ (accessed June 6, 2007).

12. Steve Rendall and Tara Broughel,

"Amplifying Officials, Squelching Dissent," 2003, http://www.fair.org/extra/0305/warstudy.html (accessed December 30, 2003).

13. Kurt Nimmo, "The Lapdog Conversion of CNN," August 23, 2002, http://www.counterpunch.org/nimmo08 23.html (accessed May 10, 2007).

14. "Buying the War," Bill Moyers Journal, PBS, April 25, 2007.

15. Nancy Snow and Philip M. Taylor, "The Revival of the Propaganda State: US Propaganda at Home and Abroad since 9/11," International Communication Gazette 68, nos. 5–6 (2006): 389–407, 403.

16. Danny Schechter, "Selling the Iraq War: The Media Management Strategies We Never Saw," in War, Media, and Propaganda: A Global Perspective, eds. Yahya R. Kamalipour and Nancy Snow (Boulder, CO: Rowman & Littlefield, 2004), 26.

17. Elisabeth Bumiller, "Bush Aides Set Strategy to Sell Policy on Iraq," New York Times, September 7, 2002, A1.

18. Andrew Calabrese, "Causus Belli: US Media and the Justification of the Iraq War," Television and New Media 6, no. 2 (2005): 153–175, 157. See also Joseph Cirincione et al., "WMD in Iraq: Evidence and Implications," January 8, 2004, http://www.carnegieendowment.org/publications/index.cfm?fa=view&id=143 5&prog=zgp&proj=znpp (accessed December 18, 2010).

19. Thomas P. Joyner, "C.S.I.: Crime Scene Iraq," PopPolitics.com, March 24, 2003, http://www.poppolitics.com/articles/2003-03-24-crimesceneiraq .shtml (accessed April 4, 2005).

20. "Powell Reversed the Trend but Not the Tenor of Public Opinion," February 14, 2003, http://people-press .org/commentary/display.php3?Analysis ID=62 (accessed August 7, 2007).

21. On the military's assistance, see Maria Pia Mascaro and Jean-Marie Barrère, "Hollywood and the Pentagon: A Dangerous Liaison," in Passionate Eye (CBC Newsworld, 2003). For a deconstruction of the Lynch episode, see John Kampfner, "The Truth about Jessica," May 15, 2003, http://www .guardian.co.uk/Iraq/Story/0,2763,95625 5,00.html (accessed December 10, 2004). For more on the made-for-TV-movie, see Stacy Takacs, "Jessica Lynch and the Regeneration of American Identity and Power Post-9/11," Feminist Media Studies 5, no. 3 (2005): 297–310.

22. David Zucchino, "US Military, Not Iraqis, behind Toppling of Statue," July 5, 2004, http://the.honoluluadvertiser .com/article/2004/Jul/05/mn/mn03a .html (accessed April 9, 2007).

23. Stephen D. Cooper and Jim A. Kuypers, "Embedded Versus Behind-the-Lines Reporting on the 2003 Iraq War," in Global Media Go to War: Role of News and Entertainment Media during the 2003 Iraq War, ed. Ralph Berenger (Spokane, WA: Marquette Books, 2004), 169.

24. James Castonguay, "Intermedia and the War on Terrorism," in Rethinking Global Security: Media, Popular Culture, and the "War on Terror," eds. Andrew Martin and Patrice Petro (New Brunswick, NJ: Rutgers University Press, 2006), 151.

25. Matt Kempner, "TV Seeks Soothing Touch," Atlanta Journal-Constitution, October 24, 2001, E1.

26. "Terror Coverage Boosts News Media's Images, but Military Censorship Backed," November 28, 2001, http://people-press.org/reports/display.php3?PageID=9 (accessed June 20, 2007).

27. Rendall and Broughel, "Amplifying Officials."

28. Veronica Forwood, "Censorship of News in Wartime Is Still Censorship," October 15, 2001, http://media.guardian.co.uk/print/0,,4277504-108927,00.html (accessed April 25, 2007).

29. Matthew Fraser, *Weapons of Mass Distraction: Soft Power and American Empire* (New York: St. Martin's Press, 2003), 170.

30. David Altheide, "Consuming Terrorism," *Symbolic Interaction* 27, no. 3 (2004): 289–308, 298.

31. Christopher Campbell, "Commodifying September 11: Advertising, Myth, and Hegemony," in *Media Representations of September 11*, eds. Steven Chermak, Frankie Y. Bailey, and Michelle Brown (Westport, CT: Praeger, 2003), 52.

32. George W. Bush, "Address to a Joint Session of Congress and the American People (September 20, 2001)," in *History and September 11*, ed. Joanne Meyerowitz (Philadelphia: Temple University Press, 2003), 242.

33. Ibid.

34. Clear Channel executives deny having banned any songs, but they did allow local stations to set their own policies, which resulted in an informal ban. Censorship activities undertaken by Cumulus were more top-down, perhaps because the network had close ties to the Bush administration and the military. See William Hart, "The Country Connection: Country Music, 9/11, and the War on Terrorism," in *The Selling of 9/11: How a National Tragedy Became a Commodity*, ed. Dana Heller (New York Palgrave MacMillan, 2005); Jeffrey Melnick, *9/11 Culture* (Malden, MA: Wiley-Blackwell, 2009).

35. Quoted in Castonguay, "Intermedia," 161.

36. Stephen Kline, Nick Dyer-Whiteford, and Greig De Peuter, *Digital Play: The Interaction of Technology, Culture, and Marketing* (Montreal: McGill University Press, 2003), 179–183.

37. James Der Derian, *Virtuous War: Mapping the Military-Industrial-Media-Entertainment Network* (New York: Basic Books, 2001); Jonathon Burston, "War and the Entertainment Industries: New Research Priorities in an Era of Cyber-Patriotism," in *War and the Media*, eds. Daya Kishan Thussu and Des Freedman (Thousand Oaks, CA: Sage, 2003).

38. Roger Stahl, "Have You Played the War on Terror?," *Cultural Studies* 23, no. 2 (2006): 112–130, 123. See also Stahl, *Militainment, Inc.: War, Media, and Popular Culture* (New York: Routledge, 2009).

39. Seth Schiesel, "On Maneuvers with the Army's Game Squad," February 17, 2005, http://www.nytimes.com/2005/02/17/technology/circuits/17army.html (accessed March 29, 2008).

40. Stahl, "Have You Played the War on Terror," 121.

41. Ibid., 113.

42. Jennifer Terry, "Killer Entertainments," *Vectors* 5 (2007), http://vectors.usc.edu/issues/5/killerentertainments/.

43. Steve O'Hagan, "Recruitment Hard Drive," June 19, 2004, http://www.guardian.co.uk/theguide/features/story/0,14671,1242262,00.html (accessed June 7, 2007).

44. Bill Schneider and Anne McDermott, "Uncle Sam Wants Hollywood," November 9, 2001, http://archives.cnn.com/2001/SHOWBIZ/Movies/11/09/hollywood.war/ (accessed March 13, 2007).

45. Quoted in Justin Lewis, Richard Maxwell, and Toby Miller, "9-11,"

Television and New Media 3, no. 2 (2002): 125–131, 126.

46. Ibid.

47. See Richard A. Clarke, *Against All Enemies: Inside America's War on Terrorism* (New York: Free Press, 2004).

48. Susan Faludi, *Terror Dream: Fear and Fantasy in Post-9/11 America* (New York: Henry Holt, 2007), 50.

49. This is not surprising, given that the film was produced by conservative filmmaker Lionel Chetwynd (of *Hanoi Hilton* fame) and vetted by neoconservative stalwarts Fred Barnes, Morton Kondracke, and Charles Krauthammer, who receive thanks for their "advice and consultation" in the closing credits.

50. For more on the film, see Faludi, *Terror Dream*; Stephen Prince, *Firestorm: American Film in the Age of Terrorism* (New York: Columbia University Press, 2009).

51. Pat Aufderheide, "Good Soldiers," in *Seeing through Movies*, ed. Mark Crispin Miller (New York: Pantheon Books, 1990), 82.

52. Anthony Giardina, "The Lives They Lived: Branding Brotherhood," *New York Times Magazine*, December 29, 2002, 52.

53. Aufderheide, "Good Soliders," 89.

54. For a more complete overview of film-making post-9/11, see David Holloway, *Cultures of the War on Terror: Empire, Ideology and the Remaking of 9/11* (Montreal: McGill University Press, 2008), especially chapter 4; Douglas Kellner, *Cinema Wars: Hollywood Film and Politics in the Bush-Cheney Era* (Malden, MA: Wiley-Blackwell, 2010); Prince, *Firestorm*.

55. Anthony Grajeda, "The Winning and Losing of Hearts and Minds: Vietnam, Iraq and the Claims of the War Documentary," *Jump Cut* 49 (2007), http://www.ejumpcut.org/archive/jc49.2007/Grajeda/index.html.

56. "US Military Uses YouTube to Get Its Story Out," May 2, 2007, http://www.npr.org/templates/story/story.php?storyId=9966124&ft=1&f=1001 (accessed May 8, 2007).

57. Tech. Sgt. Pat McKenna, "Flights! Camera! Action!: Air Force Takes Wing on the Silver Screen," June 1997, http://www.af.mil/news/airman/0697/movie2.htm (accessed April 16, 2007).

58. David Robb, *Operation Hollywood: How the Pentagon Shapes and Censors the Movies* (Amherst, NY: Prometheus Books, 2004).

59. Doug Davis, "Future-War Storytelling: National Security and Popular Film," in *Rethinking Global Security: Media, Popular Culture, and the "War on Terrorism,"* eds. Andrew Martin and Patrice Petro (New Brunswick, NJ: Rutgers University Press, 2006), 17.

60. George W. Bush, "The President's State of the Union Address," January 29, 2002, http://georgewbush-whitehouse.archives.gov/news/releases/2002/01/20020129-11.html (accessed October 7, 2011).

61. Davis, "Future-War Story Telling," 31.

62. Ibid., 15.

63. See, for example, Der Derian, *Virtuous War*; Castonguay, "Intermedia"; Burston, "War and the Entertainment Industries."

64. Christopher Sharrett, "9/11, the Useful Incident, and the Legacy of the Creel Committee," *Cinema Journal* 43, no. 4 (2004): 125–131, 127.

65. David Nasaw, *Going Out: The Rise and Fall of Public Amusements* (Cambridge, MA: Harvard University Press, 2002), 215.

66. Theodore Wilson, "Selling America Via the Silver Screen? Efforts to Manage the Projection of American Culture Abroad, 1942–1947," in *"Here, There, and Everywhere": The Foreign Politics of American Popular Culture*, eds. Reinhold Wagnleitner and Elaine Tyler May (Hanover: University Press of New England, 2000), 87.

67. McKenna, "Flights! Camera! Action!"

68. Ibid.

69. Robb, *Operation Hollywood*, 27.

70. Lewis, Maxwell, and Miller, "9-11," 128.

71. Castonquay, "Intermedia," 171.

72. Gunaratna, *Inside Al Qaeda*, 305.

73. See, for example, "Black Hawk Down HPA Edition," 2006, http://video.google.com/videoplay?docid=156833016427820258# (accessed May 10, 2011).

74. Lynn Spigel, "Entertainment Wars: Television Culture after 9/11," *American Quarterly* 56, no. 2 (June 2004): 235–270, 256.

75. Raymond Williams, *Marxism and Literature* (London: Oxford University Press, 1977), 132.

76. See, for example: Brigitte L. Nacos, *Mass-Mediated Terrorism: The Central Role of the Media in Terrorism and Counter-Terrorism* (Lanham, MD: Rowman & Littlefield, 2002); Danny Schechter, *Media Wars: News at a Time of Terror* (Lanham: Rowman & Littlefield, 2003); Nancy Snow, *Information War: American Propaganda, Free Speech, and Opinion Control since 9/11* (New York: Seven Stories Press, 2003); and the following anthologies: Ralph Berenger, ed. *Global Media Go to War: Role of News and Entertainment Media during the 2003 Iraq War* (Spokane, WA: Marquette Books, 2004); Steven Chermak, Frankie Y. Bailey, and Michelle

Brown, eds., *Media Representations of September 11* (Westport, CT: Praeger, 2003); Bradley S. Greenberg, ed. *Communication and Terrorism: Public and Media Responses to 9/11* (Cresskill, NJ: Hampton Press, 2002); Pippa Norris, Montague Kern, and Marion Just, eds., *Framing Terrorism: The News Media, the Government and the Public* (New York: Routledge, 2003); Daya Kishan Thussu and Des Freedman, eds., *War and the Media: Reporting Conflict 24/7* (Thousand Oaks, CA: Sage Publications, 2003).

77. See, for example, Wheeler Winston Dixon, ed. *Film and Television after 9/11* (Carbondale: Southern Illinois University Press, 2004); Dana Heller, ed. *The Selling of 9/11: How a National Tragedy Became a Commodity* (New York: Palgrave MacMillan, 2005); Holloway, *Cultures of the War on Terror*; Kellner, *Cinema Wars*; Andrew Martin and Patrice Petro, eds., *Rethinking Global Security: Media, Popular Culture, and the War on Terrorism* (New Brunswick, NJ: Rutgers University Press, 2006); Melnick, *9/11 Culture*; Prince, *Firestorm*; Karen Randell and Sean Redmond, *The War Body on Screen* (London: Continuum, 2008); Karen Randell, Anna Froula, and Jeff Birkenstein, eds., *Reframing 9/11: Film, Popular Culture and the "War on Terror"* (New York: Continuum Press, 2010); Stahl, *Militainment, Inc.*; Susan Willis, *Portents of the Real: A Primer for Post-9/11 America* (New York: Verso, 2005).

78. See Jonathan Bignell, *Big Brother: Reality TV in the Twenty-First Century* (New York: Palgrave MacMillan, 2005); Anita Biressi and Heather Nunn, *Reality TV: Realism and Revelation* (New York: Wallflower Press, 2005).

79. Melani McAlister, *Epic Encounters: Culture, Media, and US Interests in the Middle*

East since 1945, updated ed. (Berkeley: University of California Press, 2005), 307.

80. Richard Jackson, Writing the War on Terrorism: Language, Politics, and Counter-Terrorism (Manchester: Manchester University Press, 2005), 22.

81. Ibid., 20.

82. Michel Foucault, "Truth and Power," in Michel Foucault Power/Knowledge: Selected Interviews and Other Writings, 1972–1977, ed. Colin Gordon (New York: Pantheon, 1980), 119.

83. Michel Foucault, The History of Sexuality, vol. 1: An Introduction (New York: Vintage, 1990), 93.

84. Bethami A. Dobkin, Tales of Terror: Television News and the Construction of the Terrorist Threat (New York: Praeger, 1992); Jackson, Writing the War; Joseba Zulaika and William A. Douglass, Terror and Taboo: The Follies, Fables and Faces of Terrorism (New York: Routledge, 1996).

85. Alexis de Tocqueville, Democracy in America, ed. J. P. Mayer, trans. George Lawrence, vol. 2 (New York: Harper Perennial, 1988), 444. On the political utility of fear, see Frank Furedi, Culture of Fear Revisited: Risk-Taking and the Morality of Low Expectation (New York: Continuum, 2006); Barry Glassner, Culture of Fear: Why Americans Are Afraid of the Wrong Things (New York: Basic Books, 2000); Brian Massumi, "Fear (the Spectrum Said)," positions 13, no. 1 (2005): 31–48; Corey Robin, Fear: The History of a Political Idea (New York: Oxford University Press, 2004); Peter Stearns, American Fear: The Causes and Consequences of High Anxiety (New York: Routledge, 2006).

86. David Campbell, Writing Security: United States Foreign Policy and the Politics of Identity, rev. ed. (Minneapolis: University of Minnesota Press, 1998), 202.

87. See Dana Nelson, National Manhood: Capitalist Citizenship and the Imagined Fraternity of White Men (Durham, NC: Duke University Press, 1998).

88. James E. Garcia, "Arabs, Latinos and the Culture of Hate," September 18, 2001, http://www.alternet.org /911oneyearlater/11530/arabs,_latinos_ and_the_culture_of_hate/ (accessed October 18, 2004).

89. Robert Putnam, "Bowling Together," February 11, 2002, http://www .prospect.org/cs/articles?article=bowling _together (accessed November 1, 2005).

90. This was particularly true during the early days of the medium. See, for example, Jane Feuer, "The Concept of Live Television: Ontology as Ideology," in Regarding Television: Critical Approaches, ed. E. Ann Kaplan (Frederick, MD: University Publications of America and the University Film Institute, 1983); Alan Nadel, Television in Black-and-White America: Race and National Identity (Lawrence, KS: University of Kansas Press, 2005); Lynn Spigel, Make Room for TV: Television and the Family Ideal in Postwar America (Chicago: University of Chicago Press, 1992).

91. John Hutcheson et al., "US National Identity, Political Elites, and a Patriotic Press Following September 11," Political Communication 21 (2004): 27–50, 47.

92. See Steven Wildman and Stephen Siwek, "The Economics of Trade in Recorded Media Products in a Multilingual World: Implications for National Media Policies," in The International Market in Film and Television Programs, eds. Eli Noam and Joel Millonzi (Norwood, NJ: Ablex Publishing, 1993); Toby Miller et al., eds., Global Hollywood 2, rev. ed. (Berkeley: University of California Press, 2005).

93. On the changing state of the television industry, see Michael Curtin, "On Edge: Culture Industries in the Neo-Network Era," in *Making and Selling Culture*, ed. Richard Ohmann (Hanover, NH: Univesity Press of New England, 1996); Amanda Lotz, *The Television Will Be Revolutionized* (New York: New York University Press, 2007).

94. Henry Jenkins, *Convergence Culture: Where Old and New Media Collide* (New York: New York University Press, 2006), 3.

95. Andrew Martin, "Popular Culture and Narratives of Insecurity," in *Rethinking Global Security: Media, Popular Culture, and the War on Terrorism*, eds. Andrew Martin and Patrice Petro (New Brunswick, NJ: Rutgers University Press, 2006), 108.

96. Richard Grusin, *Premediation: Affect and Mediality after 9/11* (New York: Palgrave Macmillan, 2010), 4.

97. Chris Hedges, *War Is a Force That Gives Us Meaning* (Garden City, NY: Anchor Books, 2003).

98. Castonguay, "Intermedia," 165.

99. Joseba Zulaika, "The Self-Fulfilling Prophecies of Counter-Terrorism," *Radical History Review* 85 (2003): 191–199, 197.

100. Horace Newcomb and Paul M. Hirsch, "Television as a Cultural Forum," in *Television: The Critical View*, ed. Horace Newcomb (New York: Oxford University Press, 2000).

101. Amanda Lotz, "Using 'Network' Theory in the Post-Network Era: Fictional 9/11 US Television Discourse as a 'Cultural Forum,'" *Screen* 45, no. 4 (2004): 423–438.

102. Michael Kackman, "Introduction," in *Flow TV: Television in the Age of Media Convergence*, eds. Michael Kackman et al. (New York: Routledge, 2010).

Chapter 1. 9/11 and the Trauma Frame

1. Kirsten Mogenson et al., "How TV News Covered the Crisis: The Content of CNN, CBS, ABC, NBC and Fox," in *Communication and Terrorism: Public and Media Responses to 9/11*, ed. Bradley S. Greenberg (Cresskill, NJ: Hampton Press, 2002), 120.

2. Allen Meek, *Trauma and Media: Theories, Histories, and Images* (New York: Routledge, 2009), 173. John Ellis, *Seeing Things: Television in the Age of Uncertainty* (London: I. B. Tauris, 2000), 98.

3. See Brian Monohan, *Shock of the News: Media Coverage and the Making of 9/11* (New York: New York University Press, 2010).

4. Neil Smelser, "September 11, 2001, as Cultural Trauma," in *Cultural Trauma and Collective Identity*, eds. Jeffrey Alexander et al. (Berkeley, CA: University of California Press, 2004), 279.

5. Monohan, *Shock of the News*, 172.

6. Josef Adalian and Michael Schneider, "Plots Are Hot Spots for Nets," September 23, 2001, http://www.variety.com/article/VR1117853005.html?categoryid=14&cs=1&query=Plots+are+hot+spots+for+nets (accessed August 30, 2008).

7. This has been the conclusion of the bulk of studies on the media's coverage of 9/11. See, for example, David Altheide, "Consuming Terrorism," *Symbolic Interaction* 27, no. 3 (2004): 289–308; Carolyn Kitch, "'Mourning in America': Ritual, Redemption, and Recovery in News Narrative after September 11," *Journalism Studies* 4, no. 2 (2003): 213–224; Jack Lule, "Myth and Terror on the Editorial Page: The New York Times Responds to September 11, 2001," *Journalism and Mass Communications*

Quarterly 79, no. 2 (2002): 275–293; Monohan, *Shock of the News*; and the various essays collected in Steven Chermak, Frankie Y. Bailey, and Michelle Brown, eds., *Media Representations of September 11* (Westport, CT: Praeger, 2003).

8. On the social function of melodrama, see Peter Brooks, "The Melodramatic Imagination," in *Imitations of Life: A Reader on Film and Television Melodrama*, ed. Marcia Landy (Detroit: Wayne State University Press, 1991), 64.

9. Amy Reynolds and Brooke Barnett, "'America under Attack': CNN's Verbal and Visual Framing of September 11," in *Media Representations of September 11*, eds. Steven Chermak, Frankie Y. Bailey, and Michelle Brown (Westport, CT: Praeger, 2003), 92.

10. Quoted in Monohan, *Shock of the News*, 117.

11. The most famous such series was the *New York Times* "Portraits of Grief." See Jeffrey Melnick, *9/11 Culture* (Malden, MA: Wiley-Blackwell, 2009).

12. See, for example, Tracy Conner, "Running Late Saved Them from Trade Center Death," *New York Daily News*, September 8, 2002, 8–9; Donna St. George, "Lives Spared through Mysterious Good Fortune," *Washington Post*, September 15, 2001, B01; Robert Tomsho, Barbara Carton, and Jerry Guidera, "Twists of Fate Saved Lives of Many on 9/11," *Wall Street Journal*, November 22, 2001, F02.

13. Susan Faludi, *Terror Dream: Fear and Fantasy in Post-9/11 America* (New York: Henry Holt, 2007), 101.

14. Ibid., 100–101.

15. Ibid., 6. Faludi was not alone in this observation. See Melani McAlister, "A Cultural History of the War without End," in *History and September 11*, ed.

Joanne Meyerowitz (Philadelphia: Temple University Press, 2003); Emily Rosenberg, "Rescuing Women and Children," in *History and September 11*, ed. Joanne Meyerowitz (Philadelphia: Temple University Press, 2003); Elisabeth Anker, "Villains, Victims, and Heroes: Melodrama, Media and September 11," *Journal of Communication* 55, no. 1 (2005): 22–37. On the mythic resonance of such tales, see Richard Slotkin, *Regeneration through Violence: The Mythology of the American Frontier, 1600–1860* (Middletown, CT: Wesleyan University Press, 1973), 5.

16. Letters to the editor of *USA Today* demonstrated a similar reluctance to overreact in the days following 9/11. Nina Duseja of Chicago, Illinois, for example, questioned the strategic value of declaring "war" on terrorism: "Declaring war against terrorism is entirely different from declaring war on a country. . . . The people of Afghanistan will feel the pain. The terrorists who orchestrated the attacks Tuesday will not" (*USA Today*, Sept. 19, 2001, A14). Glen Allport of Williams, Oregon, advocated taking a good hard look at U.S. foreign policy: "Whatever we do in response to Tuesday's attacks, it is time to rethink our foreign policies. Those policies have not kept America safe—they have made us a target" (ibid.). For a similar analysis of letters to the editor of the *New York Times*, see Brigitte L. Nacos, *Mass-Mediated Terrorism: The Central Role of the Media in Terrorism and Counter-Terrorism* (Lanham, MD: Rowman & Littlefield, 2002), 156–157.

17. Mogenson et al., "How TV News Covered the Crisis"; Sandra Silberstein, *War of Words: Language, Politics and 9/11* (New York: Routledge, 2002).

18. Reynolds and Barnett, "America under Attack," 92.

19. For an in-depth analysis of the National Day of Prayer, see John Shelton Lawrence, "Rituals of Mourning and National Innocence," *Journal of American Culture* 28, no. 1 (2005): 35–48; Silberstein, *War of Words*, ch. 2.

20. Sacvan Bercovitch, *The American Jeremiad* (Madison: University of Wisconsin Press, 1978).

21. George W. Bush, "Statement by the President in His Address to the Nation," September 11, 2001, http://www.whitehouse.gov/news/releases/2001/09/20010911-16.html (accessed September 27, 2006).

22. Lule, "Myth and Terror on the Editorial Page," 285.

23. Anker, "Villains, Victims, and Heroes," 36.

24. Monohan, *Shock of the News*, 27.

25. Bethami A. Dobkin, *Tales of Terror: Television News and the Construction of the Terrorist Threat* (New York: Praeger, 1992), 40.

26. Melani McAlister, *Epic Encounters : Culture, Media, and US Interests in the Middle East since 1945*, updated ed. (Berkeley: University of California Press, 2005), 208.

27. Ibid., 200.

28. Dobkin, *Tales of Terror*, 81.

29. George P. Shultz, "Terrorism and the Modern World," *Studies in Conflict and Terrorism* 7, no. 4 (1985): 431–447.

30. Meaghan Morris, "Banality in Cultural Studies," in *Logics of Television: Essays in Cultural Criticism*, ed. Patricia Mellencamp (London: BFI Publishing, 1990), 18.

31. Bill Keveney, "Viewers Embrace Late-Night Talk Shows," *USA Today*, September 19, 2001, D4.

32. James Poniewozik et al., "What's Entertainment Now?" *Time*, October 1, 2001.

33. Todd Purdum, "Hollywood Rallies Round the Homeland," *New York Times*, February 2, 2003, B18.

34. Robert J. Bresler, "The End of the Silly Season," *USA Today Magazine*, November, 2001. See also David Ansen, "Finding Our New Voice," *Newsweek*, October 1, 2001; Poniewozik, "What's Entertainment?"

35. Ari Fleischer, "Press Conference," September 26, 2001, http://www.whitehouse.gov/news/releases/2001/09/20010926-5.html#BillMaher-Comments (accessed May 25, 2004).

36. See Silberstein, *War of Words*; Lynn Spigel, "Entertainment Wars: Television Culture after 9/11," *American Quarterly* 56, 2 (2004): 235–270.

37. Alan Nadel, *Television in Black-and-White America: Race and National Identity* (Lawrence: University of Kansas Press, 2005), 6.

38. John Corner, *Television Form and Public Address* (New York: St. Martin's Press, 1995), 32. See also John Caughie, *Television Drama: Realism, Modernism, and British Culture* (New York: Oxford University Press, 2000).

39. Mark Armstrong, "Fox's 'Most Wanted' Targets Terrorism," October 11, 2001, http://www.eonline.com/news/article/index.jsp?uuid=0c901834-320f-4b86-ba05-95c405329f38 (accessed July 23, 2007).

40. Julia Kristeva, *Powers of Horror: An Essay on Abjection* (New York: Columbia University Press, 1982), 4.

41. Franklin Gilliam and Shanto Iyengar, "Prime Suspects: The Influence of Local Television News on the Viewing Public," *American Journal of Political Science* 44, no. 3 (2000): 560–573.

42. Armstrong, "Fox's 'Most Wanted.'"

43. John Ashcroft et al., "September 11, 2001: Attack on America," October 10, 2001, http://www.yale.edu/lawweb/avalon/sept_11/doj_brief015.htm (accessed July 24, 2007).

44. See, for example, Mackubin T. Owens, "Real Liberals Versus the 'West Wing,'" February, 2001, http://www.ashbrook.org/publicat/oped/owens/01/liberals.html (accessed July 23, 2007). While The West Wing was certainly more supportive of liberal ideology overall, there was still much in the program that conservatives could embrace. Creator, writer, and producer Aaron Sorkin describes The West Wing as "a show that has no gratuitous violence, no gratuitous sex. It has featured the character of the president of the United States kneeling on the floor of the Oval Office and praying. This, I would think, would be exactly what conservative Republicans would want to see on television." Quoted in Terence Smith, "Online Focus: Aaron Sorkin," September 27, 2000, http://www.pbs.org/newshour/media/west_wing/sorkin.html (accessed July 23, 2007).

45. David Holloway, Cultures of the War on Terror: Empire, Ideology and the Remaking of 9/11 (Montreal: McGill University Press, 2008), 83.

46. According to Huntington, the Creed expresses a shared faith in "individualism, liberty, equality, democracy and the rule of law under a constitution" (14). It is open and flexible enough to be used to express all sorts of political positions, both supportive of power and antithetical to it. See Samuel P. Huntington, American Politics: The Promise of Disharmony (Cambridge, MA: Belknap Press, 1981).

47. Gail Shister, "'West Wing' Will Address Tragedy in a Special Episode," Philadelphia Inquirer, September 25, 2001, C05; Adalian and Schneider, "Plots Are Hot."

48. Peter Jonge, "Aaron Sorkin Works His Way through the Crisis," October 28, 2001, http://www.nytimes.com/2001/10/28/magazine/aaron-sorkin-works-his-way-through-the-crisis.html (accessed August 30, 2008).

49. A succinct rundown of popular commentary, both before and after the episode aired, can be found at: http://www.westwingepguide.com/S3/Episodes/45_IAI.html.

50. Robert Bianco, "'West Wing' Lectured More Than Entertained," October 4, 2001, http://www.usatoday.com/life/television/2001-10-04-west-wing.htm (accessed March 2, 2011); James Poniewozik, "'West Wing': Terrorism 101," October 4, 2001, http://www.time.com/time/columnist/poniewozik/article/0,9565,178042,00.html (accessed August 30, 2008).

51. Roger Catlin, "This Is Not the Real World," September 7, 2002, http://articles.courant.com/2002-09-07/features/0209071713_1_president-josiah-bartlet-west-wing-fictional-heroes.

52. Jasbir K. Puar and Amit S. Rai, "Monster, Terrorist, Fag: The War on Terrorism and the Production of Docile Patriots," Social Text 20, no. 3 (2002): 130.

53. "Epic theatre" sought to distance the audience from any identification with the characters or messages of the play by jolting them out passivity. Bertolt Brecht is most famously associated with this movement. Bertolt Brecht, Brecht on Theatre, trans. John Willett (London: Methuen, 1964). For an elaboration of how such modernist techniques have

historically been used in TV drama, see Caughie, *Television Drama*.

54. On enlightened false consciousness, see Peter Sloterdijk, *Critique of Cynical Reason* (Minneapolis: University of Minnesota Press, 1989). On the Bush administration's use of such cynicism post-9/11, see Thomas Foster, "Cynical Nationalism," in *The Selling of 9/11: How a National Tragedy Became a Commodity*, ed. Dana Heller (New York: Palgrave MacMillan, 2005).

55. Puar and Rai, "Monster, Terrorist, Fag," 134.

56. Isabelle Freda, "Survivors in the West Wing: 9/11 and the United States of Emergency," in *Film and Television after 9/11*, ed. Wheeler Winston Dixon (Carbondale: Southern Illinois University Press, 2004), 230.

57. Puar and Rai, "Monster, Terrorist, Fag," 130.

58. Lawrence, "Rituals of Mourning," 36.

59. They echoed conservative Israeli discourses on terror, in other words. The quotation comes from Benjamin Netanyahu, "Terrorism: How the West Can Win," in *Terrorism: How the West Can Win*, ed. Benjamin Netanyahu (New York: Farrar, Straus, Giroux, 1983), 204.

60. Melani McAlister coined the term "post-Orientalism" to describe how the simple binary of United States versus Middle East has progressively broken down over the years since 1945. See McAlister, *Epic Encounters*.

61. Richard Jackson, *Writing the War on Terrorism: Language, Politics, and Counter-Terrorism* (Manchester: Manchester University Press, 2005), 2.

62. For more on *South Park*, see the epilogue.

63. Spigel, "Entertainment Wars," 258–259.

64. Ibid., 257.

65. Kurt Nimmo, "The Lapdog Conversion of CNN," August 23, 2002, http://www.counterpunch.org/nimmo08 23.html (accessed May 10, 2007); "Roger's Balancing Act: Fox's Ailes Shakes up the News Status Quo," October 27, 2003, http://www.broadcast ingcable.com/article/print/151239- Roger_s_Balancing_Act.php (accessed March 4, 2011).

66. Paula Bernstein, "TV Newsies Skip Bush Speech Live," *Daily Variety*, November 9, 2001.

67. Bryce Zabel, "Guest Commentary: Television and the War on Terrorism," *Electronic Media*, November 19, 2001, 9.

68. John Higgins and Allison Romano, "The New Economics of Terror," *Broadcasting and Cable*, September 24, 2001, 4.

69. Charles Isherwood, "The 53rd Annual Primetime Emmy Awards, " *Daily Variety*, November 5, 2001, 2–3.

70. Michael Freeman and Chris Pursell, "Hollywood Notes," *Electronic Media*, January 7, 2002, 29.

71. Purdum, "Hollywood Rallies," B18.

72. Brian Massumi, "Fear (the Spectrum Said)," *positions* 13, no. 1 (2005): 32.

Chapter 2. Spy Thrillers and the Politics of Fear

1. Jennie Carlsten, "Constructing the Terrorist Subject: *Michael Collins* and the Terrorist as Models of Agonistic Pluralism," in *The War Body on Screen*, eds. Karen Randell and Sean Redmond (New York: Continuum, 2008).

2. Bethami A. Dobkin, *Tales of Terror: Television News and the Construction of the Terrorist Threat* (New York: Praeger, 1992); Melani McAlister, *Epic Encounters: Culture,*

Media, and US Interests in the Middle East
since 1945, updated ed. (Berkeley:
University of California Press, 2005).

3. Joseba Zulaika, "The Self-Fulfilling
Prophecies of Counter-Terrorism,"
Radical History Review 85 (2003): 191–199.

4. Dobkin identified such elasticity as
a trait of 1980s antiterrorist discourse,
too: "In official discourse, terrorism is
redefined . . . by its opposition to the
interests of the United States. Specific
ideologies and aims of individual
terrorist groups [are] conflated and
homogenized . . . subsumed . . . under
one 'over-arching goal of destroying
what we are seeking to build.'" Dobkin,
Tales of Terror, 86.

5. Zulaika, "Self-Fulfilling
Prophecies," 194.

6. Jasbir K. Puar, *Terrorist Assemblages:
Homonationalism in Queer Times* (Durham,
NC: Duke University Press, 2007), 5.

7. Zulaika, "Self-Fulfilling
Prophecies," 194.

8. For histories of the genre, see
Michael Kackman, *Citizen Spy: Television,
Espionage and Cold War Culture*
(Minneapolis: University of Minnesota
Press, 2005); Wesley Alan Britton, *Spy
Television* (Westport, CT: Praeger
Publishing, 2004).

9. We might add to this list the
Pentagon drama *E-Ring* and the special
forces drama *The Unit* (CBS, 2006–2009),
both of which treated special forces
soldiers as intelligence agents and
frequently dispatched them to distant
locales such as Afghanistan and Iraq to
uncover, detain, and interrogate
terrorists. The blurring of the boundaries
between the spy thriller and the military
drama responds to a blurring of the
boundaries between these agencies in
real life. See James Risen, *State of War: The
Secret History of the CIA and the Bush
Administration* (New York: Free Press,
2006).

10. Espionage thrillers in all media

"appeal directly to the . . . dream of
decisive, successful action in a situation
of significance beyond [an individual's]
own destiny." Ralph Harper, *The World of
the Thriller* (Cleveland, OH: Press of Case
Western Reserve University, 1969), 103.

11. Quoted in Laura Jackson, "Kiefer
Sutherland: Born to Play Jack Bauer," in
*Secrets of 24: The Unauthorized Guide to the
Political and Moral Issues behind TV's Most
Riveting Drama*, eds. Dan Burstein and
Arne J. De Keijzer (New York: Sterling
Publishing, 2007), 76.

12. Tricia Jenkins, "Get Smart: A Look
at the Current Relationship between
Hollywood and the CIA," *Historical Journal
of Film, Radio and Television* 29, no. 2
(2009): 236.

13. In reality, intelligence experts
insist the money is being misspent to
enhance electronic and satellite
intelligence at the expense of human
intelligence. See Risen, *State of War*.

14. George W. Bush, "Announcement
of Strikes against Afghanistan," October
7, 2001, http://archives.cnn.com/
2001/US/10/07/ret.bush.transcript/
(accessed November 12, 2009).

15. Jackson, "Kiefer Sutherland," 78.

16. Jenkins, "Get Smart."

17. DVD commentary, *The Grid*,
episode 3 (Century City, CA: Twentieth
Century Fox, 2005).

18. Paige Albiniak, "Post-9/11
Becomes a Television Plot," *Broadcasting
and Cable*, October 13, 2003.

19. DVD extra: "Know Your Enemy,"
Sleeper Cell (Showtime Entertainment,
2006). *24*'s reliance on the military is
near constant. Day 5, for example, used
substantial assistance from the navy,
including episodes of Marine One being
piloted by navy personnel, an episode in
which navy F/A-18 Hornet fighter jets are
scrambled to shoot down a plane piloted
by Bauer (episode 17: "3–4 am"), and two
episodes that take place aboard a
submarine stationed at Naval Base Loma

Point (episode 23: "5–6 am" and episode 24: "6–7 am"). Day 4 featured the use of an air force stealth fighter jet and pilot (episode 16: "10–11 pm"), and Day 6 included the use of an army C-130 cargo plane and crew (episode 1: "6–7 am"). And these are just the most obvious examples.

20. Matthew Baum, *Soft News Goes to War: Public Opinion and American Foreign Policy in the New Media Age* (Princeton, NJ: Princeton University Press, 2003).

21. Jenkins, "Get Smart." See also Kackman, *Citizen Spy*.

22. Manny Coto, Howard Gordon, and Evan Katz, "A Fictional Version of Issues You Read about on the Op-Ed Page: Three Members of 24's Creative Team Discuss the Stories They Tell and How They Tell Them," in *Secrets of 24*, 98.

23. Alessandra Stanley, "The War on Terrorism without the Wrangling," September 18, 2003, http://www.nytimes.com/2003/09/18/arts/television-review-the-war-on-terrorism-without-the-wrangling.html (accessed March 12, 2009).

24. Rick Kissell, "'Champ' on the Ropes Right Away," September 8, 2004, http://www.variety.com/index.asp?layout=print_story&articleid=VR1117910135&categoryid=1236 (accessed December 27, 2006).

25. *The Grid* averaged a 2.8 rating over its six episodes. *Threat Matrix* was pulling a dismal 1.4 by the time of its cancellation. See, respectively, R. Thomas Umstead, "Appeal without Limits: USA's 'The 4400,' TNT's 'The Grid' Propel Format," *Multichannel News*, August 16, 2004; "Shorts: ABC Sprinkles 'Millionaire' Pixie Dust on Sweeps," January 26, 2004, http://www.medialifemagazine.com/news2004/jan04/jan26/1_mon/news8monday.html (accessed December 12, 2009).

26. While *Alias* is a liminal case—mixing real geopolitical references into a

largely fantastic story—the series' creator, J. J. Abrams, insisted, "[We] were never doing a show about real-life intelligence agencies or the actual terrorists they might be pursuing." I take him at his word. Simon Brown and Stacey Abbott, "Introduction: 'Serious Spy Stuff?' The Cult Pleasures of *Alias*," in *Investigating Alias*, eds. Simon Brown and Stacey Abbott (New York: I. B. Tauris, 2007), 6.

27. George W. Bush, "Address to a Joint Session of Congress and the American People (September 20, 2001)," in *History and September 11*, ed. Joanne Meyerowitz (Philadelphia: Temple University Press, 2003), 241.

28. Robert Jewett and John Shelton Lawrence, *Captain America and the Crusade against Evil: The Dilemma of Zealous Nationalism* (Grand Rapids, MI: William B. Eerdmans Publishing, 2003). See also Matthew Hill, "Tom Clancy, 24 and the Language of Autocracy," in *The War on Terror and American Popular Culture*, eds. Andrew Schopp and Matthew B. Hill (Teaneck, NJ: Fairleigh Dickinson University Press, 2009); Tricia Rose, "24 and the American Tradition of Vigilantism," in *Secrets of 24*.

29. Jenkins, "Get Smart."

30. David Grove, "The Agency: Review," 2001, http://www.popmatters.com/pm/review/agency (accessed November 1, 2009); Lynette Rice, "Rescue Mission," September 13, 2002, http://www.ew.com/ew/article/0,,348195,00.html (accessed November 4, 2009).

31. *The Agency* had 10.3 million viewers compared to *Alias*'s 9.7 and 24's 8.6 million. Rice, "Rescue Mission." On 24's ranking relative to other pickups for 2002, see Tara McPherson, "Techno-Soap: 24, Masculinity and Hybrid Form," in *Reading 24: TV against the Clock*, ed. Steven Peacock (New York: I. B. Tauris, 2007).

32. Hill, "Tom Clancy, 24 and the Language of Autocracy."

33. Rice, "Rescue Mission."

34. Hill, "Tom Clancy, 24, and Langauge of Autocracy," 140.

35. Sharon Sutherland and Sarah Swan, "The Good, the Bad, and the Justified: Moral Ambiguity in *Alias*," in *Investigating Alias*; Sharon Sutherland and Sarah Swan, "'Tell Me Where the Bomb Is, or I Will Kill Your Son': Situational Morality on 24," in *Reading 24*.

36. Ann Donahue, "Review: *Threat Matrix*," September 12, 2003, http://www.variety.com/review/VE111792 1824.html?categoryid=32&cs=1&query=t hreat+matrix (accessed December 14, 2009).

37. Christopher Gair, "24 and Post-National American Identities," in *Reading 24*; Hill, "Tom Clancy, 24 and the Language of Autocracy."

38. Susan Faludi, *Terror Dream: Fear and Fantasy in Post-9/11 America* (New York: Henry Holt, 2007), ch. 1.

39. The actress who played the deaf analyst, Shoshannah Stern, would later appear as a feature character in the postapocalyptic series *Jericho* (CBS). See chapter 6.

40. DVD extra, "Know Your Enemy."

41. Jon Cassar, *24: Behind the Scenes* (San Rafael, CA: Insight Editions, 2006), 30.

42. Donahue, "Review: Threat Matrix."

43. Alexander, DVD commentary, *The Grid*, episode 3.

44. DVD extra: "Know Your Enemy."

45. Richard Jackson, *Writing the War on Terrorism: Language, Politics, and Counter-Terrorism* (Manchester: Manchester University Press, 2005), 64.

46. Bill O'Reilly used this phrase in his "debate" with the national legal director of the Council on American Islam Relations, Arsalan Iftikhar, in 2004. The interview may be viewed at: http://www.youtube.com/watch?v=EW2t ujZISvc.

47. *The National Security Strategy of the United States of America* (Washington, DC: White House, 2002), 3.

48. Sara Ahmed, "Affective Economies," *Social Text* 22, no. 2 (2004): 117–139; Inderpal Grewal, "Transnational America: Race, Gender and Citizenship after 9/11," *Social Identities* 9, no. 4 (2003): 535–561; Puar, *Terrorist Assemblages*. For a more historical take on this development, see McAlister, *Epic Encounters*, especially ch. 6.

49. Laura Bush, "Radio Address on Women in Afghanistan (November 17, 2001)," in *History and September 11*, ed. Joanne Meyerowitz (Philadelphia: Temple University Press, 2003); George W. Bush, "President Bush Discusses Freedom in Iraq and Middle East: Remarks by the President at the Twentieth Anniversary of the National Endowment for Democracy," November 6, 2003, http://www.whitehouse.gov/ news/releases/2003/11//20031106-2.html (accessed December 1, 2004).

50. Ahmed, "Affective Economies," 134.

51. Alexander, DVD commentary, *The Grid*, episode 3.

52. DVD extra: "Know Your Enemy."

53. Ahmed, "Affective Economies," 122.

54. Puar, *Terrorist Assemblages*, 187.

55. McAlister, *Epic Encounters*.

56. For a full accounting of how race, religion, and sexuality work together to constitute "terrorist subjects," see Puar, *Terrorist Assemblages*.

57. Puar, *Terrorist Assemblages*, 57.

58. Ibid.

59. Ibid., 185.

60. Alexis de Tocqueville, *Democracy in America*, ed. J. P. Mayer, trans. George Lawrence, vol. 2 (New York: Harper Perennial, 1988), 44.

61. See Lisa Parks, *Cultures in Orbit: Satellites and the Televisual* (Durham: Duke University Press, 2005), especially ch. 3.

62. Puar, *Terrorist Assemblages*, 152.

63. In 2001, the Bush administration created an Information Awareness Office, whose mission was to coordinate the application of new information technologies to help counter terrorism and other asymmetrical threats to national security. The goal was "Total Information Awareness." Critics feared it would lead to a massive and indiscriminate surveillance of U.S. citizens, so they pushed Congress to cut off funding for the program, which they did in 2003. Many of the functions of the ominously titled office were simply split up and redistributed among existing intelligence and security services, however. For criticism of the "Total Information Awareness Program," see William Safire, "You Are a Suspect," November 14, 2002, http://www.nytimes.com/2002/11/14/opinion/14SAFI.html (accessed January 12, 2010).

64. Puar, *Terrorist Assemblages*, 150.

65. Douglas Howard, "'You're Going to Tell Me Everything You Know': Torture and Morality on Fox's *24*," in *Reading 24*, 137.

66. "Primetime Torture," 2005, http://www.humanrightsfirst.org/us_law/etn/primetime/index.asp (accessed November 1, 2009).

67. Quoted in Jane Mayer, "Whatever It Takes: The Politics of the Man behind *24*," in *Secrets of 24*, 24.

68. Slavoj Zizek, "*24*, or Himmler in Hollywood," in *Secrets of 24*, 202–206.

69. Joel Surnow, "There Is Nothing Like It on TV: An Interview with Joel Surnow," in *Secrets of 24*, 88–91.

70. Robert Cochran, "A Creator's View: Interview with Robert Cochran," in *Secrets of 24*, 93, 94.

71. See, for example, the essays by John Leonard, Dorothy Rabinowitz, Sarah Vowell, and Judith Warner in *Secrets of 24*.

72. Jacqueline Furby, "Interesting Times: The Demands *24*'s Real Time Format Makes on Its Audience," in *Reading 24*, 69.

73. Dan Burstein and Arne J. de Keijzer, "How Well Does *24* Reflect the Real World?," in *Secrets of 24*, 158.

74. Steven Peacock, "*24*: Status and Style," in *Reading 24*, 29. See also Daniel Chamberlain and Scott Ruston, "*24* and Twenty-First Century Quality Television," in *Reading 24*.

75. Chamberlain and Ruston, "*24* and Twenty-First Century Quality Television," 20–21.

76. Deborah Jermyn, "Reasons to Split Up: Interactivity, Realism and the Multiple-Image Screens in *24*," in *Reading 24*, 55–56.

77. Scott McCloud, *Understanding Comics* (New York: Harper Perennial, 1994), ch. 3.

78. Jermyn, "Reasons to Split Up," 52.

79. McPherson, "Techno-Soap," 179.

80. Franklin Gilliam and Shanto Iyengar, "Prime Suspects: The Influence of Local Television News on the Viewing Public," *American Journal of Political Science* 44, no. 3 (2000): 560–573.

81. Shohreh Aghdashloo, "I Choose All My Roles with a Pair of Tweezers: An Interview with Shohreh Aghdashloo," in *Secrets of 24*, 113. The connection between "foreignness" and "danger" was heightened by the casting of a Persian actress (Aghdashloo) and a Hispanic actor (Nestor Serrano) in the roles of the Arab parents.

82. Spencer Ackerman, "How Real Is *24*?" May 16, 2005, http://www.salon.com/ent/feature/2005/05/16/24/index.html?tag=news_list%3btitle%3b1 (accessed January 20, 2010).

83. Excerpts included in Rush Limbaugh, "*24* and America's Image in Fighting Terrorism: Fact, Fiction or Does It Matter?," in *Secrets of 24*. Video available at: http://www.heritage.org/Press/Events/ev062306.cfm.

84. David Holloway, *Cultures of the War on Terror: Empire, Ideology and the Remaking of 9/11* (Montreal: McGill University Press, 2008), 83.

85. Limbaugh, "24 and America's Image in Fighting Terrorism," 156.

86. Surnow, "There Is Nothing Like It on TV," 89.

87. "'24': An Hour of Realism," April 29, 2005, http://www.washingtontimes.com/news/2005/apr/27/20050427-085529-9412r//print/ (accessed Jan 20, 2010).

88. Lindsey Coleman, "'Damn You for Making Me Do This': Abu Ghraib, 24, Torture and Television Sadomasochism," in *The War Body on Screen*, 202–203.

89. Ibid., 203.

90. Sarah Vowell, "Down with Torture! Gimme Torture!" in *Secrets of 24*, 43.

91. Coleman, "'Damn You For Making Me Do This,'" 204.

92. Surnow, "There Is Nothing Like It on TV," 90.

93. Jerome E. Copulsky, "King of Pain: The Political Theologies of 24," in *Secrets of 24*, 57.

94. Timothy Dunn, "Torture, Terrorism and 24: What Would Jack Bauer Do?," in *Homer Simpson Goes to Washington: American Politics through Popular Culture*, ed. Joseph J. Foy (Lexington: University of Kentucky Press, 2008), 175.

95. Ahmed, "Affective Economies," 119.

96. On *The Grid*, see James Castonguay, "Intermedia and the War on Terrorism," in *Rethinking Global Security: Media, Popular Culture, and the "War on Terror,"* eds. Andrew Martin and Patrice Petro (New Brunswick, NJ: Rutgers University Press, 2006). On *MI5/Spooks*, see Elizabeth Jane Evans, "Character, Audience Agency and Transmedia Drama," *Media, Culture, Society* 30, no. 2 (2008): 197–213.

97. 24's show runner Howard Gordon, quoted in Mayer, "Whatever It Takes," 26. On the use of 24 as a model for Abu Ghraib, see Tony Lagouranis, "An Army Interrogator's Dark Journey through Iraq: An Interview with Tony Lagouranis," in *Secrets of 24*, 198–199.

98. See "Conservatives Continue to Use Fox's 24 to Support Hawkish Policies," February 2, 2007, http://media matters.org/research/200702020015 (accessed January 12, 2010); Rosa Brooks, "The GOP's Torture Enthusiasts," May 18, 2007, http://www.latimes.com/news/opinion/la-oe-brooks18may18,0,5960407.column?coll=la-opinion-center (accessed January 12, 2010).

99. You can view the video at: http://www.youtube.com/watch?v=am6f5 EdHUpU.

100. Giorgio Agamben, *State of Exception*, trans. Kevin Attell (Chicago: University of Chicago Press, 2005), 22.

101. Leerom Medevoi, "Global Society Must Be Defended: Biopolitics without Boundaries," *Social Text* 25, no. 2 (2007): 53–79.

102. Roger Stahl, *Militainment, Inc.: War, Media, and Popular Culture* (New York: Routledge, 2009), 37.

103. "A Conversation about the Hit Show '24,'" *Charlie Rose* (PBS, 2005).

Chapter 3. Reality Militainment and the Virtual Citizen-Soldier

1. Michael Walzer, *Just and Unjust Wars: A Moral Argument with Historical Illustrations*, 3rd ed. (New York: Basic Books, 2000). For applications of the doctrine to the wars in Afghanistan and Iraq, see Jean Bethke Elshtain, *Just War against Terror: The Burden of America Power in a Violent World* (New York: Basic Books, 2003); Michael Walzer, *Arguing about War* (New Haven, CT: Yale University Press, 2004).

2. Rahul Mahajan, *The New Crusade: America's War on Terrorism* (New York: Monthly Review Press, 2002), 30.

3. Nina J. Easton, "Blacked Out," March 2002, http://www.ajr.org/article_printable.asp?id=2460 (accessed March 13, 2009); Neil Hickey, "Access Denied: Pentagon's War Reporting Rules Are Toughest Ever," *Columbia Journalism Review* 40, no. 5 (2002): 26–31.

4. Hickey, "Access Denied," 27.

5. Easton, "Blacked Out."

6. Al Jazeera and other international media outlets presented a very different image of the conflict. For more, see David Dadge, "Al Jazeera: A Platform of Controversy," in *Casualty of War: The Bush Administration's Assault on a Free Press*, ed. David Dadge (Amherst, NY: Prometheus Books, 2004), 66.

7. Barbie Zelizer, "Death in Wartime: Photographs and the 'Other War' in Afghanistan," *Press/Politics* 10, no. 3 (2005): 34.

8. The tactics of "mediated distanciation" were honed during the 1991 Persian Gulf War, about which see Peter Van Der Veer, "War Propaganda and the Liberal Public Sphere," in *Media, War, and Terrorism: Responses from the Middle East and Asia*, eds. Peter Van Der Veer and Shoma Munshi (New York: Routledge, 2004), 11; Andrew Hoskins, *Televising War: From Vietnam to Iraq* (New York: Continuum, 2004).

9. Caryn James, "British Take Blunter Approach to War Reporting," November 9, 2001, http://query.nytimes.com/gst/fullpage.html?res=9802E5D61638F93AA35752C1A9679C8B63&pagewanted=print (accessed March 13, 2008).

10. Elizabeth Croad, "US Public Turns to Europe for News," February 21, 2003, http://www.journalism.co.uk/2/articles/5576.php (accessed March 16, 2009).

11. Souheila Al-Jadda, "Does Al-Jazeera Belong in the USA?," December 19, 2007, http://www.usatoday.com/printedition/news/20071219/opledejazeera.art.htm?loc=interstitialskip (accessed March 16, 2009).

12. Hickey, "Access Denied," 27. Dadge, "Al Jazeera," 66.

13. Matt Wells, "How Smart Was This Bomb?," November 19, 2001, http://www.guardian.co.uk/media/2001/nov/19/mondaymediasection.afghanistan (accessed March 16, 2009).

14. Van Der Veer, "War Propaganda," 11.

15. Roger Stahl, "Have You Played the War on Terror?" *Cultural Studies* 23, no. 2 (2006): 113. See also Roger Stahl, *Militainment, Inc.: War, Media, and Popular Culture* (New York: Routledge, 2009).

16. Richard Jackson, *Writing the War on Terrorism: Language, Politics, and Counter-Terrorism* (Manchester: Manchester University Press, 2005), 147.

17. Stahl, "Have You Played the War on Terror," 114.

18. Ibid.

19. Roger Stahl, *Militainment, Inc.: Militarism and Pop Culture* (Northampton, MA: Media Education Foundation, 2006); "We Pause Now for a Word about the War . . . ," March 26, 2003, http://www.imdb.com/news/ni0103796/ (accessed June 20, 2008).

20. Robert Ito, "Theater of War," *Los Angeles Magazine*, November 2006, 108.

21. U.S. spy agencies have, likewise, sought to publicize their activities through entertainment media, setting up their own liaisons to Hollywood, beginning with the Federal Bureau of Investigations in the 1930s. The CIA put out its shingle in 1995, and the Department of Homeland Security opened an office in Hollywood in 2005. Tricia Jenkins, "Get Smart: A Look at the Current Relationship between Hollywood and the CIA," *Historical Journal of Film, Radio and Television* 29, no. 2 (2009): 229–243; "Department of Homeland Security Hires Hollywood

Liaison," May 2005, http://www.house
.gov/hensarling/rsc/doc/100406_holly
wood_liaison.doc. (accessed March 13,
2009).

22. David Robb, *Operation Hollywood:
How the Pentagon Shapes and Censors the
Movies* (Amherst, NY: Prometheus Books,
2004), 307.

23. Andrew Bacevich, *The New
American Militarism: How Americans Are
Seduced by War* (New York: Oxford
University Press, 2005), 34–68.

24. Andrew Grossman, "ABC Set to
Salute West Point," October 24, 2001,
http://www.allbusiness.com/services/mo
tion-pictures/4852640-1.html (accessed
February 5, 2009).

25. For more on these reality series,
see Stahl, *Militainment, Inc.: War, Media,
and Popular Culture*, especially ch. 3.

26. Stahl, *Militainment, Inc.: Militarism
and Pop Culture*.

27. "CBS Sues Fox over 'Boot Camp,'"
April 11, 2001, http://abcnews.go.com/
Entertainment/story?id=106967&page=1
(accessed February 5, 2009).

28. Jonathan Bignell, *Big Brother:
Reality TV in the Twenty-First Century* (New
York: Palgrave Macmillan, 2005), 62.

29. Stahl, *Militainment, Inc.: Militarism
and Pop Culture*. One of Burnett's first
contestants was Scott Helvenston, who
was later killed in the real war in Iraq as a
contractor for Blackwater. His body is
one of those dragged through the streets
of Fallujah and hung from a bridge. See
Stahl, *Militainment, Inc.: War, Media, and
Popular Culture*, 76–77.

30. Bignell, *Big Brother*, 25, 62.

31. Ibid., 5. For more on this
subgenre, see Anita Biressi and Heather
Nunn, *Reality TV: Realism and Revelation*
(New York: Wallflower Press, 2005).

32. Bignell, *Big Brother*, 63.

33. Amy Sims, "Military Reality
Shows Battle in Prime Time," April 8,
2002, http://www.foxnews.com/story/

0,2933,49730,00.html (accessed
February 28, 2009).

34. Jim Schiff, "'American Fighter
Pilot' Heavy Handed with Patriotism,"
March 29, 2002, http://www.michigan
daily.com/content/american-fighter-
pilot-heavy-handed-patriotism (accessed
March 17, 2009).

35. Producers Jesse Negron and Tony
Scott, quoted in ibid.

36. Bacevich, *The New American
Militarism*, 158–174.

37. On immediacy and hypermediacy,
see Jay Bolter and Richard Grusin,
Remediation: Understanding New Media
(Cambridge, MA: MIT Press, 2000).

38. David Bianculli, "This Pilot
Doesn't Fly: 'Jag'-Ged around Edges and
Too Hyper," *New York Daily News*, March
28, 2002, 111.

39. Maria Pia Mascaro and Jean-Marie
Barrère, "Hollywood and the Pentagon:
A Dangerous Liaison," *Passionate Eye*.
CBC News, December 15, 2003.

40. Rear Admiral Craig Quigley,
assistant secretary of defense for public
affairs, quoted in Josh Grossberg, "War's
Not Hell, It's Entertainment!" February
22, 2002, http://www3.eonline.com/
uberblog/b42902_wars_not_hell_its_
entertainment.html (accessed February
28, 2009).

41. Mascaro and Barrère, "Hollywood
and the Pentagon."

42. Sims, "Military Reality."

43. "Profiles from the Front Line,"
November 21, 2006, http://abc.go.com/
primetime/profiles/ (accessed November
5, 2006).

44. Xan Brooks, "That's
Militainment," May 22, 2002, http://
www.guardian.co.uk/film/2002/may/22/
artsfeatures.afghanistan (accessed
February13, 2009).

45. Josef Adalian and Michael
Schneider, "ABC Brings Home
Battlefront Reality," February 20, 2002,

http://story.news.yahoo.com/news?tmpl =story&u=/nm/20020220/tv_nm/televisi on_battlefront_dc_1&printer=1 (accessed May 10, 2004).

46. Quoted in Steve Gorman, "US Network Plans Controversial Wartime 'Reality' Show," February 21, 2002, http://sg.news.yahoo.com/reuters/asia-90594.html (accessed May 10, 2004).

47. James Poniewozik, "That's Militainment! The War on Terror Gets the Cops Treatment," March 4, 2002, http://www.time.com/time/magazine/ article/0,9171,1001943,00.html (accessed November 7, 2006).

48. Erin Martin Kane, "Frontline to Viewers: ABC Series with Similar Title, Branding Not Associated with PBS's Award-Winning Documentary Series," February 24, 2003, http://www.pbs.org/ wgbh/pages/frontline/us/press/abc.html (accessed February 28, 2009).

49. Quoted in Andrea Lewis, "Lights, Camera, Military Action!," April 1, 2003, http://www.articlearchives.com/humaniti es-social-science/visual-performing-arts-visual/864709-1.html (accessed October 28, 2004).

50. Mascaro and Barrère, "Hollywood and the Pentagon."

51. Bignell, Big Brother, 41.

52. Joy Press, "The Axers of Evil," March 5–11, 2003, http://www.villagevoice com/ issues/0310/tv.php (accessed May 5, 2004).

53. R. D. Heldenfels, "On the 'Front Line,'" February 27, 2003, http://www .ohio.com/beaconjournal/entertainment/ 5273901.htm?template=contentModules/ printstory.jsp (accessed March 3, 2009).

54. Mascaro and Barrère, "Hollywood and the Pentagon."

55. "We Pause Now."

56. Press, "Axers of Evil."

57. See, for example, Poniewozik, "That's Militainment!"

58. Josef Adalian, "Cutler Brings Battle to VH1," February 20, 2002, http:/ /variety.com/article/VR1117861131.html? categoryid=1201&ref=ra&cs=1 (accessed May 5, 2008).

59. "Members of America's Armed Forces Chronicle Their Lives and Their Passion for Music in New VH1 Series 'Military Diaries,'" May 15, 2002, http:// www.viacom.com/press.tin?ixPress Release=80003806 (accessed May 10, 2004); "Forget Boot Camp—It's Time to Get Really Real," Entertainment Weekly, June 14, 2002, 54.

60. Poniewozik, "That's Militainment!"; Sims, "Military Reality."

61. Cori Marshall, "VH1's Military Diaries Not All Pro-War," June 8, 2002, http://www.pww.org/article/view/1363/1/ 90/ (accessed May 10, 2004).

62. See the Frontline documentary "Merchants of Cool" (PBS, 2/27/2001).

63. Biressi and Nunn, Reality TV, 13.

64. Anthony Grajeda, "The Winning and Losing of Hearts and Minds: Vietnam, Iraq and the Claims of the War Documentary," Jump Cut 49 (2007), http://www.ejumpcut.org/archive/jc49 .2007/Grajeda/index.html.

65. Madeleine Holt, "Is Truth a Victim?" May 16, 2002, http://news.bbc .co.uk/2/hi/programmes/newsnight/1991 885.stm (accessed November 7, 2006).

66. "Members of America's Armed Forces."

67. Stahl, Militainment, Inc.: War, Media, and Popular Culture, 82.

68. Bacevich, New American Militarism, 98.

69. Stahl, Militainment, Inc.: War, Media, and Popular Culture, 82.

70. Larry Gross, "Out of the Mainstream: Sexual Minorities and the Mass Media," in Media and Cultural Studies, ed. Douglas Kellner and Meenakshi Gigi Durham (Malden, MA: Blackwell Publishing, 2001), 406.

71. Stahl, Militainment, Inc.: War, Media, and Popular Culture, 37–38.

72. Richard Grusin, *Premediation: Affect and Mediality after 9/11* (New York: Palgrave Macmillan, 2010), 2.

Chapter 4. Fictional Militainment and the Justification of War

1. Robin Andersen, "That's Militainment! The Pentagon's Media-Friendly 'Reality' War," 2003, http://www.fair.org/index.php?page=1141 (accessed November 7, 2006); Jonathon Burston, "War and the Entertainment Industries: New Research Priorities in an Era of Cyber-Patriotism," in *War and the Media*, eds. Daya Kishan Thussu and Des Freedman (Thousand Oaks, CA: Sage, 2003); James Castonguay, "Intermedia and the War on Terrorism," in *Rethinking Global Security: Media, Popular Culture, and the "War on Terror,"* eds. Andrew Martin and Patrice Petro (New Brunswick, NJ: Rutgers University Press, 2006); James Der Derian, "Imaging Terror: Logos, Pathos, Ethos," *Third World Quarterly* 26, no. 1 (2005): 23–37; Justin Lewis, Richard Maxwell, and Toby Miller, "9-11," *Television and New Media* 3, no. 2 (2002): 125–131.

2. Discovery Channel spokesman Matt Katzive acknowledges the importance of prestige value when he says, "We . . . pride ourselves on being the gold standard in nonfiction TV." Quoted in Gabriel Spitzer, "Top Scores for Some Rookie Cable Networks," July 12, 2001, http://www.medialifemagazine.com/news2001/july01/july09/4_thurs/news2thursday.html (accessed March 26, 2009).

3. Amy Sims, "Military Reality Shows Battle in Prime Time," April 8, 2002, http://www.foxnews.com/story/0,2933,49730,00.html (accessed February 28, 2009).

4. Kenneth Li, "Television Executives Reach for Reset Button," August 31, 2009, http://www.ft.com/intl/cms/s/0/d9286d90-9643-11de-84d1-00144feabdc0.html#axzz1NBSZ2GnB (accessed September 7, 2009).

5. David Stout, "Ace Sleuths Driven by Honor Truth," November 29, 1998, http://www.nytimes.com/1998/11/29/tv/cover-story-ace-sleuths-driven-by-honor-truth.html (accessed March 27, 2009).

6. See, for example, Francis Fukuyama, *The End of History and the Last Man* (New York: Avon, 1993); Thomas Friedman, *The Lexus and the Olive Tree: Understanding Globalization* (New York: Anchor Books, 2000).

7. Andrew Bacevich, *The New American Militarism: How Americans Are Seduced by War* (New York: Oxford University Press, 2005), 43.

8. Though critical reviews of the program are rare, see Julian Delasantellis, "Above the Rest," January 13, 2003, http://www.poppolitics.com/archives/2003/01/Above-the-Rest (accessed May 5, 2004). On the show's popularity, see Wayne Friedman, "CBS Still Oldest Median Age Network: UPN Now the Youngest," July 11, 2005, http://www.mediapost.com/publications/?fa=Articles.showArticle&art_aid=31939 (accessed March 27, 2009).

9. Bellisario, quoted in Sims, "Military Reality Shows."

10. Richard Huff, "After 10 Seasons, 'Jag' Is Discharged . . ." *New York Daily News*, April 24, 2005, 2.

11. The Tailhook Association was a social group comprised of current and former U.S. Navy and Marine Corps personnel associated with battle carrier groups. At their 1991 symposium, dozens of men and women reported being

groped, verbally abused, and sexually assaulted by Tailhook members. One hundred servicemen, including over fifty officers, were disciplined for their roles in the incident, and the navy instituted new, more stringent policies on sexual harassment and gender equity in response. See Neil A. Lewis, "Tailhook Affair Brings Censure of 3 Admirals," October 16, 1993, http:// www.nytimes .com/1993/10/16/us/tail hook-affair-brings-censure-of-3-admirals.html (accessed February 28, 2009); "Frontline: 'The Navy Blues,'" PBS, October 1996, http://www.pbs.org/wgbh/ pages/frontline/shows/navy/ (accessed September 7, 2009).

12. Katherine Seelye, "Pentagon Plays Role in Fictional Terror Drama," New York Times, March 31, 2002, A12; Sims, "Military Reality Shows."

13. Broadcast networks are always vague about the rationale for cancellations, but in JAG's case ratings and ad revenue were down, and David James Elliott's contract had become too expensive. See Huff, "After 10 Seasons." On the final ratings, see Marc Bermen, "National Ratings in Primetime—Week of April 25, 2005," May 4, 2005, http:// www.mediaweek.com/mw/search/ article_display.jsp?vnu_content_id= 1000909803 (accessed March 27, 2009).

14. Such sporadic assistance was due largely to the short timetable of television production. Lt. Col. Todd Breasseale, "Personal Interview," (Army Public Affairs—Los Angeles Branch, 2007). David Robb discusses an exceptional case where the Marine Corps demanded and received script changes on an episode designed to burnish the military's image, but such intervention was rare. More often than not, when the

producers requested the use of military equipment, locations, or personnel, they were given such access because their stories were already "ship-shape." See David Robb, *Operation Hollywood: How the Pentagon Shapes and Censors the Movies* (Amherst, NY: Prometheus Books, 2004), 133–136.

15. Nat Hentoff, "Seeking Justice: Administration Marginalizes Jags," *Washington Post*, September 11, 2006, A21; Seelye, "Pentagon Plays Role."

16. Richard Grusin, *Premediation: Affect and Mediality after 9/11* (New York: Palgrave Macmillan, 2010), 34.

17. Seelye, "Pentagon Plays Role."

18. Hentoff, "Seeking Justice."

19. Of course, the Smith-Mundt Act was composed at a time when the global integration of media systems was not well advanced, so it draws neat distinctions between "here" and "there" that can no longer be sustained. Messages disseminated to "foreign" publics can now be easily picked up by U.S. consumers with access to satellite TV and Internet connections. The act also fails to recognize how public diplomacy and propaganda have been conflated in the War on Terrorism. Propaganda once referred to messages designed to deceive or create a false impression, whereas public diplomacy referred to "open communication in a global communication arena." Today, false information is mixed with true information and planted in both foreign and domestic media to serve U.S. interests. For examples, see Benjamin Isakhan, "Manufacturing Consent in Iraq: Interference in the Post-Saddam Media Sector," *International Journal of Contemporary Iraqi Studies* 3, no. 1 (2009): 7–26. On the difference between public

diplomacy and propaganda, see R. S. Zaharna, "From Propaganda to Public Diplomacy in the Information Age," in *War, Media, and Propaganda: A Global Perspective*, eds. Yahya R. Kamalipour and Nancy Snow (New York: Rowman & Littlefield, 2002), 223.

20. Nicholas D. Kristof, "Beating Specialist Baker," *New York Times*, June 5, 2004, A15; Rebecca Leung, "G.I. Attacked during Training," November 3, 2004, http://www.cbsnews.com/stories/2004/11/02/60II/main652953.shtml (accessed May 30, 2009).

21. Kristof, "Beating Specialist Baker."

22. For an analysis of how the Bush administration used such cynicism to cement its hold on power post-9/11, see Thomas Foster, "Cynical Nationalism," in *The Selling of 9/11: How a National Tragedy Became a Commodity*, ed. Dana Heller (New York: Palgrave Macmillan, 2005).

23. "US Bomb Kills Allies in Afghanistan," April 18, 2002, http://news.bbc.co.uk/2/hi/south_asia/1936589.stm (accessed June 15, 2009).

24. "Pilots Blamed for 'Friendly Fire' Deaths," June 28, 2002, http://news.bbc.co.uk/2/hi/americas/2073024.stm (accessed May 30, 2009).

25. Kevin Sites, Jim Miklaszewski, and Alex Johnson, "U.S. Probes Shooting at Fallujah Mosque," November 16, 2004, http://www.msnbc.msn.com/id/6496898/ (accessed June 20, 2009).

26. Andrew Hoskins, *Televising War: From Vietnam to Iraq* (New York: Continuum, 2004), 115.

27. See, for example, ibid., 76.

28. Alex Cohen, "Interview with Kevin Sites," May 10, 2005, http://www.npr.org/templates/story/story.php?storyId=4646406 (accessed June 23, 2009).

29. Susan Sontag, *Regarding the Pain of Others* (New York: Picador, 2003), 38–39.

30. Jean Bethke Elshtain, "Jean Bethke Elshtain Responds," *Dissent* (2006), http://www.dissentmagazine.org/article/?article=664.

31. President Bush, quoted in David Cole and Jules Lobel, "Why We're Losing the War on Terror," *Nation*, September 24, 2007, 18.

32. Richard Jackson, *Writing the War on Terrorism: Language, Politics, and Counter-Terrorism* (Manchester: Manchester University Press, 2005), 124.

33. See Bacevich, *The New American Militarism*, ch. 4.

34. Quoted in Seelye, "Pentagon Plays Role."

35. Ibid. See also Marita Sturken, *Tangled Memories: The Vietnam War, the AIDS Epidemic, and the Politics of Remembering* (Berkeley: University of California Press, 1997).

36. Walter Benjamin, "Theses on the Philosophy of History," in *Illuminations: Essays and Reflections*, ed. Hannah Arendt (New York: Schocken Books, 1968), 255.

37. Ulric Neisser and Nicole Harsch, "Phantom Flashbulbs: False Recollections of Hearing the News about Challenger," in *Memory Observed: Remembering in Natural Contexts*, eds. Ulric Neisser and Ira E. Hyman (San Francisco: W. H. Freeman , 1992), 91. See also Sturken, *Tangled Memories*, 37–38.

38. Seelye, "Pentagon Plays Role."

39. See, for example, "Forums: JAG," http://www.tv.com/jag/show/242/forums.html?tag=page_nav;forums (accessed April 2, 2011); "JAG Fan Forum," http://forums.usanetwork.com/index.php?showforum=14&prune_day=100&sort_by=Z-A&sort_key=last_post&topicfilter=all&st=0 (accessed April 2, 2011); "JAG

Fan Fiction Archive," http://www
.fanfiction.net/tv/JAG/ (accessed April 2,
2011).

40. On the USA forum,
"foreverJag227" liked the CIA-themed
"Tangled Webb" for its "action," while
"tshlw" liked the Iraq-themed "In
Country," not for its discussion of the
costs of the war, but for its scenes of
"cuddling in the desert."

41. Grusin, *Premediation*, 55.

42. Ibid, 79.

Chapter 5. From Virtual Citizen-Soldier to Imperial Grunt

1. Neal Gabler, "Hollywood's Shifting
Winds," *Variety*, November 23–30, 2003,
36.

2. Ruy Teixeira, "What the Public
Really Wants on Iraq," March 21, 2008,
http://www.americanprogress.org/issues
/2008/03/public_iraq.html (accessed
March 28, 2008).

3. James Der Derian, *Virtuous War:
Mapping the Military-Industrial-Media-
Entertainment Network* (New York: Basic
Books, 2001), 167. See also Pat
Aufderheide, "Good Soldiers," in *Seeing
through Movies*, ed. Mark Crispin Miller
(New York: Pantheon Books, 1990);
Susan Sontag, *Regarding the Pain of Others*
(New York: Picador, 2003).

4. On this conception of Empire as a
form of global governmentality, see
Michael Hardt and Antonio Negri, *Empire*
(Cambridge, MA: Harvard University
Press, 2001); Hardt and Negri, *Multitude:
War and Democracy in the Age of Empire*
(New York: Penguin Press, 2004);
Leerom Medevoi, "Global Society Must
Be Defended: Biopolitics without
Boundaries," *Social Text* 25, no. 2 (2007):
53–79.

5. Andrew Bacevich, *The New American
Militarism: How Americans Are Seduced by
War* (New York: Oxford University Press,
2005), 155.

6. Ibid, 170.

7. Ibid., 69–96.

8. Donald Rumsfeld, "Secretary
Rumsfeld Speaks on '21st Century'
Transformation of the U.S. Armed
Forces," January 31, 2002, http://www
.defenselink.mil/speeches/speech.aspx?s
peechid=183 (accessed September 13,
2006).

9. While General Eric Shinseki
reported to Congress that the war would
require three times the number of troops
allotted by Franks, civilian authorities at
the Pentagon refuted these claims and
won the day. Deputy Secretary of Defense
Paul Wolfowitz famously remarked to
Congress that he could not imagine how
the postwar reconstruction efforts could
possibly require more troops than the
combat operations phase. See Thomas
Ricks, *Fiasco: The American Military
Adventure in Iraq* (New York: Penguin
Press, 2006), 96–100.

10. Quoted in ibid., 151.

11. Ibid, 115.

12. Richard Slotkin, *Regeneration
through Violence: The Mythology of the
American Frontier, 1600–1860*
(Middletown, CT: Wesleyan University
Press, 1973).

13. David Swanson, quoted in Danny
Schechter, "It's Time for a Sequel: 'Over
Here,'" August 1, 2005, http://www
.commondreams.org/views05/0801-20
.htm (accessed August 5, 2005).

14. Quoted in ibid.

15. DVD commentary, *Generation Kill*,
episode 1 DVD (Santa Monica, CA: HBO,
2008).

16. See, for example, Adam Buckman,

"War Bonding: Young Marines in the Kill Zone," July 9, 2008, http://www.nypost.com/seven/07092008/tv/war_bonding_119066.htm (accessed July 22, 2009); Nancy Franklin, "The Road to Baghdad: David Simon's *Generation Kill*," July 21, 2008, http://www.newyorker.com/arts/critics/television/2008/07/21/080721crte_television_franklin (accessed July 21, 2009); Troy Patterson, "Band of Lunkheads: The Aggro Marines of *Generation Kill*," *Slate.com*, July 11, 2008, http://www.slate.com/ id/2195145/ (accessed July 22, 2009). Most critics lauded the series for its realistic and complex portrayal of contemporary warfare, however. See David Bianculli, "HBO's 'Generation Kill' Gamble," *Broadcasting and Cable* 138, no. 26 (2008): 3; Jonathon Finer, "'Generation Kill' Captures War's Lulls and Horrors," *Washington Post*, July 12, 2008, C01; Brian Lowry, "Generation Kill Review," July 9, 2008, http://www.variety.com/review/VE1117937679.html?categoryid=32&cs=1 (accessed July 22, 2009); Ken Tucker, "TV Review: Generation Kill," July 4, 2008, http://www.ew.com/ew/article/0,20210425,00.html (accessed July 22, 2009).

17. DVD commentary, episode 1.

18. Buckman, "War Bonding."

19. For an alternate perspective on *Over There*, see Anna Froula, "Political Amnesia Over Here and Imperial Spectacle *Over There*," paper presented at the Society for Cinema and Media Studies, Vancouver, BC, March 2–5, 2006.

20. Nathaniel Fick, *One Bullet Away: The Making of a Marine Officer* (New York: Houghton Mifflin, 2005), 126.

21. The roadblock narrative is based on an incident recorded in Wright's book, which the series *Generation Kill* also includes. In GK, however, the girl's head remains intact, and the scene is not nearly as gory. In general, *Over There* is the more gruesome of the two series, fetishizing the wounded and dead bodies of both U.S. soldiers and Iraqi soldiers and civilians. In the voice-over for the pilot episode of *Over There*, Chris Gerolmo, one of the producers, acknowledges attempting to use bloody imagery to push viewers' buttons. For example, Private Bo Rider (Josh Henderson) gets his leg blown off at the end of that episode, and the soundtrack fills with nothing but Bo's screams for about five minutes. "We wanted to rub your face in it," says Gerolmo, "we just wanted to be relentless in this moment about the devastation that war causes." *Generation Kill* includes numerous disturbing shots, but the producers do not tend to linger on them in the way that *Over There* does.

22. Ricks, *Fiasco*, 145.

23. Moral courage is one of the traits Marine Corps officers are supposed to embody, according to Nate Fick. See Fick, *One Bullet Away*, 48.

24. Ricks, *Fiasco*, especially chs. 7–10.

25. Evan Wright, *Generation Kill: Devil Dogs, Iceman, Captain America and the New Face of American War* (New York: Berkeley Caliber, 2004), 5.

26. Christian Christensen, "'Hey Man, Nice Shot': Setting the Iraq War to Music on Youtube," in *The Youtube Reader*, eds. Pelle Snickars and Patrick Vonderau (Stockholm: National Library of Sweden, 2010), 212. See also Kari Andén-Papadopoulos, "US Soldiers Imaging the Iraq War on Youtube," *Popular Communication* 7, no. 1 (2009): 17–27; Christian Christensen, "Uploading

Dissonance: Youtube and the US Occupation of Iraq," *Media, War and Conflict* 2 (2008): 155–175; Jennifer Terry, "Killer Entertainments," *Vectors* 5 (2007), http://vectors.usc.edu/issues/5/killer entertainments/.

27. Wright, *Generation Kill*, 55. The treatment of Trombley in the series is much more two-dimensional than Wright's treatment of him in the book. In the series, Trombley really is little more than a violence-obsessed kid, inured to human suffering by too many war films and video games. In the book, none of the marines really fits Wright's description of them as "America's first generation of disposable children" (5). Even Trombley is a student of the warrior lifestyle and learns to channel his energies to enhance his precision and lethality. The term "Generation Kill," if it applies at all, applies to the ordinary soldiers and reservists who surround and endanger the recon marines.

28. Ricks, *Fiasco*, 234.

29. Max Boot, *The Savage Wars of Peace: Small Wars and the Rise of American Power* (New York: Basic Books, 2003); Robert Kaplan, *Imperial Grunts: The American Military on the Ground* (New York: Random House, 2005).

30. Kaplan, *Imperial Grunts*, 4, 10.

31. Ibid., 369.

32. Ibid., 6.

33. *The National Security Strategy of the United States of America* (Washington, DC: White House, 2002).

34. Kaplan, *Imperial Grunts*, 40.

35. On biopolitics, see Michel Foucault, *"Society Must Be Defended"*: *Lectures at the College De France, 1975–1976*, eds. Mauro Bertani and Alessandro Fontana, trans. David Macey (New York: Picador, 2003). For a similar indictment

of Kaplan's take on life, see Andrew Bacevich, "Robert Kaplan: Empire without Apologies," September 8, 2005, http://www.thenation.com/doc/20050926/ bacevich/single (accessed August 5, 2009).

36. Kaplan, *Imperial Grunts*, 269.

37. Ibid., 181.

38. This analysis is inspired by Stanley Corkin's astute examination of Cold War westerns and themes of empire. Stanley Corkin, *Cowboys and Cold Warriors: The Western and US History* (Philadelphia: Temple University Press, 2004).

39. Foucault, quoted in Medevoi, "Global Society," 57.

40. George W. Bush, "Address of the President to a Joint Session of Congress," September 20, 2001, http://www.c-span .org/executive/transcript.asp?cat=current _event&code=bush_admin&year=0901 (accessed April 11, 2009).

41. Medevoi, "Global Society," 73.

42. Thomas Friedman, *The Lexus and the Olive Tree: Understanding Globalization* (New York: Anchor Books, 2000), 239.

43. Kaplan, *Imperial Grunts*, 296.

44. Anna Mulrine, "New Army Manual Shows War's Softer Side with Focus on Nation-Building," October 10, 2008, http://www.usnews.com/articles/news/ national/2008/10/10/new-army-manual-shows-wars-softer-side-with-focus-on-nation-building.html (accessed August 5, 2009).

45. Peter Van Der Veer, "War Propaganda and the Liberal Public Sphere," in *Media, War, and Terrorism: Responses from the Middle East and Asia*, eds. Peter Van Der Veer and Shoma Munshi (New York: Routledge, 2004), 11.

46. Foucault first described politics as the extension of war by other means. See Foucault, *"Society Must Be Defended,"* 268.

47. Roger Stahl, *Militainment, Inc.: War, Media, and Popular Culture* (New York: Routledge, 2009), 59.

48. Ibid., 140.

49. Ibid., 127.

50. Andén-Papadopoulos, "US Soldiers Imaging the Iraq War," 17.

51. Numerous scholars have argued that screen cultures play an important role in producing subjects invested in and by the system of neoliberal capitalism. See, for example, Mark Andrejevic, *Reality TV: The Work of Being Watched* (New York: Rowman & Littlefield, 2004); Lee Grieveson, "On Governmentality and Screens," *Screen* 50, no. 1 (2009): 180–187; James Hay, "Extreme Makeover: Iraq Edition—'TV Freedom' and Other Experiments for 'Advancing' Liberal Government in Iraq," in *Flow TV: Television in the Age of Media Convergence*, eds. Michael Kackman et al. (New York: Routledge, 2010); Anna McCarthy, *The Citizen Machine: Governing by Television in 1950s America* (New York: New Press, 2010).

52. Anthony Swofford, *Jarhead : A Marine's Chronicle of the Gulf War and Other Battles* (New York: Scribner, 2003).

Chapter 6. Contesting the Politics of Fear

1. George W. Bush, "President Bush Meets with National Security Team," September 12, 2001, http://www.white house.gov/news/releases/2001/09/ (accessed September 30, 2007).

2. On "super-empowered" individuals, see Thomas Friedman, *The Lexus and the Olive Tree: Understanding Globalization* (New York: Anchor Books, 2000). On citizens as the "eyes and ear of our law enforcement agencies," see Bill Frist, *When Every Moment Counts: What You Need to Know about Bioterrorism from the Senate's Only Doctor* (New York: Rowman & Littlefield, 2002).

3. James Hay and Mark Andrejevic, "Toward an Analytic of Governmental Experiments in These Times: Homeland Security as the New Social Security," *Cultural Studies* 20, nos. 4–5 (2006): 331–348, 341.

4. "Bush's Iraq Policies 'Atrocious,' Gore Says," May 27, 2004, http://articles.latimes.com/2004/may/27/nation/na-gore27 (accessed December 27, 2010).

5. Jim VandeHei, "Kerry Vows to Rebuild Alliances, Confront Terrorism," *Washington Post*, May 28, 2004, A09.

6. Peter Wallsten, "Despite Criticism, Patriot Act Gaining Popularity," April 26, 2004, http://community.seattletimes.nwsource.com/archive/?date=20040426&slug=patriot26 (accessed December 27, 2010). Kerry and the Democrats quickly abandoned the tough rhetoric when polls suggested broad support for the Patriot Act.

7. Richard A. Clarke, *Against All Enemies: Inside America's War on Terrorism* (New York: Free Press, 2004), 267.

8. Ibid., xiii.

9. For an extended account of the shift in political rhetoric from 2004 to 2006, see chapter 2 in David Holloway, *Cultures of the War on Terror: Empire, Ideology and the Remaking of 9/11* (Montreal: McGill University Press, 2008).

10. The most thorough account of how these changes have affected TV is Amanda Lotz, *The Television Will Be Revolutionized* (New York: New York University Press, 2007).

11. John Higgins, "Fast Forward: With Scant Notice, TV-DVD Sales Top $1

Billion and Begin to Affect Scheduling, Financing," December 22, 2003, http://www.broadcastingcable.com/article/151823-Fast_Forward.php (accessed December 28, 2010). More recent data suggest DVD sales have declined, but the decline coincides with the emergence of Blu-ray and digital distribution. See Claire Atkins, "DVD Back End Is Dwindling," March 30, 2009, http://www.broadcastingcable.com/article/190848-DVD_Backend_Is_Dwindling.php (accessed December 28, 2010).

12. Lotz, Television Will Be Revolutionized, 129–130.

13. On this series, see Stacy Takacs, "Burning Bush: Sitcom Treatments of the Bush Presidency," Journal of Popular Culture 44, no. 2 (2011): 417–435.

14. "September 11, 2001," The Daily Show with Jon Stewart, Comedy Central, 2001.

15. James Poniewozik et al., "What's Entertainment Now?," Time, October 1, 2001, 108; David Ansen, "Finding Our New Voice," Newsweek, October 1, 2001, 6.

16. Robert J. Bresler, "The End of the Silly Season," USA Today Magazine, November 2001, 17.

17. Tim Goodman, "Jon Stewart, Seriously, Here to Stay," October 29, 2004, http://www.sfgate.com/cgi-bin/article.cgi?f=/c/a/2004/10/29/DDGSO9HI5F17.DTL&ao=all#ixzz19WDgz7tP (accessed December 29, 2010). It has since doubled its ratings again and is as popular as ever under the Obama regime. Michael Starr, "Jon's Got Game!" September 25, 2010, http://www.nypost.com/p/entertainment/tv/item_ARuthNhfEWo9txbCOTBNkO;jsessionid=5C26B60B79A5E8E5CB441F3B0D7A5FE4 (accessed December 29, 2010).

18. In a high-profile interview on CNN's Crossfire, Stewart called hosts Tucker Carlson and Paul Begala "hacks" hired to perform political theater rather than promote deliberative debate. The video is a available at: http://www.youtube.com/watch?v=vmj6JADOZ-8.

19. When Stephen Colbert left The Daily Show to create his own "fake news" program, this time a satire of opinion-driven news programs such as The O'Reilly Factor, he would make this critique of jingoism a centerpiece of the show. Like Stewart, Colbert uses his fake news persona to chastise politicians and the media for providing the public with "mood politics," rather than food for thought.

20. Geoffrey Baym, "The Daily Show: Discursive Integration and the Reinvention of Political Journalism," Political Communication 22 (2005): 259–276, 264–267.

21. "Interview with Hillary Rodham Clinton," The Today Show, NBC, 1998.

22. Jim Rutenberg, "TV Shows Take on Bush, and Pull Few Punches," April 2, 2004, http://www.nytimes.com/2004/04/02/politics/campaign/02TUBE.html (accessed April 3, 2004).

23. "Whoopi: Bush 'Doing to Bathroom What He's Done to the Economy!'" October 15, 2003, http://www.mediaresearch.org/cyberalerts/2003/cyb20031015.asp#3 (accessed April 3, 2004).

24. "Whoopi: On Her New Show, Patriotism and Hollywood," October 2003, http://msnbc.msn.com/id/3080555/ (accessed April 3, 2004).

25. Adam Lisberg, "'Whoopi' Cancelled after Disappointing First Season," New York Daily News, May 17, 2004; "'Arrested Development' Struggles to Survive," February 17, 2005, http://

www.usatoday.com/life/television/news/
2005-02-17-arrested-ends_x.htm
(accessed January 2, 2010); Maureen
Ryan, "There's Always Money in the
Banana Stand: 'Arrested Development's'
Stealth Success," October 21, 2005,
http://featuresblogs.chicagotribune.com/
entertainment_tv/2005/10/theres_always
_m.html (accessed January 2, 2010).

26. M. Keith Booker, *Science Fiction
Television* (Westport, CT: Praeger, 2004).

27. Holloway, *Cultures of the War on
Terror*, 78.

28. Heather Havrilesky, "White-
Knuckle TV," September 12, 2005, http://
dir.salon.com/story/ent/feature/2005/09/
12/fear/index.html (accessed July 20,
2006).

29. "The Threshold Brain Trust," in
Threshold: The Complete Series (Hollywood,
CA: Paramount Home Video, 2006). The
creators of *Threshold, Invasion, Battlestar
Galactica,* and *Jericho* all acknowledge in
either online commentary or DVD extras
that 9/11 was a source of inspiration.

30. "9/11 Five Years Later: President
Bush One-on-One," *The Today Show*,
NBC, September 11, 2006.

31. Corey Robin, *Fear: The History of a
Political Idea* (New York: Oxford
University Press, 2004), 33.

32. Ibid., 47.

33. As one critic put it, "There isn't a
moment of wonder or suspense in
Surface, or a single performance or
character that is even remotely
involving—and that includes the slimy,
electrically charged, amphibious
monsters." Rob Bianco, "You May Be
Scared Silly by NBC's *Surface*," September
18, 2005, http://www.usatoday.com/
life/television/reviews/2005-09-18-
surface_x.htm (accessed July 20, 2006).

34. Susan Faludi, *Terror Dream: Fear and
Fantasy in Post-9/11 America* (New York:
Henry Holt, 2007); Julie Drew, "Identity
Crisis: Gender, Public Discourse and
9/11," *Women and Language* 27, no. 2
(2004): 71–77.

35. For a different view of the series,
see Cynthia Fuchs, "Surface," September
19, 2005, http://popmatters.com/tv/
reviews/s/surface-050919.shtml
(accessed June 1, 2006).

36. "Invading the Mind of Shaun
Cassidy," *Invasion: The Complete Series*
(Burbank, CA: Warner Home Video,
2006).

37. Ibid.

38. Dana Polan, "Eros and
Syphilization: The Contemporary Horror
Film," in *Planks of Reason: Essays on the
Horror Film*, eds. Barry Keith Grant and
Christopher Sharrett (Lanham, MD:
Scarecrow Press, 2004), 143.

39. Donald Rumsfeld, "Secretary
Rumsfeld Speaks on '21st Century'
Transformation of the U.S. Armed
Forces," January 31, 2002,
http://www.defense link.mil/speeches/
speech.aspx?speechid=183 (accessed
September 13, 2006).

40. See John Arquilla and David
Ronfeldt, "The Advent of Netwar
(Revisited)," in *Networks and Netwars: The
Future of Terror, Crime, and Militancy*, eds.
John Arquilla and David Ronfeldt
(Washington, DC: National Defense
Research Institute, 2001), 15.

41. Noel Carroll, *The Philosophy of
Horror or Paradoxes of the Heart* (New York:
Routledge, 1990), 208.

42. Philip E. Agre, "Imagining the
Next War: Infrastructural Warfare and the
Conditions of Democracy," September
15, 2001, http://polaris.gseis.ucla.edu/
pagre/ (accessed August 30, 2006).

43. Zbigniew Brzezinski, "Terrorized

by 'War on Terror,'" *Washington Post*, March 25, 2007, B01.

44. "The Making of Jericho," *Jericho: The First Season* (Hollywood, CA: Paramount Home Video, 2007).

45. Respectively, James Poniewozik, "Postapocalypse Now," *Time*, October 23, 2006, 94; Tad Friend, "Lost Generation," *New Yorker*, October 16, 2006, 189; Ginia Bellafante, "Little Panic on the Prairie: The Odd World of 'Jericho,'" February 19, 2008, http://www.nytimes.com/2008/02/19/arts/television/19bell.html?_r=1&scp=1&sq=little%20panic%20on%20the%20prairie&st=cse (accessed January 4, 2010).

46. Bellafante, "Little Panic."

47. Samuel P. Huntington, *American Politics: The Promise of Disharmony* (Cambridge, MA: Belknap Press, 1981), 14.

48. Bellafante, "Little Panic."

49. Ronald Moore, "Podcast: Epiphanies," January 20, 2005, http://www.syfy.com/battlestar/downloads/podcast/mp3/213/bsg_ep213_1of5.mp3 (accessed January 15, 2011).

50. This might explain why philosophers have been so fascinated with the program. See Josef Steiff and Tristan Tamplin, eds., *Battlestar Galactica and Philosophy: Mission Accomplished or Mission Frakked Up?* (Chicago: Open Court, 2008); Jason T. Eberl, ed., *Battlestar Galactica and Philosophy: Knowledge Here Begins Out There* (Malden, MA: Wiley-Blackwell, 2008).

51. See, for example, Gavin Edwards, "Intergalactic Terror," *Rolling Stone*, January 27, 2006, 32; Nancy Franklin, "Across the Universe: A Battlestar Is Reborn," January 26, 2006, http://www.newyorker.com/archive/2006/01/23060123crte_television?currentPage=all

(accessed January 3, 2011); Jonathan Glater, "Retooling a 70's Sci-Fi Relic for the Age of Terror," January 13, 2005, http://www.nytimes.com/2005/01/13/arts/television/13gala.html?sq=glater%20&st=Search%22re-tooling%2070s%20science%20fiction=&scp=1&pagewanted=all&position= (accessed January 3, 2011); and the essays collected in Eberl, *Battlestar Galactica and Philosophy*; Tiffany Potter and C. W. Marshall, eds., *Cylons in America: Critical Studies in Battlestar Galactica* (New York: Continuum, 2007); Steiff and Tamplin, *Battlestar Galactica and Philosophy*. For the phrase "The West Wing in space," see "Man of Duty: Gateworld Talks with Jami Bamber," 2006, http://www.gateworld.net/galactica/articles/bamber02.shtml (accessed January 18, 2011).

52. Glater, "Retooling a 70's Sci-Fi Relic."

53. Ronald Moore, "Podcast: Colonial Day," March 18, 2005, http://www.syfy.com/battlestar/downloads/podcast/mp3/111/bsg_ep111_1of5.mp3 (accessed January 15, 2011).

54. Isabel Pineda, "Playing with Fire without Getting Burned: Blowback Re-Imagined," in *Battlestar Galactica and Philosophy: Mission Accomplished or Mission Frakked Up?*

55. Eric Greene, "The Mirror Frakked: Reflections on *Battlestar Galactica*," in *So Say We All: An Unauthorized Collection of Thoughts and Opinions on Battlestar Galactica*, ed. Richard Hatch (Dallas: Benbella Books, 2006), 9.

56. Daniel Solove, "Interview with Ron Moore and David Eick," March 2, 2008, http://www.concurringopinions.com/archives/2008/03/battlestar_gala_5.html (accessed January 18, 2011).

57. Greene, "The Mirror Frakked," 9.

58. See, for example, the fan discussions on *Galactic Watercooler* (http://forum.galacticwatercooler.com), and the following press pieces: Joshua Alston, "The Way We Were: Art and Culture in the Bush Era—*Battlestar Galactica*," December 13, 2008, http://www.newsweek.com/2008/12/12/the-way-we-were.html (accessed January 19, 2011); Edwards, "Intergalactic Terror"; Franklin, "Across the Universe"; Mike Hale, "The Things You Can't Know about 'Galactica,'" January 15, 2009, http://www.nytimes.com/2009/01/16/arts/television/16batt.html (accessed January 19, 2011).

59. Greene, "The Mirror Frakked," 6.

60. Alston, "The Way We Were."

61. Brian Ott, "(Re)Framing Fear: Equipment for Living in a Post-9/11 World," in *Cylons in America*, 14.

62. Ibid., 19.

63. Jason Mittell, *Television and American Culture* (New York: Oxford University Press, 2009), 77. See also Eileen Meehan, *Why TV Is Not Our Fault: Television Programming, Viewers, and Who's Really in Control* (Lanham, MD: Rowman & Littlefield, 2005).

64. Derek Kompare, "More 'Moments of Television': Online Cult Television Authorship," in *Flow TV: Television in the Age of Media Convergence*, eds. Michael Kackman et al. (New York: Routledge, 2011), 98.

65. Even *Whoopi* had an active online fan base who compared it favorably to *All in the Family*, engaged with its topical issues, and understood the program's cancellation as a function of conservative backlash. See, for example, Comedicman, "Re: Why Was Whoopi Canceled," August 31, 2005, http://www.imdb.com/title/tt0364902/board/nest/24213397?d=25402392&p=1#25402392

(accessed January 17, 2011). See also the *Whoopi* forums at http://www.sitcomsonline.com/.

66. Ryan, "Always Money in the Banana Stand." In 2011, online video provider Netflix announced plans to stream original episodes of *Arrested Development* as part of its expansion into the content provision business. See "The Bluths Are Back and Only on Netflix," November 18, 2011, http://news.morningstar.com/all/ViewNews.aspx?article=PR/20111118SF10170_univ.xml (accessed November 19, 2011).

67. Scott Mayerowitz, "Nutty 'Jericho' Fans Make CBS Reconsider Canceling Show," June 6, 2007, http://abcnews.go.com/Business/FunMoney/story?id=3214156&page=1 (accessed January 17, 2011).

68. "Jericho Fans About to Go 'Nutty' over Hollywood Billboard," June 3, 2008, http://www.24-7pressrelease.com/press-release/jericho-fans-about-to-go-nutty-over-hollywood-billboard-52122.php (accessed January 17, 2011).

69. Goodman, "Jon Stewart." Late-night broadcast programs such as *The Tonight Show with Jay Leno* or *The Late Show with David Letterman* regularly pull 3–4 million viewers.

70. "Americans Spending More Time Following the News," September 12, 2010, http://people-press.org/report/?pageid=1792 (accessed January 21, 2011).

71. Ivan Askwith, "Deconstructing the Lost Experience: In-Depth Analysis of an ARG," 2008, www.ivanaskwith.com/writing/IvanAskwith_TheLostExperience.pdf (accessed August 15, 2010).

72. Books include the *Lost Encyclopedia*, several tie-in novels, and companion guides to all six seasons. There were also six albums of music

from the series, one for each season. The magazine ran from 2005 to 2010. Complete issue details are available on the *Lostpedia* website (http://lostpedia .wikia.com/wiki/). About the auction, see "Lost: Official Show Auction and Exhibit," 2010, http://abc.go.com/shows/lost/auction (accessed January 20, 2011).

73. "What's the Per Episode Cost of the Television Show Lost?" 2008, http://wiki.answers.com/Q/Whats_the_cost_per_episode_of_the_televison_show_lost (accessed January 20, 2011).

74. See the thread "Lost: A Ponzi Scheme" at http://www.buddyTV.com/discuss/lost-discuss.aspx.

75. Askwith, "Deconstructing the Lost Experience"; Groshan Fabiola, "The Lost Experience—Failure of Plot, Success of Commercialism," 2004, http://Ezine Articles.com/?expert=Groshan_Fabiola (accessed January 21, 2011).

76. Ian Maull and David Lavery, "Battlestar Galactica," in *The Essential Cult TV Reader*, ed. David Lavery (Lexington: University Press of Kentucky, 2009), 49.

77. Quoted in Suzanne Scott, "Authorized Resistance: Is Fan Production Frakked?," in *Cylons in America*, 219.

78. Ibid., 217.

79. Ott, "(Re)Framing Fear," 14.

80. Lynn Spigel, "Entertainment Wars: Television Culture after 9/11," *American Quarterly* 56, no. 2 (2004): 235–270.

Chapter 7: The Body of War and the Collapse of memory

1. Richard Grusin, *Premediation: Affect and Mediality after 9/11* (New York: Palgrave Macmillan, 2010), 12.

2. Stephen D. Cooper and Jim A. Kuypers, "Embedded Versus Behind-the-Lines Reporting on the 2003 Iraq War," in *Global Media Go to War: Role of News and Entertainment Media during the 2003 Iraq War*, ed. Ralph Berenger (Spokane, WA: Marquette Books, 2004).

3. Andrew Hoskins, *Televising War: From Vietnam to Iraq* (New York: Continuum, 2004), 65.

4. Toby Miller, *Cultural Citizenship: Cosmopolitanism, Consumerism, and Television in a Neoliberal Age* (Philadelphia: Temple University Press, 2007), 89.

5. Hoskins, *Televising War*, 95.

6. Michael McCarthy, "Violence in Iraq Puts Advertisers on Edge," USA Today, May 18, 2004, B2.

7. Hoskins, *Televising War*, 78.

8. "US and Coalition Casualties," March 28, 2008, http://www.cnn.com/SPECIALS/2003/iraq/forces/casualties/ (accessed March 28, 2008); David Brown, "Study Claims Iraq's 'Excess' Death Toll Has Reached 655,000," *Washington Post*, October 11, 2006, A12; David Brown and Joshua Partlow, "New Estimate of Violent Deaths among Iraqis Is Lower," *Washington Post*, January 10, 2008, A18.

9. Sam Gardiner, "The Enemy Is Us," September 22, 2004, http://www.salon.com/news/opinion/feature/2004/09/22/psychological_warfare/index.html (accessed April 19, 2011).

10. Paul Janensch, "War in Iraq Kept Away from Public," March 17, 2008, http://www.connpost.com//ci_8577853?IADID (accessed March 18, 2008). See also David Bauder, "Iraq War Disappears as TV Story," March 17, 2008, http://www.miamiherald.com/entertainment/tv/story/458872.html (accessed March 18, 2008).

11. Susan Sontag, *Regarding the Pain of Others* (New York: Picador, 2003), 89.

12. For an analysis of how

traumatized war bodies relate to fictions of national sovereignty, see Kaja Silverman, *Male Subjectivity at the Margins* (New York: Routledge, 1992).

13. Sontag, *Regarding the Pain*, 38.

14. On the "shout-out," see Jeffrey Melnick, *9/11 Culture* (Malden, MA: Wiley-Blackwell, 2009), 143.

15. Amanda Lotz, *The Television Will Be Revolutionized* (New York: New York University Press, 2007); Jason Mittell, "Narrative Complexity in Contemporary American Television," *Velvet Light Trap* 58 (2006): 29–40.

16. Michael Curtin, "Feminine Desire in the Age of Satellite Television," *Journal of Communication* 49, no. 2 (1999): 55–70, 60.

17. Amanda Lotz, "Using 'Network' Theory in the Post-Network Era: Fictional 9/11 US Television Discourse as a 'Cultural Forum,'" *Screen* 45, no. 4 (2004): 423–438, 431.

18. This analysis is inspired by John Ellis's discussion of the "mundane witnessing" that occurs in and through everyday media encounters. He argues that TV continues to play a key role in the formation of social reality by providing viewers with resources from which they can craft their identities and relations. John Ellis, *Seeing Things: Television in the Age of Uncertainty* (London: I. B. Tauris, 2000); John Ellis, "Mundane Witness," in *Media Witnessing: Testimony in the Age of Mass Communication*, eds. Paul Frosh and Amit Pinchevski (New York: Palgrave Macmillan, 2009).

19. On televisual melodrama, see Lynne Joyrich, *Re-Viewing Reception: Television, Gender, and Postmodern Culture* (Bloomington: Indiana University Press, 1996); David Thorburn, "Television Melodrama," in *Television: The Critical View*, ed. Horace Newcomb (New York: Oxford University Press, 2000).

20. Indeed, the show would eventually be canceled due to Williams's crusade. In February 2008, Williams appeared on the Fox News Channel program *Fox and Friends* and criticized the program for ignoring the deaths of U.S. soldiers while providing wall-to-wall coverage of actor Heath Ledger's overdose. Williams's contract was canceled days later after several Fox affiliates dropped the series in protest.

21. See, for example, Dana Cloud, *Control and Consolation in American Culture and Politics* (Thousand Oaks, CA: Sage Publications, 1998); Mimi White, *Tele-Advising: Therapeutic Discourse in American Television* (Chapel Hill: University of North Carolina Press, 1992).

22. Marita Sturken, *Tourists of History: Memory, Kitsch, and Consumerism from Oklahoma City to Ground Zero* (Durham, NC: Duke University Press, 2007), 9.

23. Andrew Bacevich, *The New American Militarism: How Americans Are Seduced by War* (New York: Oxford University Press, 2005).

24. Sontag, *Regarding the Pain*, 38.

25. John Shelton Lawrence, "Rituals of Mourning and National Innocence," *Journal of American Culture* 28, no. 1 (2005): 35–48.

26. Gaylyn Studlar and David Desser, "Never Having to Say You're Sorry: Rambo's Rewriting of the Vietnam War," in *From Hanoi to Hollywood: The Vietnam War in American Film*, eds. Linda Dittmar and Gene Michaud (New Brunswick, NJ: Rutgers University Press, 1990), 104.

27. Sturken, *Tourists of History*, 16.

28. Anna McCarthy, "Reality TV: A Neoliberal Theatre of Suffering," *Social Text* 25, no. 4 (2007): 17–41, 17.

29. Jennifer Gillan, "Extreme Makeover

Homeland Security Edition," in *The Great American Makeover: Television, History, Nation*, ed. Dana Heller (Gordansville, VA: Palgrave Macmillan, 2006), 205.

30. Ibid., 196.

31. Ibid., 199.

32. On TV as a site of national pedagogy, see Lauren Berlant, *The Queen of America Goes to Washington: Essays on Sex and Citizenship* (Durham, NC: Duke University Press, 1997); Lila Abu Lughod, *Dramas of Nationhood: The Politics of TV in Egypt* (Chicago: University of Chicago Press, 2001).

33. Gillan, "Extreme Makeover," 195.

34. E. Ann Kaplan, *Trauma Culture: The Politics of Terror and Loss in Media and Literature* (New Brunswick, NJ: Rutgers University Press, 2005), 93.

35. The relevant episodes are: *Bones*, "Soldier on the Grave" (2006); *Boston Legal*, "Witches of Mass Destruction" (2005); *Cold Case*, "The War at Home" (2006); *Crossing Jordan*, "With Honor" (2002) and "Deja Past" (2004); *Las Vegas*, "Have You Ever Seen the Rain" (2004), *Law & Order*, "Veteran's Day" (2004) and "Paradigm" (2004); *Law & Order: SVU*, "Goliath" (2005); *NYPD Blue*, "Sgt. Sipowicz's Lonely Hearts Club Band" (2005); *Without a Trace*, "Gung-Ho" (2004). Wounded vets have also shown up in unexpected places, such as in the gay soap opera *The L Word* (Showtime, especially 2007), the paranormal series *The Ghost Whisperer* (CBS, "Pilot," 2005), the dramedy *The Gilmore Girls* (WB/CW, "We Got Us a Pippi Virgin," 2004), and the soap opera *All My Children* (ABC), which cast real-life Iraq War veteran J. R. Martinez as "Brot Monroe," a disfigured veteran who returns to Pine Valley to reclaim the woman he loves after years in hiding (2008–2011).

36. Thorburn, "Television Melodrama," 605.

37. This concept is inspired by Paul Gilroy, *Postcolonial Melancholia* (New York: Columbia University Press, 2006). Gilroy argues that the failure of postcolonial Britain to own up to its responsibility for the oppression of others has led to a repetition of the nation's violent, antidemocratic tendencies. He borrowed the concept of collective melancholia from Alexander and Margarete Mitscherlich's analysis of post-WWII German society. Alexander Mitscherlich and Margarete Mitscherlich, *The Inability to Mourn*, trans. Beverley R. Placzek (New York: Grove Press, 1975).

38. Edward Said, *Culture and Imperialism* (New York: Vintage Books, 1993), xiii.

39. Jack Shaheen, *Reel Bad Arabs: How Hollywood Vilifies a People* (New York: Olive Branch Press, 2001), 22.

40. This tendency to imagine Americans as the victims of a violence they have perpetrated on others is not new. See Tom Engelhardt, *The End of Victory Culture* (Amherst: University of Massachusetts Press, 1995).

41. On the tension between openness and closure on TV, see Jane Feuer, "Narrative Form in American Network Television," in *High Theory/Low Culture*, ed. Colin McCabe (Manchester: Manchester University Press, 1986); Thorburn, "Television Melodrama."

42. Lughod, *Dramas of Nationhood*, 107.

43. Kaplan, *Trauma Culture*, 196.

44. Interestingly, the narratives remain the same even when the soldier-victims are female or nonwhite. *Cold Case*, *Crossing Jordan*, and *Law & Order* all feature female victims who are treated no differently, except that "sexist soldiers"

constitute a new pool of suspects. Sexism is presented as the idiosyncratic failing of individual soldiers, rather than a structural feature of military institutions, however, and in none of these cases does the sexist character commit the crime. The message is that female soldiers are equally heroic and constitute no problem for the culture of the military. In *Bones*, it is a black soldier who is murdered to cover up the crimes of his white compatriots. It is also a black general who gives the FBI jurisdiction to arrest the guilty white captain on charges of obstruction of justice. Thus, black soldiers also easily assume the mantle of military heroism and can function unproblematically as representatives of the nation.

45. Kaplan, *Trauma Culture*, 74.

46. Marita Sturken, *Tangled Memories: The Vietnam War, the Aids Epidemic, and the Politics of Remembering* (Berkeley: University of California Press, 1997), 16.

47. "Without a Trace," 2008, http:// www.tv.com/without-a-trace/show/7449/ summary.html?q=without%20a%20trace &tag=search_results;title;1 (accessed February 25, 2008).

48. While military recruiters now find this term offensive and insist that they do not target "poor" kids because they lack desirable educational backgrounds, other data suggest that they do target individuals from small towns with below-average per capita incomes. Moreover, many soldiers report joining the military because they could not otherwise afford to go to college. For a nice summary of the arguments in support of the persistence of a poverty draft, see Jorge Mariscal, "The Poverty Draft," *Sojourners Magazine*, June 2007, http://www.sojo.net/index.cfm?action=

magazine.article&issue=soj0706&article =070628 (accessed October 16, 2011).

49. Sturken, *Tangled Memories*, 122.

50. On closure in episodic TV, see Jason Mittell, "Soap Operas and Primetime Seriality," July 29, 2007, http://justtv.wordpress.com/2007/07/29/ soap-operas-and-primetime-seriality/ (accessed May 8, 2008); Thorburn, "Television Melodrama." On redemptive narratives, see Frank Kermode, *The Sense of an Ending: Studies in the Theory of Fiction* (New York: Oxford University Press, 1967); Dominic LaCapra, *Writing History, Writing Trauma* (Baltimore: Johns Hopkins University Press, 2001).

51. Lotz, *Television Will Be Revolutionized*, 15.

52. Mittell, "Narrative Complexity," 31.

53. Annalee Newitz, "ER, Professions, and the Work-Family Disaster," *American Studies* 39, no. 2 (1998): 93–105.

54. Kaplan, *Trauma Culture*, 125.

55. Sturken, *Tourists of History*, 6.

56. Kaplan, *Trauma Culture*, 125.

57. On post-sentimentality, see Lauren Berlant, "Poor Eliza," *American Literature* 70, no. 3 (1998): 635–668.

58. Lotz, *Television Will Be Revolutionized*, 219–220.

59. Mittell, "Narrative Complexity," 35.

60. For more on how confession functions as a technique of subject formation, see Michel Foucault, *The History of Sexuality*, vol. 1: *An Introduction* (New York: Vintage, 1990).

61. Berlant, *Queen of America*, 187.

62. HBO's other major Iraq War documentary, *Baghdad ER* (2006), works in a similar fashion, showing us how bodies-at-war are treated either as machines to be tinkered with or trash to

be thrown out. See Linda Robertson, "Baghdad ER: Subverting the Mythic Gaze upon the Wounded and the Dead," in The War Body on Screen, eds. Karen Randall and Sean Redmond (New York: Continuum, 2008). The "I'm a Civilian Again" episode of the MTV series True Life (2006) works in a similar fashion. The episode followed three young soldiers recently returned from Iraq, including a multiple amputee and a young man with severe PTSD facing redeployment after only a few months home. Collectively, these "documentaries" confront us with the sheer weight of the brutality involved in war and enjoin us to get angry and to act to redress the injustices on display.

63. Susan Murray, "'I Think We Need a New Name for It': The Meeting of Documentary and Reality TV," in Reality TV: Remaking Television Culture, eds. Susan Murray and Laurie Ouelette (New York: New York University Press, 2004), 42.

64. See Lotz, Television Will Be Revolutionized, 235–238.

65. The Post did not run its series on the deplorable conditions at Walter Reed until February of 2007. See Dana Priest and Anne Hull, "Soldiers Face Neglect, Frustration at Army's Top Medical Facility," Washington Post, February 18, 2007, A01; Anne Hull and Dana Priest, "The Hotel Aftermath," Washington Post, February 19, 2007, A01.

66. For an analysis of these documentaries, see Anthony Grajeda, "The Winning and Losing of Hearts and Minds: Vietnam, Iraq and the Claims of the War Documentary," Jump Cut 49 (2007), http://www.ejumpcut.org/archive/jc49.2007/Grajeda/index.html.

67. Lotz, Television Will Be Revolutionized, 236.

68. On the "criminal vet," see Michael Lee Lanning, Vietnam at the Movies (New York: Fawcett Columbine, 1994).

69. Numerous TV reviewers noted the connection between The Kill Point and Dog Day Afternoon. See, for example, Bill Keveney, "SPIKE's Aiming Higher with 'The Kill Point,'" July 20, 2007, http://www.usatoday.com/life/television/news/2007-07-19-kill-point_N.htm (accessed July 5, 2008). Star Donnie Wahlberg also gave interviews that played up the connection. Donnie Wahlberg, "Donnie Wahlberg Back on TV as a Good Guy . . . Or Is He?" July 16, 2007, http://television.aol.com/tv-celebrity-interviews/donnie-wahlberg (accessed July 20, 2008).

70. Jeffrey Alexander, "Toward a Theory of Cultural Trauma," in Cultural Trauma and Collective Identity, eds. Jeffrey Alexander et al. (Berkeley, CA: University of California Press, 2004), 22.

71. Melnick, 9/11 Culture, 12.

72. Lotz, "Using 'Network' Theory," 429.

73. Arguably, though, no cultural site has ever offered such an ideal space of disinterested exchange. On the public sphere, see Jurgen Habermas, The Structural Transformation of the Public Sphere, trans. Thomas Burger (Cambridge, MA: MIT Press, 1993). For critiques of the concept, see the essays in Craig Calhoun, ed., Habermas and the Public Sphere (Cambridge, MA: MIT Press, 1993).

74. Ellis, Seeing Things, 80.

75. Hoskins, Televising War, 134.

Epilogue: Trauma and Memory Ten Years After

1. Scott Wilson and Al Kamen, "'Global War on Terror' Is Given New Name," Washington Post, March 25, 2009.

2. Lev Grossman, "Time's Person of

the Year: You," December 13, 2006, http://www.time.com/time/magazine/article/ 0,9171,1569514,00.html (accessed May 31, 2011).

3. Ibid.

4. Jeffrey Melnick, *9/11 Culture* (Malden, MA: Wiley-Blackwell, 2009), ch.7.

5. Lynn Spigel, "Entertainment Wars: Television Culture after 9/11," *American Quarterly* 56, no. 2 (2004): 235–270., 258.

6. Susan Faludi, *Terror Dream: Fear and Fantasy in Post-9/11 America* (New York: Henry Hol , 2007), 5.

7. For a firsthand account of some of these unhealthy behaviors, see William Langewische, *American Ground: Unbuilding the World Trade Center* (New York: North Point Press, 2002).

8. Robert Jay Lifton, *Superpower Syndrome: America's Apocalyptic Confrontation with the World* (New York: Thunder's Mouth Press/Nation Books, 2003).

9. John Ellis, *Seeing Things: Television in the Age of Uncertainty* (London: I. B. Tauris, 2000), 78–82.

BIBLIOGRAPHY

"'24': An Hour of Realism." April 29, 2005. http://www.washingtontimes.com/news/2005/apr/27/20050427-085529-9412r//print/.

Ackerman, Spencer. "How Real Is 24?" May 16, 2005. http://www.salon.com/ent/feature/2005/05/16/24/index.html?tag=news_list%3btitle%3b1.

Adalian, Josef. "Cutler Brings Battle to Vh1." February 20, 2002. http://variety.com/article/VR1117861131.html?categoryid=1201&ref=ra&cs=1.

Adalian, Josef, and Michael Schneider. "ABC Brings Home Battlefront Reality." February 20, 2002. http://story.news.yahoo.com/news?tmpl=story&u=/nm/20020220/tv_nm/television_battlefront_dc_1&printer=1.

———. "Plots Are Hot Spots for Nets." September 23, 2001. http://www.variety.com/article/VR1117853005.html?categoryid=14&cs=1&query=Plots+are+hot+spots+for+nets.

Agamben, Giorgio. *State of Exception.* Trans. Kevin Attell. Chicago: University of Chicago Press, 2005.

Aghdashloo, Shohreh. "I Choose All My Roles with a Pair of Tweezers: An Interview with Shohreh Aghdashloo." In *Secrets of 24: The Unauthorized Guide to the Political and Moral Issues behind TV's Most Riveting Drama*, eds. Dan Burstein and Arne J. de Keijzer, 111–115. New York: Sterling Publications, 2007.

Agre, Philip E. "Imagining the Next War: Infrastructural Warfare and the Conditions of Democracy." September 15, 2001. http://polaris.gseis.ucla.edu/pagre/.

Ahmed, Sara. "Affective Economies." *Social Text* 22, no. 2 (2004): 117–139.

Albiniak, Paige. "Post-9/11 Becomes a Television Plot." *Broadcasting and Cable*, October 13, 2003, 22.

Alexander, Jeffrey. "Toward a Theory of Cultural Trauma." In *Cultural Trauma and Collective Identity*, eds. Jeffrey Alexander, Ron Eyerman, Bernhard Giesen, Neil Smesler, and Piotr Szomptka, 1–30. Berkeley, CA: University of California Press, 2004.

Al-Jadda, Souheila. "Does Al-Jazeera Belong in the USA?" December 19, 2007. http://www.usatoday.com/printedition/news/20071219/opledejazeera.art.htm?loc=interstitialskip.

Alston, Joshua. "The Way We Were: Art and Culture in the Bush Era—*Battlestar Galactica*." December 13, 2008. http://www.newsweek.com/2008/12/12/the-way-we-were.html.

Altheide, David. "Consuming Terrorism." *Symbolic Interaction* 27, no. 3 (2004): 289–308.

"Americans Spending More Time Following the News." September 12, 2010. http://people-press.org/report/?pageid=1792.

Andén-Papadopoulos, Kari. "US Soldiers Imaging the Iraq War on Youtube." *Popular Communication* 7, no. 1 (2009): 17–27.

Andersen, Robin. "That's Militainment! The Pentagon's Media-Friendly 'Reality' War." 2003. http://www.fair.org/index.php?page=1141.

Andrejevic, Mark. *Reality TV: The Work of Being Watched*. New York: Rowman & Littlefield, 2004.

Anker, Elisabeth. "Villains, Victims, and Heroes: Melodrama, Media and September 11." *Journal of Communication* 55, no. 1 (2005): 22–37.

Ansen, David. "Finding Our New Voice." *Newsweek*, October 1, 2001.

Appadurai, Arjun. *Modernity at Large: Cultural Dimensions of Globalization*. Minneapolis: University of Minnesota Press, 1996.

Armstrong, Mark. "Fox's 'Most Wanted' Targets Terrorism." October 11, 2001. http://www.eonline.com/news/article/index.jsp?uuid=0c901834-320f-4b86-ba05-95c405329f38.

Arquilla, John, and David Ronfeldt. "The Advent of Netwar (Revisited)." In *Networks and Netwars: The Future of Terror, Crime, and Militancy*, eds. John Arquilla and David Ronfeldt, 1–25. Washington, DC: National Defense Research Institute, 2001.

"'Arrested Development' Struggles to Survive." February 17, 2005. http://www.usatoday.com/life/television/news/2005-02-17-arrested-ends_x.htm.

Ashcroft, John, George W. Bush, Colin Powell, and Robert Mueller. "September 11, 2001: Attack on America." October 10, 2001. http://www.yale.edu/lawweb/avalon/sept_11/doj_brief015.htm.

Askwith, Ivan. "Deconstructing the Lost Experience: In-Depth Analysis of an ARG." 2008. www.ivanaskwith.com/writing/IvanAskwith_TheLostExperience.pdf.

Atkins, Claire. "DVD Back End Is Dwindling." March 30, 2009. http://www.broadcastingcable.com/article/190848-DVD_Backend_Is_Dwindling.php.

Aufderheide, Pat. "Good Soldiers." In *Seeing through Movies*, ed. Mark Crispin Miller, 81–111. New York: Pantheon Books, 1990.

Bacevich, Andrew. *The New American Militarism: How Americans Are Seduced by War*. New York: Oxford University Press, 2005.

———. "Robert Kaplan: Empire without Apologies." September 8, 2005. http://www
.thenation.com/doc/20050926/bacevich/single.

Barker, Michael. "Democracy or Polyarchy? US-Funded Media Developments in
Afghanistan and Iraq Post-9/11." *Media, Culture and Society* 30, no. 1 (2008): 109–130.

Bauder, David. "Iraq War Disappears as TV Story." March 17, 2008. http://www
.miamiherald.com/entertainment/tv/story/458872.html.

Baudrillard, Jean. "L'esprit Du Terrorisme." *South Atlantic Quarterly* 101, no. 2 (2002):
403–416.

Baum, Matthew. *Soft News Goes to War: Public Opinion and American Foreign Policy in the
New Media Age.* Princeton, NJ: Princeton University Press, 2003.

Baym, Geoffrey. "The Daily Show: Discursive Integration and the Reinvention of
Political Journalism." *Political Communication* 22 (2005): 259–276.

Bellafante, Ginia. "Little Panic on the Prairie: The Odd World of 'Jericho.'" February
19, 2008. http://www.nytimes.com/2008/02/19/arts/television/19bell.html?_r=
1&scp=1&sq=little%20panic%20on%20the%20prairie&st=cse.

Benjamin, Walter. "Theses on the Philosophy of History." In *Illuminations: Essays and
Reflections*, ed. Hannah Arendt, 253–264. New York: Schocken Books, 1968.

Bercovitch, Sacvan. *The American Jeremiad.* Madison: University of Wisconsin Press,
1978.

Berenger, Ralph, ed. *Global Media Go to War: Role of News and Entertainment Media during
the 2003 Iraq War.* Spokane, WA: Marquette Books, 2004.

Berlant, Lauren. "Poor Eliza." *American Literature* 70, no. 3 (1998): 635–668.

———. *The Queen of America Goes to Washington: Essays on Sex and Citizenship.* Durham,
NC: Duke University Press, 1997.

Bermen, Marc. "National Ratings in Primetime—Week of April 25, 2005." May 4,
2005. http://www.mediaweek.com/mw/search/article_display.jsp?vnu_content_id
=1000909803.

Bernstein, Paula. "TV Newsies Skip Bush Speech Live." *Daily Variety*, November 9,
2001, 2–3.

Bianco, Robert. "You May Be Scared Silly by NBC's *Surface*." September 18, 2005.
http://www.usatoday.com/life/television/reviews/2005-09-18-surface_x.htm.

———. "'West Wing' Lectured More Than Entertained." October 4, 2001. http://www
.usatoday.com/life/television/2001-10-04-west-wing.htm.

Bianculli, David. "HBO's 'Generation Kill' Gamble." *Broadcasting and Cable* 138, no. 26
(2008): 3.

———. "This Pilot Doesn't Fly: 'Jag'-Ged around Edges and Too Hyper." *New York
Daily News*, March 28, 2002, 111.

Bignell, Jonathan. *Big Brother: Reality TV in the Twenty-First Century.* New York: Palgrave Macmillan, 2005.

Biressi, Anita, and Heather Nunn. *Reality TV: Realism and Revelation.* New York: Wallflower Press, 2005.

"Black Hawk Down HPA Edition." 2006, Accessed May 10, 2011. http://video.google.com/videoplay?docid=15683301642782025 8#.

"The Bluths Are Back and Only on Netflix," November 18, 2011, accessed November 19, 2011. http://news.morningstar.com/all/ViewNews.aspx?article=/PR/20111118SF 10170_univ.xml.

Bolter, Jay, and Richard Grusin. *Remediation: Understanding New Media.* Cambridge, MA: MIT Press, 2000.

Booker, M. Keith. *Science Fiction Television.* Westport, CT: Praeger, 2004.

Boot, Max. *The Savage Wars of Peace: Small Wars and the Rise of American Power.* New York: Basic Books, 2003.

Breasseale, Lt. Col. Todd. "Personal Interview." Army Public Affairs—Los Angeles Branch, 2007.

Brecht, Bertolt. *Brecht on Theatre.* Trans. John Willett. London: Methuen, 1964.

Bresler, Robert J. "The End of the Silly Season." *USA Today Magazine,* November 2001, 17.

Britton, Wesley Alan. *Spy Television.* Westport, CT: Praeger Publishing, 2004.

Brooks, Peter. "The Melodramatic Imagination." In *Imitations of Life: A Reader on Film and Television Melodrama,* ed. Marcia Landy, 50–67. Detroit: Wayne State University Press, 1991.

Brooks, Rosa. "The GOP's Torture Enthusiasts." May 18, 2007. http://www.latimes.com/news/opinion/la-oe-brooks18may18,0,5960407.column?coll=la-opinion-center.

Brooks, Xan. "That's Militainment." May 22, 2002. http://www.guardian.co.uk/film/2002/may/22/artsfeatures.afghanistan.

Brown, David. "Study Claims Iraq's 'Excess' Death Toll Has Reached 655,000." *Washington Post,* October 11, 2006, A12.

Brown, David, and Joshua Partlow. "New Estimate of Violent Deaths among Iraqis Is Lower." *Washington Post,* January 10, 2008, A18.

Brown, Simon, and Stacey Abbott. "Introduction: 'Serious Spy Stuff?' The Cult Pleasures of *Alias.*" In *Investigating Alias,* ed. Simon Brown and Stacey Abbott, 1–8. New York: I. B. Tauris, 2007.

Brzezinski, Zbigniew. "Terrorized by 'War on Terror.'" *Washington Post,* March 25, 2007, B01.

Buckman, Adam. "War Bonding: Young Marines in the Kill Zone." July 9, 2008. http://www.nypost.com/seven/07092008/tv/war_bonding_119066.htm.

Bumiller, Elisabeth. "Bush Aides Set Strategy to Sell Policy on Iraq." *New York Times*, September 7, 2002, A1.

Burstein, Dan, and Arne J. de Keijzer. "How Well Does 24 Reflect the Real World?" In *Secrets of 24: The Unauthorized Guide to the Political and Moral Issues behind TV's Most Riveting Drama*, eds. Dan Burstein and Arne J. de Keijzer, 158–159. New York: Sterling Publications, 2007.

Burston, Jonathon. "War and the Entertainment Industries: New Research Priorities in an Era of Cyber-Patriotism." In *War and the Media*, eds. Daya Kishan Thussu and Des Freedman, 163–175. Thousand Oaks, CA: Sage, 2003.

Bush, George W. "Address to a Joint Session of Congress and the American People (September 20, 2001)." In *History and September 11*, ed. Joanne Meyerowitz, 241–243. Philadelphia: Temple University Press, 2003.

———. "Announcement of Strikes against Afghanistan." October 7, 2001. http://archives.cnn.com/2001/US/10/07/ret.bush.transcript/.

———. "President Bush Discusses Freedom in Iraq and Middle East: Remarks by the President at the Twentieth Anniversary of the National Endowment for Democracy." November 6, 2003. http://www.whitehouse.gov/news/releases/2003/11/20031106-2.html.

———. "President Bush Discusses Importance of Democracy in Middle East." February 4, 2004. http://www.whitehouse.gov/news/releases/2004/02/20040204-4 .html.

———. "President Bush Meets with National Security Team." September 12, 2001. http://www.whitehouse.gov/news/releases/2001/09/.

———. "Statement by the President in His Address to the Nation." September 11, 2001. http://www.whitehouse.gov/news/releases/2001/09/20010911-16.html.

Bush, Laura. "Radio Address on Women in Afghanistan (November 17, 2001)." In *History and September 11*, ed. Joanne Meyerowitz, 249–250. Philadelphia: Temple University Press, 2003.

"Bush's Iraq Policies 'Atrocious,' Gore Says." May 27, 2004. http://articles.latimes .com/2004/may/27/nation/na-gore27.

"Buying the War." *Bill Moyers Journal*. PBS, April 25, 2007.

Calabrese, Andrew. "Causus Belli: US Media and the Justification of the Iraq War." *Television and New Media* 6, no. 2 (2005): 153–175.

Calhoun, Craig, ed. *Habermas and the Public Sphere*. Cambridge, MA: MIT Press, 1993.

Campbell, Christopher. "Commodifying September 11: Advertising, Myth, and Hegemony." In *Media Representations of September 11*, eds. Steven Chermak, Frankie Y. Bailey, and Michelle Brown, 47–66. Westport, CT: Praeger, 2003.

Campbell, David. *Writing Security: United States Foreign Policy and the Politics of Identity*. Rev. ed. Minneapolis: University of Minnesota Press, 1998.

Carlsten, Jennie. "Constructing the Terrorist Subject: *Michael Collins* and the Terrorist as Models of Agonistic Pluralism." In *The War Body on Screen*, eds. Karen Randell and Sean Redmond, 154–164. New York: Continuum, 2008.

Carroll, Noel. *The Philosophy of Horror or Paradoxes of the Heart.* New York: Routledge, 1990.

Cassar, Jon. *24: Behind the Scenes.* San Rafael, CA: Insight Editions, 2006.

Castonguay, James. "Intermedia and the War on Terrorism." In *Rethinking Global Security: Media, Popular Culture, and the "War on Terror,"* eds. Andrew Martin and Patrice Petro, 151–178. New Brunswick, NJ: Rutgers University Press, 2006.

Catlin, Roger. "This Is Not the Real World." September 7, 2002. http://articles .courant.com/2002-09-07/features/0209071713_1_president-josiah-bartlet-west-wing-fictional-heroes.

Caughie, John. *Television Drama: Realism, Modernism, and British Culture.* New York: Oxford University Press, 2000.

"CBS Sues Fox over 'Boot Camp.'" April 11, 2001. http://abcnews.go.com/ Entertainment/story?id=106967&page=1.

Chamberlain, Daniel, and Scott Ruston. "*24* and Twenty-First Century Quality Television." In *Reading 24: TV against the Clock*, ed. Steven Peacock, 13–24. New York: I. B. Tauris, 2007.

Chermak, Steven, Frankie Y. Bailey, and Michelle Brown, eds. *Media Representations of September 11.* Westport, CT: Praeger, 2003.

Christensen, Christian. "'Hey Man, Nice Shot': Setting the Iraq War to Music on Youtube." In *The Youtube Reader*, eds. Pelle Snickars and Patrick Vonderau, 204–217. Stockholm: National Library of Sweden, 2010.

———. "Uploading Dissonance: Youtube and the US Occupation of Iraq." *Media, War and Conflict* 2 (2008): 155–175.

Cirincione, Joseph, Jessica Tuchman Mathews, George Perkovich, and Alexis Orton. "WMD in Iraq: Evidence and Implications." January 8, 2004. http://www.carnegie endowment.org/publications/index.cfm?fa=view&id=1435&prog=zgp&proj=znpp.

Clarke, Richard A. *Against All Enemies: Inside America's War on Terrorism.* New York: Free Press, 2004.

Cloud, Dana. *Control and Consolation in American Culture and Politics.* Thousand Oaks, CA: Sage Publications, 1998.

Cochran, Robert. "A Creator's View: Interview with Robert Cochran." In *Secrets of 24: The Unauthorized Guide to the Political and Moral Issues behind TV's Most Riveting Drama*, eds. Dan Burstein and Arne J. de Keijzer, 92–96. New York: Sterling Publications, 2007.

Cohen, Alex. "Interview with Kevin Sites." May 10, 2005. http://www.npr.org/ templates/story/story.php?storyId=4646406.

Cole, David, and Jules Lobel. "Why We're Losing the War on Terror." *Nation*, September 24, 2007, 11–18.

Coleman, Lindsey. "'Damn You for Making Me Do This': Abu Ghraib, 24, Torture and Television Sadomasochism." In *The War Body on Screen*, eds. Karen Randell and Sean Redmond, 199–214. New York: Continuum, 2008.

Comedicman. "Re: Why Was Whoopi Canceled." August 31, 2005. http://www.imdb .com/title/tt0364902/board/nest/24213397?d=25402392&p=1#25402392.

Conner, Tracy. "Running Late Saved Them from Trade Center Death." *New York Daily News*, September 8, 2002, 8–9.

"Conservatives Continue to Use Fox's 24 to Support Hawkish Policies." February 2, 2007. http://mediamatters.org/research/200702020015.

"A Conversation about the Hit Show '24.'" *Charlie Rose*. PBS, 2005.

Cooper, Stephen D., and Jim A. Kuypers. "Embedded Versus Behind-the-Lines Reporting on the 2003 Iraq War." In *Global Media Go to War: Role of News and Entertainment Media during the 2003 Iraq War*, ed. Ralph Berenger, 161–171. Spokane, WA: Marquette Books, 2004.

Copulsky, Jerome E. "King of Pain: The Political Theologies of 24." In *Secrets of 24: The Unauthorized Guide to the Political and Moral Issues behind TV's Most Riveting Drama*, eds. Dan Burstein and Arne J. de Keijzer, 55–59. New York: Sterling Publications, 2007.

Corkin, Stanley. *Cowboys and Cold Warriors: The Western and US History*. Philadelphia: Temple University Press, 2004.

Corner, John. *Television Form and Public Address*. New York: St. Martin's Press, 1995.

Coto, Manny, Howard Gordon, and Evan Katz. "A Fictional Version of Issues You Read About on the Op-Ed Page: Three Members of 24's Creative Team Discuss the Stories They Tell and How They Tell Them." In *Secrets of 24*, eds. Dan Burstein and Arne J. de Keijzer, 97–100. New York: Sterling Publications, 2007.

Croad, Elizabeth. "US Public Turns to Europe for News." February 21, 2003. http:// www.journalism.co.uk/2/articles/5576.php.

Curtin, Michael. "Feminine Desire in the Age of Satellite Television." *Journal of Communication* 49, no. 2 (1999): 55–70.

———. "On Edge: Culture Industries in the Neo-Network Era." In *Making and Selling Culture*, ed. Richard Ohmann, 181–202. Hanover, NH: University Press of New England, 1996.

Dadge, David. "Al Jazeera: A Platform of Controversy." In *Casualty of War: The Bush Administration's Assault on a Free Press*, ed. David Dadge, 49–76. Amherst, NY: Prometheus Books, 2004.

Davis, Doug. "Future-War Storytelling: National Security and Popular Film." In *Rethinking Global Security: Media, Popular Culture, and the "War on Terrorism,"* eds.

Andrew Martin and Patrice Petro, 13–44. New Brunswick, NJ: Rutgers University Press, 2006.

Delasantellis, Julian. "Above the Rest." January 13, 2003. http://www.poppolitics.com/archives/2003/01/Above-the-Rest.

"Department of Homeland Security Hires Hollywood Liaison." May 2005. http://www.house.gov/hensarling/rsc/doc/100406_hollywood_liaison.doc.

Der Derian, James. "Imaging Terror: Logos, Pathos, Ethos." *Third World Quarterly* 26, no. 1 (2005): 23–37.

———. *Virtuous War: Mapping the Military-Industrial-Media-Entertainment Network.* New York: Basic Books, 2001.

Dixon, Wheeler Winston, ed. *Film and Television after 9/11.* Carbondale: Southern Illinois University Press, 2004.

Dobkin, Bethami A. *Tales of Terror: Television News and the Construction of the Terrorist Threat.* New York: Praeger, 1992.

Donahue, Ann. "Review: Threat Matrix." September 12, 2003. http://www.variety.com/review/VE1117921824.html?categoryid=32&cs=1&query=threat+matrix.

Drew, Julie. "Identity Crisis: Gender, Public Discourse and 9/11." *Women and Language* 27, no. 2 (2004): 71–77.

Dunn, Timothy. "Torture, Terrorism and 24: What Would Jack Bauer Do?" In *Homer Simpson Goes to Washington: American Politics through Popular Culture,* ed. Joseph J. Foy, 171–184. Lexington: University of Kentucky Press, 2008.

Easton, Nina J. "Blacked Out." March 2002. http://www.ajr.org/article_printable.asp?id=2460.

Eberl, Jason T., ed. *Battlestar Galactica and Philosophy: Knowledge Here Begins Out There.* Malden, MA: Wiley-Blackwell, 2008.

Edwards, Gavin. "Intergalactic Terror." *Rolling Stone,* January 27, 2006, 32.

Ellis, John. "Mundane Witness." In *Media Witnessing: Testimony in the Age of Mass Communication,* eds. Paul Frosh and Amit Pinchevski, 73–88. New York: Palgrave Macmillan, 2009.

———. *Seeing Things: Television in the Age of Uncertainty.* London: I. B. Tauris, 2000.

Elshtain, Jean Bethke. "Jean Bethke Elshtain Responds." *Dissent.* 2006. http://www.dissentmagazine.org/article/?article=664.

———. *Just War against Terror: The Burden of America Power in a Violent World.* New York: Basic Books, 2003.

Engelhardt, Tom. *The End of Victory Culture.* Amherst: University of Massachusetts Press, 1995.

Evans, Elizabeth Jane. "Character, Audience Agency and Transmedia Drama." *Media, Culture, Society* 30, no. 2 (2008): 197–213.

Fabiola, Groshan. "The Lost Experience—Failure of Plot, Success of Commercialism." 2004. http://EzineArticles.com/?expert=Groshan_Fabiola.

Faludi, Susan. *Terror Dream: Fear and Fantasy in Post-9/11 America.* New York: Henry Holt, 2007.

Feuer, Jane. "The Concept of Live Television: Ontology as Ideology." In *Regarding Television: Critical Approaches,* ed. E. Ann Kaplan, 12–21. Frederick, MD: University Publications of America and the University Film Institute, 1983.

———. "Narrative Form in American Network Television." In *High Theory/Low Culture,* ed. Colin McCabe, 101–114. Manchester: Manchester University Press, 1986.

Fick, Nathaniel. *One Bullet Away: The Making of a Marine Officer.* New York: Houghton Mifflin, 2005.

Finer, Jonathon. "'Generation Kill' Captures War's Lulls and Horrors," July 12, 2008. http://www.washingtonpost.com/wp-dyn/content/article/2008/07/11/AR20080711 03372_pf.html.

Fleischer, Ari. "Press Conference." September 26, 2001. http://www.whitehouse.gov/news/releases/2001/09/20010926-5.html#BillMaher-Comments.

Folkenflik, David. "US Raising New Voices to Counter Arab Media: Old VOA Hands Say Alhurra TV, Radio Sawa Are Less News Than Propaganda." August 1, 2004. http:// www.baltimoresun.com/features/arts/bal-as.alhurra01aug01,1,2238783 .story.

"Forget *Boot Camp*—It's Time to Get Really Real." *Entertainment Weekly,* June 14, 2002, 54.

Forwood, Veronica. "Censorship of News in Wartime Is Still Censorship." October 15, 2001. http://media.guardian.co.uk/print/0,,4277504-108927,00.html.

Foster, Thomas. "Cynical Nationalism." In *The Selling of 9/11: How a National Tragedy Became a Commodity,* ed. Dana Heller, 254–287. New York: Palgrave Macmillan, 2005.

Foucault, Michel. *The History of Sexuality.* Vol. 1: *An Introduction.* New York: Vintage, 1990.

———. *"Society Must Be Defended": Lectures at the College De France, 1975–1976.* Eds. Mauro Bertani and Alessandro Fontana, trans. David Macey. New York: Picador, 2003.

———. "Truth and Power." In *Michel Foucault Power/Knowledge: Selected Interviews and Other Writings, 1972–1977,* ed. Colin Gordon, 109–133. New York: Pantheon, 1980.

Franklin, Nancy. "Across the Universe: A Battlestar Is Reborn." January 26, 2006. http://www.newyorker.com/archive/2006/01/23/060123crte_television?currentPage =all.

———. "The Road to Baghdad: David Simon's *Generation Kill.*" July 21, 2008. http:// www.newyorker.com/arts/critics/television/2008/07/21/080721crte_television_ franklin.

Fraser, Matthew. *Weapons of Mass Distraction: Soft Power and American Empire*. New York: St. Martin's Press, 2003.

Freda, Isabelle. "Survivors in the West Wing: 9/11 and the United States of Emergency." In *Film and Television after 9/11*, ed. Wheeler Winston Dixon, 226–244. Carbondale: Southern Illinois University Press, 2004.

Freeman, Michael, and Chris Pursell. "Hollywood Notes." *Electronic Media*, January 7, 2002, 29.

Friedman, Thomas. *The Lexus and the Olive Tree: Understanding Globalization*. New York: Anchor Books, 2000.

Friedman, Wayne. "CBS Still Oldest Median Age Network: UPN Now the Youngest." July 11, 2005. http://www.mediapost.com/publications/?fa=Articles.showArticle& art_aid=31939.

Friend, Tad. "Lost Generation." *New Yorker*, October 16, 2006, 188–190.

Frist, Bill. *When Every Moment Counts: What You Need to Know about Bioterrorism from the Senate's Only Doctor*. New York: Rowman & Littlefield, 2002.

"Frontline: 'The Navy Blues.'" PBS, October 15, 1996. http://www.pbs.org/wgbh/pages/ frontline/shows/navy/.

Froula, Anna. "Political Amnesia Over Here and Imperial Spectacle *Over There*." Paper presented at the Society for Cinema and Media Studies, Vancouver, BC, March 2–5, 2006.

Fuchs, Cynthia. "Surface." September 19, 2005. http://popmatters.com/tv/reviews/s/ surface-050919.shtml.

Fukuyama, Francis. *The End of History and the Last Man*. New York: Avon, 1993.

Fullerton, Jamie, and Alice Kendrick. *Advertising's War on Terrorism: The Story of the U.S. State Department's Shared Values Initiative*. Spokane, WA: Marquette Books, 2006.

Furby, Jacqueline. "Interesting Times: The Demands 24's Real Time Format Makes on Its Audience." In *Reading 24: TV against the Clock*, ed. Steven Peacock, 59–70. New York: I. B. Tauris, 2007.

Furedi, Frank. *Culture of Fear Revisited: Risk-Taking and the Morality of Low Expectation*. New York: Continuum, 2006.

Gabler, Neal. "Hollywood's Shifting Winds." *Variety*, November 23–30, 2003, 20 +.

Gair, Christopher. "24 and Post-National American Identities." In *Reading 24: TV against the Clock*, ed. Steven Peacock, 201–208. New York: I. B. Tauris, 2007.

Garcia, James E. "Arabs, Latinos and the Culture of Hate." September 18, 2001. http:// www.alternet.org/911oneyearlater/11530/arabs,_latinos_and_the_culture_of_hate/.

Gardiner, Sam. "The Enemy Is Us." September 22, 2004. http://www.salon.com/ news/opinion/feature/2004/09/22/psychological_warfare/index.html.

Gerth, Jeff, and Scott Shane. "US Is Said to Pay to Plant Articles in Iraq Papers."

December 1, 2005. http://www.nytimes.com/2005/12/01/politics/01propaganda
.html.

Giardina, Anthony. "The Lives They Lived: Branding Brotherhood." *New York Times
Magazine*, December 29, 2002, 52.

Gillan, Jennifer. "*Extreme Makeover* Homeland Security Edition." In *The Great American
Makeover: Television, History, Nation*, ed. Dana Heller, 193–209. Gordansville, VA:
Palgrave Macmillan, 2006.

Gilliam, Franklin, and Shanto Iyengar. "Prime Suspects: The Influence of Local
Television News on the Viewing Public." *American Journal of Political Science* 44, no. 3
(2000): 560–573.

Gilroy, Paul. *Postcolonial Melancholia*. New York: Columbia University Press, 2006.

Glassner, Barry. *Culture of Fear: Why Americans Are Afraid of the Wrong Things*. New York:
Basic Books, 2000.

Glater, Jonathan. "Retooling a 70's Sci-Fi Relic for the Age of Terror." January 13,
2005. http://www.nytimes.com/2005/01/13/arts/television/13gala.html?sq=glater
%20&st=Search%22re-tooling%2070s%20science%20fiction=&scp=1&page
wanted=all&position=.

Goodman, Tim. "Jon Stewart, Seriously, Here to Stay." October 29, 2004.
http://www.sfgate.com/cgi-bin/article.cgi?f=/c/a/2004/10/29/DDGSO9HI5F17
.DTL&ao=all#ixzz19WDgz7tP.

Gorman, Steve. "US Network Plans Controversial Wartime 'Reality' Show." February
21, 2002. http://sg.news.yahoo.com/reuters/asia-90594.html.

Grajeda, Anthony. "The Winning and Losing of Hearts and Minds: Vietnam, Iraq and
the Claims of the War Documentary." *Jump Cut* 49 (2007). http://www.ejumpcut
.org/archive/jc49.2007/Grajeda/index.html.

Greenberg, Bradley S., ed. *Communication and Terrorism: Public and Media Responses to
9/11*. Cresskill, NJ: Hampton Press, 2002.

Greene, Eric. "The Mirror Frakked: Reflections on *Battlestar Galactica*." In *So Say We All:
An Unauthorized Collection of Thoughts and Opinions on Battlestar Galactica*, ed. Richard
Hatch, 5–22. Dallas: Benbella Books, 2006.

Grewal, Inderpal. "Transnational America: Race, Gender and Citizenship after 9/11."
Social Identities 9, no. 4 (2003): 535–561.

Grieveson, Lee. "On Governmentality and Screens." *Screen* 50, no. 1 (2009): 180–187.

Gross, Larry. "Out of the Mainstream: Sexual Minorities and the Mass Media." In
Media and Cultural Studies, eds. Douglas Kellner and Meenakshi Gigi Durham, 405–
423. Malden, MA: Blackwell Publishing, 2001.

Grossberg, Josh. "War's Not Hell, It's Entertainment!" February 22, 2002. http://
www3.eonline.com/uberblog/b42902_wars_not_hell_its_entertainment.html.

Grossman, Andrew. "ABC Set to Salute West Point." October 24, 2001. http://www
.allbusiness.com/services/motion-pictures/4852640-1.html.

Grossman, Lev. "Time's Person of the Year: You." December 13, 2006. http://www
.time.com/time/magazine/article/0,9171,1569514,00.html.

Grove, David. "The Agency: Review." 2001. http://www.popmatters.com/pm/review/
agency.

Grusin, Richard. *Premediation: Affect and Mediality after 9/11.* New York: Palgrave
Macmillan, 2010.

Gunaratna, Rohan. *Inside Al Qaeda: Global Network of Terror.* New York: Berkeley Books,
2002.

Habermas, Jurgen. *The Structural Transformation of the Public Sphere.* Trans. Thomas
Burger. Cambridge, MA: MIT Press, 1993.

Hale, Mike. "The Things You Can't Know about 'Galactica.'" January 15, 2009. http://
www.nytimes.com/2009/01/16/arts/television/16batt.html.

Hardt, Michael, and Antonio Negri. *Empire.* Cambridge, MA: Harvard University Press,
2001.

———. *Multitude: War and Democracy in the Age of Empire.* New York: Penguin Press, 2004.

Harper, Ralph. *The World of the Thriller.* Cleveland, OH: Press of Case Western Reserve
University, 1969.

Hart, William. "The Country Connection: Country Music, 9/11, and the War on
Terrorism." In *The Selling of 9/11: How a National Tragedy Became a Commodity,* ed.
Dana Heller, 155–173. New York: Palgrave Macmillan, 2005.

Havrilesky, Heather. "White-Knuckle TV." September 12, 2005. http://dir.salon.com/
story/ent/feature/2005/09/12/fear/index.html.

Hay, James. "Extreme Makeover: Iraq Edition—'TV Freedom' and Other Experiments
for 'Advancing' Liberal Government in Iraq." In *Flow TV: Television in the Age of Media
Convergence,* eds. Michael Kackman, Marnie Binfield, Matthew Thomas Payne,
Allison Perlman, and Bryan Sebok, 217–241. New York: Routledge, 2010.

Hay, James, and Mark Andrejevic. "Toward an Analytic of Governmental Experiments
in These Times: Homeland Security as the New Social Security." *Cultural Studies* 20,
nos. 4–5 (2006): 331–348.

Hedges, Chris. *War Is a Force That Gives Us Meaning.* Garden City, NY: Anchor Books,
2003.

Heldenfels, R. D. "On the 'Front Line.'" February 27, 2003. http://www.ohio.com/
beaconjournal/entertainment/5273901.htm?template=contentModules/printstory
.jsp.

Heller, Dana, ed. *The Selling of 9/11: How a National Tragedy Became a Commodity.* New
York: Palgrave Macmillan, 2005.

Hentoff, Nat. "Seeking Justice: Administration Marginalizes Jags." *Washington Post*, September 11, 2006, A21.

Hickey, Neil. "Access Denied: Pentagon's War Reporting Rules Are Toughest Ever." *Columbia Journalism Review* 40, no. 5 (Jan.–Feb. 2002): 26–31.

Higgins, John. "Fast Forward: With Scant Notice, TV-DVD Sales Top $1 Billion and Begin to Affect Scheduling, Financing." December 22, 2003. http://www.broad castingcable.com/article/151823-Fast_Forward.php.

Higgins, John, and Allison Romano. "The New Economics of Terror." *Broadcasting and Cable*, September 24, 2001, 4.

Hill, Matthew. "Tom Clancy, 24 and the Language of Autocracy." In *The War on Terror and American Popular Culture*, eds. Andrew Schopp and Matthew B. Hill, 127–148. Teaneck, NJ: Fairleigh Dickinson University Press, 2009.

Holloway, David. *Cultures of the War on Terror: Empire, Ideology and the Remaking of 9/11*. Montreal: McGill University Press, 2008.

Holt, Madeleine. "Is Truth a Victim?" May 16, 2002. http://news.bbc.co.uk/2/hi/ programmes/newsnight/1991885.stm.

Hoskins, Andrew. *Televising War: From Vietnam to Iraq*. New York: Continuum, 2004.

Howard, Douglas. "'You're Going to Tell Me Everything You Know': Torture and Morality on Fox's 24." In *Reading 24: TV against the Clock*, ed. Steven Peacock, 133–145. New York: I. B. Tauris, 2007.

Huff, Richard. "After 10 Seasons, 'Jag' Is Discharged . . ." *New York Daily News*, April 24, 2005, 2.

Hull, Anne, and Dana Priest. "The Hotel Aftermath." *Washington Post*, February 19, 2007, A01.

Huntington, Samuel P. *American Politics: The Promise of Disharmony*. Cambridge, MA: Belknap Press, 1981.

Hutcheson, John, David Domke, Andre Billeaudeux, and Philip Garland. "US National Identity, Political Elites, and a Patriotic Press Following September 11." *Political Communication* 21 (2004): 27–50.

Isakhan, Benjamin. "Manufacturing Consent in Iraq: Interference in the Post-Saddam Media Sector." *International Journal of Contemporary Iraqi Studies* 3, no. 1 (2009): 7–26.

Isherwood, Charles. "The 53rd Annual Primetime Emmy Awards." *Daily Variety*, November 5, 2001, 2–3.

Ito, Robert. "Theater of War." *Los Angeles Magazine*, November 2006, 106–114.

Jackson, Laura. "Kiefer Sutherland: Born to Play Jack Bauer." In *Secrets of 24: The Unauthorized Guide to the Political and Moral Issues behind TV's Most Riveting Drama*, eds. Dan Burstein and Arne J. De Keijzer, 72–79. New York: Sterling Publishing, 2007.

Jackson, Richard. *Writing the War on Terrorism: Language, Politics, and Counter-Terrorism*. Manchester: Manchester University Press, 2005.

James, Caryn. "British Take Blunter Approach to War Reporting." November 9, 2001. http://query.nytimes.com/gst/fullpage.html?res=9802E5D61638F93AA35752C1A9 679C8B63&pagewanted=print.

Janensch, Paul. "War in Iraq Kept Away from Public." March 17, 2008. http://www .connpost.com//ci_8577853?IADID.

Jenkins, Henry. *Convergence Culture: Where Old and New Media Collide.* New York: New York University Press, 2006.

Jenkins, Tricia. "Get Smart: A Look at the Current Relationship between Hollywood and the CIA." *Historical Journal of Film, Radio and Television* 29, no. 2 (2009): 229–243.

"Jericho Fans About to Go 'Nutty' over Hollywood Billboard." June 3, 2008. http:// www.24-7pressrelease.com/press-release/jericho-fans-about-to-go-nutty-over-hollywood-billboard-52122.php.

Jermyn, Deborah. "Reasons to Split Up: Interactivity, Realism and the Multiple-Image Screens in 24." In *Reading 24: TV against the Clock,* ed. Steven Peacock, 49–58. New York: I. B. Tauris, 2007.

Jewett, Robert, and John Shelton Lawrence. *Captain America and the Crusade against Evil: The Dilemma of Zealous Nationalism.* Grand Rapids, MI: William B. Eerdmans Publishing, 2003.

Jonge, Peter. "Aaron Sorkin Works His Way through the Crisis." October 28, 2001. http:// www.nytimes.com/2001/10/28/magazine/aaron-sorkin-works-his-way-through-the-crisis.html.

Joyner, Thomas P. "C.S.I.: Crime Scene Iraq." March 24, 2003. http://www.poppolitics .com/articles/2003-03-24-crimesceneiraq.shtml.

Joyrich, Lynne. *Re-Viewing Reception: Television, Gender, and Postmodern Culture.* Bloomington: Indiana University Press, 1996.

Kackman, Michael. *Citizen Spy: Television, Espionage and Cold War Culture.* Minneapolis: University of Minnesota Press, 2005.

———. "Introduction." In *Flow TV: Television in the Age of Media Convergence,* eds. Michael Kackman, Marnie Binfield, Matthew Thomas Payne, Allison Perlman, and Bryan Sebok, 1–10. New York: Routledge, 2010.

Kampfner, John. "The Truth about Jessica." May 15, 2003. http://www.guardian.co .uk/Iraq/Story/0,2763,956255,00.html.

Kane, Erin Martin. "Frontline to Viewers: ABC Series with Similar Title, Branding Not Associated with PBS's Award-Winning Documentary Series." February 24, 2003. http://www.pbs.org/wgbh/pages/frontline/us/press/abc.html.

Kaplan, E. Ann. *Trauma Culture: The Politics of Terror and Loss in Media and Literature.* New Brunswick, NJ: Rutgers University Press, 2005.

Kaplan, Robert. *Imperial Grunts: The American Military on the Ground*. New York: Random House, 2005.

Kellner, Douglas. *Cinema Wars: Hollywood Film and Politics in the Bush-Cheney Era*. Malden, MA: Wiley-Blackwell, 2010.

Kempner, Matt. "TV Seeks Soothing Touch." *Atlanta Journal-Constitution*, October 24, 2001, E1+.

Kermode, Frank. *The Sense of an Ending: Studies in the Theory of Fiction*. New York: Oxford University Press, 1967.

Keveney, Bill. "SPIKE's Aiming Higher with 'The Kill Point.'" July 20, 2007. http://www.usatoday.com/life/television/news/2007-07-19-kill-point_N.htm.

———. "Viewers Embrace Late-Night Talk Shows." *USA Today*, September 19, 2001, D4.

Kissell, Rick. "'Champ' on the Ropes Right Away." September 8, 2004. http://www.variety.com/index.asp?layout=print_story&articleid=VR1117910135&categoryid=1236.

Kitch, Carolyn. "'Mourning in America': Ritual, Redemption, and Recovery in News Narrative after September 11." *Journalism Studies* 4, no. 2 (2003): 213–224.

Kline, Stephen, Nick Dyer-Whiteford, and Greig De Peuter. *Digital Play: The Interaction of Technology, Culture, and Marketing*. Montreal: McGill University Press, 2003.

Kompare, Derek. "More 'Moments of Television': Online Cult Television Authorship." In *Flow TV: Television In the Age of Media Convergence*, eds. Michael Kackman, Marnie Binfield, Matthew Thomas Payne, Allison Perlman, and Bryan Sebok, 95–113. New York: Routledge, 2011.

Kristeva, Julia. *Powers of Horror: An Essay on Abjection*. New York: Columbia University Press, 1982.

Kristof, Nicholas D. "Beating Specialist Baker." *New York Times*, June 5, 2004, A15.

LaCapra, Dominic. *Writing History, Writing Trauma*. Baltimore: Johns Hopkins University Press, 2001.

Lagouranis, Tony. "An Army Interrogator's Dark Journey through Iraq: An Interview with Tony Lagouranis." In *Secrets of 24: The Unauthorized Guide to the Political and Moral Issues behind TV's Most Riveting Drama*, eds. Dan Burstein and Arne J. de Keijzer, 196–201. New York: Sterling Publications, 2007.

Langewische, William. *American Ground: Unbuilding the World Trade Center*. New York: North Point Press, 2002.

Lanning, Michael Lee. *Vietnam at the Movies*. New York: Fawcett Columbine, 1994.

Lawrence, John Shelton. "Rituals of Mourning and National Innocence." *Journal of American Culture* 28, no. 1 (2005): 35–48.

Leonard, John. "Rush Hour." In *Secrets of 24: The Unauthorized Guide to the Political and*

Moral Issues behind TV's Most Riveting Drama, eds. Dan Burstein and Arne J. de
  Keijzer, 48–49. New York: Sterling Publications, 2007.

Leung, Rebecca. "G.I. Attacked during Training." November 3, 2004. http://www
  .cbsnews.com/stories/2004/11/02/60II/main652953.shtml.

Lewis, Andrea. "Lights, Camera, Military Action!" April 1, 2003. http://www.article
  archives.com/humanities-social-science/visual-performing-arts-visual/864709-1
  .html.

Lewis, Justin, Richard Maxwell, and Toby Miller. "9-11." *Television and New Media* 3, no.
  2 (2002): 125–131.

Lewis, Neil A. "Tailhook Affair Brings Censure of 3 Admirals." October 16, 1993.
  http://www.nytimes.com/1993/10/16/us/tailhook-affair-brings-censure-of-3-
  admirals.html.

Li, Kenneth. "Television Executives Reach for Reset Button." August 31, 2009. http://
  www.ft.com/intl/cms/s/0/d9286d90-9643-11de-84d1-00144feabdc0.html#axzz1
  NBSZ2GnB.

Lifton, Robert Jay. *Superpower Syndrome: America's Apocalyptic Confrontation with the World.*
  New York: Thunder's Mouth Press/Nation Books, 2003.

Limbaugh, Rush. "24 and America's Image in Fighting Terrorism: Fact, Fiction or
  Does It Matter?" In *Secrets of 24: The Unauthorized Guide to the Political and Moral Issues
  behind TV's Most Riveting Drama*, eds. Dan Burstein and Arne J. de Keijzer, 151–157.
  New York: Sterling Publications, 2006.

Lisberg, Adam. "'Whoopi' Cancelled after Disappointing First Season." *New York Daily
  News*, May 17, 2004.

"Lost: Official Show Auction and Exhibit." 2010. http://abc.go.com/shows/lost/
  auction.

Lotz, Amanda. *The Television Will Be Revolutionized.* New York: New York University
  Press, 2007.

———. "Using 'Network' Theory in the Post-Network Era: Fictional 9/11 US
  Television Discourse as a 'Cultural Forum.'" *Screen* 45, no. 4 (2004): 423–438.

Lowry, Brian. "Generation Kill Review." July 9, 2008. http://www.variety.com/review/
  VE1117937679.html?categoryid=32&cs=1.

Lughod, Lila Abu. *Dramas of Nationhood: The Politics of TV in Egypt.* Chicago: University
  of Chicago Press, 2001.

Lule, Jack. "Myth and Terror on the Editorial Page: *The New York Times* Responds to
  September 11, 2001." *Journalism and Mass Communications Quarterly* 79, no. 2 (2002):
  275–293.

Mahajan, Rahul. *The New Crusade: America's War on Terrorism.* New York: Monthly Review
  Press, 2002.

"Man of Duty: Gateworld Talks with Jami Bamber." 2006. http://www.gateworld.net/galactica/articles/bamber02.shtml.

Mariscal, Jorge. "The Poverty Draft." *Sojourners Magazine*. June 2007. http://www.sojo.net/index.cfm?action=magazine.article&issue=soj0706&article=070628.

Marshall, Cori. "VH1's Military Diaries Not All Pro-War." June 8, 2002. http://www.pww.org/article/view/1363/1/90/.

Martin, Andrew. "Popular Culture and Narratives of Insecurity." In *Rethinking Global Security: Media, Popular Culture, and the War on Terrorism*, eds. Andrew Martin and Patrice Petro, 104–116. New Brunswick, NJ: Rutgers University Press, 2006.

Martin, Andrew, and Patrice Petro, eds. *Rethinking Global Security: Media, Popular Culture, and the War on Terrorism*. New Brunswick, NJ: Rutgers University Press, 2006.

Mascaro, Maria Pia, and Jean-Marie Barrère. "Hollywood and the Pentagon: A Dangerous Liaison." *Passionate Eye*. CBC News, december 15, 2003.

Massumi, Brian. "Fear (the Spectrum Said)." *positions* 13, no. 1 (2005): 31–48.

Maull, Ian, and David Lavery. "*Battlestar Galactica*." In *The Essential Cult TV Reader*, ed. David Lavery, 44–50. Lexington: University Press of Kentucky, 2009.

Mayer, Jane. "Whatever It Takes: The Politics of the Man behind 24." In *Secrets of 24: The Unauthorized Guide to the Political and Moral Issues behind TV's Most Riveting Drama*, eds. Dan Burstein and Arne J. de Keijzer, 22–36. New York: Sterling Publications, 2007.

Mayerowitz, Scott. "Nutty 'Jericho' Fans Make CBS Reconsider Canceling Show." June 6, 2007. http://abcnews.go.com/Business/FunMoney/story?id=3214156&page=1.

McAlister, Melani. "A Cultural History of the War without End." In *History and September 11*, ed. Joanne Meyerowitz, 94–116. Philadelphia: Temple University Press, 2003.

———. *Epic Encounters : Culture, Media, and US Interests in the Middle East since 1945*. Updated ed. Berkeley: University of California Press, 2005.

McCarthy, Anna. *The Citizen Machine: Governing by Television in 1950s America*. New York: New Press, 2010.

———. "Reality TV: A Neoliberal Theatre of Suffering." *Social Text* 25, no. 4 (2007): 17–41.

McCarthy, Michael. "Violence in Iraq Puts Advertisers on Edge." *USA Today*, May 18, 2004, B2.

McCloud, Scott. *Understanding Comics*. New York: Harper Perennial, 1994.

McKenna, Tech. Sgt. Pat. "Flights! Camera! Action!: Air Force Takes Wing on the Silver Screen." June 1997. http://www.af.mil/news/airman/0697/movie2.htm.

McPherson, Tara. "Techno-Soap: 24, Masculinity and Hybrid Form." In *Reading 24: TV against the Clock*, ed. Steven Peacock, 173–190. New York: I. B. Tauris, 2007.

Medevoi, Leerom. "Global Society Must Be Defended: Biopolitics without Boundaries." *Social Text* 25, no. 2 (2007): 53–79.

Meehan, Eileen. *Why TV Is Not Our Fault: Television Programming, Viewers, and Who's Really in Control.* Lanham, MD: Rowman & Littlefield, 2005.

Meek, Allen. *Trauma and Media: Theories, Histories, and Images.* New York: Routledge, 2009.

Melnick, Jeffrey. *9/11 Culture.* Malden, MA: Wiley-Blackwell, 2009.

"Members of America's Armed Forces Chronicle Their Lives and Their Passion for Music in New VH1 Series 'Military Diaries.'" May 15, 2002. http://www.viacom.com/press.tin?ixPressRelease=80003806.

"Merchants of Cool." *Frontline.* PBS, February 27, 2001.

Miller, Toby. *Cultural Citizenship: Cosmopolitanism, Consumerism, and Television in a Neoliberal Age.* Philadelphia: Temple University Press, 2007.

Miller, Toby, Nitin Govil, John McMurria, Richard Maxwell, and Ting Wang, eds. *Global Hollywood 2.* Rev. ed. Berkeley: University of California Press, 2005.

Mitscherlich, Alexander, and Margarete Mitscherlich. *The Inability to Mourn.* Trans. Beverley R. Placzek. New York: Grove Press, 1975.

Mittell, Jason. "Narrative Complexity in Contemporary American Television." *Velvet Light Trap* 58 (2006): 29–40.

———. "Soap Operas and Primetime Seriality." July 29, 2007. http://justtv.wordpress.com/2007/07/29/soap-operas-and-primetime-seriality/.

———. *Television and American Culture.* New York: Oxford University Press, 2009.

Mogenson, Kirsten, Laura Lindsey, Xigen Li, Jay Perkins, and Mike Beardsley. "How TV News Covered the Crisis: The Content of CNN, CBS, ABC, NBC and Fox." In *Communication and Terrorism: Public and Media Responses to 9/11,* ed. Bradley S. Greenberg, 101–120. Cresskill, NJ: Hampton Press, 2002.

Monohan, Brian. *Shock of the News: Media Coverage and the Making of 9/11.* New York: New York University Press, 2010.

Moore, Ronald. "Podcast: Colonial Day." March 18, 2005. http://www.syfy.com/battlestar/downloads/podcast/mp3/111/bsg_ep111_10f5.mp3.

———. "Podcast: Epiphanies." January 20, 2005. http://www.syfy.com/battlestar/downloads/podcast/mp3/213/bsg_ep213_10f5.mp3.

Morris, Meaghan. "Banality in Cultural Studies." In *Logics of Television: Essays in Cultural Criticism,* ed. Patricia Mellencamp, 14–43. London: BFI Publishing, 1990.

Mulrine, Anna. "New Army Manual Shows War's Softer Side with Focus on Nation-Building." October 10, 2008. http://www.usnews.com/articles/news/national/2008/10/10/new-army-manual-shows-wars-softer-side-with-focus-on-nation-building.html.

Murray, Susan. "'I Think We Need a New Name for It': The Meeting of Documentary and Reality TV." In *Reality TV: Remaking Television Culture*, eds. Susan Murray and Laurie Ouelette, 40–56. New York: New York University Press, 2004.

Nacos, Brigitte L. *Mass-Mediated Terrorism: The Central Role of the Media in Terrorism and Counter-Terrorism*. Lanham, MD: Rowman & Littlefield, 2002.

Nadel, Alan. *Television in Black-and-White America: Race and National Identity*. Lawrence: University of Kansas Press, 2005.

Nasaw, David. *Going Out: The Rise and Fall of Public Amusements*. Cambridge, MA: Harvard University Press, 2002.

The National Security Strategy of the United States of America. Washington, DC: White House, 2002.

Neisser, Ulric, and Nicole Harsch. "Phantom Flashbulbs: False Recollections of Hearing the News about Challenger." In *Memory Observed: Remembering in Natural Contexts*, eds. Ulric Neisser and Ira E. Hyman, 75–104. San Francisco: W. H. Freeman, 1992.

Nelson, Dana. *National Manhood: Capitalist Citizenship and the Imagined Fraternity of White Men*. Durham, NC: Duke University Press, 1998.

Netanyahu, Benjamin. "Terrorism: How the West Can Win." In *Terrorism: How the West Can Win*, ed. Benjamin Netanyahu, 199–226. New York: Farrar, Straus, Giroux, 1983.

Newcomb, Horace, and Paul M. Hirsch. "Television as a Cultural Forum." In *Television: The Critical View*, ed. Horace Newcomb, 561–573. New York: Oxford University Press, 2000.

Newitz, Annalee. "ER, Professions, and the Work-Family Disaster." *American Studies* 39, no. 2 (1998): 93–105.

Nimmo, Kurt. "The Lapdog Conversion of CNN." August 23, 2002. http://www .counterpunch.org/nimmo0823.html.

Norris, Pippa, Montague Kern, and Marion Just, eds. *Framing Terrorism: The News Media, the Government and the Public*. New York: Routledge, 2003.

O'Hagan, Steve. "Recruitment Hard Drive." June 19, 2004. http://www.guardian.co .uk/theguide/features/story/0,14671,1242262,00.html.

Ott, Brian. "(Re)Framing Fear: Equipment for Living in a Post-9/11 World." In *Cylons in America: Critical Studies in Battlestar Galactica*, eds. Tiffany Potter and C. W. Marshall, 13–26. New York: Continuum, 2008.

Owens, Mackubin T. "Real Liberals Versus the 'West Wing.'" February 2001. http:// www.ashbrook.org/publicat/oped/owens/01/liberals.html.

Parks, Lisa. *Cultures in Orbit: Satellites and the Televisual*. Durham, NC: Duke University Press, 2005.

Patterson, Troy. "Band of Lunkheads: The Aggro Marines of *Generation Kill*." July 11, 2008. http://www.slate.com/ id/2195145/.

Peacock, Steven. "24: Status and Style." In *Reading 24: TV against the Clock*, ed. Steven Peacock, 25–34. New York: I. B. Tauris, 2007.

"Pilots Blamed for 'Friendly Fire' Deaths." June 28, 2002. http://news.bbc.co.uk/2/hi/ americas/2073024.stm.

Pineda, Isabel. "Playing with Fire without Getting Burned: Blowback Re-Imagined." In *Battlestar Galactica and Philosophy: Mission Accomplished or Mission Frakked Up?* eds. Josef Steiff and Tristan Tamplin, 173–184. Chicago: Open Court, 2008.

Polan, Dana. "Eros and Syphilization: The Contemporary Horror Film." In *Planks of Reason: Essays on the Horror Film*, eds. Barry Keith Grant and Christopher Sharrett, 142–152. Lanham, MD: Scarecrow Press, 2004.

Poniewozik, James. "Postapocalypse Now." *Time*, October 23, 2006, 94.

———. "That's Militainment! The War on Terror Gets the Cops Treatment." March 4, 2002. http://www.time.com/time/magazine/article/0,9171,1001943,00.html.

———. "'West Wing': Terrorism 101." October 4, 2001. http://www.time.com/time/ columnist/poniewozik/article/0,9565,178042,00.html.

Poniewozik, James, et al. "What's Entertainment Now?" *Time*, October 1, 2001, 108–112.

Potter, Tiffany, and C. W. Marshall, eds. *Cylons in America: Critical Studies in Battlestar Galactica*. New York: Continuum, 2007.

"Powell Reversed the Trend but Not the Tenor of Public Opinion." February 14, 2003. http://people-press.org/commentary/display.php3?AnalysisID=62.

Press, Joy. "The Axers of Evil." March 5–11, 2003. http://www.villagevoice.com/issues/ 0310/tv.php.

Priest, Dana, and Anne Hull. "Soldiers Face Neglect, Frustration at Army's Top Medical Facility." *Washington Post*, February 18, 2007, A01.

"Primetime Torture." 2005. http://www.humanrightsfirst.org/us_law/etn/primetime/ index.asp.

Prince, Stephen. *Firestorm: American Film in the Age of Terrorism*. New York: Columbia University Press, 2009.

"Profiles from the Front Line." November 21, 2006. http://abc.go.com/primetime/ profiles/.

Puar, Jasbir K. *Terrorist Assemblages: Homonationalism in Queer Times*. Durham, NC: Duke University Press, 2007.

Puar, Jasbir K., and Amit S. Rai. "Monster, Terrorist, Fag: The War on Terrorism and the Production of Docile Patriots." *Social Text* 20, no. 3 (2002): 117–148.

Purdum, Todd. "Hollywood Rallies Round the Homeland." *New York Times*, February 2, 2003, B1+.

Putnam, Robert. "Bowling Together." February 11, 2002. http://www.prospect.org/cs/
articles?article=bowling_together.

Rabinowitz, Dorothy. "Full-Voltage Shocks: The 24 Addiction." In *Secrets of 24: The
Unauthorized Guide to the Political and Moral Issues behind TV's Most Riveting Drama*, eds.
Dan Burstein and Arne J. de Keijzer, 40–42. New York: Sterling Publications, 2007.

Randell, Karen, Anna Froula, and Jeff Birkenstein, eds. *Reframing 9/11: Film, Popular
Culture and the "War on Terror."* New York: Continuum Press, 2010.

Randell, Karen, and Sean Redmond, eds. *The War Body on Screen*. London: Continuum,
2008.

Ravault, Rene-Jean. "Is There a Bin Laden in the Audience? Considering the Events of
September 11 as a Possible Boomerang Effect of the Globalization of US Mass
Communication." *Prometheus* 20, no. 3 (2002): 295–300.

Rendall, Steve, and Tara Broughel. "Amplifying Officials, Squelching Dissent." 2003.
http://www.fair.org/extra/0305/warstudy.html.

Rice, Lynette. "Rescue Mission." September 13, 2002. http://www.ew.com/ew/article/
0,348195,00.html.

Ricks, Thomas. *Fiasco: The American Military Adventure in Iraq*. New York: Penguin Press,
2006.

Risen, James. *State of War: The Secret History of the CIA and the Bush Administration*. New
York: Free Press, 2006.

Robb, David. *Operation Hollywood: How the Pentagon Shapes and Censors the Movies*.
Amherst, NY: Prometheus Books, 2004.

Robertson, Linda. "Baghdad ER: Subverting the Mythic Gaze upon the Wounded and
the Dead." In *The War Body on Screen*, eds. Karen Randall and Sean Redmond, 64–
78. New York: Continuum, 2008.

Robin, Corey. *Fear: The History of a Political Idea*. New York: Oxford University Press, 2004.

"Roger's Balancing Act: Fox's Ailes Shakes Up the News Status Quo." October 27,
2003. http://www.broadcastingcable.com/article/print/151239-Roger_s_Balancing
_Act.php.

Rose, Tricia. "24 and the American Tradition of Vigilantism." In *Secrets of 24: The
Unauthorized Guide to the Political and Moral Issues behind TV's Most Riveting Drama*, ed.
Dan Burstein and Arne J. de Keijzer, 130–133. New York: Sterling Publications,
2007.

Rosenberg, Emily. "Rescuing Women and Children." In *History and September 11*, eds.
Joanne Meyerowitz, 81–93. Philadelphia: Temple University Press, 2003.

Rumsfeld, Donald. "Secretary Rumsfeld Speaks on '21st Century' Transformation of
the U.S. Armed Forces." January 31, 2002. http://www.defenselink.mil/speeches/
speech.aspx?speechid=183.

Rutenberg, Jim. "TV Shows Take on Bush, and Pull Few Punches." April 2, 2004. http://www.nytimes.com/2004/04/02/politics/campaign/02TUBE.html.

Ryan, Maureen. "There's Always Money in the Banana Stand: 'Arrested Development's' Stealth Success." October 21, 2005. http://featuresblogs.chicago tribune.com/entertainment_tv/2005/10/theres_always_m.html.

Safire, William. "You Are a Suspect." November 14, 2002. http://www.nytimes.com/2002/11/14/opinion/14SAFI.html.

Said, Edward. *Culture and Imperialism.* New York: Vintage Books, 1993.

Savage, Charlie, and Alan Wirzbicki. "White House-Friendly Reporter under Scrutiny." February 2, 2005. http://www.boston.com/news/nation/articles/2005/02/02/white_house_friendly_reporter_under_scrutiny/.

Schechter, Danny. "It's Time for a Sequel: 'Over Here.'" August 1, 2005. http://www.commondreams.org/views05/0801-20.htm.

———. *Media Wars: News at a Time of Terror.* Lanham, MD: Rowman & Littlefield, 2003.

———. "Selling the Iraq War: The Media Management Strategies We Never Saw." In *War, Media, and Propaganda: A Global Perspective,* eds. Yahya R. Kamalipour and Nancy Snow, 25–32. Boulder, CO: Rowman & Littlefield, 2004.

Schiesel, Seth. "On Maneuvers with the Army's Game Squad." February 17, 2005. http://www.nytimes.com/2005/02/17/technology/circuits/17army.html.

Schiff, Jim. "'American Fighter Pilot' Heavy Handed with Patriotism." March 29, 2002. http://www.michigandaily.com/content/american-fighter-pilot-heavy-handed-patriotism.

Schneider, Bill, and Anne McDermott. "Uncle Sam Wants Hollywood." November 9, 2001. http://archives.cnn.com/2001/SHOWBIZ/Movies/11/09/hollywood.war/.

Scott, Suzanne. "Authorized Resistance: Is Fan Production Frakked?" In *Cylons in America: Critical Studies in Battlestar Galactica,* eds. Tiffany Potter and C. W. Marshall, 210–235. New York: Continuum, 2008.

Seelye, Katherine. "Pentagon Plays Role in Fictional Terror Drama." *New York Times,* March 31, 2002, A12.

Shaheen, Jack. *Reel Bad Arabs: How Hollywood Vilifies a People.* New York: Olive Branch Press, 2001.

Sharrett, Christopher. "9/11, the Useful Incident, and the Legacy of the Creel Committee." *Cinema Journal* 43, no. 4 (2004): 125–131.

Shister, Gail. "'West Wing' Will Address Tragedy in a Special Episode." *Philadelphia Inquirer,* September 25, 2001, C05.

"Shorts: ABC Sprinkles 'Millionaire' Pixie Dust on Sweeps." January 26, 2004. http://www.medialifemagazine.com/news2004/jan04/jan26/1_mon/news8monday.html.

Shultz, George P. "Terrorism and the Modern World." *Studies in Conflict and Terrorism* 7, no. 4 (1985): 431–447.

Silberstein, Sandra. *War of Words: Language, Politics and 9/11.* New York: Routledge, 2002.

Silverman, Kaja. *Male Subjectivity at the Margins.* New York: Routledge, 1992.

Sims, Amy. "Military Reality Shows Battle in Prime Time." April 8, 2002. http://www .foxnews.com/story/0,2933,49730,00.html.

Sites, Kevin, Jim Miklaszewski, and Alex Johnson. "U.S. Probes Shooting at Fallujah Mosque." November 16, 2004. http://www.msnbc.msn.com/id/6496898/.

Sloterdijk, Peter. *Critique of Cynical Reason.* Minneapolis: University of Minnesota Press, 1989.

Slotkin, Richard. *Regeneration through Violence: The Mythology of the American Frontier, 1600–1860.* Middletown, CT: Wesleyan University Press, 1973.

Smelser, Neil. "September 11, 2001, as Cultural Trauma." In *Cultural Trauma and Collective Identity,* eds. Jeffrey Alexander, Ron Eyerman, Bernard Giesen, Neil Smesler, and Piotr Sztompka, 264–282. Berkeley, CA: University of California Press, 2004.

Smith, Terence. "Online Focus: Aaron Sorkin." September 27, 2000. http://www.pbs .org/newshour/media/west_wing/sorkin.html.

Snow, Nancy. *Information War: American Propaganda, Free Speech, and Opinion Control since 9/11.* New York: Seven Stories Press, 2003.

Snow, Nancy, and Philip M. Taylor. "The Revival of the Propaganda State: US Propaganda at Home and Abroad since 9/11." *International Communication Gazette* 68, nos. 5–6 (2006): 389–407.

Solove, Daniel. "Interview with Ron Moore and David Eick." March 2, 2008. http:// www.concurringopinions.com/archives/2008/03/battlestar_gala_5.html.

Sontag, Susan. *Regarding the Pain of Others.* New York: Picador, 2003.

Spigel, Lynn. "Entertainment Wars: Television Culture after 9/11." *American Quarterly* 56, no. 2 (2004): 235–270.

———. *Make Room for TV: Television and the Family Ideal in Postwar America.* Chicago: University of Chicago Press, 1992.

Spitzer, Gabriel. "Top Scores for Some Rookie Cable Networks." July 12, 2001. http:// www.medialifemagazine.com/news2001/july01/july09/4_thurs/news2thursday .html.

St. George, Donna. "Lives Spared through Mysterious Good Fortune." *Washington Post,* September 15, 2001, B01.

Stahl, Roger. "Have You Played the War on Terror?." *Cultural Studies* 23, no. 2 (2006): 112–130.

———. *Militainment, Inc.: Militarism and Pop Culture.* Northampton, MA: Media Education Foundation, 2006.

———. *Militainment, Inc.: War, Media, and Popular Culture.* New York: Routledge, 2009.

Stanley, Alessandra. "The War on Terrorism without the Wrangling." September 18, 2003. http://www.nytimes.com/2003/09/18/arts/television-review-the-war-on-terrorism-without-the-wrangling.html.

Starr, Michael. "Jon's Got Game!" September 25, 2010. http://www.nypost.com/p/entertainment/tv/item_ARuthNhfEWo9txbCOTBNkO;jsessionid=5C26B60B79A5E8E5CB441F3B0D7A5FE4.

Stearns, Peter. *American Fear: The Causes and Consequences of High Anxiety.* New York: Routledge, 2006.

Steiff, Josef, and Tristan Tamplin, eds. *Battlestar Galactica and Philosophy: Mission Accomplished or Mission Frakked Up?* Chicago: Open Court, 2008.

Stout, David. "Ace Sleuths Driven by Honor, Truth." November 29, 1998. http://www.nytimes.com/1998/11/29/tv/cover-story-ace-sleuths-driven-by-honor-truth.html.

Studlar, Gaylyn, and David Desser. "Never Having to Say You're Sorry: *Rambo's* Rewriting of the Vietnam War." In *From Hanoi to Hollywood: The Vietnam War in American Film,* eds. Linda Dittmar and Gene Michaud, 101–112. New Brunswick, NJ: Rutgers University Press, 1990.

Sturken, Marita. *Tangled Memories: The Vietnam War, the AIDS Epidemic, and the Politics of Remembering.* Berkeley: University of California Press, 1997.

———. *Tourists of History: Memory, Kitsch, and Consumerism from Oklahoma City to Ground Zero.* Durham, NC: Duke University Press, 2007.

Surnow, Joel. "There Is Nothing Like It on TV: An Interview with Joel Surnow." In *Secrets of 24: The Unauthorized Guide to the Political and Moral Issues behind TV's Most Riveting Drama,* eds. Dan Burstein and Arne J. de Keijzer, 88–91. New York: Sterling Publications, 2007.

Sutherland, Sharon, and Sarah Swan. "The Good, the Bad, and the Justified: Moral Ambiguity in *Alias.*" In *Investigating Alias,* eds. Simon Brown and Stacey Abbott, 119–132. New York: I. B. Tauris, 2007.

———. "'Tell Me Where the Bomb Is, or I Will Kill Your Son': Situational Morality on *24.*" In *Reading 24: TV against the Clock,* ed. Steven Peacock, 119–132. New York: I. B. Tauris, 2007.

Swofford, Anthony. *Jarhead : A Marine's Chronicle of the Gulf War and Other Battles.* New York: Scribner, 2003.

Takacs, Stacy. "Burning Bush: Sitcom Treatments of the Bush Presidency." *Journal of Popular Culture* 44, no. 2 (2011): 417–435.

———. "Jessica Lynch and the Regeneration of American Identity and Power Post-9/11." *Feminist Media Studies* 5, no. 3 (2005): 297–310.

Teixeira, Ruy. "What the Public Really Wants on Iraq." March 21, 2008. http://www.americanprogress.org/issues/2008/03/public_iraq.html.

"Terror Coverage Boosts News Media's Images, but Military Censorship Backed." November 28, 2001. http://people-press.org/reports/display.php3?PageID=9.

Terry, Jennifer. "Killer Entertainments." *Vectors* 5 (2007). http://vectors.usc.edu/issues/5/killerentertainments/.

Thorburn, David. "Television Melodrama." In *Television: The Critical View*, ed. Horace Newcomb, 595–608. New York: Oxford University Press, 2000.

Thussu, Daya Kishan, and Des Freedman, eds. *War and the Media: Reporting Conflict 24/7*. Thousand Oaks, CA: Sage Publications, 2003.

Tocqueville, Alexis de. *Democracy in America*. Ed. J. P. Mayer, trans. George Lawrence. Vol. 2. New York: Harper Perennial, 1988.

Toppo, Greg. "Education Dept. Paid Commentator to Promote Law." January 7, 2005. http://www.usatoday.com/news/washington/2005-01-06-williams-whitehouse_x.htm.

Tomsho, Robert, Barbara Carton, and Jerry Guidera. "Twists of Fate Saved Lives of Many on 9/11." *Wall Street Journal*, November 22, 2001, F02.

Tucker, Ken. "TV Review: Generation Kill." July 4, 2008. http://www.ew.com/ew/article/0,20210425,00.html.

Umstead, R. Thomas. "Appeal without Limits: USA's 'The 4400,' TNT's 'The Grid' Propel Format." *Multichannel News*, August 16, 2004, 12.

"US and Coalition Casualties." March 28, 2008. http://www.cnn.com/SPECIALS/2003/iraq/forces/casualties/.

"US Bomb Kills Allies in Afghanistan." April 18, 2002. http://news.bbc.co.uk/2/hi/south_asia/1936589.stm.

"US Military Uses YouTube to Get Its Story Out." May 2, 2007. http://www.npr.org/templates/story/story.php?storyId=9966124&ft=1&f=1001.

VandeHei, Jim. "Kerry Vows to Rebuild Alliances, Confront Terrorism." *Washington Post*, May 28, 2004, A09.

Van Der Veer, Peter. "War Propaganda and the Liberal Public Sphere." In *Media, War, and Terrorism: Responses from the Middle East and Asia*, eds. Peter Van Der Veer and Shoma Munshi, 9–21. New York: Routledge, 2004.

Vowell, Sarah. "Down with Torture! Gimme Torture!" In *Secrets of 24: The Unauthorized Guide to the Political and Moral Issues behind TV's Most Riveting Drama*, eds. Dan Burstein and Arne J. de Keijzer, 43–45. New York: Sterling Publications, 2007.

Wahlberg, Donnie. "Donnie Wahlberg Back on TV as a Good Guy . . . Or Is He?" July 16, 2007. http://television.aol.com/tv-celebrity-interviews/donnie-wahlberg.

Wallsten, Peter. "Despite Criticism, Patriot Act Gaining Popularity." April 26, 2004. http://community.seattletimes.nwsource.com/archive/?date=20040426&slug=patriot26.

Walzer, Michael. *Arguing about War.* New Haven, CT: Yale University Press, 2004.

———. *Just and Unjust Wars: A Moral Argument with Historical Illustrations.* 3rd ed. New York: Basic Books, 2000.

Warner, Judith. "Jonesing for More 24." In *Secrets of 24: The Unauthorized Guide to the Political and Moral Issues behind TV's Most Riveting Drama,* eds. Dan Burstein and Arne J. de Keijzer, 134–136. New York: Sterling Publications, 2007.

"We Pause Now for a Word About the War . . ." March 26, 2003. http://www.imdb.com/news/ni0103796/.

Wells, Matt. "How Smart Was This Bomb?" November 19, 2001. http://www.guardian.co.uk/media/2001/nov/19/mondaymediasection.afghanistan.

"What's the Per Episode Cost of the Television Show Lost?" 2008. http://wiki.answers.com/Q/Whats_the_cost_per_episode_of_the_televison_show_lost.

White, Mimi. *Tele-Advising: Therapeutic Discourse in American Television.* Chapel Hill: University of North Carolina Press, 1992.

"Whoopi: Bush 'Doing to Bathroom What He's Done to the Economy!'" October 15, 2003. http://www.mediaresearch.org/cyberalerts/2003/cyb20031015.asp#3.

"Whoopi: On Her New Show, Patriotism and Hollywood." October 2003. http://msnbc.msn.com/id/3080555/.

Wildman, Steven, and Stephen Siwek. "The Economics of Trade in Recorded Media Products in a Multilingual World: Implications for National Media Policies." In *The International Market in Film and Television Programs,* eds. Eli Noam and Joel Millonzi, 13–40. Norwood, NJ: Ablex Publishing, 1993.

Williams, Raymond. *Marxism and Literature.* London: Oxford University Press, 1977.

Willis, Susan. *Portents of the Real: A Primer for Post-9/11 America.* New York: Verso, 2005.

Wilson, Scott, and Al Kamen. "'Global War on Terror' Is Given New Name." March 25, 2009. http://www.washingtonpost.com/wp-dyn/content/article/2009/03/24/AR2009032402818.html.

Wilson, Theodore. "Selling America Via the Silver Screen? Efforts to Manage the Projection of American Culture Abroad, 1942–1947." In *"Here, There, and Everywhere": The Foreign Politics of American Popular Culture,* eds. Reinhold Wagnleitner and Elaine Tyler May, 83–99. Hanover, NH: University Press of New England, 2000.

"Without a Trace." 2008. http://www.tv.com/without-a-trace/show/7449/summary.html?q=without%20a%20trace&tag=search_results;title;1.

Wright, Evan. *Generation Kill: Devil Dogs, Iceman, Captain America and the New Face of American War.* New York: Berkeley Caliber, 2004.

Zabel, Bryce. "Guest Commentary: Television and the War on Terrorism." *Electronic Media*, November 19, 2001, 9.

Zaharna, R. S. "From Propaganda to Public Diplomacy in the Information Age." In *War, Media, and Propaganda: A Global Perspective*, eds. Yahya R. Kamalipour and Nancy Snow, 219–224. New York: Rowman & Littlefield, 2002.

Zelizer, Barbie. "Death in Wartime: Photographs and the 'Other War' in Afghanistan." *Press/Politics* 10, no. 3 (2005): 26–55.

Zizek, Slavoj. "24, or Himmler in Hollywood." In *Secrets of 24: The Unauthorized Guide to the Political and Moral Issues behind TV's Most Riveting Drama*, eds. Dan Burstein and Arne J. de Keijzer, 202–206. New York: Sterling Publications, 2007.

Zucchino, David. "US Military, Not Iraqis, Behind Toppling of Statue." July 5, 2004. http://the.honoluluadvertiser.com/article/2004/Jul/05/mn/mn03a.html.

Zulaika, Joseba. "The Self-Fulfilling Prophecies of Counter-Terrorism." *Radical History Review* 85 (2003): 191–199.

Zulaika, Joseba, and William A. Douglass. *Terror and Taboo: The Follies, Fables and Faces of Terrorism.* New York: Routledge, 1996.

TELEVISION BIBLIOGRAPHY

24. Fox, November 6, 2001–May 24, 2010.

"9/11 Five Years Later: President Bush One-on-One." *Today Show*. NBC, September 11, 2006.

"A Conversation about the Hit Show '24.'" *Charlie Rose*. PBS, May 20, 2005.

The Agency. CBS, September 28, 2001–May 17, 2003.

Alias. ABC, September 30, 2001–May 22, 2006.

Alive Day Memories: Home From Iraq. DVD. Santa Monica, CA: HBO Films, 2007.

AFP: American Fighter Pilot. CBS, March 26, 2002–April 5, 2002.

AFP: American Fighter Pilot. DVD. Century City, CA: Twentieth Century Fox, 2005.

"After Time." *Third Watch*. NBC, October 29, 2001.

America's Most Wanted: Terrorists. Fox, October 12, 2001.

Arrested Development. Fox, November 2, 2003–February 1, 2006.

Baghdad ER. DVD. Santa Monica, CA: HBO Films, 2006.

Battlestar Galactica. Sci Fi, January 14, 2005–March 20, 2009.

Battlestar Galactica: Miniseries. Sci Fi, December 8–December 10, 2003.

Boot Camp. Fox, March 28–May 23, 2001.

"Buying the War." *Bill Moyers Journal*. PBS, April 25, 2007.

"Camp Delta." *JAG*. CBS, November 19, 2004.

Combat Missions. USA, January 16–April 17, 2002.

The Daily Show with Jon Stewart. Comedy Central, January 11, 1999–present.

"Death at the Mosque." *JAG*. CBS, April 1, 2005.

"Deja Past." *Crossing Jordan*. NBC, October 17, 2004.

E-Ring. NBC, September 21, 2005–February 1, 2006.

"Everyone's Waiting." *Six Feet Under*. HBO, August 21, 2005.

"First Casualty." *JAG*. CBS, March 26, 2002.

"Friendly Fire." *JAG*. CBS, February 11, 2003.

Generation Kill. HBO, June 20, 2008–August 24, 2008.

Generation Kill. DVD. Santa Monica, CA: HBO Films, 2008.

"Goliath." *Law & Order: SVU*. NBC, May 24, 2005.

The Grid. TNT, July 19–August 9, 2004.

The Grid. DVD. Century City, CA: Twentieth Century Fox, 2005.

"Gung-Ho." *Without a Trace*. February 26, CBS, 2004.

"Have You Ever Seen the Rain." *Las Vegas*. NBC, September 13, 2004.

Homeland Security. NBC, April 11, 2004.

"I'm a Little Bit Country." *South Park*. Comedy Central, April 29, 2003.

"In Their Own Words." *Third Watch*. NBC, October 15, 2001.

"Interview with Dan Rather." *Late Show with David Letterman*. CBS, September 17, 2001.

"Interview with Dick Cheney." *Meet the Press*, September 16, 2001.

"Interview with Hillary Rodham Clinton." *The Today Show*. NBC, January 27, 1998.

"Invading the Mind of Shaun Cassidy." *Invasion: The Complete Series*. DVD. Burbank, CA: Warner Home Video, 2006.

Invasion. ABC, September 21, 2005–May 17, 2006.

Invasion: The Complete Series. DVD. Burbank, CA: Warner Home Video, 2006.

"Isaac and Ishmael." *The West Wing*. NBC, October 3, 2001.

JAG. CBS, September 23, 1995–April 29, 2005.

Jericho. CBS, September 20, 2006–March 25, 2008.

Jericho: The First Season. DVD. Hollywood, CA: Paramount Home Video, 2007.

Jericho: The Second Season. DVD. Hollywood, CA: Paramount Home Video, 2008.

The Kill Point. SPIKE, July 22–August 26, 2007.

"Know Your Enemy." *Sleeper Cell*. DVD. Hollywood, CA: Showtime Entertainment, 2006.

The L Word. Showtime, January 8, 2004–March 8, 2009.

Lost. CBS, September 22, 2004–May 23, 2010.

Making Marines. Discovery Channel, May 30–June 16, 2002.

Making Marines. DVD. Hollywood, CA: Image Entertainment, 2003.

"The Making of Jericho." *Jericho: The First Season*. DVD. Hollywood, CA: Paramount Home Video, 2007.

MI5 (Spooks). BBC1, May 13, 2003–present.

Military Diaries. VH1, May 27–June 24, 2002.

"The Mission." *JAG*. CBS, February 26, 2002.

"Mystery of the Urinal Deuce." *South Park*. Comedy Central, October 11, 2006.

"The New Forgotten." *The Montel Williams Show*. CBS Television Distribution, May 27, 2005.

"A New Life." *JAG*. CBS, September 23, 1995.

Off to War. Discovery-Times, April 20, 2004–December 24, 2005.

"Osama Bin Laden Has Farty Pants." *South Park*. Comedy Central, November 7, 2001.

Over There. FX, July 27, 2005–October 26, 2006.

Over There. DVD. Century City, CA: Twentieth Century Fox, 2006.

"Paradigm." *Law & Order*. NBC, September 22, 2004.

"People v. SecNav." *JAG*. CBS, February 6, 2004.

"Pilot." *Ghost Whisperer*. CBS, September 23, 2005.

Profiles from the Front Line. ABC, February 27–March 13, 2003.

"Red Sleigh Down." *South Park*. Comedy Central, December 11, 2002.

Rescue Me. FX, July 21, 2004–2011.

Saving Jessica Lynch. NBC, November 9, 2003.

"September 10." *Third Watch*. October 22, 2001.

"Sergeant Sipowicz's Lonely Heart's Club Band." *NYPD Blue*. ABC, February 8, 2005.

Sleeper Cell. Showtime, December 4–December 18, 2005.

Sleeper Cell. DVD. Hollywood, CA: Showtime Entertainment, 2006.

Sleeper Cell: American Terrorist. Showtime, December 10–December 17, 2006.

Sleeper Cell: American Terrorist. DVD. Hollywood, CA: Showtime Entertainment, 2007.

"The Soldier on the Grave." *Bones.* Fox, May 10, 2006.

"Static." *Six Feet Under.* HBO, August 14, 2005.

Surface. NBC, September 19, 2005–February 6, 2006.

Surface: The Complete Series. DVD. Universal City, CA: Universal Studios Home Entertainment, 2006.

Threat Matrix. ABC, September 18, 2003–January 29, 2004.

Threshold. CBS, September 16–November 22, 2005.

Threshold: The Complete Series. DVD. Hollywood, CA: Paramount Home Video, 2006.

"The Threshold Brain Trust." *Threshold: The Complete Series.* Hollywood, CA: Paramount Home Video, 2006.

"Tribunal." *JAG.* CBS, April 30, 2002.

The Unit. CBS, March 7, 2006–May 10, 2009.

"Veteran's Day." *Law & Order.* NBC, February 18, 2004.

"The War at Home." *Cold Case.* CBS, October 1, 2006.

War Games. TBS, March 25, 2001.

"We Got Us a Pippi Virgin." *Gilmore Girls.* WB, October 19, 2004.

Whoopi. NBC, September 9, 2003–April 20, 2004.

"Witches of Mass Destruction." *Boston Legal.* ABC, November 1, 2005.

"With Honor." *Crossing Jordan.* NBC, March 18, 2002.

INDEX

A&E, 103

ABC
  collaboration with the U.S. military,
    102–103
  military docusoaps, 109–114, 115
  revitalization of spy programs, 60
Abizaid, Gen. John, 148
"About-to-die" photos, 99
Abraham Lincoln (USS), 5
Abrams, J. J., 257n26
Abtahi, Omid, 165
Abu Ghraib scandal, 8, 95, 125, 168
Academy of Motion Picture Arts and
    Sciences, 17
"Acting out," 243
Ad Council, 7
Advertising industry, 7
Aerial bombardment
  in Afghanistan, 147
  in Iraq, 147
  JAG's justification of, 131–133
  Revolution in Military Affairs and,
    146–147
Affleck, Ben, 15
Afghanistan
  alternative media networks created by
    the U.S., 2
  Bush administration rhetoric on the
    invasion of, 73
Afghanistan War
  aerial bombardment in, 147
  Barack Obama and, 238
  Bush administration rhetoric on the
    invasion, 73

friendly-fire deaths, 219
information warfare and, 100
JAG's justification of combat tactics
    in, 131–133
JAG's mediation of the cultural
    memory of, 140–141
Just War theory and Bush's
    declaration of war, 97–98
military docusoaps and, 105–119
news media presentation and
    coverage, 98–100
re- and premediation of news
    accounts, 121
AFP: American Fighter Pilot (docusoap), 101,
    105, 106–109, 122
Against All Enemies (Clarke), 169
Agamben, Giorgio, 96
Agency, The (television series)
  assistance from the CIA and, 62,
    63
  female agents and characters, 70
  impact of 9/11 on, 38
  multicultural orientation, 71
  number of viewers, 257n31
  original conception of, 61
  promotional material for, 66
  in the revitalization of spy programs,
    60
  vigilante heroism and, 65–68
Aghdashloo, Shohreh, 91
Ahmed, Sara, 72, 75, 94
Al Arabiya, 99
Alexander, Tracey, 71, 73
Alhurra, 2

Alias (television series)
   female agents, 69
   J. J. Abrams on the intent of,
      257n26
   number of viewers, 257n31
   original conception of, 61
   perspective on the spy game, 63
   in the revitalization of spy programs,
      60
   video game spinoffs, 94
   vigilante heroism and, 65
Alive Day Memories (HBO documentary),
      226–227
Al Jazeera, 56, 99–100, 261n6
Allard, Kenneth, 166
"Allegory lite" aesthetics, 91–92
Al Qaeda, 238
   The Agency TV show and, 66
   depiction in science fiction TV
      programs, 178, 186
   "oppositional" reading of U.S. pro-
      militarist films, 17–18
   pathologization and
      decontextualization of, 59–60
   propaganda efforts, 1–2
   September 11 attacks as media
      events, 1
   See also Terrorism/Terrorists
Alston, Joshua, 199
Alternate reality games (ARGs), 202–203
Amazing Race, The (reality television
      show), 120
Ambrose, Lauren, 233
American citizenship
   in contrast to "alienness," 69
   redefined in special TV episodes
      following 9/11, 39–54
American Creed
   interrogation by *Battlestar Galactica*,
      194–200
   Samuel Huntington on, 254n46
American Embassy, The (television series),
      57
"American Empire," 161

American exceptionalism
   comic interrogation by *South Park*, 54–55
   reaffirmed in melodramas of soldier-
      suffering, 216
   religious rhetoric and, 36
American Fighter Pilot. See AFP: American
      Fighter Pilot
American High (docusoap), 114
American identity
   the discourse of security and, 22–23
   media invocations in the coverage of
      9/11, 34–35
   multiculturalist construction in spy
      TV programs, 69–72
   redefined in 9/11 special TV episodes,
      39–45, 46, 47–53
American Muslims
   depiction in 24, 91
   depiction in spy TV programs, 70–71
America's Army (video game), 9
America's Most Wanted (television series),
      31, 42–47, 52–53
"America the Beautiful" (song), 56
Andén-Papadopoulos, Kari, 166
Anthrax scares, 66
Appadurai, Arjun, 2
Arab Americans
   racial profiling in 9/11 special TV
      episodes and, 50–52
   TV as a fear-machine, 58
Arab TV characters, 71–72
Arkansas National Guard, 228
Arrested Development (television series),
      172–173, 174–175, 201
Ashcroft, John, 42–43, 45
Asteroid (television miniseries), 17
Asymmetric Warfare Environment (video
      game), 10
Atkins, Sharif, 224
Aufderheide, Pat, 13
Azizi, Anthony, 71

Bacevich, Andrew, 107, 123, 146
"Backdraft," 2

Baghdad ER (HBO documentary), 278n62

Baker, Sean, 129

Band of Brothers (television series), 13–14

Barnett, Brooke, 33, 35

Battaglia, Matt, 219

Battlestar Galactica (television series), 176, 188–189, 194–200, 202–204

Baudrillard, Jean, 1

Baym, Geoffrey, 172

BBC America, 99

BBC News Online, 99

Beach, Michael, 41

Beck, Glenn, 8

Bee, Samantha, 171

Beers, Charlotte, 2–3

Beetem, Chris, 135

Begala, Paul, 271n18

Bell, Catherine, 122–123

Bell, Lake, 178

Bellafante, Ginia, 190, 191

Bellisario, Donald, 123, 124, 128, 140, 141

Bellows, Gil, 67

Benjamin, Walter, 141

Bernard, Carlos, 71

Beyer, Brad, 192

Bianco, Robert, 48

Bianculli, David, 108

Bill Moyers Journal (PBS television show), 4

Bin Laden, Osama
   The Agency TV show and, 66
   assassination of, 238
   comic depiction on *South Park*, 55
   depicted in spy TV programs, 78–79
   pathologized by George W. Bush, 59
   Russian-brokered deal for the surrender of, 98
   September 11 attacks as media events, 1

Biressi, Anita, 118

Black Hawk Down (film), 13, 14, 15, 17, 18

Black soldiers, 278n44

Blitzer, Wolf, 35

"Blowback," 195

Bochco, Steven, 145

Bones (television series), 217, 219–223, 278n44

Booker, Keith, 175

Boot, Max, 160

Boot Camp (reality militainment series), 104

Boreanaz, David, 219

Boykin, Gen. William G., 72

Brandon, Chase, 62, 65

Braverman, Chuck and Alex, 105

Brecht, Bertolt, 254n53

Bresler, Robert, 39

Brown, Aaron, 32, 33

Brown, Wren T., 174

Bruckheimer, Jerry, 110, 113–114

Brzezinski, Zbigniew, 188–189

Buckman, Adam, 151

Bureau of Motion Pictures (BMP), 16

Burnett, Mark, 104

Burns, Ed, 145, 149, 150, 155

Bush, George W.
   American desire for vengeance and action following 9/11 and, 65
   appearance on the *Rush Limbaugh Show*, 8
   assertions regarding U.S. intelligence and law enforcement, 61
   declaration of war against Afghanistan, 97–98
   defense of waterboarding, 177
   depicted in *DC 9/11: Time of Crisis*, 11, 12–13
   flexibly expansive definition of "terrorists," 60
   image portrayed during the war in Iraq, 5
   invocations of loyalty to in the coverage of 9/11, 34, 35
   on the legitimacy of the Iraq War, 137–138
   on the need for preemption in the War on Terrorism, 15
   paternal authority assigned to, 52, 59

Bush, George W., *continued*
  September 20 speech pathologizing
    and decontextualizing terrorism,
    59–60
  War on Terrorism conceived as the
    defense of global society, 164
Bush administration
  Abu Ghraib scandal and, 168
  America's Most Wanted 9/11 special
    episode and, 42–47
  collaboration with the producers of
    JAG, 124, 125–126
  cooptation of the entertainment
    media in the War on Terrorism, 5–
    8, 10–15, 31, 39, 102
  cooptation of the news media in the
    War on Terrorism, 6
  depoliticization of terrorism, 60
  embedded journalists and
    information management in Iraq, 5
  ethic of "proactive defense," 95
  halt of press conferences on the Iraq
    War, 207
  image management during the war in
    Iraq, 4–5
  imposition of special powers of
    authority, 60
  infantilization of the American
    public, 52
  Information Awareness Office,
    259n63
  interrogated by science fiction TV
    programs, 189–200
  Just War theory and, 97–98, 139–140
  media melodramatization of 9/11 and,
    36–37
  Netwar thinking, 100
  pathologization of terrorists, 69,
    188
  patriotic TV programming and, 57–
    58
  personalization of fear and, 177
  political criticism of, 168–169
  politics of fear and, 53–54
  rhetoric of multicultural American
    identity, 69
  rhetoric on the invasion of
    Afghanistan, 73
  satirization of, 172–175, 240
  selling of the war in Afghanistan
    through militainment, 100–101
  selling of the war in Iraq, 3–4
  selling of the War on Terrorism, 2–5,
    81
  strategic use of fictional formats,
    120–121
Bush Doctrine, 38, 123
  See also Preventative warfare
Business as War (Allard), 166

Cable television
  decline in coverage of the Iraq War,
    208
  FCC regulations and, 225
  migration of reality militainment to,
    120
  post-sentimentality in complex
    modes of storytelling,
    225–235
"Campaign for Freedom," 7
Campbell, David, 22
Capra, Frank, 16
Caraccioli, Laura, 57
Carafano, James, 91–92
Card, Andrew, 4
Carlson, Amy, 41
Carlson, Tucker, 271n18
Carnegie Endowment for International
  Peace, 4
Carry, Julius, 130
Carson, Silas, 87
Carter, Graydon, 172
Carter, Sgt. Stephen, 116, 117
Casabani, Marc, 126
Cash, Johnny, 159
Cassar, Jon, 62
Castonguay, James, 5, 17
Casualties of War (film), 13

Censorship
  banning of songs, 8, 247n34
  following the 9/11 attacks, 6
  of Iraq War news coverage, 207
  JAG on, 134–135
  self-censorship in the news media, 3
Central Intelligence Agency (CIA)
  The Agency TV show and, 65–67
  assistance to The Sum of All Fears, 15
  liaison to the film industry, 261n21
  spy television programs and, 61–62
Chamberlain, Daniel, 89
Channing, Stockard, 52
Chaos (television show), 60
Chen, Joey, 33
Cheney, Dick, 8, 11, 12
Cheney, Liz, 95–96
Chinese Muslims, 129
Choudhury, Sarita, 215
Cibrian, Eddie, 183
Civilian casualties
  defended on JAG, 127
  news coverage of Afghanistan, 3
  treatment in Generation Kill and Over
    There, 152–154, 165
Clarke, Richard, 12, 169
Clarke, Victoria "Torie," 5, 98–99
Clear Channel, 7–8, 247n34
Clinton, Hillary Rodham, 35, 173
Clooney, George, 39
CNN
  Al Jazeera feed, 56
  melodramatic framing of 9/11 in
    "Breaking News" coverage, 32–33
  religious references during the
    coverage of 9/11, 35–36
Coalition Provisional Authority, 148
Cochran, Robert, 87–88
Colbert, Stephen, 171, 271n19
Colbert Report, The (television show), 120,
  202
Cold Case (television series), 277n44
Coleman, Lindsey, 92–93
"Collateral damage," 132, 133

Combat Diary: The Marines Lima Company
  (documentary film), 13, 229
Combat Missions (gamedoc), 104
Comedy Central, 54, 120, 202
Comedy television programs
  influence and survival in the new
    media context, 200–202
  interrogation of American innocence
    and exceptionalism, 54–55
  in the plurality of the commercial
    media systems, 204–205
  political dissent and, 170–175
"Comfort culture," 225
Comic books, 203
Committee on Public Information, 16
Conflict: Desert Storm (video game), 9
Consumption, linked to patriotism, 7
Cooper, Stephen, 5
Corner, John, 40
Coulter, Anne, 92
Council on American-Islamic Relations
  (CAIR), 91
Counterinsurgency doctrine
  David Petraeus and, 160
  neoconservative conceptualization of,
    160–162
  promotion by television shows, 145
Counterterrorism, 18–19
  See also Spy TV programs
Couric, Katie, 33
"Cowboys," 162–163
Creel Committee, 16
"Criminal vets," 230–232
Critical media literacy, 172
Cronkite, Walter, 56
Cross, David, 173
Cross, Roger, 71
Crossfire (television news show), 271n18
Crossing Jordan (television series), 277n44
CSI: New York (television series), 57
Cumulus, 7–8, 247n34
Cure (music group), 8
Curry, Ann, 174
Cutler, R. J., 114–115, 116, 117

Daily Show with Jon Stewart, The (television show), 4, 170–172, 175, 200, 201–202

Daniel, Sean, 38

Davis, Doug, 15

DC 9/11: Time of Crisis (television docudrama), 11–13

DeGeneres, Ellen, 56

Denton, James, 68

De Palma, Brian, 144

Department of Defense
    coercion of entertainment media, 17
    collaboration with the entertainment media, 6, 102–104, 124
    Office for Motion Picture Production, 102
    propaganda efforts in Iraq, 2
    reality militainment programs and, 101
    Revolution in Military Affairs, 146–148

Department of Homeland Security, 63, 261n21

Desante, Michael, 75

Deschanel, Emily, 219

Detention practices, JAG's defense of, 125–131

Devane, William, 85

"Direct cinema," 14

"Dirty wars," 160

Discourse of security
    American national identity and, 22–23
    entertainment TV and, 20–21

Discovery Channel, 122, 264n2

Discovery Times, 120, 227

Dispersed surveillance, 83–84

Dissent. *See* Political dissent

Dixie Chicks, 8, 54

Djalili, Omid, 173

Dobkin, Bethami, 37–38, 256n4

Docudramas, 11–13

Documentarism, 40, 42

Documentary realism, 14

Docusoaps, 227
    concept of, 104–105
    military, 105–119

Dog Day Afternoon (film), 230

Douglas, Aaron, 198

Dunn, Timothy, 93

Ealy, Michael, 70

Edison Company, 102

Elliott, David James, 122, 265n13

Ellis, John, 236, 244, 276n18

Embedded reporting
    in the Iraq War, 5, 120, 206–207
    JAG on, 134

Emma Brody (television series), 57

Emmy Awards of 2001, 56–57

Enemy aliens, depicted in science fiction TV programs, 175, 178–179, 181, 182–184, 185, 186, 188

"Enhanced interrogation." *See* Torture

Entertainment media
    collaboration with the U.S. military, 102–104
    cooptation by the Bush administration in the War on Terrorism, 5–8, 10–15, 102
    critical depiction of the Iraq War, 144–145
    "military-industrial-entertainment" complex, 16–18, 24
    popularization of the citizen as an agent of government, 168
    See also Entertainment television; Film industry

Entertainment television
    complex modes of storytelling in the "post-network" system, 223–225
    concept of, 20
    creation of a climate of fear, 53–54
    desacralization of the War on Terrorism, 240–244
    in the discourse of security in the War on Terrorism, 20–21

documentarism in 9/11 special episodes, 40, 42

historical witnessing and, 235–237

images of soldier-suffering, 209 (*see also* Soldier-suffering)

impact of 9/11 on themes and emphases in programming, 38–39

infantilization of the American public, 51–52

militainment (*see* Militainment)

pathologization of terrorists, 44–46, 50–52, 53–54

patriotic programming following 9/11, 55–58

redefining of American identity in 9/11 special episodes, 39–45, 46, 47–53

See also Comedy television programs; Reality television; Science fiction TV programs; Spy TV programs

"Epic theatre," 254n53

E-Ring (television series), 256n9

ER (television series), 223–225

Espionage thrillers, 256n10

See also Spy TV programs

ESPN, 103

ESPN SportsCenter, 120

ESPN: The Magazine, 103

Ethical responsibility, interrogated in science fiction TV programs, 196–197

Ethnocentrism, 215

Executive authority, interrogated in science fiction TV programs, 189, 191–192, 195, 196–197

Extreme Makeover: Home Edition (reality television show), 120, 212–214, 223, 227, 229

Faber, George, 159

Fallujah, 10, 135, 137

Fallujah: Operation Al Fajr (video game), 10

"False consciousness," 143

Faludi, Susan, 12, 33, 34, 68–69

Family life, personalization of fear and, 177–184

"Family under siege," 59

Fan campaigns, 201

Fan interaction, science fiction TV programs and, 202–204

FCC regulations, 225

Fear
personalization of, 177–184
Zbigniew Brzezinski on, 188–189
See also Politics of fear

Federal Bureau of Investigation (FBI)
assistance to spy TV programs, 61, 62
liaison to the film industry, 261n21
meeting with film industry executives following 9/11, 10–11

Fehr, Oded, 70, 72

Femininity, depicted in science fiction TV programs, 179–180, 182

Ferguson, Jay, 178

Few Good Men, A (film), 130

Fiasco (Ricks), 160

Fichtner, William, 182

Fictional formats, strategic use by the Bush administration, 120–121

Field of Honor: 100 Years of Army Football (documentary), 103

Film industry
collaboration with the U.S. government and military, 10–11, 16–17, 102–103
critical depiction of the Iraq War, 144
DC 9/11: Time of Crisis, 11–13
films on the Vietnam War, 13
liaisons from U.S. intelligence agencies, 261n21
military-themed films following 9/11, 13–14
"oppositional" reading of pro-militarist films, 17–18
"strategic fictions" supporting the War on Terrorism, 14–15

1st Motion Picture Unit (U.S. Army), 16

Flashbulb memory, 141

Flashframe memory, 135, 141

Fleischer, Ari, 10–11, 39, 80

"Foreignness," American national identity and, 22–23, 69

Foreign policy, 22

Foucault, Michel, 21, 269n46

"Four Minute Men," 16

Fox and Friends (television news show), 276n20

Fox News Channel, 56, 57, 133, 276n20

Fox Television, 60, 104

Frain, James, 183

Franks, Gen. Tommy, 147

Friend, Tad, 190

Friendly fire deaths, 98, 132–133, 157, 207, 219–220

Frontier mythology, 162–163

Frontline (television news show), 111

Full Spectrum Warrior (video game), 11

Furby, Jacqueline, 88

FX, 230, 240

Gabler, Neal, 144

Gadinsky, Brian, 106

Gamedocs, military-themed, 104

Gandolfini, James, 226

Garner, Jennifer, 62, 69

Gaston, Michael, 191

Gates, Robert, 151

Gender politics
    the melodramatic framing of 9/11 by television news and, 33–34
    science fiction TV programs and, 179–181

General Motors, 7, 207

Generation Kill (television series), 268n21, 269n27
    after-action review of the Iraq invasion, 145, 148, 149–151, 152–156, 158–160
    Billy Lush, 232, 233, 236
    on the economic motivations for war, 164–165
    melodrama in scripted treatments of soldier-suffering, 230
    moral thinking solicited by, 167
    origin of, 144–145
    promotion of counterinsurgency doctrine, 145
    promotion of war as an instrument of peace, 165–166
    recuperation of militarism and, 121
    rejection of frontier mythology, 162–163
    vaunting of the professional soldier, 163–165

"Generation Kill" (term), 269n27

Gerolmo, Chris, 268n21

Gibson, Mel, 64

Gillan, Jennifer, 213

Gillman, Lt. Col. Bruce, 14

Gilroy, Paul, 277n37

Gods and Generals (film), 13

Goldberg, Whoopi, 173, 174

Good Morning America (television show), 103

Google Video, 14

Gordon, Howard, 61

Gore, Al, 168

"Government Information Manual for the Motion Picture Industry," 16

Goyer, David, 176

Great Raid, The (film), 13

Green, Sgt. Laurie, 116, 117

Greene, Eric, 195, 199

Grewal, Inderpal, 72

Grid, The (television series), 57
    action-oriented heroism in, 68
    assistance from the NSA, 62
    depiction of racial profiling, 77
    depiction of surveillance technologies, 83
    depiction of terrorism as a contagion, 73–74
    female agents, 69
    justification of dispersed surveillance, 84

logic of suspicion in, 80
multicultural orientation, 71–72
normalization of the state of
    exception, 95
ratings, 64, 257n25
in the revitalization of spy programs,
    60
static between intelligence agencies
    incorporated in, 63
treatment of torture in, 87
video game spinoffs, 94
whitening of the terrorist figures, 77
Grusin, Richard, 121, 142
Guantanamo Bay, 129–130
Guardian Online, 99
Gugino, Carla, 185
Gummersall, Devon, 217
Gunner Palace (film), 13

Hall, Michael C., 233
Halliburton, 192
Harris, Laura, 77
Haysbert, Dennis, 71
HBO, programming formula, 225–226
HDNet, 144
Healthcare, interrogated on ER, 223–224
Heldenfels, R. D., 114
Helvenston, Scott, 262n29
Henderson, Josh, 268n21
Heroism
    expanded conceptualization of, 68–
        73
    vigilante heroism in spy TV
        programs, 65–68
High-School Boot Camp (docusoap), 105
Hill, Mathew, 67
Hill and Knowlton public relations firm,
    5
History Channel, 103
Hobbes, Thomas, 177
Hogan, Michael, 198
Holden, William, 16
Holloway, David, 47, 92
Hollywood. See Film industry

Homeland Security, interrogated by
    Threshold, 185–188
Homeland Security (television series)
    depiction of racial profiling in, 74–75
    "deviant sexuality" as a signifier of
        perversity, 78–79
    propaganda function of, 63
    in the revitalization of spy programs,
        60
    weak audience penetration, 64
Homestead (Florida), 182
Hoskins, Andrew, 207
Huertas, Jon, 164
Human rights discourse, 80–81
Human Rights First, 85
Huntington, Samuel, 47, 254n46
Hussein, Saddam, 17

Iftikhar, Arsalan, 258n46
"I'm on Fire" (song), 8
"Imperial grunts," 161
Imperial Grunts (Kaplan), 161
Imperial melancholia, 215
Information Awareness Office, 259n63
Information warfare
    Netwar thinking by the Bush
        administration, 100
    re- and premediation of news
        accounts, 121
Institute for Creative Technologies, 8–9
Intelligence agencies
    liaisons to the film industry, 261n21
    propaganda function of spy TV
        programs and, 61–65
    See also specific agencies
Invasion (television series), 176, 177, 178,
    181–184, 200, 201
Iranian hostages crisis, 37
Iraq conspiracy theories, 12
Iraqi Media Network, 2
Iraq War
    alternative media networks created by
        the U.S., 2
    American image management in, 4–5

Iraq War, *continued*
   Bush administration's selling of,
      3–4
   critical depiction by the
      entertainment media, 144–145
   decline in popular support for, 144
   George W. Bush on the legitimacy of,
      137–138
   images of soldier-suffering on
      entertainment TV, 209 (*see also*
      Soldier-suffering)
   information warfare and, 100
   initial U.S. strategy in, 147–148
   interrogated by science fiction TV
      programs, 188–200
   JAG's defense of preventative warfare,
      135–140
   JAG's justification of combat tactics
      in, 131–133
   JAG on the media's role in, 135–137
   JAG's mediation of the cultural
      memory of, 140–141
   Just War theory and, 138–140
   news coverage (*see* Iraq War news
      coverage)
   structural absence of Iraqi war victims
      on American television, 215–216
   television's after-action review, 145,
      148–160
   video games of, 10
Iraq War news coverage
   abdication of the witnessing function,
      206–207
   decline in coverage over time, 207–
      208
   embedded reporting, 5, 120,
      206–207
   government censorship and, 207
   JAG on, 135–137
   re- and premediation of news
      accounts, 121
   sanitization of the war, 207
   selective witnessing and the "collapse
      of memory," 208–209

Iraq War veterans
   Alive Day Memories documentary, 226–
      227
   depicted on talk shows and reality
      programming, 210–214
   depiction of the "criminal vet" in
      television shows, 230–232
Irelan, Lana and Wayne, 228
"Ironic" (song), 8
Isaacson, Walter, 3, 56

Jackson, John, 126
Jackson, Richard, 53, 139
JAG (television series)
   cancellation, 265n13
   collaboration with the Bush
      administration, 124, 125–126
   collaboration with the Department of
      Defense following 9/11, 124
   defense of U.S. detention practices,
      125–131
   innovation in the propagandizing of
      war, 137
   justification of combat tactics in Iraq
      and Afghanistan, 131–133
   legitimation of the doctrine of
      preventative warfare, 123, 135–140
   on the media's role in war, 134–137
   mediation of the cultural memory of
      the wars in Iraq and Afghanistan,
      140–141
   online fan forums, 142
   overview, 122–123
   premediation of future war, 121, 124–
      125, 137–140, 141–143
   ratings, 122
   remediation of flashpoints in the War
      on Terrorism, 124–133, 135–137,
      140–143
   "ripped-from-the-headlines"
      topicality, 123–124
Janensch, Paul, 208
Jarhead (film), 13
Jarhead (Swofford), 167

Jenkins, Carter, 178
Jenkins, Tricia, 63
Jericho (television series), 176, 188–194, 198, 201
Jermyn, Deborah, 89
Jewett, Robert, 65
Jones, Simon Cellan, 149
Journalists
    coverage of the war in Afghanistan, 98–99
    embedded, 5, 120, 206–207
    JAG on the journalist's role in war, 134–137
Just War theory, 97–98, 138–140

Kackman, Michael, 63
Kandahar, 98
Kaplan, E. Ann, 224, 225
Kaplan, Robert, 160–162, 164
Karbacz, Kelly, 218
Katzive, Matt, 264n2
"Keep America Safe" coalition, 95–96
Keith Olbermann Show (television show), 202
Kellogg, Brown & Root contractors, 192
Kelly, Chance, 153
Kentucky National Guard, 129
Kerry, John, 168–169, 270n6
"Killing an Arab" (song), 8
Kill Point, The (SPIKE TV series), 230–232
King, Larry, 35–36
"Know Your Enemy" (promotional video), 76
Kompare, Derek, 200
Krause, Peter, 233
Kristol, William, 95–96
Kronenfeld, Ivan, 103
Kuma/War (video game), 9–10, 11
Kuypers, Jim, 5

La Femme Nikita (television series), 60
Late Show with David Letterman, The (television show), 34
Lauer, Matt, 33

Lavery, David, 203
Law & Order (television series), 38, 215, 277n44
Lawrence, John Shelton, 65
Lawrence, Scott, 126
Leary, Denis, 241
Leguizamo, John, 230
Leonard, Lt. Col. Steve, 165
Lewis, Justin, 11
Lichter, Robert, 140–141
Lifton, Robert Jay, 243
Limbaugh, Rush, 92
Lincoln Group, 2
Line of Fire (television series), 57
Lisi, Anthony, 40
Long, Howie, 103
Loose Change (video), 239
Los Angeles Joint Terrorism Task Force, 62
Lost (television series), 175, 202–203
Lost: The Experience (alternate reality game), 202–203
Lowe, Rob, 50
Lule, Jack, 36
Lush, Billy, 154, 232, *233*, 236
Lutz, Kellan, 159
Lyman, Will, 80
Lynch, Jessica, 4, 212, 213

MacDonald, Scott, 187
Macfarlane, Luke, 153
Mad Men (television series), 240
Maher, Bill, 39, 54, 170
Maines, Natalie, 8
Making Marines (military docusoap), 101, 105–106, 122
"Man Comes Around, The" (song), 159
Marek, Piter, 71
Margulies, Julianna, 62, 69
Marshall, Andrew, 146
Massumi, Brian, 58
Matchett, Kari, 182
Mattis, Gen. James, 72
Maull, Ian, 203

Maxwell, Richard, 11

McAlister, Melani, 255n60

McCain, John, 92

McCann Erickson agency, 7

McCarthy, Ann, 212

McCombs, Phil, 34

McDermott, Dylan, 62, 68

McDonnell, Mary, 196

McPherson, Tara, 90

McRaney, Gerald, 191

Medal of Honor (video game), 9

Medevoi, Lee, 164

Media

"family under siege" trope for
   terrorism, 59

impact of media convergence on the
   significance of ratings, 200–201

impact of technological convergence
   on television, 169–170

Richard Grusin on the function of,
   142

See also Entertainment media; News
   media

Media-military collusion

in a global media environment, 18

in the War on Terrorism, 5–18

during World War I, 16

during World War II, 16–17

"Mediated distanciation," 261n8

melancholia, 232, 277n37

Melnick, Jeff, 240

Melodramas, of soldier-suffering, 214–
   223

Men of Annapolis, The (television series),
   102

MI5 (television series), 60, 94

Mickey Mouse Club, The (television show),
   102

Militainment

after-action review of the Iraq
   invasion, 145, 148–160

Bush administration promotion of
   the war in Afghanistan, 100–101

conversion into "war porn," 167

critical depiction of the Iraq War,
   144–145

durability as a vehicle for military
   propaganda, 122

enlistment of citizens in the War on
   Terrorism, 101

goals and effects of, 100

JAG (*see* JAG)

re- and premediation processes in,
   121

recuperation of militarism and, 121

See also Military docusoaps; Reality
   militainment

"Militainment, Inc.", 166

Militarism

melodramas of soldier-suffering and,
   215

melodramatic framing of 9/11 and,
   36–37

National Security Strategy Statement
   of 2002, 161–162

reality militainment programs and,
   101, 119, 121

Robert Kaplan on, 161

Military Channel, 13, 120, 122

Military Diaries (military docusoap), 101,
   114–118, 119, 122

Military discipline, 166

Military docusoaps

American Fighter Pilot, 101, 105, 106–
   109, 122

concept of, 104–105

Making Marines, 101, 105–106, 122

Military Diaries, 101, 114–118, 119, 122

Profiles from the Front Line, 101, 109–114,
   115

service to the propagandistic
   purposes of the U.S. military, 118–
   119

Military History Channel, 13

"Military-industrial-entertainment
   complex," 16–18, 24

Military recruiters, 278n48

Military-style boot camps, 166

Military television channels, 13
Military-themed gamedocs, 104
Military tribunals, 125–129
Miller, Toby, 11, 207
Mitchell, Kenneth, 191
Mitscherlich, Alexander and Margarete, 277n37
Mittell, Jason, 226
"Mobisodes," 203
Monica Lewinsky scandal, 173
Monohan, Brian, 37
"Monomythic hero," 65
Montel Williams Show, The (television talk show), 210–212, 223, 226, 227
Moore, Ronald, 194–195
Morales, Esai, 192
Moral responsibility, interrogated by science fiction TV programs, 196–197
Moricz, Barna, 77
Morissette, Alanis, 8
"Morning Again in America" advertising campaign, 7
Morris, Meaghan, 38
Mourning, 216–217, 243
MSNBC, 3, 56
MTV, 6, 103–104
Multiculturalism, and the construction of American identity, 69–73
"Mundane witnessing," 276n18
Murdoch, Rupert, 6, 10
Murrow, Edward R., 56
Muslim Americans, 58
Muslim TV characters, 71–72

Nagle, John, 238
Nagra, Parminder, 224
National security
    construction of terrorism as a state problem, 21–22
    depicted in Threshold, 185–188
National Security Agency, 61, 62
National Security Strategy Statement of 2002, 81, 139, 161–162

Negron, Jesse, 106
Netwar, 100
New media, 239
"New" Revolution in Military Affairs, 145, 160–165
News media
    censorship following the 9/11 attacks, 6
    cooptation by the Bush administration, 6
    embedded reporting in Iraq, 5, 120, 206–207
    emphasis on personal stories from 9/11, 33
    JAG on the media's role in war, 134–137
    management by the Bush administration in Iraq, 5
    presentation and coverage of the war in Afghanistan, 98–100
    priming function in the War on Terrorism, 6
    satirization of, 171–172, 174
    self-censorship following the 9/11 attacks, 3
    See also Iraq War news coverage; Television news
New York City firefighters, 34
New York Times (newspaper), 2, 4
Nichols, Marisol, 71
Nicholson, Jack, 130
Nielsen ratings, 169–170, 200–201
Nightline (television show), 103
"9/11 Shout-outs," 240
9/11 Truth Movement, 239, 240
"Noble grunt" films, 13–14
Noonan, Peggy, 34
Norman, David, 40
Nunn, Heather, 118

Obama, Barack, 238
Occupation Dreamland (documentary film), 13, 229

Office for Motion Picture Production (Department of Defense), 102
Office of Diplomacy and Public Affairs, 2–3
Office of War Information, 16
Off to War (television documentary series), 227–229
Olmos, Edward James, 195
O'Mara, Jason, 67
100 Hours (video), 95–96
Online podcasts, 194–195
"Operational aesthetic," 226
Operation Enduring Freedom, 147
    depicted in *Profiles from the Front Line*, 113–114
    See also Afghanistan War
O'Reilly, Bill, 133, 258n46
Orientalism, 53
Oscar Awards, 17
Ott, Brian, 200
Over There (FX television series), 230, 268n21
    after-action review of the Iraq invasion, 145, 148–149, 150, 151–153, 156–158
    on the economic motivations for war, 164–165
    origin of, 144–145
    promotion of counterinsurgency doctrine, 145
    promotion of war as an instrument of peace, 165–166
    recuperation of militarism and, 121
    vaunting of the professional soldier, 163–165

Palladino, Erik, 157
Parents Television Council, 85
Parker, Trey, 55
Parks, Lisa, 82
Pate, Josh and Jonah, 178
Paternal/patriarchal authority
    assigned to Bush by TV, 52
    depicted in science fiction TV programs, 179–181

"family under siege" mentality and, 59
Patriot, The (film), 64
Patriot Act, 81–82, 169, 173, 270n6
Patriotism
    linked through advertising to consumption, 7
    TV programming following 9/11 and, 55–58
"Peace Train" (song), 8
Peacock, Steven, 89
Pearl Harbor (film), 13
Peel, Maj. Kevin, 116
Pentagon Channel, 13, 120
Personalization of fear, 177–184
Peters, Evan, 183
Petraeus, David, 160
Petrelli, John, 130
Piestewa family, 212–213
Platoon (film), 13
"Pluralism," 47, 48–49
Podcasts, 195, 203–204
Political dissent
    effect of reality militainment on, 120
    as "immoral" and "un-American," 37
    John Kerry's criticism of the Bush administration, 168–169
    satire in comedy television shows, 170–175
    in science fiction TV programs (*see* Science fiction TV programs)
Politically Incorrect (television series), 54, 170
Political satire, 170–175
Politics of fear
    depiction of terrorism as a contagion in spy TV programs, 73–80
    impact on human rights discourse in spy TV programs, 80–81
    interrogation by science fiction TV programs, 175–177, 188
    justifications for torture in spy TV programs, 84–87

logic of "preventative defense" in spy
    TV programs, 81–87
Poniewozik, James, 48, 189, 190
Post-Orientalism, 53, 77, 255n60
Powell, Anne, 103
Powell, Colin, 3, 6, 46
Power
    capillary and arterial models of, 24
    exercising through biopolitical
        mechanisms, 162
Power relations
    in American national identity and the
        discourse of security, 22–23
    construction of terrorism as a state
        problem and, 21–22
    Foucault's conceptualizations of, 21
    in a "neo-network" model of
        television, 23–25
Premediation
    concept of, 121
    JAG and, 121, 124–125, 137–140, 141–
        143
    purpose of, 141–142
Premium television channels
    FCC regulations and, 225
    post-sentimentality in complex
        modes of storytelling, 225–235
Preventative warfare
    JAG's exoneration of, 123, 135–140
    logic of preventative defense in spy
        TV programs, 81–87
    See also Bush Doctrine
Private contractors, 191–192
"Proactive defense," 95
Professional soldiers, 163–165
Profiles from the Front Line (military
    docusoap), 101, 109–114, 115
Puar, Jasbir, 49, 72, 78, 82
Public opinion, on the media's handling
    of 9/11, 6
Putnam, Robert, 23

Qaddafi, Muammar, 38
Queer identity, 79

Racial profiling
    depicted in spy TV programs, 74–75,
        77
    depicted in West Wing, 50–52
Radio industry, 7–8
Radio Sawa, 2
Rai, Amit, 49
"Rallies for America," 8
Rambo (films), 17–18
Ransone, James, 164
Rather, Dan, 34, 112
Ratings, 169–170, 200–201
Raver, Kim, 85
Reagan, Ronald, 16
Reality militainment
    Combat Missions, 104
    consequences for citizen identity,
        119–120
    docusoaps and the war in
        Afghanistan, 104–119
    enlistment of citizens in the War on
        Terrorism, 101
    Fox television and Boot Camp, 104
    logic of militarism as a regime of
        conduct, 101
    low viewer ratings and, 122
    normalization of militarism and, 119
    recategorized as a niche
        phenomenon, 120
Reality television
    blurring of the boundary between
        information and entertainment,
        20
    depiction of soldier-suffering on, 210,
        212–214
    following the 9/11 attacks, 6
    military veterans in, 120
    See also Reality militainment
Real World/Road Rules Challenge (MTV
    series), 103–104
Redacted (film), 144
"Redemptive narratives," 222–223
Redgrave, Jemma, 69
Redstone, Sumner, 10

Religion, 35–36

Remediation
   concept of, 121
   JAG and, 124–133, 135–137, 140–143
   purpose of, 141–142

Rescue Me (FX series), 240–244

Reuben, Gloria, 70

Revolution in Military Affairs (RMA)
   applied to Afghanistan, 147
   critiqued by television shows, 145,
      148–160
   failure in Iraq, 147–148
   origin of, 146–147

Reynolds, Amy, 33, 35

Rhys, Phillip, 77

Rice, Condoleezza, 6, 168

Ricks, Thomas, 148, 160

Robb, David, 265n14

Roberts, Julia, 39

Robinson, Keith, 153

Rocque, Francisco Silva, 23

Ross, Kathleen Canham, 110

Rove, Karl, 3–4, 10

Ruivivar, Anthony, 41

Rumsfeld, Donald
   Abu Ghraib scandal and, 168
   briefings on the war in Afghanistan,
      98
   criticism of press coverage of the war
      in Afghanistan, 100
   enlistment of citizens in the War on
      Terrorism, 96
   influence on the wars in Afghanistan
      and Iraq, 147
   JAG and, 125, 140, 141
   portrayed in *DC 9/11: Time of Crisis*, 12
   Profiles from the Front Line and, 110

Rumsfeld v. Hamden, 129

Rush Limbaugh Show (radio show), 8

Rustin, Scott, 89

Rutherford, Kelly, 68

Sands, Stark, 152

Satellite news channels, 99

Satire, 170–175

Saving Private Ryan (film), 13

Savior-figures, 61

Schiff, Richard, 50

Schlamme, Thomas, 182

Schultz, George, 38

Science fiction TV programs
   depiction of enemy aliens, 175, 178–
      179, 181, 182–184, 185, 186, 188
   depiction of femininity, 179–180, 182
   depiction of the national security
      state in *Threshold*, 185–188
   influence and survival in the new
      media context, 200–201, 202–204
   interrogation of the politics of fear,
      175–177, 188
   interrogation of U.S. political culture
      following the occupation of Iraq,
      188–200
   limit-cases, 189
   personalization of fear, 177–184
   in the plurality of the commercial
      media systems, 204–205
   processes of defamiliarization and
      displacement in, 176

Sci Fi cable channel, 176, 204. *See also*
   Syfy channel

Scott, Suzanne, 203

Scott, Tony and Ridley, 106

Scurti, John, 243

Seaquist, Larry, 62

Season Zero (comic book), 203

Seattle Times (newspaper), 207

Secret agents, as savior-figures, 61

September 11 attacks
   American desire for vengeance and
      action following, 65
   "Breaking News" format of coverage,
      6, 30, 33–35
   as media events, 1
   news media construction as a
      national trauma, 30–31
   portrayed as a national trauma, 238–
      239

September 11 babies, 41–42

Sexism, 277–278n44

Sexual attitudes, as signifiers of terrorists, 78–79

Sheen, Martin, 52

Shields, Blake, 77

Shinseki, Gen. Eric, 267n9

Shout-outs, 240

Showtime docudramas, 11–13

Simon, David, 145, 149, 150, 151, 155, 159

Simpsons, The (television series), 240

Sites, Kevin, 135, 137

Six Feet Under (HBO series), 232–235, 236

Skarsgård, Alexander, 152

Skerritt, Tom, 75

"Sleeper" agents, 189

Sleeper Cell (television series)
  American Muslim hero in, 70–71
  assistance from intelligence agencies, 62
  depiction of racial profiling, 77
  depiction of surveillance technologies, 82–83
  depiction of terrorism as a contagion, 73–74, 75, 76
  justifications for torture, 84–85, 86–87
  logic of suspicion in, 80
  multicultural orientation, 71, 72
  normalization of the state of exception, 95
  in the revitalization of spy programs, 60
  sexual attitudes and the determinants of terrorists, 79
  whitening of the terrorist figures, 77

"Smart" weapons, 146

Smelser, Neil, 30

Smith-Mundt Act, 126, 265n19

Social engineering, 164–165

Sodhi, Balbir Singh, 23

"Soldier personalities," 162

Soldiers, professional, 163–165

Soldier-suffering
  complex modes of storytelling in the "post-network" system, 223–225
  depicted on talk shows and reality programming, 210–214
  television and the historical witnessing of, 209, 235–237
  television melodramas of, 214–223

Soldier videos, 166–167

Songs, banning of, 8, 247n34

Sontag, Susan, 208, 210

Sorkin, Aaron, 47, 48, 254n44

South Park (television series), 54–55, 240

Spencer, John, 49

Spigel, Lynn, 18, 55

SPIKE TV, 230

Spooks (television series). *See MI5*

Springsteen, Bruce, 8

Spy satellites, 82

Spy TV programs
  depiction of racial profiling, 74–75, 77
  depiction of terrorism as a contagion, 73–80
  "deviant sexuality" as a signifier of perversity, 78–79
  enlistment of citizens in the War on Terrorism and, 96
  female agents and characters, 69–70
  human rights discourse portrayed as obstructive, 80–81
  justifications for surveillance, 81–84
  justifications for torture, 84–87
  logic of "preventative defense" in, 81–87
  logic of suspicion in, 80
  multiculturalist identity and the expansion of heroic agency, 69–72
  normalization of the state of exception, 87, 95
  propaganda function for the state, 61–65
  revitalization of, 60–61
  secret agents as savior-figures, 61

Spy TV programs, *continued*
  variations between, 63–64
  video game spinoffs, 94
  vigilante heroism and, 65–68
  whitening of the terrorist figure, 76–77
  See also 24
Stability Operations Field Manual (U.S. Army), 165
Stahl, Roger, 9, 100, 119, 166
Stamberg, Josh, 156
Stanley, Alessandra, 64
Stapf, David, 67
Star-Spangled Banner (silent film), 102
State of exception
  interrogated by science fiction TV programs, 189–200
  normalized by spy TV programs, 87, 95
"Stealth terrorist," 77
Stevens, Cat, 8
Stewart, Jon, 170–172, 202, 271n18
Stockwell, Dean, 138
Stone, Matt, 55
Strub, Phil, 102
Sturken, Marita, 211
Subpopulations, 164
Sudduth, Skipp, 40
Sum of All Fears, The (film), 14–15
"Superpower Syndrome," 243
Surface (television series), 176, 177–181, 201, 272n33
Surnow, Joel, 87, 92, 93
Surveillance, 45–46, 81–84
Sutherland, Kiefer, 61–62, 91, 96
Sweeney, D. B., 192
Swofford, Anthony, 167
Syfy channel, 201, 204. *See also* Sci Fi cable channel

Tailhook Association, 264–265n11
Taliban
  "about-to-die" photos of fighters, 99
  Bush's declaration of war against, 97–98

Talk shows, 210–212
Tambor, Jeffrey, 172
Team America: World Police (film), 55
Technological warfare, JAG's justification of, 131–133
Television industry
  after-action review of the Iraq invasion, 145, 148–160
  American national identity and, 23
  blurring of the informational and entertainment properties of, 19–20
  commercial nature of in the modern plurality of media systems, 204–205
  contemporary trends in the desacralization of the War on Terrorism, 240–244
  critical depiction of the Iraq War, 144–145
  historical witnessing and, 235–237
  military channels, 13 (*see also* Militainment; Reality militainment)
  power relations in a "neo-network" model of, 23–25
  technological convergence of media and, 169–170
  See also Entertainment television; Reality television
Television news
  blurring of the boundary between information and entertainment, 19–20
  "Breaking News" coverage of 9/11, 6, 30, 33–35
  commercialization of news production, 37
  construction of 9/11 as a national trauma, 30–31
  coverage of terrorism in the 1980s, 37–38
  melodramatic framing of 9/11, 31, 32–38

as a "shock absorber," 30
See also Iraq War news coverage; News media
Tenet, George, 168
Tennessean (newspaper), 3
Tergesen, Lee, 150
Terrorism/Terrorists
  Bush's flexibly expansive definition of, 60
  construction as an American state problem, 21–22
  depicted as a contagion on spy TV programs, 73–80
  depicted as enemy aliens in science fiction TV programs, 175, 178–179, 181, 182–184, 185, 186, 188
  "family under siege" trope employed by the media, 59
  "naturalization" of in the 1980s, 37–38
  1980s antiterrorist discourse, 256n4
  pathologization in 9/11 special TV episodes, 44–46, 50–52, 53–54
  pathologized and decontextualized by the Bush administration, 59–60, 69, 188
  See also Al Qaeda; War on Terrorism
Terry, Jennifer, 10
That's My Bush (television series), 170
Thin Red Line (film), 13
Third Infantry Division (U.S. Army), 147–148
Third Watch (television series), 31, 40, 41–42, 52–53, 240
36th Engineering Brigade (Arkansas National Guard), 228
Thompson, Fred, 215
Threat Matrix (television series)
  action-oriented heroism in, 68
  assistance from intelligence agencies, 62
  cancellation of, 64
  celebration of the Patriot Act and surveillance, 81–82

depiction of Islam and Muslims, 77–78
depiction of terrorism as a contagion, 73–74, 75–76
female agents and characters, 69–70
human rights discourse portrayed as obstructive, 80–81
justification of dispersed surveillance, 84
justification of torture, 84
logic of suspicion in, 80
multicultural orientation, 71
propaganda function of, 63
ratings, 257n25
in the revitalization of spy programs, 60
"We are making progress" message, 63
Threshold (television series), 176, 185–188, 201
Tillman, Pat, 220
Time magazine, 239
Tocqueville, Alexis de, 81
Today Show, The (television show), 177
Top Gun (film), 107
Torture
  depoliticized by 24, 92–94
  interrogated by science fiction TV programs, 196
  justified by spy TV programs, 84–87
  treatment by JAG, 127–128, 130–131
"Total Information Awareness" program, 259n63
Tribute to Heroes (telethon), 56
True Life (MTV series), 278–279n62
Turteltaub, Jon, 189
24 (television series)
  "allegory lite" aesthetics, 92
  conscription of viewers into the War on Terrorism, 88–94
  cultural legacy of, 95–96
  depiction of racial profiling, 74
  depiction of surveillance technologies, 82

24 (television series), *continued*
 female agents and characters, 70
 future-oriented conception of fear, 87
 impact of 9/11 on, 38
 multicultural orientation, 71
 normalization of the state of
  exception, 87, 95
 number of viewers, 257n31
 original conception of, 61
 ratings in 2002, 67
 real-time conceit, 87–89
 reliance on the military, 256–257n19
 serial form of, 90
 shifting perspective through time,
  63–64
 use of information deficits, 91–92
 use of split-screens and narrative
  gaps, 89–90
 use of torture in, 92–94
 video game spinoff, 94
 vigilante heroism and, 65
 whitening of the terrorist figure, 76–
  77
24: *The Game* (video game), 94
Tyndall Air Force Base, 106

Uighurs, 129
Ulrich, Skeet, 191
Unit, The (television series), 256n9
United States Air Force, 17
United States government
 censorship of news media following
  the 9/11 attacks, 6
 image management during the war in
  Iraq, 4–5
 propaganda efforts in the War on
  Terrorism, 2–5
 propaganda function of spy TV
  programs and, 61–65
 selling of the war in Iraq, 3–4
 See also Bush administration
United States military
 collaboration with entertainment
  media, 102–104

collaboration with the video game
 industry, 8–10, 11
embedded journalists and information
 management in Iraq, 5
film unit in World War II, 16
media-military collusion in the War
 on Terrorism, 5–18
military docusoaps, 105–119
"military-industrial-entertainment"
 complex, 16–18, 24
promotion of the military lifestyle
 through entertainment media,
 103–104
Revolution in Military Affairs, 146–148
Stability Operations Field Manual, 165
video games created by, 9, 10
U.S. Air Force, 105, 106–109
USA Patriot Act, 81–82, 169, 173, 270n6
USA *Today* (newspaper), 252n16
U.S. Information and Educational
 Exchange Act of 1948, 126
U.S. Marine Corps
 collaboration with the entertainment
  media, 102, 103, 104, 265n14
 military docusoaps and, 105–106
U.S. Military Academy at West Point,
 102–103
U.S. Supreme Court, 129

Valenti, Jack, 10, 11
Van Munster, Bertram, 109–111, 112, 113–
 114
Video games
 created by the U.S. military, 9, 10
 industry collaboration with the
  military, 8–10, 11
 spinoffs from spy TV programs, 94
Vietnam War, 13, 146
Vigilante heroism, 65–68
Voris, Cyrus, 76
Vowell, Sarah, 93

Wahlberg, Donnie, 230
Walsh, Bill, 40

Walsh, John, 43, 44, 45
Walt Disney Corporation, 102–103
Walzer, Michael, 97
Warfront/Zeal Picture, 107
War Games (television series), 103
War on Terrorism
    Barack Obama and, 238
    Bush administration's cooptation of
        the entertainment media and, 5–8,
        10–15, 102
    Bush's September 20, 2001 speech
        on, 59–60
    construction of terrorism as a state
        problem, 21–22
    contemporary television's
        desacralization of, 240–244
    as the defense of global society, 164
    enlistment of citizens in, 96
    entertainment TV and the discourse
        of security, 20–21
    expanded conceptualization of heroic
        agency, 68–73
    in a global media environment, 18
    imposition of special powers of
        authority by the Bush
        administration, 60
    as information warfare, 100
    JAG's remediation of flashpoints in,
        124–133, 135–137, 140–143
    media-military collusion in, 5–18
    militainment and, 100–101
    multiculturalism in the rhetorical
        construction of America, 72–73
    narratives of 9/11 special TV episodes
        and, 42–53
    the new media and, 239
    patriotic TV programming and, 57–58
    politics of fear and, 53–54
    portrayed as a moral struggle by the
        Bush administration, 81
    Robert Kaplan on, 161
    social mechanisms in the
        militarization of counterterrorism,
        18–19

    video games of, 9–10, 11
    See also Terrorism/Terrorists
War Tapes, The (film), 13
Waterboarding, 177, 196
Watson, Alberta, 85
Web 2.0, 239
Wells, John, 31, 47
Wersching, Annie, 70
West Point Military Academy, 102–103
"West Point Minute," 103
West Point Story (television series), 102, 103
West Wing, The (television series), 42, 47–
    53, 254n443I
We Were Soldiers (film), 13
What Price Glory? (film), 102
White, Susanna, 149–150
Whitford, Bradley, 49
Whoopi (television series), 172, 173–175,
    274n65
Why We Fight (training/propaganda
    series), 16
Wiles, Jason, 42
Williams, Montel, 210–211, 276n20
Wilson, Woodrow, 16
Windtalkers (film), 13
Winthrop, John, 36
Without a Trace (television series), 217–
    219, 223
With the Marines at Tarawa (film), 17
Wolfowitz, Paul, 12, 15, 267n9
Woodruff, Judy, 32–33, 36
World War I, 16
World War II, 16–17
Wright, Evan, 145

Young America Salutes West Point (television
    documentary), 102–103
YouTube, 14, 166–167, 239

Zabel, Bryce, 56
Zarek (comic book), 203
Zelizer, Barbie, 99
Zucker, Jeff, 47
Zulaika, Joseba, 60